A Guide to
What's Wrong with Economics

Anthem Studies in Political
Economy and Globalization

to

Kate Fullbrook
1950–2003

A Guide to
What's Wrong with Economics

edited by
EDWARD FULLBROOK

Anthem Press
London

This edition first published by Anthem Press 2004

Anthem Press is an imprint of
Wimbledon Publishing Company
75-76 Blackfriars Road
London SE1 8HA
or
PO Box 9779, London SW19 7QA

British Library Cataloguing in Publication Data
Data available

Library of Congress in Publication Data
A catalogue record has been applied for

2 4 6 8 10 9 7 5 3 1

ISBN 1 84331 148 8 (Pbk)

Typeset by Pentagon Graphics Pvt. Ltd., Chennai, India
Printed in Great Britain by Cromwell Press

CONTENTS

Introduction: Broadband Versus Narrowband Economics

EDWARD FULLBROOK

UNIVERSITY OF THE WEST OF ENGLAND, UK

Theories, scientific and otherwise, do not represent the world as it is but, rather, highlight certain aspects of it while leaving others in the dark. It may be the case that two theories highlight the same aspects of some corner of reality but offer different conclusions. In the last century, this type of situation preoccupied the philosophy of science. The book you are reading, however, addresses a different kind of situation: one where one theory, that illuminates a few facets of its domain rather well, wants to suppress other theories that would illuminate some of the many facets that it leaves in the dark. This theory is neoclassical economics. Because it has been so successful at sidelining other approaches, it also is called 'mainstream economics'.

From the 1960s onward, neoclassical economists have increasingly managed to block the employment of non-neoclassical economists in university economics departments and to deny them opportunities to publish in professional journals. They also have narrowed the economics curriculum that universities offer students. At the same time they have increasingly formalized their theory, making it progressively irrelevant to understanding economic reality. And now they are even banishing economic history and the history of economic thought from the curriculum, these being places where the student might be exposed to non-neoclassical ideas. Why has this tragedy happened?

Many factors have contributed; I will mention only three. First, neoclassical economists have as a group deluded themselves into believing that all you need for an exact science is mathematics, and never mind about whether the symbols used refer quantitatively to the real world. What began as an indulgence became an addiction, leading to a collective fantasy of scientific achievement where in most cases none exists. To preserve their illusions, neoclassical economists have found it increasingly necessary to isolate themselves from non-believers.

Second, as Joseph Stiglitz has observed, economics has suffered 'a triumph of ideology over science'.[1] Instead of regarding their theory as a tool in the pursuit of knowledge, neoclassical economists have made it the required viewpoint from which, at all times and in all places, to look at all economic phenomena. This is the position of neo-liberalism.

Third, today's economies, including the societies in which they are embedded, are very different from those of the nineteenth century for which neoclassical economics was invented to describe. These differences become more pronounced every decade as new aspects of economic reality emerge, for example: consumer societies, corporate globalization, economically induced environmental disasters and impending ecological ones, the accelerating gap between the rich and poor, and the movement for equal-opportunity economies. Consequently neoclassical economics sheds light on an ever-smaller proportion of economic reality, leaving more and more of it in the dark for students permitted only the neoclassical viewpoint. This makes the neoclassical monopoly more outrageous and costly every year, requiring of it ever more desperate measures of defense, like eliminating economic history and history of economics from the curriculum.

But eventually reality overtakes time-warp worlds like mainstream economics and the Soviet Union. The moment and place of the tipping point, however, nearly always takes people by surprise. In June 2000, a few economics students in Paris circulated a petition calling for the reform of their economics curriculum. One doubts that any of those students in their wildest dreams anticipated the effect their initiative would have. Their petition was short, modest and restrained. Its first part, 'We wish to escape from imaginary worlds', summarizes what they were protesting against.

> Most of us have chosen to study economics so as to acquire a deep understanding of the economic phenomena with which the citizens of today are confronted. But the teaching that is offered, that is to say for the most part neoclassical theory or approaches derived from it, does not generally answer this expectation. Indeed, even when the theory legitimately detaches itself from contingencies in the first instance, it rarely carries out the necessary return to the facts. The empirical side (historical facts, functioning of institutions, study of the behaviors and strategies of agents...) is almost non-existent. Furthermore, this gap in the teaching, this disregard for concrete realities, poses an enormous problem for those who would like to render themselves useful to economic and social actors.

The students asked instead for a broad spectrum of analytical viewpoints.

Too often the lectures leave no place for reflection. Out of all the approaches to economic questions that exist, generally only one is presented to us. This approach is supposed to explain everything by means of a purely axiomatic process, as if this were THE economic truth. We do not accept this dogmatism. We want a pluralism of approaches, adapted to the complexity of the objects and to the uncertainty surrounding most of the big questions in economics (unemployment, inequalities, the place of financial markets, the advantages and disadvantages of free trade, globalization, economic development, etc.)[2]

The Parisian students' complaint about the narrowness of their economics education and their desire for a broader approach to economics teaching that would enable them to connect constructively and comprehensively with the complex economic realities of their time hit a chord with French news media. Major newspapers and magazines gave extensive coverage to the students' struggle against the 'autistic science'. Economics students from all over France rushed to sign the petition. Meanwhile a growing number of French economists dared to speak out in support and even launched a parallel petition of their own. Finally the French government stepped in. The Minister of Education set up a high level commission to investigate the students' complaints.

News of these events in France spread quickly via the Web and email around the world. The distinction drawn by the French students between what could be called 'narrowband' and 'broadband' approaches to economics, and their plea for the latter, found support from large numbers of economics students and economists in many countries. In June 2001, almost exactly a year after the French students had released their petition, 27 PhD candidates at Cambridge University in the UK launched their own, titled 'Opening Up Economics'. Besides reiterating the French students' call for a broadband approach to economics teaching, the Cambridge students also champion its application to economic research:

This debate is important because in our view the status quo is harmful in at least four respects. Firstly, it is harmful to students who are taught the 'tools' of mainstream economics without learning their domain of applicability. The source and evolution of these ideas is ignored, as is the existence and status of competing theories. Secondly, it disadvantages a society that ought to be benefiting from what economists can tell us about the world. Economics is a social science with enormous potential for making a difference through its impact on policy debates. In its present form its effectiveness in this arena is limited by the uncritical application of mainstream methods. Thirdly, progress towards a deeper understanding of many important aspects of economic life is being held back. By restricting research done in economics to that based on one approach only, the development of competing research programs is seriously hampered or prevented altogether. Fourth and finally, in the current situation an economist who does not do economics in the prescribed way finds it very difficult to get recognition for her research.

In August of the same year economics students from 17 countries who had gathered in the USA in Kansas City, released their International Open Letter to all economics departments calling on them to reform economics education and research by adopting the broadband approach. Their letter includes the following seven points.

1. **A broader conception of human behavior.** The definition of *economic man* as an autonomous rational optimizer is too narrow and does not allow for the roles of other determinants such as instinct, habit formation and gender, class and other social factors in shaping the economic psychology of social agents.

2. **Recognition of culture.** Economic activities, like all social phenomena, are necessarily embedded in culture, which includes all kinds of social, political and moral value-systems and institutions. These profoundly shape and guide human behavior by imposing obligations, enabling and disabling particular choices, and creating social or communal identities, all of which may impact on economic behavior.

3. **Consideration of history.** Economic reality is dynamic rather than static—and as economists we must investigate how and why things change over time and space. Realistic economic inquiry should focus on process rather than simply on ends.

4. **A new theory of knowledge.** The positive vs. normative dichotomy which has traditionally been used in the social sciences is problematic. The fact-value distinction can be transcended by the recognition that the investigator's values are inescapably involved in scientific inquiry and in making scientific statements, whether consciously or not. This acknowledgement enables a more sophisticated assessment of knowledge claims.

5. **Empirical grounding.** More effort must be made to substantiate theoretical claims with empirical evidence. The tendency to privilege theoretical tenets in the teaching of economics without reference to empirical observation cultivates doubt about the realism of such explanations.

6. **Expanded methods.** Procedures such as participant observation, case studies and discourse analysis should be recognized as legitimate means of acquiring and analyzing data alongside econometrics and

formal modelling. Observation of phenomena from different vantage points using various data-gathering techniques may offer new insights into phenomena and enhance our understanding of them.

7. **Interdisciplinary dialogue.** Economists should be aware of diverse schools of thought within economics, and should be aware of developments in other disciplines, particularly the social sciences.

In March 2003 economics students at Harvard launched their own petition, demanding from its economics department an introductory course that would have 'better balance and coverage of a broader spectrum of views' and that would 'not only teach students the accepted modes of thinking, but also challenge students to think critically and deeply about conventional truths.'

Students have not been alone in mounting increasing pressure on the status quo. Thousands of economists from scores of countries have also in various forms taken up the cause for broadband economics under the banner 'Post-Autistic Economics' and the slogan 'sanity, humanity and science' (www.paecon.net).[3] The PAE movement, or, if you prefer, the Broadband Economics movement, is not about trying to replace neoclassical economics with another partial truth, but rather about reopening economics for free scientific inquiry, making it a pursuit where empiricism outranks *a priorism* and where critical thinking rules instead of ideology.[3]

Against this background of accelerating momentum for radical change, 27 economists and two mathematicians, many of them internationally renowned, representing eight countries and five continents, have come together to create this book. It aims to provide you, the student, with three things.

First, it offers you some protection against the indoctrination process to which you are likely to be subjected as an economics student. There are many things that your teachers should tell you about the brand of economics they are teaching you, but, in most cases, will not. This book will make you aware of some of the many worldly and logical gaps in neoclassical economics, and also its hidden ideological agendas, its disregard for the environment and inability to consider economic issues in an ecological context, its habitual misuse of mathematics and statistics, its inability to address the major issues of economic globalization, its ethical cynicism concerning poverty, racism and sexism, and its misrepresentation of economic history.

Second, if you are brave you may want to bring up some of the points raised in this book in your classes. It is sure to make them more interesting. It may even provoke lively discussion and, for a while at least, convert the indoctrination process into an educational one. If it does you will be doing a good thing: we live in a time when bad economics probably kills more people and causes more suffering than armaments.

Third, this book is intended to appeal to your imagination and humanity by showing you how interesting and relevant, even exciting, economics can be when it is pursued, not as the defense of an antiquated and blinkered system of belief, but as a no-holds-barred inquiry looking for real-world truths.

PART I

BASIC PROBLEMS

1

The Quarrelsome Boundaries of Economics

Hugh Stretton

University of Adelaide, Australia

Nothing's *necessarily* wrong with economics. But there isn't a one-and-only *right* way to learn it. It can't help being a controversial subject. Let us begin by looking at some of the reasons for that.

COMPLEXITY, INVENTION, CONFLICT AND COOPERATION

When a new drug saves an unemployed worker's child from a dangerous disease, is that because the doctor knows how to prescribe it, or the chemist shop stocks it, or the pharmaceutical company manufactures it, or clinical researchers have tried and proved it, or because biomedical researchers have invented it, because their scientific education equipped them to do that, or because the government financed their university education and research, or indeed because our history has given us a culture and values which prompt us to vote for politicians who will tax us to finance medical and hospital services to our citizens? Since every one of those contributing causes has its own causal conditions and history, how many of those other histories do we also need to know in order to understand why the poor kid got help his parents could not pay for?

The question is ridiculous. Some knowledge is its own reward: you hunt histories, biographies, fiction, poetry and other arts for whatever grabs you. But if you want 'useful' knowledge – to serve other purposes rather than to enjoy for its own sake – what you look for depends on what you want to do with it. Like many other human activities, economic activity is so complicated that any study of it has to be selective. Investigators' values have to combine with their skills in deciding what's important, what questions to ask, what sort of answers to look for, which causal conditions and processes to explore. For example, researchers who want to reduce inequality and researchers who want to increase efficiency may ask some different questions, and focus on different causes of some effects that interest them both. They may also disagree about the best way to *measure* the inequality or the efficiency of an economic system. Those differences reflect their values and social concerns, which are allowed to differ in a free country – and in its universities.

Economic behavior is also changeable, and can be inventive. So experts disagree about *how* best to understand it. Can a general theory explain most of what people do in getting an income and deciding how to spend it? Most of what public and private firms do in order to produce goods and services for you? Most of what governments can and can't do about their national economic systems? Some neoclassical and some Marxist economists believe that their theories distil important regularities to be found in all or most economic activity. Learn the theory at college, and it should equip you to deal professionally with whatever economic activity concerns you in your working life: understand it, measure it, explain its causes, assess its efficiency, and so on.

Or does economic activity vary so much with time and place that to know how any particular industry or market or national economy is working, what you chiefly need is an open mind, local knowledge, and the skills of a tough investigator? Institutional economists and economic historians tend to work like that, using theory to prompt some of their questions but not to dictate the answers to them.

Besides being complex and changeable, economic life also has elements of both conflict and cooperation. Conflicts can be driven by material self-interest. They can also reflect religious beliefs, and unselfish disagreements about freedom, justice, social duty, quality of life. Cooperation can also be for selfish or friendly or high-principled purposes, or for mixtures of all three. Must economists therefore study all the individual and cooperative, selfish and unselfish purposes at work if they are to understand why economic systems work as they do? Or can they safely confine themselves to so-called strictly 'economic' purposes? Assume that material self-interests prevail? That's not a safe assumption about how people choose to earn, or to vote about economic policies. The most famous economist of all, Adam Smith, believed that humans feel and act with considerable sympathy for each others' pains and pleasures. A lot of modern economic theory avoids the problem by assuming that people seek 'utility', meaning whatever turns them on. But to know your business as an economist, and to understand or predict particular economic activities, or the different capacities of the four productive sectors, or the development of public opinion and economic policy, you may often need to look outside the boundary of economics for some of the forces that drive the behavior inside it.

MEASUREMENT

There are also boundaries within economics. Some of them make it hard to measure economic performance. The most-used measures of national economic activity – gross domestic product, gross national product, net national income, economic growth – only count goods and services that sell for money. They don't count household output: the work people do at home as unpaid labor, the goods and services they produce for their own use rather than for sale. Valued at market prices (how much a restaurant would charge for the cooking you do, a house-cleaner charge for the cleaning you do, and so on) what households make and do for themselves averages a third or more of all production in rich countries.

If rich households pay servants to do their cooking and housework and child care and gardening and book-keeping, those services are counted as economic output. Why not when household members do the work for themselves and one another? If Australian mothers stopped breast-feeding their babies, economists would increase national income by $2.2 billion for producing the equivalent artificial milk and another billion or so for doctoring more sick infants. Extra costs and worse health would count as economic growth. (So of course do efforts to cope with other unhealthy habits.)

EQUALITY

Besides affecting measures of output, the boundary between paid and unpaid work also affects measures of economic inequality. Rich and poor households don't only differ in their money income. They usually also have unequal household capital. Poor households may not have the means of producing much for themselves. Middle-income families can afford bigger houses with well-equipped kitchens, laundries, storage spaces, gardens and workshops and sheds if they want them, games, books and magazines, computers and internet access. They can equip themselves to do much more for themselves than poor households can. If measures of inequality included household output, they might show greater material inequality between the poor and the middle class, but less within the middle class. Once households have a standard outfit of home space and equipment, the difference between cheap and expensive cars, furniture, plumbing, kitchen equipment (and so on) may not make much difference to what they can make and do for themselves. Through the top two-thirds or so of incomes, similar home output of goods and services may often reduce material inequality.

To measure inequality you also have to make some other choices. Should you measure quantum differences between incomes (Brown earns $90,000 more than Smith does) or percentage differences (Smith earns only 10 per cent of

Brown's income)? Those two can give contradictory accounts of the increase or decrease of inequalities over time. Have inequalities risen or fallen, for example, if Brown's income grows from $100,000 to $180,000 while Smith's grows from $10,000 to $20,000? Work it out both ways, and decide which measure you'd use if you wanted to persuade people to reduce inequalities, and which if you didn't want to.

The choice of measures is a technical and moral choice, a task for your values as well as your skills. That's another boundary that you'll meet under various names: between facts and values, knowledge and opinion, positive and normative social science. If you were teaching first-year Economics instead of studying it, how would you mark the assignments and exam papers of students who chose to use different measures of inequality? Left-leaning student says Brown used to get $90,000 more than Smith got. Now he gets $160,000 more than Smith gets, so inequality has increased. Right-thinking student says Smith's income was 10 per cent of Brown's, now it's more than 11 per cent, so inequality is declining. (If you would give either student full marks for being quite right and the other zero for being quite wrong, please look for some other occupation than teaching. A speech-writing spin-doctor for a Left or Right politician, perhaps?)

EFFICIENCY

Measures of efficiency also depend – though in different ways – on what you choose to count. Is the cheapest way to produce a given product (without loss of quality) necessarily the most efficient?

Suppose five competing firms all manage to lower the production cost and selling price of a standard product that they all produce. One does it by cutting its workers' pay. One does it by working them longer hours. One does it by getting some of its materials at lower prices from a poorer country. One does it by replacing some of its workers by robots. One does it by inventing an improvement to some of its machinery that allows it to cut work hours with no harm to anyone – no loss of output, profit, jobs or pay. Ask which change was the most desirable, and scarcely anybody will name either of the first two. There may be votes for each of the other three, though perhaps on conditions. Were the foreign supplies produced by cruelly exploited labor, or with pollutant wastes? Could the workers displaced by robots depend on finding other jobs? Has the inventor of the improved machinery patented it, so that other firms and workers can't share its benefits? The respondents thus bring familiar social values to bear on the question.

But if you ask people to rank the firms in order of efficiency, you are likely to get responses of three kinds. Some will ask you what you mean – 'efficient at what?' Some will name the inventive firm because the benefits of its invention were impartially efficient for its workers, customers and shareholders. But many economists will find the five firms equally efficient because they produce the same product at the same cost and sell it at the same price. Smarter economists may find them equally inefficient, because each of them is neglecting four out of the five available economies.

Economists who accept the orthodox meaning of efficiency aren't necessarily blind or indifferent to the social effects of ruthless cost-cutting. They may well distinguish between good and bad social effects of efficient performance. It can still be useful to have a measure of efficiency that can be applied to the pursuit of any purpose, regardless of its morality. (There are more and less efficient ways of cheating, stealing, exploiting workers, two-timing your partner, or plagiarizing first-year Economics assignments.) But beware of combining (a) a ruthless definition of market efficiency with (b) a boundary that makes material self-interest the only motivation of economic behavior. That makes it easy for careless thinkers to assume that self-interest always prevails over other concerns in everyone's economic behavior, and is the main cause of market efficiency, which is the main cause of economic growth, which is good for everyone. Care for others, in such a view, from the world's poor to the homeless in your own neighborhood, will only encourage the government to waste your money on welfare and entice layabouts to live on it.

Worst of all, though, would be to mistake that nasty moral choice for a scientific fact you learned at university.

EXTERNALS

How much notice should economists take of the many strands of social life that can affect people's economic aims and behavior, but are conventionally the business of lawyers, political scientists, psychologists, sociologists, social philosophers rather than economists? What of those areas of life outside the boundary of economics, which can nevertheless often affect or be affected by the life inside the boundary?

The economists' concept of 'externality' assumes both a boundary around economics and a boundary within it. Suppose that an economic activity has some effects that are not bought, sold or exchanged. Smoke from a factory harms its neighbors' health. It also inspires a local artist to paint landscapes under unusual sunny/smoky skies. The factory doesn't pay the sick people's doctors' bills. The painter doesn't pay the factory for colouring the sky. So economists define both effects as external to the factory's economic business: an external economy for the painter, an external diseconomy for the neighbors. The effects themselves may or may not be economic; it doesn't matter whether or not the neighbors' ill-health harms their work and earning, or the artist's new inspiration affects the price she gets for her paintings, because the unintended effects are seen to lie beyond the boundary that economists draw around their subject.

In either case humane economists may well be concerned for the neighbors' health and the painter's inspiration. The boundary of the discipline, they would argue, doesn't limit citizens' moral responsibility for their economic actions. Should that boundary be allowed, then, to limit economists' concern for the social effects of their research and teaching which, whether they like it or not, have to be shaped by their values as well as their professional skills?

MARKET AND GOVERNMENT

Of all the economic boundaries, the most talked-about these days – and often the most misleading – is drawn between 'market' and 'government'. Economists certainly need to understand relations between business and government. But I don't believe they're best understood as dealings across a boundary. They're better understood as necessary components of most economic activity.

Don't underestimate the value of market relations. Wherever they can be free and fair exchanges they're as valuable as the business boosters claim. Don't knock the freedom to choose your occupation, choose your employer, or work independently as an artist or surgeon or shop-keeper or soccer pro. Choosing a trade that suits your tastes and talents and purposes in life can make the difference between freedom and slavery, buzz and boredom, for about a third of your waking hours through your earning years. Deciding freely how to save and spend the income, and shopping around for the best goods at the best prices and enjoying the use of them, can do wonders for the rest of your day.

But many of those blessings depend on the market exchanges being free and fair. Free, because the parties have roughly equal bargaining power, so neither can frighten or force or starve the other into a one-sided deal. Fair, because they both know what they're doing and neither can fool the other. Some of the fair dealing can come from the market conditions, some depends on government. Markets differ, and so does the government they need. When you buy socks or apples you can see what you're getting. When you buy insurance or antibiotics you can't, and only government can discipline the suppliers and make sure you get what you pay for.

As in life, so in business. All the legal powers that private firms use have to be created for them by government. Company law gives the firm its corporate identity, to exist, do business and sue or be sued apart from its owners and directors. Company law defines joint stock, requiring the firm to operate for all its shareholders and reward them in proportion to their shares of ownership. And above all company law exempts the firm's owners from paying its debts, because limited liability provides that shareholders can only lose the money that they spend to buy their shares. If the firm goes bankrupt, its creditors can't get their money back from its share-holding owners.

Those three powers are open to plenty of dishonest or incompetent abuse, so governments that create them have to police them. But they do so not only in order to protect the public; above all it's to serve the firm. Without corporate identity the firm couldn't exist. Without joint stock and limited liability it could not expect to raise capital from strangers. Without a lot of other law, honest firms would have too little protection from dishonest employees, suppliers and competitors. There is currently widespread anger, for example, at the rising scale of plunder that the law allows directors of big firms to take for themselves.

So why all the complaints that government 'intervention' in business is raising its costs, wasting its time, reducing its efficiency? In many cases it seems fair to say that business people take for granted the public services that empower and protect the firm, but resent those that police the use of their powers and protect the rights of their owners and workers and customers and suffering neighbors. That sort of spin is human, and we all do some of it. Some of the firms' workers and customers certainly do, taking their own rights for granted and accusing business of greedy, oppressive or deceptive misbehavior (and the analogy can, of course, be extended to government itself!) All involved in or affected by business need government, but government can be anywhere from good to terrible. It often enough needs criticism, reform and improvement. But it's no help to pretend that business or its workers or its customers could do better without it or (usually) with less of it.

MODES OF PRODUCTION

Meet a different set of boundaries, and some examples of their uses (good and bad) in practice. For example, we can distinguish four kinds of productive enterprise:

- Private enterprises earning profits for their private owners.
- Independent enterprises (a collective term for church and other charities, non-profit trusts with charitable or other useful purposes, and cooperative or mutual enterprises whose profits go to their workers or customers, or both).
- Public enterprises, working with varying degrees of independence from the governments that create them.
- Households cooking, washing up, laundering, ironing, bed-making, house-cleaning, mending clothes and repairing breakages, shopping, providing their own transport if they have a car and bikes, and (most demanding, time-consuming and productive) bringing up children.

One thing that's wrong with almost all economists is their habit of calling unpaid work 'consumption' rather than work. Think of that as you slave at your economics course for half your waking hours and do your share of the housework through the other half. Are you really doing nothing but consume?

Call these four the 'productive sectors'. There are various ways of estimating their shares of work and output, usually by estimating market prices for the elements of unpaid labor and unmarketed goods and services. National patterns vary and so do methods of measuring them, but a rough average might show private enterprises producing 45–50 per cent, independent enterprises 5 per cent, public enterprises 15–20 per cent, and households 30–35 per cent of the economic output – the material goods and services – of the rich Western countries.

That leaves no percentage for government? You can shave them all a few points to make room for government at 10–15 per cent. Or you can do as I did in arriving at the above percentages, which was to include what it costs to govern them in the estimate for each of the four sectors. Notice four things about them:

- They all need and get pervasive government and could not exist or do their work without it.
- The government can range from good to bad, just as the enterprises and households can.
- The sectors get some of their quality from the quality of their government, and some from other causes in their histories, their culture, and their physical, financial and human capital.
- There's busy trade and aid between the sectors. They depend on one another for many goods and services. None of them could live without some or all of the others.

Public and independent non-profit enterprises buy a lot of their material capital and consumable goods and services from the private sector, which has also contributed a good deal to developing its own productivity. But the public and independent and household sectors contribute most to the production of the human capital – the capacity and willingness to work – that in turn contributes to the productivity and purposes of all four sectors and their government. Between them the three non-profit sectors breed the people, bring them up to be willing workers, educate them in public or non-profit private schools and universities, and feed and house them throughout their working lives. The market goods and services that they buy make them as dependent on the private sector as it is on them, and as all four are on government. And the necessary government can be better or worse: wise or foolish, fair or oppressive, well or badly administered and enforced, and so on. Citizens, lawyers, politicians, business people, workers' and consumers' representatives can all contribute valuably to the debates about its quality.

As practical examples of 'market and government', from worst through average to best, two true stories – one about blood and one about oil – can end this paper. They compare different relations between the four sectors, and between each sector and government. They include a good deal of Australian material because that's what I know best.

BLOOD

A generation ago in a classic of social science and market theory Richard Titmuss explained why donated blood is safer as well as cheaper than marketed blood. People who sell their blood include some, desperate for cash, who don't mind selling infected blood.

Until 1993 Australian donors (household producers) gave their blood free to the Red Cross (an independent non-profit charity) who passed it to the Commonwealth Serum Laboratories (CSL, a public enterprise), who processed it and supplied it to doctors and hospitals (a mix of public and private enterprises). The government paid the Red Cross to collect it and CSL to process it. The supply was unusually economical: blood for medical use cost about half as much as other Western countries were paying for it. CSL also did other work, producing various kinds of serum and vaccine and selling some of them in a market way without public subsidy.

Through the 1980s the Australian government, like a lot of others, was persuaded to believe that private enterprise is always more efficient than public, and government should get out of its way. So in 1994 the government sold CSL. To get what they innocently thought was a good price for it they gave it a ten-year monopoly of Australia's blood supply at twice the price the government was currently paying for it. Its purity was to be protected by strict new regulation. (Privatization thus *increased* government 'intervention' in the business.)

Shares in the new company were offered to the public and fetched $2.30. Six years later they were fluctuating between $26 and $30. What the government had described as a profitable deal for the taxpayers had brought them just under $300 million, soon spent on buying back their freely-given blood at twice the old price. The private buyers got a capital gift of nearly $3 billion. CSL began to process a lot of foreign blood. When they repeatedly broke the safety rules in their contract, the government repeatedly forgave them. The new chief executive who had negotiated the privatization was soon a multimillionaire and moved to the United States to expand CSL's business there. Was the firm's growth a triumph of competitive private enterprise, or of private monopoly-pricing caused by bad government at the Australian taxpayers' expense? It depends whose spin you read. Better judge for yourself.

OIL

Oil was discovered off the coasts of Britain, Norway and Australia in the 1960s. Boundaries were negotiated to give each country its underwater territory. Each government then had to decide how to organize the extraction and marketing of oil from its area, and for whose benefit.

Australia was experienced at keeping gold rushes in order. Government made the rules. It specified the sizes – the surface areas – for which it would register mining claims. Registered claims were then secure against other prospectors. Similar principles were now applied to the seabed. Private enterprises paid government for rights to particular areas, and mined and marketed what they found there. The profits were private, but there were public benefits of three kinds. The oil companies paid fees for their claims and royalties on their output. They created some employment. And Australia's balance of trade and payments with the rest of the world improved as it stopped importing oil and began to export it.

The British created the British National Oil Corporation (BNOC), a public enterprise, to monopolize the mining and marketing of its North Sea oil. It got most of its work done by hiring and coordinating the work of dozens of private contractors with the specialized skills needed for the work The private operators were thus paid for the work they did, at rates which yielded them some profit. They were regulated more by contract with the public enterprise than by government. Profit from marketing the oil went to the British government as sole shareholder, who used it to cut some tax and to reduce the public debt that was also costing the taxpayers money. That could have been a continuing gain for British people, though more for the rich (because they gained more from the tax cuts) than for the poor. But in the 1980s the Thatcher government privatized the national corporation and spent the proceeds, also to reduce debt and taxes. When that lump of capital was spent, along with similar windfalls from privatizing other public enterprises, Mrs. Thatcher's conservative successors had to make the biggest peacetime tax increase in Britain's history.

Norway began as Britain did, but with a vital difference. Its government insisted that the main concern of its oil policy must be the quality of life in Norway after the oil runs out. As in Britain a public corporation was created with a monopoly of the business. About a tenth of its output, each year, was all the oil that Norway needed. The rest was exported. All the export revenue was invested abroad, permanently. Only the interest and dividends from that investment are for current Norwegian use. When in due course the oil is all mined and sold, its financial benefits can continue forever in the specially valuable form of foreign income.

Think about that. The British politicians were competing for public favor by spending the oil revenue on what could only be temporary tax cuts. The end of the oil must bring both less income and higher taxes or poorer public services, or both. Are British people, or just their politicians, greedier and stupider than Norwegians? It's hard to know about the people, because their politicians never offered them the Norwegian option. Instead they spent what could have been a great capital resource.

Keep thinking. Could the Norwegians have done even better? It's all very well to be prudent with the oil money. Why not with the oil itself? Extract only what Norway needs each year, and the supply could continue much longer. Norway could still be oil-fired, and could be running the world's last airline, after the rest of the world is back to coal-fired industry and rail and sea transport. Or Norway could be selling the last of its oil at fantastic prices. Why not? Keep thinking. It's only by local international agreement that Norway owns that oil. Would you trust the rest of the world when the rest of its oil was gone? When its navies, refitted with coal-fired boilers, are capable of clearing the North Sea of Norwegians in a week? Perhaps in the course of a third world war for the last of the black gold? Norway may have been prudent to turn its oil into money after all. Iran and Saudi Arabia too, perhaps, before long.

KEEP AT IT

Thinking about the capacities of the different productive sectors, their trade with each other and their relations with government, the toughest lesson seems to me to be this: The four sectors do have different capacities. It can be important to have each do what it can do better than the others can. But their type of ownership is not a sure guarantee of their performance. Each of them – governments, public enterprises, private enterprises, independent non-profits, households – can vary from best to worst, and for a variety of reasons. One of the reasons is the quality and competence of their people, which can also vary, over time and between countries. In the oil business Norway seems to have had both the policy-making and the engineering and commercial work in good hands. Britain also had an efficient public corporation, but improvident politicians.

Some free traders think the world would be richer without national economic boundaries. For once, this chapter defends the boundaries. Of the many reasons for them, two will do. With no sign yet of effective world democracy, national democracy is the only democracy we have, and its electors are entitled to decide what government they need. And no country has ever got rich without protecting the early development of its industries. Britain, France, Germany, Italy, Scandinavia, the United States, Canada, Australia, Japan all did it, and still do a good deal of it. To force free trade and unhindered foreign ownership and policy-making on the remaining poor countries must keep many of them poor, and powerless over vital elements of their social life and environmental care.

Economic activity depends, in varying degrees, on its surroundings: on natural resources, law, culture, experience, know-how, mutual trust or distrust, and so on. It is a part of life as a whole. It can be affected in many ways by the political, intellectual, social and global conditions around it. Hence the advice earlier in this chapter. Don't let the boundaries of your economics curriculum – or of any other social science – blind you to that interdependence. To know how any particular industry or market or national economy is working, or how to improve it, you may often need 'an open mind, local knowledge, and the skills of a tough investigator', besides, and sometimes instead of, whatever theory you learned in college.

RECOMMENDED FURTHER READING

Richard Titmuss *The Gift Relationship* [1930], new edn with additional chapters edited by Ann Oakley and John Ashton, London: LSE, 1997.

Paul Streeten *Strategies for Human Development: Global Poverty and Unemployment*, Copenhagen: Handelshojskolens Forlag, 1994.

Jonathan B. Wight *Saving Adam Smith: A Tale of Wealth, Transformation and Virtue*, London: Prentice Hall, 2000.

Hugh Stretton *Economics: A New Introduction*, London and Sterling, VA: Pluto Press and Sydney: UNSW Press 1999.

David Donnison *Policies for a Just Society*, Basingstoke: Macmillan 1998.

2
Modern Economics:
the Problem and a Solution[1]

TONY LAWSON

CAMBRIDGE UNIVERSITY, UK

Modern economics is not very successful as an explanatory endeavour. This much is accepted by most serious commentators on the discipline, including many of its most prominent exponents (See, for example, Rubinstein 1995: 12; Lipsey 2001: 173; Friedman 1999: 137; Coase 1999: 2; Leontief 1982: 104). In the words of Mark Blaug, 'modern economics is sick' (Blaug 1997: 3). Certainly it seems desirable that we do better.

In order to determine whether we *can* do better, however, we need first to be clear *how* modern economics goes wrong and then to explain *why* it does. Once this is achieved, once we have identified the nature and cause(s) of the problem, we will be better placed to determine whether the failings of the discipline are in fact remediable. I briefly consider each of these three issues here.

THE PROBLEM

So how does modern economics go wrong? It does so, I contend, simply through its practitioners seeking to utilise methods of analysis that are largely inappropriate for addressing material of the sort that lies within the social domain.

A fundamental insight here is that, for any method to be able to illuminate a domain of reality, the *nature* of the phenomena of that domain must be of a sort to render this feasible. There is a sense in which method must fit with the nature of its object. We can easily see, for example, that the nature of glass in the window is such as to allow a cotton cloth, but *not* a pneumatic drill, to serve as an appropriate tool for cleaning it. In similar fashion, for a social research method to be relevant in a specific context the material to be studied must be of a sort that makes feasible the method's application. The problem of modern economics, as I am interpreting it, stems from a neglect of this insight. Rather than starting with a question about an aspect of social reality and determining an appropriate method, modern economists usually start with a particular type of method and presume, mistakenly, that it must be appropriate to all social contexts. The result is that modern economists end up distorting social phenomena just to render them open to treatment by their chosen approach.

What is this type of methodology that is not entirely suitable, but which is effectively universally recommended even prior to determining the research question to be addressed? If we open almost any modern economics textbook we quickly find references to procedures of formalistic economic modelling, central to which is the reliance upon functional relations. To the extent that economists concern themselves with phenomena such as consumption, production, investment or human well-being, standard economic analyses involve the formulation of consumption, production, investment and utility *functions* respectively. It is this emphasis upon functional relations that I shall argue is inappropriate to the analysis of most social phenomena.

It does not take too much reflection to see that if an approach to economics that utilises mathematical functions is to be everywhere appropriate then social events must relate to each other in very specific (stable) ways. A function is formally defined as follows: if X is a set of numbers x and Y is a set of numbers y, and if rules are given by which, to each x in X, a corresponding y in Y is assigned, these rules determine a *function* defined for x in X. Typically the value y that a function f takes for a particular x in X is written $f(x)$, so that $y=f(x)$. The point, clearly, is that if a reliance on functions is to be an appropriate way to proceed in economics, event-regularities or event correlations, i.e., regularities of the form 'whenever event x (or state of affairs) then event (or state of affairs) y', must be a commonplace in the social realm.

FUNCTIONAL FELATIONS AND SOCIAL PHENOMENA

What are the reasons for supposing the emphasis on functional relations to be misplaced in economics?

One is simply empirical. Attempts so far to identify non-trivial, stable correlations between economic variables have mostly not succeeded. This is so despite the high-powered techniques of econometrics available to modern economists. Typically, no sooner is an event-regularity reported for the social realm than it is found to break down (see Lawson 1997, chapter 7). Actually, event-regularities are rather rare in the natural sciences too. To be precise, most stable correlations that hold in the natural realm are restricted to situations of experimental control. For example, a table-tennis ball will fall with a constant rate of acceleration when dropped in an experimentally produced vacuum, but rarely does so outside the experimental set-up.

Why is this? It is simply because outside the experimental laboratory any object that is 'dropped' tends, in its movement, to be influenced by a range of causal factors. The wind, thermal forces, table-tennis bats and much else may affect the movement of the ball. The point of an experimental set-up is precisely to isolate a stable causal mechanism from the influence of countervailing mechanisms in order to better identify its properties. The event-regularity produced correlates a triggering of a mechanism with its (isolated) effects. Of course if gravity were not a stable force an experimental event-regularity would not occur anyway.

Such considerations suggest a second, more fundamental, reason for expecting the emphasis on functional relations in economics to be misplaced. For consideration of the experimentally produced event-regularity leads us to recognise that at least three conditions must be satisfied if event-regularities of the sort presupposed by the use of functional relations are to be guaranteed (as opposed to emerging fortuitously). And these seem unlikely to occur in the social realm, as we shall see.

What are the three conditions for an event-regularity to be guaranteed? Simply put, the relevant domain of reality must consist of factors that are 1) intrinsically stable, 2) isolatable and 3) actually acting in a condition of isolation. Notice the last requirement is not superfluous to 2). We may be able experimentally to isolate gravitational forces, aerodynamic forces, thermal forces, and so on. However outside the laboratory all such forces and untold others simultaneously act on the autumn leaf making its actual path unpredictable. If an event-regularity is to be achieved then isolation (and not just isolatability) at some level is required. We might take note at this stage that, in the relevant philosophy-of-science literature, a situation in which many and changing causal mechanisms determine the course of events is referred to as open, whereas one in which a single mechanism is isolated, and an event-regularity produced, is usually described as closed.

We are now in a position to see rather easily why economics, with its emphasis on functional relations, and so a presumption of event-regularities, does so poorly. First of all, even if economic forces were intrinsically stable and isolatable there could be no presumption that they act in isolation. As I say, even in the natural realm, experimental intervention is required to achieve conditions of isolation. Thus in seeking to apply their modelling methods to all social situations economists are overlooking the special conditions required for such regularities even within natural science.

But the situation is more complex still. For rarely are social phenomena found to be either intrinsically stable in the way that some natural mechanisms seem to be, or isolatable. Consider, first, the question of intrinsic stability. Now more or less by definition, social phenomena depend on us for their existence. Without us there would still be natural forces like gravity, but no social phenomena like tables, chairs, cars, markets, universities, language systems, and so forth. Let us consider the latter more closely. A language system is given to us at any moment and facilitates our speech-acts. But, as I say, it also depends on us. And through drawing on it when speaking, individuals, in total, come to reproduce the system in question. In part, we also transform it; whether intentionally or through error we continually change parts of it. The point is that the language system exists as something being continually reproduced and transformed. This is its mode of being, as a process of reproduction and transformation; a language system is intrinsically dynamic in nature. And a moment's reflection helps us realise that so too is the market, the school curriculum, ultimately the school itself, and everything else that is social; all social phenomena are processual in nature. Although aspects of social life may be reproduced over sometimes significant regions of time and space, the sort of stability we attribute, say, to gravitational forces on the surface of the earth are unlikely to prevail.

The remaining requirement for the guarantee of an event-regularity, namely that social causes be isolatable, appears to be at least as unlikely to be satisfied; the social realm seems intrinsically open and interconnected. Firms, money, markets, institutions, social relations, even individual identities, cannot be experimentally isolated from each other. Indeed most, if not all, social phenomena are actually *constituted* in their relations to something else. We cannot have employers without employees, teachers without students, parents without children, and so on; whenever any of us move into new positions, as students, employees, trade union members, etc., what we can and cannot do is determined by our relations to others.

In short, even opportunities for achieving event-regularities within the confines of experimental analyses, conditions that are already rare in the natural sciences, seem unlikely in social research. Yet economists assume they occur anyway, and without any need for experimental intervention.

ECONOMICS AS SCIENCE

But is this analysis not rather debilitating for economics? Does it not undermine any hope that economics can be a science in the sense of natural science, or even a serious discipline at all? Actually this does not follow. Remember that even in natural scientific work the event-regularities produced are mostly restricted to laboratory experiments. Yet this has not prevented the results of natural science, including experimental ones, being used successfully outside the experimental laboratory, in such activities as building bridges and sending rockets to the moon.

The reason this is possible is simply that even where experimental event-regularities are produced these are not actually the real or primary objects of science. For the preceding discussion of experimental activity suggests that the primary objects of science are the underlying mechanisms that govern the directly perceivable events and states of affairs of the world. The experimentally produced event-regularities merely enable us to identify the underlying mechanisms experimentally isolated. And a point of significance here is that, unlike the experimentally restricted event-regularities, the mechanisms responsible may operate inside and outside the experimental set-up alike. Thus the gravitational mechanism operates on autumn leaves (and table tennis balls) even as they fly over roofs and chimneys.

The working of a mechanism that so has its effects and makes its impact whatever the actual outcome (co-determined by countervailing factors) can be referred to as a *tendency*. It is clearly a knowledge of the gravitational mechanism or tendency, and not of events and their patterns *per se,* that helps us build bridges and send rockets to the moon.

So if the primary goal of science is not after all the sorts of event-regularities produced in conditions of experimental control, (but, to repeat, the uncovering of causal mechanisms, like gravity, that govern the phenomena we can, or may be able to, experience directly, such as movements in table tennis balls and autumn leaves) the failure to turn up many event-regularities in the social realm clearly ought not to be viewed as an automatic bar to economics being a serious discipline or even scientific, in the sense of natural science. This failure does, though, render the insistence of modern economic modellers on analysing the economy in terms of functional relations somewhat questionable.

If event-regularities are mostly restricted to experimental situations we shall see below that non-experimental ways of identifying causal factors are perfectly feasible and common. Their uncovering is something that economics can succeed in as well as any other area of research.

EXPLAINING THE PROBLEM

The question that arises at this stage is why we are in the situation in which we find ourselves. If the activity of economic modelling using functional relations is so unsuccessful, and on reflection understandably so, why do economists persist in their modelling activities? The answer is quite simple. Economists very much want to be viewed as scientific. But for reasons that I explore elsewhere (see Lawson 2003, chapter 10) economists take the view that research can only qualify as scientific if it is formulated mathematically. And a deductive mathematics based on functional relations is the sort of mathematical system that economists have found easiest to handle.

Thus whilst other disciplines tend to be defined in terms of the nature of the materials or principles that are studied (for example chemistry is concerned with understanding the chemical aspect of the physical world including living organisms), economists mistakenly conceive of their discipline in terms of their chosen methodological approach.

Of course, we can now see that the belief that maths is essential to science is mistaken. As the discussion of experimental achievements above has suggested, if there is any practice that is essential to science it is that of seeking to identify causes of phenomena of interest. This clearly depends on creativity, imagination, analogy and metaphor and so forth. The use of mathematics cannot take us from falling leaves to gravity, from an increase in human bodily temperature to the virus responsible, from a phenomenon of one type to its cause of a different type. Mathematics, certainly of the sort used by economists, is incidental to this causal-explanatory endeavour, being mostly restricted to analysing cases of stable correlations. As we have also already seen such stable correlations are rare in the natural realm and even more so in the social.

It is likely that the fact that various phenomena regarded as economic are measurable encourages the misapprehension that a mathematical discipline of relevance is possible. But beyond appreciating this fact of the situation, I suspect that most economists never for a moment question whether their preferred (mathematical) methods are appropriate to the material they address. They take it for granted that their methods and social reality 'fit' and that they themselves can be scientists in line with their own (mistaken) image of it, and thereafter they focus mostly on the potentialities of their chosen methods and such like. This indeed, is similar to an assessment made by Alfred Marshall rather a long time ago:

> [The mathematician's] concern is to show the potentialities of mathematical methods on the supposition that material appropriate to their use had been supplied by economic study. He takes no technical responsibility for the material, and is often unaware how inadequate the material is to bear the strains of his powerful machinery. (Marshall 1920: 644)

DOING BETTER

The final question to address is whether, or better, how, it is actually possible to do better. One conceivable justification for the insistence on mathematical modelling in economics that I want to dispose of quickly is that there just is no other way of proceeding.

Some commentators have reasoned that if each social phenomenon is really governed by many causal factors, where we cannot experimentally isolate the effects of any one of them, the only option available is to pretend that any social phenomenon of interest can be treated *as if* generated under conditions of the controlled experiment. But there is a sense in which we often *can* isolate the effects of a single causal mechanism in such an open system. The controlled experiment is but a special case of a method I want to describe here, a method that, in its most abstract formulation, is appropriate to natural and social contexts alike. This is the method of *contrast explanation*. All we need for this method to work is a situation in which i) two outcomes are different ii) in conditions where it was expected that they would have been the same, resting on an assessment that they shared the same, or a sufficiently similar, causal history. Alternatively put, in contrast explanation we seek *not* to explain some X, but to explain why some 'X rather than Y' occurred in a situation where Y was expected (given our understanding of the causal history of the relevant phenomenon). In such a situation we do not seek all the causes of X but the one that made it different from the Y that was anticipated.

Consider the onset of 'mad cow disease'. In the late 1980s in the UK, a group of cows surprised everyone and confounded expectations in displaying unusual symptoms of illness (such as wobbling their heads and falling over). Cows are complex animals, and many factors influence their behaviour. However, by comparing the conditions of the affected cows with others that revealed no symptoms, it was possible to standardise for the causes common to both groups, creating a situation in which it was possible in effect to isolate and identify the cause of the difference, i.e., of the phenomenon of interest.

In the social realm specifically, surprises triggering explanatory endeavour often occur when we move to contexts (regions, countries, institutions, cultures) other than those with which we are very familiar. On doing so we may discover practices, ceremonies, meanings, and orientations, which are at variance with those with which we are acquainted. Of course, we usually find very many commonalities too, suggesting similar causal conditions to those operating in our more familiar context. By standardising for the latter when focusing on a specific contrastive experience, we can often figure out the causes (different rule systems, institutions, or social relations) for the unexpected outcomes. Thus, for example, if we travel, we may find that the inhabitants of some countries drive on a different side of the road to ourselves, treat as equal those who in our own locality are discriminated against (or vice versa), eat differently, etc., all of which allow us to infer something of the operative local rules and social relations.

Note too, that we can also seek to identify more than one of the various causes of any phenomenon. We can do this by comparing a given phenomenon with an array of different contrasts or 'foils', where feasible, considered one at a time. Elsewhere, for example, I have focussed on the immediate post-Second World War productivity growth in the UK and contrasted this with different foils. When the foil utilised was the pre-war productivity experience of the UK then the post-war experience was found to be strikingly higher. This contrast can be explained by the post-war specific expansion in world demand. When, however, the chosen foil was the rate of post-war productivity growth in other comparable industrial countries, such as that of the old West Germany, the UK comparative experience was found to be strikingly poorer. This contrast now highlighted can be explained by the localised nature of collective bargaining in the UK compared to the centralised systems in West Germany and elsewhere (see Lawson 1997, chapter 18 for detail).

EXPERIMENTAL WORK AS A SPECIAL CASE OF CONTRASTIVE EXPLANATION

We can now see that controlled experiments constitute a special case of contrast explanation. For example, in outdoor research, such as in plant breeding experiments, a field may be divided into numerous plots with, say, some chemical compound applied to some plots only. If the average yield is higher in the plots where the compound is allocated we can conclude that it acts as a fertilizer, that it explains not the level of yield but the yield differential (our contrast). In such an outdoor experiment, the conditions in the field can vary throughout the growing season. The method works just because at any point in time the effects are the same throughout the field, except for the chemical compound whose properties are under investigation.

The indoor laboratory experiment is different only in that the background conditions are held constant throughout the period of the experiment, allowing a meaningful contrast between what happens prior to, and what occurs with, a mechanism being triggered.

But these experimental scenarios, though useful in science, are not necessary for success using the contrast explanatory approach. Often all we need is an informed perspective giving us reason to expect two outcomes to be the same in a situation where the latter are found to be different. In that situation there is *prima facie* reason to suppose a single causal factor is responsible, and reason to expect that it can be identified (for a longer more detailed discussion, see Lawson, 2003, chapter 4).

I have run through the method of contrast explanation first and foremost to indicate that causal analysis can proceed in the absence of closed systems. However, I should emphasise that explanatory analysis required to render any chosen contrast phenomenon of interest intelligible can take many forms. It may involve the identification of a hitherto non-existent local mechanism or set of conditions, or a reworking of previous understandings, including seeing connections or relations previously unnoticed, or even the elaboration of a highly abstract account of the workings of a system in its entirety. It all depends on context.

If, for example, the chosen contrast is highly context-specific, say two local traders are selling the same product at different prices, the causal explanation is likely also to be a relatively localised factor. If instead, the contrast is of a sort that interested Marx, namely that after a point in history goods were mostly being produced for exchange in the marketplace (i.e., as commodities) rather than, as previously, for immediate use, the explanation (in Marx's case his theory of the emergence and nature of the capitalist mode of production), will be rather more extensive in its scope or reach of relevance.

APPLIED ECONOMICS

Now economics is not restricted to the identification of causal tendencies, of course, whether these involve reference to simple mechanisms or economic totalities or systems. Economists may also be interested in specific outcomes.

Can we say much about concrete events? After an event has occurred it may be possible to work out how the different known mechanisms combined to produce it (much as English weather can be explained after it has happened). How about before the event? Can anything be said? The answer depends on context. If the situation is one in which two or three mechanisms or tendencies are thought to dominate a phenomenon of interest, perhaps a range of likely outcomes can be safely speculated.

More typically, though, it will be possible, in a given context, to identify little more than the workings of a specific tendency of import and perhaps speculate as to some of the likely countervailing tendencies. At the level of outcomes there is no option but to wait and see (notice that even this may be enough for policy purposes. Even if we do not know the workings of all mechanisms we may be able to identify those that work to produce greater unemployment, poverty, discrimination and other undesirable features, and so work on undermining their supporting conditions).

It is the deeper, more abstract structures which, though never fixed, seem to be the more enduring. The price mechanism is more enduring than a set of prices; typically the university outlives any specific courses given. In serious economic research it is often the case that deeper structures will be taken as momentarily given and perhaps used to frame more detailed studies, although the insights of the latter will often facilitate a better or revised understanding of the former.

What does all this entail for economists who wish to give a broader picture? It means they will need to move between different levels of abstraction, at some moments descending to speculations of concrete outcomes where it is believed the major forces of determination are fairly stable and mostly known; at other moments identifying the operation of significant tendencies in play and perhaps also noting offsetting counter-tendencies; and at further moments retreating to yet higher levels of abstraction, specifically where the context makes so much difference both to precise outcomes and to the causal factors in play that little can be said short of empirically examining the details in context (and perhaps alerting the reader to this fact).

The above overview, though not comprehensive, indicates the sorts of analytical procedures that the best of economists have mostly tended to draw upon, most specifically those now associated with the modern heterodox traditions. Let me finish by giving some brief illustrations.

When Thorstein Veblen, the figurehead of the (old) institutionalist school of economics (a heterodox tradition opposed to the modern mainstream), argued a century ago that social life was in large part a process, and specifically constituted by evolutionary processes of cumulative causation, he never tried to generalise the concrete details of social processes. Clearly to suggest that social life is largely processual is to generalise at a relatively high level of abstraction. However, Veblen was clear that if his general claim was correct, and that an evolutionary economics was inevitable, a turn to the latter actually meant abandoning the search for highly general self-contained systems of substantive economic theory (such as modern day economists mostly do pursue with their reliance on functional relations). Indeed, Veblen concluded that an evolutionary economics would need to be highly empirical in nature, concerned with determining how actual social phenomena grow and change (he also erroneously thought that 'the body of economists' appreciated this and were already carrying it through):

> Self-contained systems of economic theory, balanced and compendious, are no longer at the focal centre of attention; nor is there a felt need of such.... Meantime, detailed monographic and itemised inquiry, description, analysis, and appraisal of particular processes going forward in industry and business, are engaging the best attention of economists; instead of that meticulous reconstruction and canvassing of schematic theories that once was of great moment and that brought comfort and

assurance to its adepts and their disciples. There is little prospect that the current generation of economists will work out a compendious system of economic theory at large ...

...The question now before the body of economists is not how things stabilise themselves in a 'static state,' but how they endlessly grow and change. (Veblen 1954 [1925]: 8)

When John Maynard Keynes, the figurehead of the post-Keynesian school of economics (a further heterodox tradition opposed to the modern mainstream), argued that social life was characterised by uncertainty, and specifically that, as a result, investment decisions were especially sensitive to the current state of markets and investor confidence, he never tried to generalise these factors at the concrete level (to make the state of investor confidence the dependent variable in a functional relation or whatever). Rather, Keynes recommended an empirical assessment of markets and actual business psychology in any relevant context. In doing so, Keynes was aware that successful analysis necessarily moved between different levels of abstraction, according to the nature of the subject-matter being considered:

There is, however, not much that can be said about the state of confidence *a priori*. Our conclusions must mainly depend on actual observations of markets and business psychology. This is the reason why the ensuing digression is on a different level of abstraction from most of the book. (Keynes 1973: 149)

And when Karl Marx theorised, and systematised as a 'general law', a mechanism working to cause profits to fall, he fully recognised that, if his theory was correct, this mechanism would typically be crossed if not annulled by countervailing forces. For this reason Marx described his law as expressing a tendency rather than an empirical actuality. Marx even stressed that in periods when profits actually fell there were likely countervailing forces preventing it falling faster. Indeed, he inquired into their nature:

There must be some counteracting influences at work, which cross and annul the effect of the general law, and which give it merely the characteristic of a tendency, for which reason we have referred to the fall of the general rate of profit as a tendency to fall.

The following are the most general counterbalancing forces: ... (Marx (1973): chapter xiv)

SUMMARY

The argument of this chapter can be put simply. It is widely recognised that economics performs badly as an explanatory endeavour. The reason for this is that modern economists all too often seek to generalise in the wrong place, and specifically, given their desire to formulate functional relations, at the level of actual outcomes and their presumed correlations. The reason for this, in turn, is a widespread insistence on using the methods of mathematical-deductive modelling. And this latter phenomenon, in its turn, is motivated by a desire on the part of economists to be 'scientific', coupled with the (erroneous) belief that mathematics is essential to all science. Once the erroneous nature of the latter belief is recognised and the straightjacket of the insistence on mathematical-deductive modelling thrown off, methods can be taken up that seem capable of allowing economics to be both explanatorily successful and even scientific in the sense of natural science.

REFERENCES

Blaug, Mark (1997) 'Ugly Currents in Modern Economics', *Options Politiques* (Septembre), 3–8.

Coase, Ronald (1999) Interview with Ronald Coase, *Newsletter of the International Society for New Institutional Economics*, Vol 2, No. 1 (Spring).

Friedman, Milton (1999) Conversation with Milton Friedman in Snowdon B. and Vane H. (eds) *Conversations with Leading Economists: Interpreting Modern Macroeconomics*, 124–44, Cheltenham: Edward Elgar.

Kay, John (1995) 'Cracks in the Crystal Ball', *Financial Times*, September 29.

Keynes, John Maynard (1973) *The Collected Writings of John Maynard Keynes*, Vol. VII, *The General Theory of Employment Interest and Money*, London: Royal Economic Society.

Lawson, Tony (1997) *Economics and Reality*, London and New York: Routledge.

Lawson, Tony (2003) *Reorienting Economics*, London and New York: Routledge.

Leontief, Wassily (1982) Letter in *Science*, 217: 104–7.

Lipsey, Richard, G. (2001) 'Successes and failures in the transformation of economics' *Journal Of Economic Methodology*, Vol. 8, No. 2 (June): 169–202.

Marshall, A. (1920) *The Principles of Economics*, 8th Edition, London: Macmillan.

Marx, Karl (1974) *Capital: A Critique of Political Economy, Volume III: The Process of Capitalist Production as a Whole*, Edited by Engels F., London: Lawrence and Wishart.

Rubinstein, Ariel (1995) 'John Nash: the master of economic modelling', *Scandinavian Journal of Economics* 97(1): 9–13.

Veblen, Thorstein B. (1954 [1925]) 'Economic theory in the calculable future', in Ardzrooni, Leon (ed.) *Essays in our Changing Order*, New York: Viking Press [first published in *American Economic Review*, Vol. XV, No. 1, Supplement, March 1925].

3
The Pitfalls of Mainstream Economic Reasoning (and Teaching)

MICHAEL A. BERNSTEIN

UNIVERSITY OF CALIFORNIA, SAN DIEGO, USA

Most disciplines challenge an instructor to utilize decidedly unrealistic arguments as they introduce their students to its foundational ideas. In an introductory physics class, for example, students are acquainted with the simple notions of classical mechanics. They are taught that every object accelerates to the centre of gravity at the same rate. In a perfect vacuum, like that of outer space, such abstractions have direct applicability and can thus be verified by actual observation. Even so, students and instructors alike know well enough to avoid the conclusion that, in actual space and time on (say) planet Earth, a rock and a feather, when dropped from a two-story building, will hit the ground at the same time. The clearly unreal conclusions of classical reasoning are not translated directly to 'real life' and this precisely because the student (not to mention the mentor) knows from actual experience to avoid doing so.

In economics, however, just the opposite is the case. The everyday appearance of social life provides little in the way of verification for the student of basic economic ideas. The result is an analytical confusion that captivates the student more or less forever – indeed, the application of abstract ideas is no longer a means to refinement of those obviously crude first approximations. It becomes instead a continued series of reaffirmations of initial ideas that are as misleading as they are illogical.

Two features of contemporary economic reasoning powerfully constrain the ways in which students learn to think about the social world: the notions of 'perfect competition' and of 'equilibrium.' Misunderstanding what these concepts actually mean, and how their unalloyed application affects the ways in which we engage in economic analysis, constitutes the essential pitfall of mainstream reasoning in the discipline as a whole. Yet instructors rarely convey this profound warning to their introductory students. On the contrary, they invest the vast proportion of their time in deploying these concepts in uncritical and unexamined ways – actively encouraging their students to reproduce the very same lack of theoretical awareness that inflects (and infects) the use of these concepts in the first place.

For the vast majority of contemporary, mainstream economists, competition (whether of the 'perfect' or 'imperfect' variety) is a state rather than a process. They teach their students that in a market in which a large number of producers compete to produce a given good or service, a flexible price system will generate an optimal outcome in which consumer satisfaction and producer efficiency are both maximized. This characterization of a 'perfectly competitive' market rests upon the assumption that the large number of competitors within it are identical – their cost structures, techniques of production, knowledge of key market variables, and access to information are all the same. In point of fact, the 'sameness' of the competitors in this market, and the allocative situation achieved when prices competitively gravitate to an equivalence with the marginal costs of production, fully characterizes a state of affairs that will not change, barring exogenous shocks to the system as a whole.

As an initial analysis of market structure and function, the perfect competition model seems a benign starting point for investigation. Presumably students, having mastered the intricacies of the simple model, will ultimately be equipped to complicate their analysis with the empirical refinements of the 'real' world. Much like a physicist taking into account the realities of friction, temperature, ambient pressure, and so forth, the apprenticed economist will over time learn to reconstitute the simple findings of the perfect competition model to make them more useful for an understanding of the social world as it actually exists. But the promise of this positivistic approach to learning is rarely realized; the reasoning that lies behind the construction of the model makes such iterative learning and growing sophistication virtually impossible. Here lies the common failure of contemporary economic reasoning and the fundamental inadequacy of its transmission to succeeding generations of students.

Ironically, the perfect competition model suffers not from being an abstraction from reality – indeed all models in all disciplines share that epistemological quality. Rather, the pitfall of utilizing the perfect competition framework as a starting point for economic reasoning is that it makes a logically coherent understanding of what competition is impossible. Competition, in any given market, is a process by which firms continually seek to re-establish the conditions of their own profitability. In other words, to compete in a market is to seek to exploit differences, among firms, in cost structures of production, in technology, in knowledge about production and distribution, in access to information, and in awareness of trends in consumption habits and volumes. These differences are the essential dimensions along which competitive decisions are made.

Firms invest in new production techniques, in new product lines, in new distributional frameworks and marketing schemes, precisely because they perceive a difference between their awareness of and access to these opportunities and those of their competitors. If in fact they saw no difference in these attributes, they would avoid strategic initiatives altogether for the simple reason that they would have no competitive advantage, over their peers, in pursuing them. The fundamental goal in capitalist competition is to be one step ahead of the 'herd,' to be the first to invest in a new technology, the first to liquidate a non-productive commitment, the first to present a novel product to the public. Failure to be first is usually the signal symptom of failure to compete. Stock and other financial markets provide the generalized corollary to this argument. In them, every investor seeks to be first – the first to buy a new stock that will then appreciate as others 'herd in' to benefit from the same opportunity and push the price higher, the first to sell equity at its peak price before others try to cash in and thus drive the price downward.

In characterizing competition as a state rather than as a process of economic change, mainstream reasoning does not erect a first approximation of reality, it rather frames a way of thinking about competitive behavior that forever and completely prevents a full understanding of the phenomenon itself. What in most disciplines are simple models to begin a kind of analysis that will lead to increasingly accurate characterizations of real-world, real-time situations becomes instead in economics an actual barrier to further elaboration of core analytical ideas. By uncritically accepting the notions of perfect competition with which they are introduced to the discipline, our students more often than not are prevented from ever developing a set of tools and theoretical protocols with which to grasp fully the workings of the competitive marketplace.

An equally unfortunate form of reasoning in economics is encountered with respect to discussions of equilibrium. Students in the introductory setting are quickly introduced to the notion of market stasis where any forces moving the market out of an equilibrium state, in which supply equals demand, are quickly counteracted such that equilibrium is once again achieved. Increases in supply will depress prices such that no excess quantities of production are left in inventory. Conversely, increases in demand will move prices upward such that unfulfilled orders or shortages are eliminated. These simple fables about equilibration in competitive markets provide the foundation of most economic reasoning with which introductory students are acquainted in their first courses of study in the discipline.

Yet far from being an approximation of reality that may subsequently be complicated by 'real life' frictions, distortions, and contingencies, the idea of equilibrium with which mainstream economists first train their students lays the foundation for an enduring and vastly confusing methodological practice– that of comparative statics. This is to say that, much like the confusions introduced in the discussion of perfect competition, mainstream economic reasoning encourages the student to mistake the presence of an equilibrium for the means by which equilibrium is achieved. For example, a model of a perfectly competitive labor market shows that at a low wage more labor is employed. This market-in-stasis paradigm is then compared with an alternative state, one in which the wage is high and the amount of labor employed is less. A comparison of these two static equilibrium positions affords the student an appreciation of the market-clearing function of a price (in this case, the 'wage') in a competitive environment. While such a teaching strategy may be unobjectionable on its face, it is the source of grave misunderstanding when improperly used–as it most often is in introductory courses.

As the late Joan Robinson (a celebrated Cambridge University economist who died in 1983) once pointed out, the comparison of two equilibrium positions is not the same as explaining the process by which one moves from one equilibrium position to another. Contrasting a low-wage/high-employment equilibrium, in the case of the example above, with a high-wage/low-employment state does not allow one to conclude that rising (or falling) wages will lead to lower (or higher) employment. Yet it is just this sort of reasoning with which most introductory economics students are endowed by the time they conclude their studies. Their approach to understanding dynamic market processes are thus forever constrained by the confusion their initial training instills in their minds.

A critique of the wage/employment model derived from comparative static methodology is rather straightforward; indeed, it is the core of the devastating critique of mainstream economic reasoning advanced by John Maynard Keynes in the middle of the twentieth century. Let us assume that, in a given labor market, the prevailing wage is high and equilibrium employment is low. A simple comparative statics analysis would suggest that a remedy to the low employment problem thus encountered would be to provoke a fall in the wage. Such a reduction could be the result of competition by unemployed workers willing to labor for lower pay. It could, perhaps, be the consequence of limiting the power of labor unions to militate for and sustain higher wage-rates, or it could be the result of reducing or eliminating minimum-wage floors in public policy legislation itself. But if we then closely examine the *process* by which the wage change affects the market under analysis, we discover that the employment result may be just the opposite of what a comparative statics perspective would suggest.

Let us examine the effects of a falling wage in the market imagined above. A lower wage will reduce the incomes of those employed. Lower wage earnings will translate into falling demand as income constraints make themselves increasingly felt in households. Falling demand in the marketplace will yield lower sales revenues for competing firms in that market. Firms will react to falling sales revenues by reducing the level of their operations. Their demand for labor inputs will consequently fall. Rising unemployment will be the necessary result. By closely and logically examining the ways in which markets work, and in which market actors respond to changing variables, we have discovered that a falling wage might very well lead to a *decrease* in employment. In other words, comparative statics, if improperly applied to the analysis of market processes, will actually lead us to a finding diametrically opposed to what logic and formal consistency in our reasoning would suggest. Yet this lesson is more often than not ignored in a mainstream introductory course in economics.

Another example in this vein concerns price controls. Introductory students are vigorously taught that any attempt to control prices will yield perverse results. The classic example mobilized in the introductory economics curriculum pertains to rent control. If legislation limits the cost of rental housing below its 'equilibrium' level, so the argument goes, the lower revenues earned by housing contractors will discourage them from building more housing stock. The result will be a greater shortage of housing, a scarcity that will ultimately increase the price of housing over time. Hence rent controls should be avoided by policy-makers.

Consider, however, an alternative view of how the housing market works. Lower rents will allow rental dwellers higher levels of discretionary income as their housing costs are reduced. These higher residual incomes will generate more purchasing of other goods and services, as well as allow most consumers the opportunity to save more as the margin between essential and discretionary expenditures is widened. Greater purchases of goods and services will improve overall economic growth, employment, and spending; greater savings by a larger proportion of the population will yield a larger supply of loanable funds in banks and credit unions. Terms of borrowing will improve as interest rates fall in response to the increased supply of savings. Building contractors, impressed by improving macroeconomic conditions generally (due to the increased purchases of goods and services obtaining in most markets), and stimulated by the reduced costs of borrowing, will increase their investment in the production of new housing. Construction housing starts will thus increase. Once again, a more thorough examination and application of plausible economic principles yields altogether different conclusions from those typically conveyed in the mainstream introductory classroom.

To these criticisms of mainstream economic reasoning, and of their transmission to new generations of students, the instinctive and obvious retort of many will be that science must proceed first on the basis of abstractions that are, by their nature, unreal. Only through the successive and iterative approximation of reality can models of particular processes, in this case social ones, be made more realistic, concrete, and accurate. This is the essential claim of any positivistic approach to the accumulation of knowledge and it is, indeed, the foundation of a remarkable defense of mainstream economics mobilized five decades ago by Milton Friedman in his *Essays in Positive Economics*.[1] But a concern with the pitfalls of mainstream economic reasoning goes far beyond a naïve anxiety about realism in scientific analysis. It instead condemns forms of analysis and techniques of persuasion that serve to enfeeble our students' capacity to engage in a coherent examination of society itself.

The lessons of classical mechanics in an introductory physics course, far from disabling the student's ability to refine and elaborate their learning, actually serve to warn them that foundational models of motion are only a first step in winning a full understanding of the physical world. Indeed, precisely because the student *knows* from actual experience that a rock and a feather will not hit the ground at the same time, when dropped from an equal height, Newton's equations showing the existence of a gravitational constant term may be understood as only the beginning in the study of mass and motion. Yet the innate knowledge of the social world that the student brings to the introductory economics classroom is not only less useful than this, it is also actually quite misleading.

The disjunction between appearance and reality lies at the center of all processes of knowledge creation and accumulation. What *seems* to be true must be, in any disciplinary context, constantly questioned, examined, and challenged. In physics, we thus ultimately learn, through the important analytical lessons of classical mechanics, that while the rock will hit the ground before the feather in a simple experiment in actual experience, the rate of acceleration toward the center of mass, for these (and all) objects, is the same when friction, wind velocity, and ambient pressure are taken out of account. No such correction of misunderstanding in the social sciences is so readily available. Our students suffer as a result of the fact that what *appears* to be true, when uncritically examined in everyday life, is unthinkingly assumed to be true in its essence. The simple models that introduce students to the subject-matter of economics then become not the initial starting point of an investigation soon to be complicated, refined, and reorganized by subsequent analysis, but rather the conclusion of the overall analysis as a whole.

An insightful critic of mainstream economics once said that in the discipline there is nothing more complicated than the simplest of ideas, and nothing simpler than the most complicated representation of those ideas in mathematical models.[2] Perhaps it is this paradox that, above all, best exemplifies what is wrong with mainstream economic reasoning (and teaching) today.

Simple models that delimit the ways in which we introduce our students to our discipline actually destroy their capacity to complicate in meaningful ways their understanding of economic processes overall. In fact, what we teach our students about competition and equilibrium serves to make it impossible for most of them to imagine what real competition and dynamic processes in an actual economy are like. No amount of additional 'complicating variables,' introduced into a model initially premised on false notions, can remedy this problem. Far from empowering our students in their efforts to understand the social world in which they live, we unintentionally cripple them with simple propositions that actually mislead rather than inform.

Historians and philosophers of science have long taught us that it is the articulation of a 'starting point' that encapsulates the core methodologies, questions, and practices of any discipline. For the classical economic theorists of the eighteenth and nineteenth centuries, the beginnings of their science rested in a determination to understand the 'nature and causes of the wealth of nations' as the result of the social organization of human beings to provision their needs and desires. By the twentieth century that starting point of analysis had been abandoned by mainstream theorists, replaced by a preoccupation with understanding the goal-oriented behavior of individuals in the marketplace. There was much to commend that change in emphasis – the focus on exchange behavior could yield formalized models, ones that could apparently be tested with empirical evidence, algorithms that could actually yield operational results for particular activities such as budgetary and strategic choice. But the change also had an immense cost inasmuch as it obscured from view not simply an older and meaningful tradition of analysis in the discipline, but also encouraged economists in the deployment of behavioral models that precluded further substantive examination of the mechanisms of economic change themselves.

The pitfalls of mainstream economic reasoning subsist within the flawed ways in which and by which we motivate our subject for our introductory students. We appeal to their innermost prejudices about their everyday experience of markets – that what they most desire, and what is in shortest supply, is most expensive; that what they least value, and what is amply available, has the lowest price. These appeals to their uncritically examined assumptions about the appearance of the world in which they live falsely encourage them in the idea that those assumptions, and the appearances on which they are based, are all accurate and logically robust. Our simple comparative static models of supply and demand then conform with what is, for the introductory student, a simple (and simple-minded) apprehension of reality. The quick and entirely misguided jump from the comparison of equilibrium positions to the perception of how economic processes actually work is the necessary and unfortunate result.

Social scientific perceptions of the social world do not, of course, exist outside of the political, social, economic, and cultural contexts within which they emerge. This is all to say that changing how our students examine and understand society, not to mention how they perceive the relationship between models of social processes and empirical findings about those processes, is not purely an intellectual endeavor. But within the classroom there are steps we can take to avoid misleading our students on matters of fundamental methodological importance. Avoiding the transmission of hackneyed notions about 'perfect competition' and 'equilibrium,' that have framed introductory teaching in our discipline for over a century, is a very good place to start.

4
Neoclassical Economic Theory: a Special and Not a General Case

PAUL ORMEROD

VOLTERRA CONSULTING, UK

INTRODUCTION

All theories are approximations to reality. Even the most rigorously tested theories in physics are not absolutely and completely true. Sooner or later, someone will develop a theory which explains reality just that little bit better.

The key question for the value of a theory is whether it is a good enough approximation to reality for it to be useful in practice. Neoclassical economics has its strengths. But the assumptions which it makes place limits on its usefulness.

The single most restrictive assumption of conventional economics is that the tastes and preferences of individual agents – whether people or firms – are fixed. The theory can only be a satisfactory description of reality where this assumption is reasonable. In practice, we are surrounded by situations in which the assumption is not valid. Financial markets, new technologies, films, fashionable consumer goods, crime – all these are examples of circumstances in which the behaviour of an agent can be and is directly altered by the behaviour of other agents.[1]

Models in which agents can influence directly the behaviour of others are able to subsume conventional neoclassical theory as a special case. In the latter, any potential direct influence is assumed to take the value zero. In other words, the theory presumes it does not exist. So models in which it can either be zero or greater than zero can offer a more general description of behaviour.

STRENGTHS OF ECONOMICS

Economics as an academic discipline has two valuable strengths. First, it trains people to think analytically. Second, it provides a number of important insights into how the economic and social world actually operates. But despite these advantages, students at all levels have turned away from economics in large numbers.

By far the most important idea in economics is that agents respond to incentives to prices. This is an extraordinarily powerful concept, which distinguishes economics from all other social sciences. It is here that economics comes close to positing a universal law of behaviour. In practice, of course, quantifying these effects may be very difficult, not least because the strength of the response to a given set of incentives is emphatically not universal. It varies with the social and institutional setting and with the historical context.

But the idea that agents respond to incentives has many applications. The Mayor of London – Ken Livingstone, a man of impeccable Left wing credentials – is using it to try to help solve London's traffic problems. A congestion charge has been levied on the movement of cars into Central London in the hope that this will cause a sufficient number of drivers to abandon their cars and switch to public transport. We do not have to buy into the complete package of free market ideology to recognise that incentives matter.

Yet another area where incentives are important is crime. Again, we do not have to believe wholeheartedly in rational, utility-maximising agents to recognise this. The proposition that poverty causes crime is often dismissed scornfully as a figment of the imagination of bleeding heart liberals. Look at the 1930s, it is said. People were poorer then but crime was much lower. But hard-hearted economics tells us that the *relative* set of incentives faced by agents is important. Most crime is committed by young men with low levels of skill. The widening of inequality from the 1970s onwards altered the relative set of prices which they faced and, not surprisingly, crime became a more attractive option. As the UK economy has moved back towards full employment in the 1990s and a minimum wage has been introduced, the appeal of ordinary jobs has increased, and crime has fallen.[2] Agents have responded to the price mechanism. Of course, this is by no means the whole story, but it is simply not possible to give an account of how crime changes over time without considering the role of incentives.[3]

Why, then, has the number of students choosing economics dropped sharply, and how might they be persuaded to move back? Economics can be extremely interesting, but agents in the market-students-are telling us that it is not. The set of incentives they face either discourages them from taking up economics in the first place, or leads them to abandon it as soon as possible.

DOGMATISM

I think that an important reason for this is that the teaching of economics has become too dogmatic, and too much is claimed for the achievements of the discipline. Economics should be taught instead as more of a way of thinking about the world which can be of help in understanding a wide range of business, economic and social issues. An engineer teaching students the mathematics of, say, bridge-building, can afford to be dogmatic. An enormous number of bridges has been constructed on these principles and, most of the time, most of them stay up. Economics is far from being in this position, yet it is often presented as though it is. Textbooks have come to resemble those of engineering, as if many problems have been solved and students simply need to absorb a settled body of knowledge.

A key example of this is the widespread assumption in economic theory that agents are rational maximisers. John Sutton of the London School of Economics, and now President of the Royal Economic Society, has recently reflected on this question:

> The student who comes to economics for the first time is apt to raise two rather obvious questions. The first relates to the economist's habit of assuming that agents can be treated as rational maximisers... By the time that students have advanced a couple of years, this question is forgotten. Those students that remain troubled by [it] have quit the field; those who remain are socialised and no longer ask about such things.'[4]

Some of the most interesting work in economics in the past twenty years has been on the topic not of rational maximisation, but of bounded rationality, on situations in which, for example, some or all the agents have access to incomplete information. Professional economists have gained prestige and even Nobel prizes for this work. George Akerlof and Joe Stiglitz, two of the 2001 prize winners, have pioneered this area, and have made extremely interesting contributions.[5] These models usually attempt to explain a particular question, rather than purporting to be *the* general theory of how agents behave.

But most economics courses for most students remain fixated on the old-fashioned theory based on rational maximisation which, as John Sutton notes, many students simply disbelieve. Judging by the content of the top economics journals in recent years, a lot of the big names in the profession in America do not believe it either.

MAKING ECONOMICS MORE GENERAL

In some circumstances, such as when a shopper is in a supermarket and is choosing between different brands of a product, the assumption of fixed preferences is not a bad one to make. But in a wide range of circumstance, individual agents are influenced directly by the actions of others.

In conventional theory, agents respond to the decisions of others only in so far as these affect the prices of the goods and services which the individual buys and/or sells. They do not want a Teletubbie, say, or a hula hoop or, much more seriously, a 30 year US government bond rather than a French one, simply because other people do. But in the real world this sort of behaviour is pervasive. From fashion markets to financial markets to the degree of optimism or pessimism which firms feel about the future, the opinions and behaviour of others affects directly how individuals behave. This is the key theme of my book *Butterfly Economics*.[6]

Bounded rationality, the concept which won the 2001 Nobel prize, is a distinct step forward for economics. But under this, agents still have the capacity to maximise, to find the optimal decision.

The 2002 prize went to scholars who are helping to make the discipline very much more general. Daniel Khaneman and Vernon Smith have integrated insights from psychological research into economics. A key theme of their work is the ability of agents to make judgements under uncertainty,[7] which is typically much weaker than standard economic theory presumes. Rather than assuming that 'rational' behaviour prevails, they have adopted the scientific methodology of testing empirically the validity of theoretical hypotheses.

On occasions, the postulate of the rational maximiser with fixed tastes and preferences is not rejected by the experimental evidence. In some circumstances, the approximations made by the theory are not unreasonable. Much more frequently, agents are found to operate according to simple rules of thumb. These rules seem to give fairly good outcomes and avoid obvious loss. But they are quite different from the world of the rational maximiser.

In circumstances in which agents can directly influence the tastes and preferences of others, the ability to compute optimal solutions rapidly becomes impossible. In fact, there are many examples where this is true even if we do make the assumption of fixed tastes and preferences. The classic one is of course Roy Radner's 1968 proof of the existence of general equilibrium under uncertainty.[8] He formalized the conditions required to prove the existence of such equillibrium when agents hold different views about the future. The key point about the proof is that each agent is required to have access to an infinite amount of computing power. Radner concluded that the model of general equilibrium 'breaks down completely in the face of limits on the ability of agents to compute optimal strategies'. In other words, economics has known for 35 years that general equilibrium, the central building block of conventional neoclassical theory, requires assumptions which are obviously not true.

At a less elevated level, game theory has permeated economics in the past twenty years or so. Yet consider the Prisoner's Dilemma. The rules are very simple and are time-invariant. Agents are assumed to have a great deal of information. In particular, in its simplest form, each agent is assumed to know the payoff values of his or her opponent. This is a pretty strong assumption to make when you think about it. Yet do we know the best strategy? Well, we do when we make the very specific assumption that the game will end in a fixed number of moves, and that both players know this. But we should note immediately that this assumption removes a great deal of the uncertainty that the future might hold. Most of the time, in practice, we simply do not know when a game will end. So the assumption places strong limits on the dimension of the problem from the point of view of processing information.

There is a vast literature on the Prisoner's Dilemma when it ends at random. But the optimal strategy remains unknown. The scientific community has invested a great deal of effort in trying to discover the best strategy, but still we do not know.

In models in which tastes and preference can vary according to the actions of others, there is no point at all in looking for optimal rules of behaviour. Instead, we are seeking plausible rules of thumb for agents to follow. Crucially, the outcomes of these models are almost invariably compared to the real world phenomena which they are trying to explain. From the outset, they are more scientific than conventional economic theory.

An excellent early example of such models is Alan Kirman's theory of foreign exchange markets.[9] Conventional theory finds the volatility of these markets very difficult to explain, so much so that Kenneth Arrow has described the degree of volatility as an 'empirical refutation'[10] of general equilibrium theory. In Kirman's model, the individual agents follow very simple yet plausible rules of behaviour, but the interactions between them give rise to complex behaviour of the market as a whole. Plausible rules for individual behaviour give rise to exactly the kind of high levels of volatility at the aggregate level which we observe in financial markets.

CONCLUSION

Contrary to the perceptions of many critics of economics, the discipline is in the process of re-inventing itself. An increasing number of scholars are testing empirically the postulates of conventional neoclassical theory, and finding them wanting. More and more papers allow the preferences of agents to vary as a result of the actions of others. There is a scientific imperative to relax the assumption of fixed preferences, in order to be able to give a reasonable account of important real world phenomena.

Of course, the mainstream remains powerful, with its emphasis on rational, maximising agents with fixed tastes. But it is gradually being outflanked. Vernon Smith's Nobel lecture in the *American Economic Review*[11] is a superb example in this vein.

The problem is that most academic economists are not sufficiently aware of developments in their own subject. The teaching of economics in general lags far behind the advances and developments which have taken place. A key task for critics of neoclassical orthodoxy is to reinforce the already established trend by producing more convincing models which explain reality better than those of conventional fixed-taste, rational, maximising agents. It can be done. It needs to be done.

5

Where Do Economies Come From? The Missing Story

ANNE MAYHEW

UNIVERSITY OF TENNESSEE, USA

Where do economies come from? How are the rules by which we lead our economic lives determined? If you try to answer these questions by reading one of the standard introductory economic texts, you will come away with the impression that economies take the form that they do by virtue of millions of individual human actions. In the words of one widely used text:

> Economics is the study of how society manages its scarce resources. In most societies, resources are allocated not by a single central planner but through the combined actions of millions of households and firms... There is no mystery to what an 'economy' is. Whether we are talking about the economy of Los Angeles, of the United States, or of the whole world, an economy is just a group of people interacting with one another as they go about their lives.[1]

Fine, but interactions require accepted rules, practices, customs, understandings. When is it appropriate to take a piece of food that is lying on a shelf or table and eat it? If you are a guest in a house and you see a plate of cookies on a table, you may reasonably assume that it is appropriate to take one. In many restaurants in the United States, a bowl of small candies will be at a table or desk near the entrance. You may take one without disapproval. In the U.S., grocery stores frequently have shelves of candies next to the cashier at the entrance in an arrangement that looks not unlike that of the candies in the restaurants. However, you may not take one of these pieces of candy without risk of arrest. These are trivial examples of rules and practices that we all know; it would surely be a silly waste of time if economics textbooks tried to list all such rules, much less if they tried to explain how all such rules arose.

However, not all rules and practices are trivial and the processes whereby they develop and change are important. In the remainder of this paper, the importance of rules and common practices for economic behavior and organization will be illustrated. Recent events in Iraq will be used to illustrate some of the possibilities and problems in changing such rules and practices. In the next section, some of the common causes and processes whereby rules and practices are changed will be explored. Finally, an answer to the title question will be proposed.

THE IMPORTANCE OF RULES AND COMMON PRACTICES

Let us do a thought experiment that will help explain the contention that there are rules and common practices that are not trivial in organizing human interaction. A thought experiment is a mental exercise in which we use imagination to hold some things constant and let others change in order to discover the isolated effect of the changes.

In the first thought experiment, we consider the behavior of an individual whom we imagine to have landed in a space/time capsule in the United States (or the United Kingdom, or France; depending on your choice of country, you may provide more appropriate detail). Our observed individual is a transplant from a remote time and place. This time and place could be a much earlier century on earth or in another galaxy. It does not make a lot of difference. We will assume that our subject looks much like a modern man, though his dress may be odd, and we will assume (unrealistically) that he can speak the language of the country in which he lands. He will also have all of the attributes attributed to him in the typical economics textbook.

The attributes of humans assumed in economics textbooks are those that are crucial to the kind of decision making that is the central theme of these texts. For example, in describing economics as the study of individual interaction, Mankiw lists four principles of individual decision-making: people face tradeoffs; the cost of something is what you give up to get it; rational people think at the margin; people respond to incentives.[2] We will assume that our time/space traveler shares these attributes.

However, the first problem that our space/traveler (let's call him Greg) faces is also one that all humans (and other living creatures for that matter) face. He has traveled through time and space and he is thirsty and hungry. He has landed in a city unknown to him and he needs to find food and drink. Let us say that he has landed (somehow without attracting attention) in a public park in a major city. He observes that people walk up to devices and drink the water that is produced when a button is pushed (or a handle turned). He does the same and his thirst is relieved. He also observes that there are people sitting on benches and on the grass eating food laid out beside them.. He quickly learns that it is not appropriate to do as he did with the water and help himself to the food. 'Go buy your own,' he is told rather rudely. As he walks up to a nearby food stand, it becomes obvious to him that he needs to have some of the pieces of paper and metal that people are turning over in exchange for food. When he asks a person in line at the stand for some of the pieces of metal, he is told, in an equally rude voice: 'Get a job and earn your own.'

Our time/space traveler has learned some rudimentary rules of urban living in the West in the twenty-first century: drinkable water is freely and easily available but you must purchase food, to purchase food you need money, and to get money you need a job. These rules seem so basic to those of us who live in the modern West, that we assume they are a natural part of human existence. It is hard to imagine that allocation of food could be handled differently. However, in some parts of the world today, and in most parts of the world not so many centuries ago, this was not the common pattern of food distribution. Had our space/time traveler landed in rural England or Wales or Scotland around 1500, he would have found that most food was both produced and consumed within family units.[3] To sustain himself until he could reach an urban area where food could have been purchased, he would have had to figure out the rules of being a beggar or of being adopted as part of a family unit. That would not have been an easy task. In much of the United States, even until late in the nineteenth century, local distribution of food also took place largely within the family unit which, in a world of family farms, was also the producing unit. In the rest of our world, insofar as we can reconstruct it, food distribution up until the last few centuries was primarily accomplished through complex systems of kinship obligations or, in some cases, by a kind of theocratic-state redistribution.[4]

Return now to Greg, still standing in an urban park, and in serious need of a job. How does he get a job? Would he find an answer to this question in an introductory economics text? No, for the rules and practices of job markets are also among those assumed, but largely undiscussed practices that are nevertheless crucially important. These rules and practices also change over time. In some urban areas (in the cloth trade in Flanders, now Belgium and the Netherlands, for example) casual wage employment was available as early as 1,000 years ago, but throughout most of Western Europe, employment was gained through apprenticeship or some form of agreed servitude. The carefully devised strategies of English families to place adolescent children in apprenticeships are well described by Keith Wrightson in a wonderful book about the rules of early modern England call *Earthly Necessities*.[5]

Today, there are a wide variety of ways of finding employment through the use of placement services, internet job searches, and direct application. Greg, in a twenty-first-century city, might be able to find quick, casual employment by responding to a 'Help Wanted' sign in a small retail establishment. But most employment requires that an application be submitted; to get a job you have to know where to go and how to apply. Greg would also find that even casual employment required a well-documented identity. Without a social security number, driver's license, or the various other documents that we use to establish ourselves in modern economies, Greg would find it hard to get a job. He would need to know a lot more about the rules and the practices of the place where he had landed.

Of course, people do not travel by space/time capsules and situations such as Greg's are purely imaginative. It is not uncommon for international travelers or migrants to find variation in rules and practices puzzling, but the development of very similar practices in most western countries, and the extension of those common practices to urban areas in the rest of the world (if not always to rural areas) have dulled our sense of how diverse the rules by which we interact have in fact been over human history. This has made it easier for the authors of economics texts to assume that rules are known and to go straight to analysis of a range of interactions that take place within the context of those assumed rules.

However, events do occur that make us realize how important the rules of the economy are. When the United States Armed Forces invaded Iraq, the Bush administration was faced with the task of administering a country in which both war and the overthrow of civil authority had seriously disrupted the production and distribution of goods and services. Those who planned and carried out the invasion also brought with them plans for restructuring the Iraqi economy. What this has meant is that the U.S. has imposed new rules that reflect an idealized modern U.S. economy as the basic model. In practice, many of these rules have not worked as intended; and precisely because of this, their introduction serves to illustrate the importance of rules and norms.

Before turning to some illustrations, note that there was a conscious recognition by the U.S. administration that the occupation and the restructuring of Iraqi government and economy would require the writing of new rules. The goals were explicit. In the words on the U.S. Agency for International Development website: 'Although the lifting of UN sanctions will reduce black market activities in Iraq, much more must be done to make a solid break with past practices and put the country on a solid economic and commercial footing.'[6]

Although a person reading an introductory text might have the impression that the rules governing interaction are simply those of self-interested individuals who, as Mankiw tells us, evaluate decisions at the margin and respond to incentives, there is obviously a lot more to the story than that, as the U.S. government recognized as it planned the revision of Iraqi rules. It has also become obvious that U.S. officials in Iraq underestimated the difficulty of imposing new rules and practices that often conflict with unwritten rules and practices of the Iraqi people.

One recurring difficulty, according to newspaper accounts, has been the importance of ethnic and subnational, or tribal, identity and affiliation. The difficulties faced in recruiting and keeping Iraqis in a new army had partly to do with pay that was too low and the risk of violence; but it also had to do with the fact that the Americans did not take into account the unwillingness of Iraqis to serve alongside other ethnic groups with whom they had long-standing hostile relationships.

In another instance of the importance of subnational identity and loyalty, recounted in a story in the *Washington Post*, an American diplomat posted an official notice soliciting bids to tear down a bombed-out building.[7] In doing this, he was following the rules established by the U.S. occupation authority. The initial response was what he, operating under American rules, would have expected: several sealed bids were submitted by the official deadline. The plan was to accept the lowest bid. However, as reporter Rajiv Chandrasekaran reports, a tribal sheik, having heard of the process submitted additional bids, well after the deadline, and all were substantially higher than those submitted earlier. Had the American diplomat followed the practice of accepting the lowest bid submitted by the deadline, he would have risked offending a tribal sheik whose tribesmen had been helping the Americans. Of course, if he accepted the higher bid from a political ally he would be opening himself to charges of favoritism and corruption. What he did was a compromise of sorts. He negotiated with the sheik and got the asking price down to a level closer to, if still higher than, the lowest bids. The diplomat then accepted the sheik's bid. What was the diplomat's justification? 'When we have a tribal issue at stake, we do a controlled bidding process to make sure the contract goes to the right person...' The rules of sealed bids were not the only rules operating here.

It would be easy to react to this story by saying that in a war zone bad, and probably corrupt, practice may develop and even be justified. However, consider that we also use processes of 'controlled bidding' on government contracts in the United States, though the actual rules are different. Often (though not always where political patronage is involved) this controlled bidding is a process that stands on the authority of law and is considered by many to be an enlightened process of good government. Consider the Small Business Administration which was created some fifty years ago (during the Eisenhower Administration) to assist small business in gaining access to some of the billions of dollars worth of contracts that are let by the Federal Government every year. According to a recent version of the law that governs the fairness of such awards, twenty-three percent of prime Federal contracts are to go to small businesses as defined by law, five percent to small disadvantaged businesses, five percent of prime and sub-contracts to small businesses owned by women, three percent to small businesses in HUB Zones (Historically Underutilized Business Zones), and three percent of prime- and sub-contracts to small businesses owned by service-disabled veterans.

These quotas are only one small part of the complex set of provisions that control bidding on federal contracts in the U.S. There are many, many more provisions that provide technical assistance and finance to businesses owned by Native Americans, African-Americans, women, Hispanics, and others deemed to deserve special assistance in securing business with the very large federal government. State governments in some instances have similar programs. The sheik who negotiated with the diplomat in Iraq was using his inherited political position to represent a group of followers in a negotiation for patronage, money, and jobs. He was doing this according to well-established Iraqi customs and understanding. The small business owner who negotiates with the Small Business Administration to secure favorable treatment is also in negotiation for patronage, money, and jobs for a group deemed disadvantaged. To the American reader this will likely seem fairer and more honorable than what the sheik did, but that is not the point to be made here. Here we note only that there were different rules in the two settings, but in both cases the rules were non-trivial and important for economic interaction.

One more example of the diversity and importance of rules and practices comes from the American efforts to reorganize Iraqi agriculture. According to an article in the *Washington Post* on January 22, 2004, 'Under Saddam Hussein, Iraqis depended on subsidies and handouts as a way of life. The Coalition Provision Authority [the occupying force] is determined to change that and create a capitalist economy where the state provides little, if any, support, except to the neediest.'[8] The story, in fact, is a lot more complicated. Prior to the American invasion, the Iraqi state 'provided seeds, fertilizer, pesticides, sprinklers, tractors and other necessities to farmers at a low cost, often a third or even a fourth of the market price.' It leased the land to the farmers and bought the main crops of wheat and barley at a guaranteed price. Flour, sugar, tea, and some other 'necessities' were then distributed to each Iraqi family. The plan that is being developed for a restructured Iraqi agriculture would end state provision of seed and other agricultural inputs. Prices of wheat, barley, and other agricultural produce would be de-controlled and the hope would be that the market price would cover the costs of agricultural inputs and provide an incentive for farmers to produce enough food. Of course, this would also require that the incomes of consumers be sufficient to buy food at the going prices.

In the first year of occupation, it has proven impossible to put the restructuring plan into effect because of fears of civil unrest and the difficulty of overhauling a system quickly. However, there are other problems as well, problems that can be illustrated by the complexity of the U.S. system of agricultural production. The story in the *Washington Post* makes it appear that a capitalist agricultural system such as that of the U.S. is one in which the 'state provides little, if any, support, except to the neediest.' It might lead the reader to think that the rules of agricultural production are simply the rules of the market as described in economics texts. This is certainly not true.

Since the 1930s, the United States has had a complex system of subsidies to farmers who produce selected commodities. The fundamental idea of the agricultural programs of the 1930s, an idea that has continued to be implemented in modified form today, is that producers of basic commodities (which currently include wheat, feed grains, cotton, rice, and soybeans) will be eligible for government payments when market prices fall below an established level. Because this system, in combination with changes in technology (about which more will be said later) often resulted in output in excess of national demand for these foodstuffs, farmers have also received payments for not producing. However, the direct subsidies to farmers who produce these basic commodities is only part of a complex system of government support. This support includes a program of loan guarantees, support for rural electrical projects, grants to develop new products, extension services, and many other services. Indeed, the agricultural industry has probably been the most heavily subsidized industry in the American economy over the past half century and more.

But the story does not stop there. Large, private firms often contract with farmers and supply the basic inputs as part of an arrangement whereby they also contract to buy the product of the farm. An Iraqi farmer has been quoted as saying, 'We are afraid of the free economy. We don't understand it. If we grow crops, who will help us and who will buy it?' Had that farmer known the complexity of support from public and private sources available to American farmers, he might well have added that American farmers would be afraid of the free economy as well, were they to be threatened with it.

Once again, however, the point here is not to argue whether or not the phrase 'free market' accurately describes the American economy, or whether or not the American plans for restructuring Iraqi agriculture are sound. The point is that if the goal is to create an agricultural sector that resembles that of the United States, this requires the importation of a complicated set of rules and practices. American farmers do not simply interact with one another and with their consumers in a rule-free environment. The same is true of farmers everywhere.

HOW RULES CHANGE

We began with the space/time traveler who found himself in a place where the rules and practices were quite different than those he had known. The rules and practices had changed since his time. One way in which rules and practices change is by imposition of new rules by an occupying force. This is what is happening in Iraq now where the outcome of the effort is as yet unknown. There have been other instances of imposed rules in human history. Following World War II, the Allies imposed new economic rules on both Japan and Germany. During the late nineteenth and early twentieth centuries, European nations imposed new rules on African populations by levying taxes, thereby forcing people to work for money wages in the mines and plantations that the Europeans had created.

Although it would be possible to create a much longer list of imposed changes in which a dominant, foreign power imposed new rules, by far the most common process in human history has been one whereby rules change through changing norms, conflict among interest groups, conflicts brought about by technological change, by evolution in response to new norms, and by changes in the law. The changes in American agriculture illustrate this point well. Much of the continental United States was settled by families who gained ownership through a complex of government-run auctions, purchase from their fellow farmers who became speculators, from railroads and land companies, and through land grants. In the period of initial settlement and for some time afterwards, difficulties of transportation and the social norms made the family-sufficient farm a model of existence. However, the coming of the railroads and steam ships, which opened European and other markets to the highly productive farms of the American midwest as well as the growth of industry and of cities, changed American agriculture profoundly. The consequence was a landscape of family farmers who did learn to fear the free market, and especially in the 1920s, when over-farming and -grazing led to serious problems of erosion and the creation of the infamous dust bowl, and when prices of agricultural commodities fell sharply. A program of price supports was introduced in the 1930s to alleviate farm poverty, with a program of limitations on production to restore prices to the apparently more reasonable levels that had prevailed before the disastrous 1920s.

In the decades that followed, the increasingly widespread use of chemical fertilizers and other new technologies increased the output per acre, where earlier technologies had simply increased the output per farmer (but not per acre). It no longer solved the problem of agricultural overabundance to move people off the farm, for now a very small agricultural labor force could produce vastly more output even with a smaller amount of land in production.

At that point group conflict and the politics of economic change became increasingly important. A early as the late 1940s, policy makers in Washington, remembering that the agricultural programs of the 1930s had been designed to alleviate rural poverty, noted that farm subsidies were going increasingly to farmers who were quite well off and who owned large amounts of land. They could obtain payments from the government for withholding land, something that farmers who owned small amounts of land found it hard to do. The owners of large-scale farms were also able to collect much larger federal cheques than did small-scale farmers when the market price of basic commodities fell below the guaranteed government price. The agricultural programs of the 1930s had been transformed by technological change into a program of subsidies for well-to-do farmers. Though this was widely recognized, the farmers who benefitted were able, and remain able, to exercise power through Congress and lobbying groups and the farm subsidy programs, though greatly modified in recent years, remain available.

What this last part of our story illustrates is that rules and practices that govern the human interaction that makes up economies may be kept in place by group action. New rules can also be put in place by group action. The Small Business Administration's programs for women and minority business owners are among the many changes in rules of interaction that have resulted from the Civil Rights movement and the various efforts of women who have sought economic and social equality with men. In the 1960s there was a flurry of new legislation and of court decisions that changed the rules of America so that employers could no longer refuse to hire qualified people because of race or gender. Further, in 1963, the Equal Pay Act was passed which said that employers could not pay women less than men doing the same job. Until that time, women were often paid less even when the employer recognized in writing that the jobs were the same.

It is possible to explain at least some of the power of the Civil Rights movement and of the campaigns for equal treatment and pay for women as a consequence of prior technological changes such as the tractors and mechanical cotton picker that helped feed movement of African-Americans into American cities, and of the contraceptive pill and new household technologies that allowed more women to have careers outside the homes. Nevertheless, the shape of legislation and the relatively new set of expectations of employers as they employ African-Americans and women were also the product of fierce and dedicated group action. And that observation helps us approach our concluding issue.

WHERE DO ECONOMIES COME FROM?

Mankiw, and the authors of other introductory texts, focus on individual human action. The 'combined actions of millions of households and firms' are the actions of individual firms and households interacting through supply and demand of economic goods and services. Because so little attention is given to the rules and practices that govern those interactions, there is no recognized need in the texts to deal with the processes whereby rules and practices are created: that is, there is no need to deal with collective action. But such collective action creates the all-important context in which our space/time traveler Greg, or the Iraqi farmer who fears the free market undertake the actions that make up the economy.

A major part of the story of economies has been left out of the texts. Not only are the rules and common practices left largely unspecified, but the processes whereby these rules and common practices change are left unexamined. In this chapter I have concentrated on legal rules of economies and on collective action to change the legal rules. To have the background to understand these aspects of economies a student of economics would need to study politics and political history before studying economics. In addition to the kinds of legal norms discussed above, there are important non-legal social norms that govern our action, and those social norms change in many of the same ways that legal norms change. To understand these aspects of economies a student of economics would need to study sociology and social history before studying economics. To study economics alone is simply not enough.

By focusing on individual action within an unspecified and presumably unchanging context, economics texts not only leave much to other disciplines. They also enforce either apathy or antipathy toward collective action to make economies better. If economies are simply the products of individual action, then what can one individual do? It is easy to get the sense from our modern texts that economies are as much a part of unbending nature as are the seasons of weather. There is not much that can be done. However, recognition that economies are made by humans, who collectively decide the laws and the norms of their land, frees the student of economics from this kind of fatalism. Is there poverty in some regions and among some populations? Is income distribution inconsistent with freedom of opportunity for all? Are some desirable products (say medicine or education) too highly priced to be readily available while other undesirable products that are inexpensive are overused for the good of society? These things can be fixed. There may be undesirable consequences of some fixes, but those consequences can be worked on as well.

Economies are made by human beings interacting with each other in a variety of ways. If they are made by humans, they can be changed by humans. That is the powerful message that is absent from the economics textbooks.

6

Can Economics Start From the Individual Alone?

Geoffrey M. Hodgson

University of Hertfordshire, UK

On the first page of his *Principles* (1890) Alfred Marshall gave the following definition: 'Political Economy or Economics is the study of mankind in the ordinary business of life; it examines that part of individual and social action which is most closely connected with the attainment and with the use of the material requisites of wellbeing.' Less than half a century later, the conception of the subject began to change dramatically. Inspired by nineteenth-century predecessors such as Carl Menger, Lionel Robbins in his *Essay on the Nature and Significance of Economic Science* (1932) redefined the subject as the science of individual choice. Robbins's redefinition of the subject became prevalent when Paul Samuelson adopted it in his bestselling textbook *Economics* in 1948. The 'economic problem' became one of allocation of scarce means between alternative uses, as a universal matter of choice for every individual in a world of scarcity. Instead of the whole system of production and allocation of the means of life, the choosing individual alone became the foundation stone of economic theory.

The 'economic approach' to the analysis of phenomena was seen as a method of analysing phenomena as resultants of individual choices upon given preferences. Outcomes would be 'predicted' upon the basis of given utility functions, with an individual facing specific scarcities and constraints.

In principle this approach could be extended to any phenomenon where an organism faced a 'choice' in allocating scarce means. Accordingly, Nobel Laureate Gary Becker applied the 'economic approach' to 'social' phenomena such as love and marriage, while others went even further to apply the approach to religion, suicide and even the behaviour of non-human organisms. In view of its apparent ability to 'explain' a wide range of phenomena, and with its relatively high degree of technical precision and formalism, the wide extension of the 'economic approach' was hailed as a major achievement in social science.

The purpose of this chapter is to probe the limits of this approach and to suggest that the isolated individual is not viable as an analytical starting point. We proceed at first by examining claims that the emergence of institutions can be analysed as the outcome of individual interactions. Even if we take individuals as given, the rules of their interaction cannot be exclusively explained in individual terms. The following section considers how individuals make sense of sensory stimuli and communicate with one another. Once again, explanations founder in terms of individuals alone. The next section explores the limitations of both methodological individualism and methodological collectivism. The concluding section suggests that institutions as well as individuals have to be foundational for economic analysis.

THE EVOLUTION OF INSTITUTIONS FROM INDIVIDUALS

In his classic theory of money, originally published in his *Grundsätze der Volkswirtschaftslehre* of 1871, Carl Menger saw many institutions emanating in an undesigned manner from the communications, rational decisions, and interactions of individual agents. His thought experiment started from a situation of barter, which is intrinsically inconvenient due to a general lack of the 'double coincidence of wants': swaps immediately satisfactory to both parties are not generally attainable. Consequently, for convenience, people look out for an item that is exchanged regularly, to use it as a medium of exchange. This could be pieces of precious metal or even tokens of some kind. Once such a convenient medium begins to emerge, a circular process of institutional self-reinforcement takes place. The chosen medium becomes more popular and assumes the characteristics of money. Money is chosen because it is convenient, and it is convenient because it is chosen.

Apart from the emergence of money, similar examples of institutional emergence through individual interactions are found in the later literature on institutions. Cases include driving on one side of the road, and traffic conventions at road junctions. For example, once the convention of driving on the left of the road is established, it is clearly rational for all drivers to follow the same rule. Most of the cases in this genre can be analysed technically as coordination games, where not only does each player lack any incentive to change strategy, but also each player wishes that other players keep to their strategy as well.

The value of this work should not be denied. Substantial heuristic insights about the development of institutions and conventions have been gained on the basis of the assumption of given, rational individuals. The main problem addressed here is the inherent incompleteness of the research program in its attempt to provide a general theory of the emergence and evolution of institutions from individuals alone.

In a series of articles appearing from 1974 to 1984, the American economist Alexander Field identified a fundamental criticism of this approach. He pointed out that in attempting to explain the origin of social institutions, analysts always have to presume individuals acting in a specific context. Along with the assumption of given individuals, is the assumption of given rules of behaviour governing their interaction. What is often forgotten is that in the original, hypothetical, 'state of nature' from which institutions are seen to have emerged, a number of weighty rules, institutions and cultural and social norms have already been presumed.

In game theory, for example, some norms and rules must inevitably be presumed at the start. There can be no games without rules, and thus game theory can never explain the elemental rules themselves. Game theory assumes a limited set of possible strategies, defining the arena in which the players are to compete or cooperate. The game of chess presumes the layout of the board and rules that govern the legitimate moves of the pieces. The Prisoners' Dilemma game confines its strategic options to 'cooperate' or 'defect' and excludes the possibility of digging a tunnel or bribing the guards.

Even in a sequence of repeated games, or of games about other (nested) games, at least one game or meta-game, with a structure and payoffs, must be assumed at the outset. Any such attempt to deal with history in terms of sequential or nested games is thus involved in a problem of infinite regress: even with games about games about games to the nth degree there is still one preceding game left to be explained.

Accordingly, all these explanations, including those from game theory, presume a set of rules or constraints at the outset. If we attempt to explain these elemental rules in terms of individuals alone, then we are always led into a hopeless and infinite explanatory regress. The idea of explaining institutions by beginning with individuals alone has never been successful because the starting point always involves more than individuals. In addition to individuals, some notion of rule system or social structure is implicitly or explicitly assumed. The project to explain institutions in terms of individuals alone has to be abandoned.

COGNITION AND COMMUNICATION

There are even more fundamental reasons why economics cannot start from the individual alone. Choosing requires a conceptual framework to make sense of the world. The models of human interaction that attempt to explain the emergence of institutions through the interactions of individuals all assume that individuals receive informational signals and then act rationally or appropriately. The evolution of money from barter assumes that we understand the concepts of property and contractual exchange. It also assumes that individuals perceive the medium of exchange that is used more frequently than others. The evolution of traffic conventions assumes that we understand and interpret the behaviour of other drivers, and regard them as making decisions with a concern for their own safety, rather than acting randomly or dangerously.

Acting in the world, we receive a huge amount of sense data. From this chaotic mass we have to select the more important signals and make sense of them. Individual existence and action depends on a continuous process of data selection and cognitive interpretation. A sophisticated mental apparatus of cognition is necessary for us to perceive, make sense and act in the world around us. How do we obtain such a cognitive apparatus? Some elements may be inherited, as instinctive proclivities to respond to specific stimuli. But there is no doubt that much is also learned by individuals, through their socialisation from birth, and through their interactions with parents and others in a structured social setting. We learn to categorise and to classify, typically according to prevailing cultural norms. We learn the social conventions and rules emanating from the specific institutions with which we interact. Consequently our apparatus of cognition, choice and decision-making itself bears the stamp of the specific, historically given, social world around us. Individual choice depends unavoidably on institutional and social props.

More specifically, our interaction with others requires the use of language. Language itself is a rule system, and thus an institution. We cannot understand the world without concepts and we cannot communicate without some form of language. Without the prior institutionalisation of individuals, we can neither interpret the behaviour of others nor interact meaningfully with them. The transmission of information from institution to individual is impossible without a coextensive process of enculturation, in which the individual learns the meaning and value of the sense data that are communicated. Human interaction always and necessarily involves such a process of enculturation. Without our previous immersion in a social culture we are unable to communicate and to interact with others.

Institutions are durable systems of established and embedded social rules that structure social interactions. Institutions are social structures that constrain and influence individuals. Accordingly, if there are institutional influences on individuals and their goals, then these are worthy of explanation. In turn, the explanation of those may be in terms of other purposeful individuals. In turn, these individuals would be explained in part by their institutional and cultural background.

But where should the analysis stop? If we expect to explain everything in terms of individuals (or institutions) alone, then we are led once again into an infinite regress. The purposes of an individual could be partly explained by relevant institutions, culture and so on. These, in their turn, would be partly explained in terms of other individuals. But these individual purposes and actions could then be partly explained by cultural and institutional factors, and so on, indefinitely. We are involved in something similar to the puzzle 'which came first, the chicken or the egg?' Such an analysis never reaches an end point. It is simply arbitrary to stop at one particular stage in the explanation and say 'it is all reducible to individuals' just as much as to say 'it is all social and institutional.' The key point is that in this infinite regress, neither individual nor institutional factors have legitimate explanatory primacy. The idea that all explanations have ultimately to be in terms of individuals (or institutions) is thus unfounded.

There is thus an unbreakable circle of determination. This does not mean, however, that institutions and individuals have equivalent ontological and explanatory status. Clearly, they have different characteristics. Individuals are purposeful, whereas institutions are not, at least in the same sense. Institutions have different lifespans from individuals, sometimes enduring the passing of the individuals they contain. Their mechanisms of reproduction and procreation are very different.

All theories must first build from elements which are taken as given. However, the problems identified here undermine any claim that the explanation of the emergence of institutions can start from some kind of institution-free ensemble of (rational) individuals in which there is supposedly no rule or institution to be explained. At the very minimum, explanations of the development of institutions depend upon interpersonal interpretation and communication of information. And the communication of information itself requires shared conventions, rules, routines and norms. These, in turn, have to be explained. Consequently, the project to explain the emergence of institutions on the basis of given individuals runs into difficulties, particularly with regard to the conceptualisation of the initial state from which institutions are supposed to emerge.

BEYOND METHODOLOGICAL INDIVIDUALISM AND METHODOLOGICAL
· COLLECTIVISM

The term 'methodological individualism' is widely used but less often defined. Even among its advocates, there is no consensus on the meaning of the term. Much of the confusion in the debate over methodological individualism stems from whether methodological individualism means explanations (a) in terms of individuals alone, or (b) in terms of individuals plus individual interactions or social structures.

If we follow option (a) then, in this strong and meaningful sense, methodological individualism means the doctrine that all social and economic phenomena should be explained in terms of individuals alone. But several reasons have been given above why this option is not generally available. In contrast, if we interpret methodological individualism in terms of option (b), then it is difficult to find fault with it. However, such an inclusive notion would not warrant the title of methodological individualism any more than the description 'methodological structuralism'. If social structures or interactions between individuals are also an essential part of the doctrine, then it is misleading to give the individual exclusive representation in the label.

Overall, while methodological individualism is a popular mantra, in strong and meaningful terms it is never actually achieved. Explanations are never reduced to individuals alone. The advocates of this approach fail to carry out their own prescriptions.

A polar opposite approach could be described as 'methodological collectivism' or 'methodological holism'. By reversing the aforementioned and stronger definition of methodological individualism, methodological collectivism can be defined symmetrically as the notion that *all* individual intentions or behaviour should be explained *entirely* in terms of social, structural, cultural or institutional phenomena. Methodological collectivism connotes doctrines described variously as 'structural determinism', 'cultural determinism', 'economic determinism' and 'technological determinism'. They see individual thought or behaviour as being determined largely by structural, cultural or technological factors. In turn, to make the theory work, 'structure', 'culture', 'economy' or 'technology' are often seen as having a powerful logic and dynamic of their own. Social, cultural or technological systems are seen to dominate any individual motives or behaviours. Such systems are upheld to have their own teleology, or direction. They are typically assumed to evolve in some insufficiently described way. They act somehow upon individual actors, who are dragged in their wake.

Examples or hints of methodological collectivism are found in some versions of Marxism, in the sociology of Émile Durkheim, in structuralist or functionalist sociology or anthropology, and even in some versions of postmodernism. What is common in these cases is the lack of any developed micro-theory of how social structures affect, and are affected by, individual purposes or dispositions. In some passages Marx seemed to make psychology redundant, by declaring that the human essence was nothing more than the 'ensemble of the social relations'. More explicitly, Durkheim banned psychology from social science with his famous declaration in his *Rules of Scientific Method* of 1901 that 'every time a social phenomenon is directly explained by a psychological phenomenon, we may rest assured that the explanation is false.' The consequences of such neglects or prohibitions are highly damaging for social and economic theory.

In the absence of a theory of how society may lead to the reconstitution of individual preferences or purposes, a temptation is to explain individual action primarily by reference to the *constraints* imposed by the evolving social organism upon the individual. In such a conception, institutional constraints have effects, but without necessarily changing individual inclinations. For example, the greedy behaviour of people under capitalism is explained in terms of the options and structural constraints of capitalism itself; allegedly the ruthlessly competitive will win out, and the philanthropists are less likely to prosper. The explanation here of individual behaviour devolves entirely upon the assumed character of structures and systemic constraints. Variations in individuality, and individual psychology itself, play little or no part in the explanation.

Many social theorists have criticized methodological collectivism for making the individual the mere puppet of social forces. In addition, it is argued here that the main problem is that methodological collectivism does not only diminish the individual, but that it also pays insufficient attention to the processes and mechanisms by which the individual is fundamentally altered. It also ignores crucial variations between individuals. One consequence of conflating the individual into the social structure is to lose sight, not simply of the individual, but also of the mechanisms of social power and influence that may help to reconstitute individual purposes or preferences. Because the explanation is in terms of structures and constraints alone, the ways in which institutions may actually affect individuals are ignored. It may appear paradoxical, but only by rescuing the individual from its conflation into the social, can the social determination of individuality be fully appreciated.

Part of the solution is to bring psychology back into the picture. But strangely this is absent from much of social and economic theory. Some influential economists abandoned psychology at about the same time. Robbins recast economics as 'the science of choice'. Individual ends were taken as given, economics was to be all about the rational choice of appropriate means. Because individual preferences were taken as given, psychology no longer had a significant role in this reconstruction of the subject.

After their common rejection of psychological and related underpinnings, economics and sociology went their separate ways. Proclamations of methodological individualism were more prominent in economics, and of methodological collectivism in sociology. The social sciences as a whole were characterized as an apparent dilemma between an Adam Smith-like and incentive-driven view of action in economics, and a Durkheim-like and norm-propelled view in sociology. In one discipline there appeared the 'self-contained', 'under-socialized', 'atomistic' and 'asocial' individual; in the other the individual seemed sometimes to be the 'over-socialized' puppet of 'social forces'.

However, despite the century-long battle between methodological individualists and methodological collectivists, they have much more in common than is typically admitted. Methodological individualism conflates the social into the individual, thus losing sight of key mechanisms of social influence, and is consequently impelled to take the purposes and preferences of the individual as given. Methodological collectivism conflates the individual into society and thereby lacks an explanation or adequate recognition of how individual purposes or preferences may be changed. The explanatory moves are in opposite directions but the results are similar in some vital respects: there is no adequate explanation of how social institutions may reconstitute individual purposes and preferences. Typically, both approaches disregard the value and role of psychology in the explanation of social phenomena. Both methodologies end up with a diminished concept of social power, and an analytical over-emphasis on overt coercion and constraint, rather than more subtle mechanisms of social influence. Arguably, to understand the way in which power is exercised over individuals we have to appreciate the subtle mechanisms of enculturation and persuasion, as well as the more overt sanctions and penalties that are sometimes involved.

Accordingly, as long as the debates within social and economic theory simply flips back and forth between these two opposed methodological positions, then it will be incapacitated by a failure to examine, and escape from, their common presuppositions. They are two mutually implicated poles of a misconceived and unsustainable dualism; they have both demonstrably failed to bring social theory out of its twentieth-century impasse.

CONCLUSION: A WAY FORWARD

The above argument has established the importance of avoiding the two polar extremes of methodological individualism and methodological holism. However, this does not mean that we should search for some kind of midway point between the two. A reason why such a solution would be unsatisfactory is that individual actor and social structure are not ontologically symmetrical. A sequence of prominent writers, including Auguste Comte, Karl Marx, George Henry Lewes, Émile Durkheim, Thorstein Veblen and Margaret Archer have rightly insisted that we are born into a social context that is not of our making. From birth, we are obliged to engage with particular social structures and institutions that were bequeathed by history. Of course, without individuals, social structures and institutions would not exist. But social structures and institutions precede any one individual. Hence there is a temporal asymmetry: although structures always depend for their existence on a *group* of individuals, in regard to each *single* individual, several structures precede the emergence of that agent.

Consequently, any adequate alternative to both methodological individualism and methodological holism must avoid any conflation of individual and social structure, and must acknowledge their temporal asymmetry. Instead of trying to explain all institutions in terms of individuals alone, or trying to explain all individuals in terms of institutions or structures alone, we have to understand social reality as *process*, in which at any given point, there are always individuals *and* social structures or institutions. The individual must be acknowledged as such, but always placed in his or her historical, social and institutional context.

We can take our cue here from two Nobel Laureates in economics. In an article on 'Economic History and Economics' in the May 1985 edition of the *American Economic Review*, Robert Solow declared that 'all narrowly economic activity is embedded in a web of social institutions, customs, beliefs, and attitudes'. He proceeded to draw a vital conclusion from this proposition: 'different social contexts may call for different background assumptions and therefore for different models.' He continued:

> If the proper choice of a model depends on the institutional context – and it should – then economic history performs the nice function of widening the range of observation available to the theorist... One will have to recognize that the validity of an economic model may depend on the social context.[1]

In his Nobel lecture 'Econometrics and the Welfare State' of 1989 – which was eventually published in the *American Economic Review* in December 1997 – Trygve Haavelmo proclaimed that 'existing economic theories are not good enough' because they 'start by studying the behavior of the individual under various conditions of choice' and 'then try to construct a model of the economic society in its totality by a so-called process of aggregation'. Haavelmo went on:

> I now think this is actually beginning at the wrong end... Starting with some existing society, we could conceive of it as a structure of rules and regulations within which the members of society have to operate. Their responses to these rules as individuals obeying them, produce economic results that would characterize the society.[2]

Both Nobel Laureates reached the same conclusion, concerning the inadequacy of the existing mainstream approach and the need to place the individual in a historical given context of structures and institutions. Both the options available to individuals, and the means by which they calculate their specific advantages and disadvantages, depend upon this particular social context. Individuals cannot be regarded as free-standing entities, separable from the social world, but part of it and its institutions.

Some experimental economists have developed allied thoughts. Results of many experiments suggest that the way choices and rules are framed and conceptualised affect the behaviour of human subjects. Furthermore, the very notion of what is a 'rational' calculation seems often to depend on the specific context of the experiment itself. Accordingly, it has been concluded that the results cannot be explained in terms of given individuals with fixed preference functions, but instead have to be seen in terms of individuals adopting rules of thumb specific to the structure of the decision-task in hand. Consequently, the procedures and evaluations involved are themselves context-dependent, and in part constituted by the social environment.

In sum, mainstream economics itself has pointed to the need to conceptualise individuals acting within an institutional framework, where not only institutions depend upon and are affected by individuals, but also individuals can be profoundly reconstituted by their institutional context. This general idea of individuals being affected by their institutional circumstances or social context was prominent in much of pre-Robbins economics, and is even found in the *Principles* of Marshall. It is being revived today.

The importance of institutions in understanding economic performance is now widely acknowledged. For instance, Nobel Laureates Douglass North and Ronald Coase, and influential bodies such as the World Bank, have emphasized the role that institutions play in economic development. Institutions are increasingly being acknowledged as the stuff of social and economic life. Consequently, the old idea that economic development was predominantly a matter of pecuniary investment in capital goods is being eclipsed by a notion that economic performance also depends on the system of institutions in which individuals are obliged to act, and the related incentives and values that crucially affect their motivation.

However, while bringing institutions fully back into the picture, it is important to avoid the trap of seeing individuals as puppets of social circumstances. Methodological collectivism is no improvement on methodological individualism. What is a required is a detailed causal account of how institutional or other circumstances affect individual beliefs, preferences and intentions. It is impossible to elaborate such details here, but any attempt to do so must rely in part on insights from psychology – the science that was divorced from economics as a result of the Robbinsian transformation of the discipline.

One option is to adopt some insights from the original institutional economics as developed by Veblen from the 1890s to the 1920s. Veblen relied heavily on the psychology of William James, in which both instinct and habituation are emphasised. Through our interactions with others in a specific social context we acquire habitual dispositions of thought and behaviour. In this manner, institutions can affect our preferences and purposes. The crucial mechanism that is involved in this development of our personalities is the building up of habits. These in turn are the result of repeated thoughts or behaviours motivated or constrained by the institutional context. Through the operation of institutional constraints and norms, we acquire notions of what is proper and true. But not only may the individual change through time, but also there is scope for substantial variation between individuals.

If this option and approach were viable, then it would involve a rehabilitation of Veblenian institutionalist ideas that have been long neglected and disregarded in the social sciences. It would also open up a fruitful dialogue between the old and the new institutional economics.

This approach is elaborated in Hodgson (2004). Hodgson (2003) is a wide-ranging collection of articles by different authors, touching on several of the names and themes that have been mentioned in this brief essay. Lukes (1973) remains a classic introductory account of different notions of individualism in the social sciences. It is a good starting point to begin reading on the topic, and could usefully be followed by an excursion into some of the essays in Hodgson (2003). Archer (1995) contains a very useful survey of developments in social theory that bear upon the debates concerning methodological individualism and methodological collectivism, as well as the pioneering contribution of Archer herself. Davis (2003) is the most recent and advanced text on the theory of the individual in economics, written with the benefit of a detailed expert knowledge of modern philosophy and economic theory.

REFERENCES AND SUGGESTIONS FOR FURTHER READING

Archer, Margaret S. (1995) *Realist Social Theory: The Morphogenetic Approach* (Cambridge: Cambridge University Press).

Davis, John B. (2003) *The Theory of the Individual in Economics: Identity and Value* (London and New York: Routledge).

Hodgson, Geoffrey M. (ed.) (2003) *Recent Developments in Institutional Economics* (Cheltenham: Edward Elgar).

Hodgson, Geoffrey M. (2004) *The Evolution of Institutional Economics: Agency, Structure and Darwinism in American Institutionalism* (London and New York: Routledge) in press.

Lukes, Steven (1973) *Individualism* (Oxford: Basil Blackwell).

Part II

Micro Nonsense

7

Are You Rational?

EDWARD FULLBROOK

(UNIVERSITY OF THE WEST OF ENGLAND, UK)

It is unlikely that you are 'rational' in the traditional economics meaning of
the word. And for your sake I hope that you are not. You may think that I am
mad, but by time that you have finished reading this chapter I am confident
that you will see that the madness lies elsewhere.

MAKE-BELIEVE WORLDS REQUIRE MAKE-BELIEVE PEOPLE

Neoclassical economics – that's the kind you are almost certain to be taught
as gospel truth – has strange origins. Although invented in the 1870s, it
modelled itself on seventeenth-century Newtonian mechanics instead of one
of the developing sciences of its day, like electro-magnetic physics. This meant
that it conceived of economic systems, be they individual markets or whole
economies, as self-regulating determinate mechanisms composed of atomistic
elements and tending toward equilibrium. Kenneth Arrow, a celebrated
neoclassical economist of the second half of the last century, identifies two

> aspects of the notion of general equilibrium as it has been used in
> economics: (1) the simple notion of determinateness...and (2) the more
> specific notion that each relation represents a balance of
> forces...[meaning] that a violation of any one relation sets in motion
> forces tending to restore the balance...
>
> (Arrow 1983b: 107)

As Arrow's words show, equilibrium in neoclassical economics serves as
much more than just a concept. It also is a sweeping ontological
pronouncement, expressed in strongly metaphorical language, on the nature
of economic reality and therefore offering no possibility of direct conformation

or refutation. We need to look at what this entails, especially at what kind of behaviour it demands from you if, by its lights, you are going to be judged rational.

Let's call neoclassical economics' assertion that markets and economies are determinate systems ruled by a principle of equilibrium its Equilibrium Hypothesis. (As stated by Arrow and others it does not qualify as a hypothesis but we in part are going to turn it into one.) It has two primary characteristics. One, it is presented as an *a priori* article of faith rather than the outcome of a process of scientific research. Two, as Arrow's description shows, it is a holistic metaphysic, not an individualistic one. It is first and foremost an assertion about economic systems rather than about economic agents. But for the assertion to be true, the elements comprising market systems, especially the human agents, can't be of just any kind. It might even be the case that the hypothesis is logically impossible – for example, that there exists no possible pattern of agent behaviour that would make the hypothesis true (see chapter in Section III by Gun; also Ackerman 2002).

But of course neoclassical believers try to show that their belief is logically possible, and this activity commands centre stage in microeconomics courses. It usually takes the form of mathematical models, which, although having no correspondences to empirical quantities, require a long list of stipulations regarding the microelements, including pure competition, constant coefficients of production, identical products and methods of production within an industry, perfect markets or instantaneous omniscience and perfect divisibility of goods. Some combination of these and other micro conditions must be true before the Equilibrium Hypothesis can even conceivably be true.

But even all this is not nearly enough. The Equilibrium Hypothesis requires a major subsidiary hypothesis postulating some driving force behind the putative order and this is where you come in. It asserts that the determining force is the independently 'chosen' behaviour of individual economic agents, like you, your family and your friends. Let's call this the Individual Behaviour Hypothesis. For neoclassical economists, it is agents acting individually which results in determinate equilibrium values for markets. But, as noted above, this outcome is logically possible only if the behaviour of individual agents is circumscribed by various formal properties. Therefore, 'deriving' these properties, with emphasis on the behaviour of imaginary consumers, has always stood at the centre of the neoclassical project. And it is precisely these properties and the class of behaviour that they define that the neoclassical tradition tendentiously calls 'rationality' and 'rational economic behaviour'. Likewise, behaviour inconsistent with its system of belief, it dubs 'irrational'.

Having found out what kind of individual behaviour might make the Equilibrium Hypothesis conceivably true and then having limited the definition of 'rational behaviour' to it, one further basic manoeuvre remains for the neoclassical project: it *declares* – no empirical research, please – that 'rationality' generally characterizes the actual behaviour of real economic agents like you, and furthermore that this pattern of human behaviour is context-independent.

The superstructure of the neoclassical paradigm, including the logical order of its development, is summarized as follows:

1. Equilibrium Hypothesis.
2. Individual Behaviour Hypothesis.
3. Justification of the Equilibrium and Individual Behaviour Hypotheses by:
   a. Deriving properties of individual behaviour consistent with the Equilibrium Hypothesis,
   b. The rhetorical manoeuvre of naming this set of properties 'rationality', and
   c. Assertion that 'rationality' describes real economic agents.

In the classroom, neoclassical economics usually reads its models backwards. This gives the illusion that they show the behaviour of individual economic units determining sets of equilibrium values for markets and for whole economies. It hides from you the fact that these models have been constructed not by investigating the behaviour of individual agents, but rather by analysing the logical requirements of achieving a certain aggregate or global state, that is, a market or general equilibrium. *It is the behaviour found to be consistent with these hypothetical aggregate states that is prescribed for the individual agents, rather than the other way around.* Sometimes textbook authors inadvertently call attention to how the 'individualist' rabbit really gets into the neoclassical hat. For example, consider the following passage about consumer choice from a widely used introduction to microeconomics:

> *For the purpose of our theory,* we want the preference ranking to have certain properties, which give it *a particular, useful structure. We build these properties up* by making a number of assumptions, first about the preference-indifference relation itself, and then about some aspects of the preference ranking to which it gives rise. (Gravell and Rees 1981: 56, emphasis added)

In other words, it is not the behaviour of the individual agents that determines the model's overall structure, nor even the structure of the preference ranking. *Instead it is the global requirement for a particular structure which dictates the behaviour attributed to the individual agents.* I want to consider three of these axiomatic assumptions in the light of some extremely common, everyday, real-life consumer-choice situations. First it is necessary to spell out these assumptions.

Two of these axioms are usually clearly stated in elementary textbooks, whereas the third, by tradition, is rarely mentioned. The reason for secrecy regarding the third will soon become obvious.

Transitivity Axiom

If a consumer regards good X as preferred or indifferent to Y, and Y as preferred or indifferent to Z, then the consumer regards X as preferred or indifferent to Z.

Completeness Axiom

'This assumption says in effect that the consumer is able to express a preference or indifference between any pair of consumption bundles (out of the set of all possible bundles given his/her income) however alike or unalike they may be. This ensures that there are not 'holes' in the preference ordering, points or areas to which it does not apply.' (Gravelle and Rees 1981: 56). But we will make it easier for the neoclassical case and relax this manifestly unrealistic assumption (see chapter by Keen, below) by saying that the consumer only compares the possible bundles up to the limit of his or her cognitive powers.

Independence Axiom

Almost for sure your textbooks leave unstated a third axiom for 'rationality'. Indeed, this axiom remains so well concealed that it even lacks an established name. The hidden axiom concerns the relation between the one and the many. In the words of John Hicks, another neoclassical luminary from the last century, 'economics is not, in the end, much interested in the behaviour of single individuals. Its concern is with the behaviour of groups. A study of individual demand is only a means to the study of market demand.' (Hicks 1946: 34)

Instead of taking the market demand function as a primitive concept, traditionalist economics derives market demand explicitly from what its axioms assume to be individual demand behaviour. The derivation consists of a summation of the individual demand schedules (for the same product). But these summations are logically possible only if the demand functions of the various individuals are independent of each other. Half a century ago, Oskar Morgenstern, the co-inventor of game theory, diagnosed the problem as follows:

> Collective demand is generally understood as a summation of individual demand schedules (for the same commodity)... It [this additivity] is only valid if the demand functions of the various individuals are independent of each other. This is clearly not true universally. Current theory possesses

no methods that allow the construction of aggregate demand curves when the various constituent individual demand curves are not independent of each other. The problem does not even seem to have been put. If there is interdependence among individual demand functions, it is doubtful that aggregate or collective demand functions of the conventional type exist... (Morgenstern 1948: 175)

Therefore, traditional neoclassical market demand functions implicitly assume absence of interdependence between the behaviours of individual agents. Let's call this logical requirement of the neoclassical model the Independence Axiom. It bears no relation to the narrower notion of the 'independence axiom' of expected utility theory.

However, considerations of agents' interdependence do appear in 'mainstream' literature, and some have broader relevance than just game-theoretic situations. For example, models exist which show an individual agent's preferences influenced by the behaviour of other agents. Regard for the regard of others may be treated as an argument in an agent's utility function. But without extending these exercises to market populations, *which means providing aggregate summation functions*, these endeavours remain at the level of statements about the behaviour of single individuals reacting to others rather than about the behaviour of groups. Therefore, these exercises stand off on their own, disconnected from neoclassical economics' main theoretical framework and pursuit. Indeed the primary effect, if not the intention, of these exercises may be merely to further conceal the Independence Axiom and the impasse exposed by Morgenstern.

REAL PEOPLE IN THE REAL WORLD: REAL-WORLD RATIONALITY

Now comes the fun part. We are going to apply neoclassical rationality to eight common types of consumer situations and see whether it is really fair to call it 'rationality' or whether it might be more accurate to call it 'neoclassical irrationality'. The first situation that we are going to consider is conceptually the most difficult but perhaps the most interesting.

1. Double-Bind Situations

In the real world, rationality concepts, including rational action decision theories, are applied in socio-economic contexts, and this gives them an inherently two-sided nature. Here they function as both normative and descriptive theories. Moreover, this double role invariably extends to the word 'rational' itself, whose mere sight or sound evokes meanings at both the normative and descriptive levels. The word 'rational' infers the existence of the irrational and of people so characterized. The word 'rational' and its antonym form part of the common and emotive currency of social politics. Basic categories of citizenship and personhood have always been framed, sometimes explicitly, with reference to notions of rationality. One notorious application led the authors of the Constitution of the United State of America to define a slave imported from Africa as three-fifths of a person. A standard justification for the subjugation of women has always been that they, whether due to the will of God or the whim of Nature, are not fully 'rational' beings.

These inequities, however, represent only one side of the politics of rationality. There is also the problem of maintaining the social order that those politics define. Individuals assigned to categories of sub-, partial or inferior personhood must be discouraged from subversive behaviour, that is, from manifesting more than that degree of 'rationality' commensurate with that ascribed to their social group. Through the ages, guardians of societies have devised and deployed diverse methods of discouraging the development and display of 'rationality' in selected populations. For example, the slave codes in the American South made it a crime for African-Americans to read.

The fate of these same people in the Jim Crow era (1890s to 1960s) provides another example. They were expected to show themselves inferior before whites, with failure to do so punishable by eviction, assault, torture and, on over 3000 occasions, by lynching. Similarly, the traditional choices available to women have been framed within the politics of rationality. Patriarchies everywhere established subtle, complex, and pervasive systems which reward girls and women for deferring to the 'rationality' of their male contemporaries and punish them for not doing so. These dialectics of otherness, which function to identify some social groups as more or less rational than others, have been described and analysed by innumerable women and minority writers.

I now want to bring into the foreground the paradox around which these dialectics turn. However defined, 'rational' and 'irrational' economic behaviour refer to observable patterns of behaviour, that is, to empirical phenomena. But this comes at a cost for the theoretician. It means that such behaviour by an individual stands potentially open to scrutiny, not just by possibly neutral social scientists, but also and more significantly by the immediate society in which that person lives, works and consumes. Consider any concept of rationality defined as some pattern of observable behaviour R and such that behaviour which is not R is irrational behaviour I. Assume that a person B belongs to a social category (a B-group) whose members are punished by another social category (the A-group) for R and rewarded for I. Assume that B prefers the consequences of I to those of R, and therefore chooses to behave irrationally. Assume that the concept of rationality includes the stipulation that a person chooses that behaviour whose consequences he or she prefers. Then under the concept of rationality it follows that it is irrational for B to behave rationally and vice versa.

This paradox arises because for person B the phenomenological facts surrounding choice are intermeshed with 'rationality' as a socially operative normative concept. But this concept dependence is not limited to B-group people. An A-group person's choice behaviour may also be influenced by the normative dimension of the concept of rationality because they wish to be perceived by others as 'rational'.

The paradox considered above springs from an extreme case of double-bind rationality. But, given that human groups and individuals define themselves in imitation of and in contradistinction to others, double-bind rationality necessarily shades everyone's socio-economic reality. If a society is not perfectly homogeneous, then in so far as notions of rationality become common conventions or institutions in the broad sense, they become part of decision-making situations as well as of decision procedures. This recursiveness of 'rationality', leading to *double-bind situations* of choice, falls outside the logical range of ethnocentric neoclassicalism. Rationality may in each case have a specific subjective character that depends on the individual's socio-economic situation and that commits him or her to interdependent, intransitive and/or incomplete decision behaviour. Without identifying the situational character of an individual's experience and understanding it from his or her point of view, we cannot know what, by any standard, is rational behaviour for them.

2. Social Being

The most pervasive of the classes of reasonable behaviour excluded from neoclassical analysis are consumer choices made with regard to one's *social being*. To be a social being means to have regard, sometimes positive, sometimes negative, for the behaviour, opinion and companionship of others. In a consumer society this regard inevitably extends to and mediates one's economic choices. And who wishes to deny that it is patently absurd to think that to be a social being in a consumer society is irrational? Yet that is precisely what neoclassical rationality infers when it insists that, given rational choice, the demands of individuals are independent of each other. It also infers this through its transitivity condition, because regard for social being means that changes in the norms of one's reference groups lead to intransitive choices.

The mere fact that consumers are social beings-that they care about each other-gives them many eminently sensible reasons for basing their choices, in part, on considerations of other peoples' choices. This is especially true in affluent societies where consumer demand is based increasingly on a desire to exchange in order to acquire a social identity, to be recognized by others. Desire for social identity translates into consumer desires because commodities have non-material as well as material properties. Goods carry meanings, bundles of often conflicting socio-cultural significances which change with the season and the social context and which arise from the market exchange process itself. These meanings affect consumers. Rational choice, therefore, requires choosers to give weight to the intersubjective, context-specific, market-based kaleidoscopes of meanings.

To be fashionably dressed, for example, means buying one's clothes with an eye to what other people are buying and to be ready and willing to take part in counter-trends. Likewise to dress so as to make one's self appear hireable, promotable, respectable, outrageous, youthful, etc. requires giving weight to current and ever-changing consumer patterns. Everyday sociability also entails regard for the consumption decisions of others. To be a good conversationalist – surely not an irrational desire – often depends on buying and consuming the books, films, entertainments, newspapers and the like that the people one knows buy and consume. For most people, to enjoy a night out means patronizing businesses where other people are enjoying a night out. Rare is the person who does not find it expedient to look to the choices of other consumers as guides to what they might buy. All these and other forms of imitation and interdependence enter into the decision processes of modern and post-modern consumers, from the youngest to the oldest, from the poorest to the richest, and from the rock star to the accountant, so that if these behaviours are not rational, then there exist no rational consumers, not even any who begin to or would want to approximate the neoclassical ideal.

3. Reciprocal Imitation

Long ago John Maynard Keynes noted that stock markets are dominated by 'a society of individuals each of whom is endeavouring to copy the others'. In such situations reasonableness requires the imitation of other agents who in turn are imitating other agents. If you care about the future market value of your investment, rational decision must be based on the anticipated decisions of other investors. So here rationality requires behaviour contrary to the neoclassical axiom of independence. Fashion phenomena, which becomes pervasive as societies become more affluent depend on the same intersubjective behavioural pattern.

4. Self-Referential Goods

Paper money is intrinsically worthless. Our willingness to accept it in exchange for things of intrinsic value is based entirely our belief that other people also will accept (demand) it in exchange for goods. This process of dematerialization has its parallel in the development of some contemporary consumer products. Consider the cola industry. Beginning in the 1960s, Pepsi-Cola abandoned attempts to create demand for its product on the basis of tangible properties. It turned instead, with great success, to marketing Pepsi as a symbol of membership in its *own* population of users, that is, 'the Pepsi People', 'the Pepsi Generation'. The company's advertisements and the demand that they generated could be understood only in terms of symbol.

The efficacy of such symbols *as the basis of their own market demand*, designer labels being an everyday example, is founded on people believing that other people believe that the product represents certain values or qualities. Here the communicative property of goods, whose meanings lead to the creation of market value, arises directly through the market exchange process. In such cases, the individualist point of view intersects with a holistic or collective one, giving rise to agreed social fact. Rather than being mere curiosities, as neoclassical economists claim, these and other interdependencies are central to modern consumer choice.

The chicaneries of soft drink peddling and designer fashions might be dismissed as unwholesomely manipulative, but everyone concurs with the need to maintain confidence in modern dematerialised monetary systems. When money takes the form of inconvertible paper currency and bank deposits, it exists as pure symbol, devoid of intrinsic value, a pure case of a self-referential good. But with any self-referential good, individual demands for it are fundamentally interdependent.

5. Spontaneity

Neoclassical rationality is the progeny not only of a holistic vision, but also of the more austere times in which it emerged. If the margin between survival and death is precarious, the material means of life permitting only the narrowest existence, then unbending application of neoclassical rationality may be your best strategy for making the most of your prospects. But things become radically different when affluence is gained. Then new possibilities for living emerge and the conflict between the application of neoclassical axiomatic rationality and the pursuit of leisured pleasures becomes both obvious and acute. The sybarite merely occupies the common perceptual ground in realizing that maintenance of preference consistency (transitivity) and estimation of outcomes up to the limits of one's cognitive powers (completeness) are not always consonant with 'the good life'. Indeed, allegiance to neoclassical rationality precludes several major classes of consumer pleasures in today's 'experience economy'. These include choices motivated by spontaneity, by the spirit of adventure and by the wish for change.

Firstly, consider spontaneity. Some hedonistic activities depend on it. This means there exists a logical impasse for any notion of rationality that requires agents always to work to a plan. Jon Elster explains it nicely.

Take the plan to behave spontaneously. There is nothing incoherent in the end state which defines that plan, since people often do behave spontaneously. Yet trying to be spontaneous is a self-defeating plan, since the very act of trying will interfere with the goal. There is a possible world in which I behave spontaneously, but none in which I plan to do so and succeed.

(Elster 1985: 11)

Neoclassical rationality requires choices to be made according to a preference ordering, a plan which, even when simplified to 'procedural rationality', is extremely complex. Therefore, by the lights of the neoclassical paradigm, spontaneous consumption decisions and those people who make them are irrational. The joys of carnival, the pleasures of impulse buying, and the elation of lubricated but unpremeditated conviviality are examples of categories of consumer choice founded on spontaneity or 'holes in the preference ordering' and, therefore, fall foul of the neoclassical regime of good consumership. Existence of cultural differences between 'races' regarding the value placed on spontaneity, means that the neoclassical concept of rationality/irrationality is *not* a racially neutral construct. This is a simple but important fact that you may wish to raise in your classes, especially if your university is committed to 'equal opportunities' and against the promotion of racism.

6. Adventure

Neoclassical rationality assumes that the consumer's transitive and complete preference orderings are made on the basis of perfect knowledge of future outcomes or at least some attempted approximation to it. *Adventure*, however, turns on ignorance. Without some absence of knowledge about what lies ahead, adventure is impossible. Its essence dwells in the unknownness of coming experience and of its outcome. Taste for this uncertainty is not confined to heroes and heroines. Shadows of Marco Polo and Amelia Earhart live in us all, making the pleasures of the unknown and the indeterminate universal. Even the elderly and the infirm enjoy reading a whodunit or cliffhanger. And even the tamest package holiday attracts with its promise of unknown experiences. The travel brochure's proverbial '400 cheeses to choose from', for example, aims at a consumer preference for the unknown, for the 'hole in the preference ordering'. Many everyday consumption decisions also take place under the influence of the desire for the unknown. Spectator sports, which form one of the world's largest industries, owe their massive appeal to the indeterminacy of their outcomes.

7. Free Choice

As a logical system, neoclassical rationality works by eliminating free choice from its conceptual space. It does so by proceeding on the basis of a temporal separation of the moments of preference ordering and of *what it calls* 'choice'. It defines rationality as people 'choosing' what they have *previously* decided or determined they prefer. Rationality requires, says Kenneth Arrow, that the agent's 'choices be in conformity with an ordering or a scale of preferences'. (Arrow 1983a: 49) '[T]he individual is assumed to choose among the alternatives available that one which is highest on his ranking.' (Arrow 1984b: 56) '[R]ational behaviour simply means behaviour in accordance with some ordering of alternatives in terms of relative desirability...' (Arrow 1984a: 7) This approach has no predictive power at all unless it is assumed that the preferences (i.e., prior choices) do not change over time. The theory merely freezes an agent's dispositions to choose at some time in the past. Only by separating the two acts – a prior ranking of goods (or ordering of priorities) and a subsequent buying of goods in the market place – do 'irrationality' and 'rationality' become distinguishable. Without the temporal gap, irrational behaviour is impossible under the neoclassical definition. Similarly, under the revealed preferences approach, 'rationality' assumes that no change in preferences takes place for the period in which preferences are revealed.

So the basic condition of neoclassical rationality is that individuals must *forego* choice in favour of some past reckoning, thereafter acting as automata. This conceptual elimination of freedom of choice, in both its everyday and philosophical meanings, gives neoclassical theory the hypothetical determinacy that its Newtonian inspired metaphysics require. *No indeterminacy; no choice. No determinacy; no neoclassical model.*

This postulation of a form of closed-mindedness, of being 'set in one's ways', as the ultimate meaning of rational choice is a model that you may not find appealing. Except perhaps among the very old and the clinically neurotic, dogged consistency of choice has never, outside economic theory, cut much ice as a behavioural ideal. It is at odds with the contingency and indeterminacy of human existence, with the developmental character of a healthy personality, with the humanist tradition, and, most especially, with the temper of post-traditional societies.

Choice takes place at particular points of time in the individual's life, so that what is 'rational' is *relative* to those points. A person's phenomenal world changes continuously from birth to death. If human life is a developmental process, then by definition one cannot know what one's points of view will be toward future choice situations. To imply otherwise, as the neoclassical paradigm does, is to indulge and encourage others in fantasy.

If self-identity is an ongoing, intentional, reflexive project of change – and, by implication, so too are preference orderings and meta-preferences and meta-

meta-preferences and so on – then there exists no ground for putting forward, on any timescale, consistency of choice as a maximizing principle. A further logical twist occurs when, as seems increasingly the case, people's consumption choices become 'lifestyle' choices that are about choices of self-identity. When this becomes the case, market choices determine preferences, rather than the other way around.

8. Taste for Change

But the convolutions of self-identity are not alone in turning consumer preference and choice into a reflexive process and, thereby, beyond the scope of neoclassical rationality. A century ago, Caroline Foley identified 'the taste for change' as widespread in motivating consumer choice, and, where material circumstances permit, a human universal (Foley 1893; see also Fullbrook 1998a). Foley's thesis that consumers frequently prefer something *because* hitherto they did not prefer it strikes, with the precision of a Cruise missile, the superstructure of the neoclassical theory. If a consumer has a taste for change, then some intransitivity of choice is a necessary condition for its gratification. As Foley emphasized, with the improvement of material circumstance, this taste comes increasingly into play as a criterion of consumer choice. In our time, vast industries – tourist, film, television, pop music and publishing – have prospered by catering directly to what Foley also called 'the law of variety in wants' (Foley 1893: 461).

We have considered eight broad categories of consumer decisions accepted as rational by contemporary society but which, analysis shows, violate one or more of the axioms of neoclassical rationality. These results are summarized in the following table.

Axioms Violated

Categories of Decision Behaviour	Transitivity	Completeness	Independence
Double-Bind Situations	X	X	X
Social Being	X		X
Reciprocal Imitation	X		X
Self-Referential Goods			X
Spontaneity	X	X	
Adventure		X	
Free Choice	X	X	
Taste for Change	X		

CONCLUSION

Projects to understand the logic of economic choice that do not engage with real-world situations of the same are doomed to epistemological failure and axiomatic delusions for the same reasons as are also attempts to theorize about the natural world without observing it. Economics' interest in choice behaviour has in the main been and continues to be far removed from the spirit of empirical, let alone scientific, inquiry. Each of the aspects of consumer behaviour considered above is widespread today, more or less understood by marketing professions, and influential in market outcomes and probably also in your personal life. Yet neoclassical economics, on the grounds of a logic dictated by the *a priori* foundations of its system of belief insists upon branding you and your consumer choices as irrational.

This chapter has identified eight categories of decision-making behaviour which neoclassical rationality counts as irrational, but which any person of good sense and good will would see as reasonable. What is so eminently notable about these categories is that taken together they include a very large, growing and arguably already dominant share of the decisions that consumers, particularly young ones, make in advanced economies. Rather than being obscure or far-fetched exceptions to the general rule, they characterise mainstream economic practice. Yet most economics textbooks and economics teachers remain conceptually embarrassed by their existence. This is madness.

REFERENCES

Ackerman, Frank (2002) 'Flaws in the Foundation: Consumer behavior and general equilibrium theory' in *Intersubjectivity in Economics: Agents and Structures*, ed. Edward Fullbrook, London: Routledge.

Arrow, Kenneth J. (1983a) 'The Principle of Rationality in Collective Decisions' [1952], *Collected Papers of Kenneth J. Arrow, Volume 1: Social Choice and Justice*, Cambridge, Mass.: Harvard University Press, 45–58.

—— (1983b) 'General Equilibrium' [1968], *Collected Papers of Kenneth J. Arrow, Volume 2: General Equilibrium*, Cambridge, Mass.: Harvard University Press, 107–32.

Elster, Jon (1985) *Sour Grapes: Studies in the Subversion of Rationality*. Cambridge: Cambridge University Press.

Foley, Caroline A. (1893) 'Fashion', *Economic Journal*, 3 (September): 458–74.

Fullbrook, Edward (1998a) 'Caroline Foley and the Theory of Intersubjective Demand', *Journal of Economic Issues*, Vol. XXXII, No. 3 (September): 709–31.

Gravelle, Hugh and Ray Rees (1981) *Microeconomics*, London: Longman.

Hicks, J. R. (1946) *Value and Capital: An Inquiry into some Fundamental Principles of Economic Theory* [1939], 2nd edn, Oxford: Clarendon Press.

Morgenstern, Oskar (1948) 'Demand Theory Reconsidered', *The Quarterly Journal of Economics*, February: 165–201.

8

Five Pieces of Advice for Students Studying Microeconomics

Emmanuelle Benicourt

École des Hautes Études en Sciences Sociales, France

Today most economists regard microeconomics as the core of economic theory. They nearly always present it as a theory that intends to describe and explain what happens in the real world, even if only in an approximate way. For instance, in his *Intermediate Microeconomics* Hal Varian uses a geographic metaphor:

> Economics proceeds by developing *models* of social phenomena. Think about how useless a map on a one-to-one scale would be. The same is true of an economic model that attempts to describe every aspect of reality. A model's power stems from the elimination of irrelevant details, which allows the economist to focus on essential features of the economic reality he or she is attempting to understand (Varian, 1990, 1–2).

In *Microeconomic analysis*, he uses the "friction" metaphor: "This competitive story represents a limiting case of market behaviour that is very useful for economic analysis just as the study of a frictionless system is useful for a physicist." (Varian, 1984, p. 82).

Gregory Mankiw, another popular textbook author, uses the same metaphor.

> Just as a physicist begins the analysis of a falling marble by assuming away the existence of friction, economists assume away many of the details of the economy that are irrelevant for studying the question at hand. (Mankiw, 2001, p. 23)

He adds:

Economists...approach the study of economy as a physicist approaches the study of matter and a biologist that of life: they derise theories, collect data and then analyse these data in an attempt to verify or refute the in theories. (Mankiw, 2001, p. 20)

Joseph Stiglitz uses a different metaphor for the same idea: 'Just as engineers construct models to study the characteristics of a car, economists construct, using words or equations, models describing the characteristics of an economy' (Stiglitz, 1993, p. 20).

The beginning student may then think to himself: 'Cool! I am finally going to understand what is happening in the world that surrounds me, just as the physicist or the biologist, and even more, with the rigour of mathematics!' The student then expects to go from a certain number of concrete examples (falling bodies, planet movements, electric power, or the description of the organism of this or that animal, etc.) to the theory which explains – even approximately – the observed phenomena.

Unfortunately, he soon discovers that this is not the case. Although some of the words used in his microeconomics class, like 'goods', 'commodities', 'household', 'firm', 'market', 'price' and 'supply and demand' sound familiar, he rapidly learns that the economics teacher is using them to designate objects that have practically nothing to do with what we usually mean by these words. Instead they refer to fictitious entities, and not approximations of something that really exists. This is why microeconomic textbooks almost never include data drawn from reality, from observations. They talk about a 'housing market' (Varian, 1990, p. 2) on a small campus, about an 'ice-cream seller' (Mankiw, 2001, pp. 76–87) in a 'small city', or about 'chocolate bars' (Stiglitz, 1993, pp. 87–95), but each time the data (numbers and curves) are invented by the authors. They do this not for educational reasons, but because the world about which they are reasoning is not the one we know.

FICTITIOUS AGENTS: HOUSEHOLDS AND FIRMS

Microeconomic courses all start by studying two types of agents: consumers (or households) and producers (or firms). The first are represented by a preference ordering (or a utility function) and an endowment (of goods and property rights), the latter by a production function. The student then expects that, as it occurs in physics and in biology, he will be given examples drawn from observations – of existing households or firms – even if they only focus on certain aspects.

But no example is ever given of someone's preference relation – not even those of leading neoclassical economists, whom one might think resemble the perfect consumers described by their theory. The student has to content himself with an ordering or a utility function that has a certain number of formal proprieties (monotonicity, convexity, continuity) that sometimes have an economic meaning, but which are never shown to characterize real individuals. Instead these proprieties have merely been invented so as to make possible the mathematical treatment that becomes the professor's main preoccupation: indifference maps, marginal rates of substitution, budget constraints, choice of an optimal bundle of goods, substitution and income effects, etc., and all deduced from fictitious preference relations. In the end, the student puts all his energy into trying to understand these formulas and figures. And what does all this lead to? Well, as real consumers' preferences (tastes) generally do not have these properties,[1] as households don't calculate like the economist supposes they do, as numerous motivations – which aren't included in the theory – intervene when one makes a choice, all this leads to nothing except new formulas.

It is rather striking to note that persons interested in consumers' effective choices –such as managers and marketing specialists – appeal to scholars who really observe them (psychologists, sociologists, and even, sometimes, psychoanalysts and ethnologists) and not to microeconomists, who deal with fictitious agents.

My first piece of advice to somebody obliged to study microeconomics: ask the teacher to give a real example of somebody's preference map (the teacher's perhaps) and then ask him or her to give one precise and general 'result' (which is not blatantly obvious anyway) of consumer theory.

THE CASE OF THE FIRM

The microeconomics fiction becomes pure fantasy when it turns its attention to the firm and pretends to describe it with a mathematical function linking inputs to outputs. Students may be enticed with the story of Robinson Crusoe or with a story about a one-person firm (farmer, fisherman, ice-cream seller, etc.), where inputs are either confined to two or three 'factors of production' or disappeared into a cost function with one variable. Students' attention is then directed towards the calculus-marginal productivity, rate of substitution, cost, and so on – without a word about the relevance of this approach. No examples of actual firms are given, no case made that this in anyway corresponds to and describes a known reality.

Some books – like Varian's (1984, 1990) – jump straight to a function $f(x_1, \dots, x_n)$, or $f(K,L)$, and start calculating. But often microeconomics textbooks 'invent' firms, and become ridiculous, especially when they want to give examples of 'substitutability' of inputs (or of factors of production), which are supposed to adapt 'smoothly' and instantaneously when prices change. For example, Hirshleifer and Glazer (1992, pp. 284–6) feature a 'textile' example. Between equations they talk about the production of 'shirts' from labour and 'cloth'. One is expected to imagine how the *same* shirt can be produced with little cloth and a lot of labour, or with a lot of cloth and little labour. Another frequently used example concerns substitutability between land and labour (see, for instance, the 14th edition of Samuelson's and Nordhaus' *Economics* (1992, pp. 82–3)). Here again there are numerical examples, but like events in a novel, they are inventions of the authors, rather than the result of observing and interviewing farmers.[2] Begg, Dornbush and Fisher's *Economics* provides another example of this fantasy approach. Fisher was the chief economist of the International Monetary Fund for years and Dornbusch an important member of its staff. So if real-life examples of production with substitutes exist, these men would surely know about some. But they have failed to come up with a single concrete example. Instead they ask the student to imagine a fictitious product, 'snarks', which can be produced with different proportions of machines and workers (Begg, Dombusch, Fisches, 1984, pp. 119–20).

In the real world there are practically no examples of firms whose inputs are substitutable at each moment. And for a simple reason: one cannot substitute a man (or half of a man) by, say, a tenth of a machine (or one hour of labour by two pounds of clay) and obtain the same product, say, a pot. It is why, in *all* textbooks, examples (if there are any) of firms are pure inventions when seeking justification of the book's assumption of factor substitutability.

Of course substitutability does exist in the real world, but it is of the *intertemporal* kind: as time passes, and as knowledge and techniques improve, (relatively) fewer men and more machines are used to produce the same quantity (or more) of goods. Price movements may have some influence on this substitution, but surely not in a 'smooth' way: first, men are substituted by machines, but the replacement practically never goes the other way around. Second, machines cannot be replaced 'at the margin', as they incorporate new technologies and generally suppose a different form of organising work.

Microeconomics textbooks don't say a word about these important facts that everyone can see in everyday life and by observing infant industries and bankruptcies. The textbooks sometimes allude to fixed costs, in a 'marshallian' way, but the sole purpose is to explain that 'in the long run', profits disappear if there is 'competition' (or 'free entry'). Thus, although irreversible sunk costs are one of the main problems of real firms' (and one of the main reasons of their existence), microeconomists ignore them, and prefer to focus on fictitious firms, where everything can be 'substituted', at every moment – and where calculus can be 'applied'.

My second piece of advice to students studying microeconomics: ask the teacher to give *just one* example of a production function describing, even approximately, a real life firm. You could also request a concrete example of (instantaneously) substitutable inputs. If the teacher cannot offer any examples, ask him: 'then, what is the use of all the mathematics?'

ABOUT MARKETS

Neoclassical economists know that factors (and outputs) are not really substitutes. They also know that there is not one person in the whole world who knows (or tries to know) his or her indifference map. But they say: 'Well, theories are abstractions, so we are obliged to simplify. They capture some aspects of reality, even if they are not the most important ones, and we try to deduce from them results or theorems.' In general, this is true. It supposes, however, that assumptions (or abstractions) are not in fact directly contrary to reality, as is the case with the factor substitutability assumption and, even more, with that of 'perfect markets'.

Nothing is more central to neoclassical microeconomics that the concept of a market. Yet textbooks leave its meaning up in the air. Why? Because their analysis requires a notion of a market that assumes magical properties, which any attempt to explain would cause deep embarrassment. Textbooks typically begin by assuming that prices are 'given' by the market, meaning that all agents, including producers, are 'price takers'. But if prices are given for everyone, who sets them? It also is claimed that markets add up all the individual supplies and demands and then find the equilibrium price. But who exactly performs these feats? These are essential questions. But they are forbidden because they reveal a fundamental logical inconsistency at the centre of neoclassical price theory.

Occasionally in advanced textbooks, and usually toward the end, authors may whisper a few words about this puzzle. For example, Varian, in his *Advanced Microeconomics*, after 397 pages concedes that:

> The biggest problem is one that is the most fundamental, namely the paradoxical relationship between the idea of competition and price adjustment: if all economic agents take market prices as given and outside their control, how can prices move? Who is left to adjust prices?

And what is Varian's answer to the most fundamental of questions? 'The puzzle has led to the erection of an elaborate mythology, which postulates the existence of a "Walrasian auctioneer" whose sole function is to search for the market clearing prices'(Varian, 1984, p. 244). This 'auctioneer' is of course pure fantasy. It is not only a myth but also one that is 'very unrealistic' as

Varian concedes, admitting that another theory, one without an auctioneer, is needed. But, then, why study all this stuff with price-taking agents, 'excess market demand' and so on? And why do microeconomists continue to say that this model represents 'perfect competition', or 'the perfect market'?[3]

IS A 'PERFECT MARKET' A MARKET ?

Microeconomists never define a market because it is impossible to do so in a mathematical sense. But they always refer to the 'perfect case' – the so-called perfect competition general equilibrium – and use it as a norm. Why? Because it is 'efficient' in the sense of being Pareto-optimal.[4] Why? Because the 'visible hand' of the auctioneer does the entire job and without costs. This idea is far removed from Adam Smith's 'invisible hand'-microeconomics textbooks' inescapable (and false) metaphor-and very near to the Soviet Union's planners' dream! Even neoclassical economists admit (not in microeconomics textbooks, but in macroeconomics ones, especially when they treat growth) that competitive equilibrium and a central planner's choice give the same result – which is obvious, as perfect competition *assumes* that there is an auctioneer, who acts as a central planner. However, these economists almost *never* say a word about this assumption; instead competitive prices 'emerge' from nowhere.

Do microeconomists *really* have as their ideal a system where people cannot propose prices and cannot trade directly-where they can only exchange goods at prices set by the auctioneer (or the central planner)? Do the IMF and the World Bank *really* want such a system when they say that 'efficiency' and 'competition' have to be implemented? The answer is obvious: no.

So this is all a big mess: 'perfect markets' are not at all proxies for real markets, excluding 'irrelevant details'. Indeed, they suppose an institutional form *opposed* to the idea of a market, whatever it may be. Often, it is said that perfect competition describes a 'decentralised economy', but this is the exact opposite of the truth: it describes a centralised system, where agents are only allowed to make transactions at centrally given prices.

One can perhaps accept that preference orderings and endowments are a (more or less) good abstraction of consumers and that production sets give an idea of firms' technology. However, it is *impossible* to accept that 'perfect competition' has anything to do with competition and markets, whether abstract or concrete.

RIGOUR OR CONFUSION?

Suppose that somebody teaching microeconomics started by saying: 'We are going to study a world where there is a benevolent person – called the 'auctioneer', 'market player' or 'fictitious agent' – who sets prices, finds out the exact demands and supplies of all the price-taking households and firms; etc…'. What would then happen? Students would stop him or her and say: 'Why? Please tell us why do we have to learn about this strange world?' A 'rigorous' teacher can only answer: 'For fun' or 'Because I think socialism will soon win and society is going to need planners' or 'Because it is good for you to learn to reason in an "axiomatic" way'.

But microeconomics teachers are not as rigorous as they claim, even if they do know some mathematics. To elude such a question, they *never* present the notion of perfect competition straightforwardly. Instead, like poets, they use metaphors and appeal to intuition. In the case of competition, they link it to the usual and 'obvious' opinion that the market of a good is competitive if there are many agents supplying and demanding this good, each of them being very little and atomistic. Thus, as no one can influence prices-or only in a trivial manner – all agents can be assumed to be price takers. Then perfect competition can be considered as synonymous with 'many agents', making theory and reality appear to agree.

But in fact they don't. A rigorous person will reply: 'even if there are millions of agents, if *all* of them are supposed to be price takers, then *who sets prices?* And *who changes them* when global supply is different from global demand?' At this point the neoclassical economist resorts to poetics: 'prices emerge' thanks to 'market forces' or to 'the invisible hand', etc. So much for clarity and intellectual rigour. But that is the dark power of ideology at work. Neoclassical economists are wedded to the idea that 'perfect competition' or 'frictionless markets' are 'efficient' in the sense of being Pareto-optimal. They do not want to admit that this efficiency is only possible with a costless, benevolent auctioneer doing a whole lot of things.

My third and most important piece of advice to students studying microeconomics: Each time someone speaks to you of perfect competition say: 'So, you assume that there is an auctioneer. Consequently, you are not trying to approach or abstract from the real world. You propose instead to study another kind of world. Please then stop trying to seduce us students into confusion and error by falsely comparing your 'perfect competition' with the cartographer's maps or with the physicist's frictionless models. Please propose something else, preferably something that, like mapmaking and physics, relates to the real world.

ABOUT 'IMPERFECTIONS'

Microeconomics textbooks usually present perfect competition as 'unrealistic'. But not because it assumes a central system with an authoritarian auctioneer. Instead textbooks say it is unrealistic in the sense that in the real world there can be 'a few' agents, acting in a 'strategic' way. These are 'frictions' (Varian and Mankiw) or 'imperfections' impeding efficient allocations. The textbook suddenly switches to a normative mode and says that they should be eliminated. But the very fact of speaking of imperfections means that there is a 'perfect world' that can be attained, or, at least, approximated. This 'perfect world' is of course the perfect competition model.

In this model, equilibriums are 'efficient' or 'Pareto-optimal' and so play the role of *norms*. The message is that not only can these equilibrium be attained or approximated, but they *should be*. This is why in microeconomics textbooks (and now, unfortunately, even in those of macroeconomics), all models with 'imperfections' are compared with the 'perfectly competitive' ones. This happens with models of monopoly, duopoly (or oligopoly), monopolistic competition, public goods (where efficiency can be 'restored' by 'creating markets' in relation to externalities), etc. This normative twist generates an ideological argument that has come to be very widely applied. Suppress market imperfections (frictions) wherever possible, and everything will be all right. This has become the 'economist's message', implicit in the analysis and recommendations of the IMF, the World Bank, the OECD, the central banks, etc.. And it is so simple: suppress 'rigidities', especially in labour markets, (re-)establish 'flexibility', and then an ('efficient') equilibrium will, 'smoothly', be attained. Perhaps, but we ask again: do these people *really* want to implement a centralised system of the 'perfect competition' kind-the only one where 'efficiency' can be obtained?

My *fourth piece of advice to students studying microeconomics*: when a teacher proposes to study more 'realistic' models, of the 'imperfect competition' kind, tell him: 'All right, but models without an auctioneer and, thus, with at least some price-making agents'. Then, wait and see'.

ABOUT 'MARKET FAILURES'

Often microeconomics textbooks have one or two chapters about 'market failures'. What they mean is that there are goods (or 'evils') that are consumed (voluntarily or not) without being exchanged through a price system. Externalities (like pollution) and public goods (goods that can be consumed at the same time by many persons, such as street lighting) are classic examples of 'market failures'.

Microeconomists then propose to 'create markets' with the purpose of implementing 'efficiency' (Pareto-optimality). In other words, their approach is clearly normative. How do they propose to do this? Some, like Ronald Coase (1960), consider it enough to attribute property rights to agents and to let them bargain, as (competitive) prices 'emerge'. It is suggested that 'markets' will do the job-efficiently, of course. How? Well, because efficiency requires price-taking agents, it is (implicitly) supposed that there is somebody setting them, and so on, i.e., that all the institutional arrangements of 'perfect competition' are implemented. But when neoclassical economists speak of 'markets' and 'efficiency', they almost always are unconsciously referring to a centralised system. They want to show that 'markets' can solve problems without government intervention, but what they propose is a system where a government, or some other power-collects supply and demand statistics and finds and sets equilibrium prices.

Often, textbooks give the 'example' of a polluter and a polluted, and propose the 'perfect competitive' (and thus, efficient) solution, in total contradiction with what they have said in preceding chapters, where perfect competition was identified with many and atomistic agents on each side.[5] In fact, nowhere has this kind of 'solution' ever been really implemented. It is true that some countries, or American States, have organised 'tradable pollution permit markets' (for example, sulphur oxide emissions by electric power plants). But this requires lots of controls and, because there is no auctioneer, 'efficient' or 'equilibrium' prices don't 'emerge' spontaneously. This is not surprising: how can traders discover the 'good' price, even if there is lots of (costly) bilateral bargaining? Indeed, some people will trade, others not, and prices of goods will depend on the way people meet, on their aptitude (or desire) for bargaining, etc. Generally, the same good will have a different price in different places and at different times.

In fact, the problem posed by this kind of 'market' is the same as for other markets: how are prices formed when there is no auctioneer?

THE MAIN PROBLEM: BARGAINING IS INDETERMINATE

Suppose that there is no auctioneer. Then at least some agents must set prices. If this happens for the seller and the buyer of the same good, there is no reason that they both propose the same price. They will then bargain, the buyer trying to get a price as low as possible and the seller the opposite. In our societies, however, most people are price takers: they buy in shops at given prices. But shopkeepers' prices depend on the prices of the wholesalers and/or producers. At some moment, there will be a bargain: between dealers and wholesalers (or producers), or between wholesalers and producers. In fact, *there is always a bargain* (often between groups as lobbies, syndicates, trade unions, etc) *in price formation.*

But when one bargains and trades, it is because one wants to get an advantage (more satisfaction, or profit, after trade, than before). How will the total 'surplus' from trade be distributed? There is no simple answer to this question because traders' payoffs depend on their bargaining power, on their information about others' situations (especially on their reservation price), on norms imposed by society (or 'internalised' by traders), etc.

Take as an example a bargaining process between a worker and an employer. Suppose that both are interested in making a deal (a job for the worker, profit for the boss), the gain from trade being given by what Marx called 'surplus value'. The boss will try to keep the worker's wage as low as possible and the worker will try the opposite. The result of this process will depend on a variety of factors such as the level of unemployment, the existence and power of unions, and the laws, conventions, customs, etc. to which the parties are subject.[6] Most of these factors cannot be reduced to variables in equations; the result of bargaining is indeterminate.

What can a theorist then do? The answer seems obvious: observe what happens (or has happened) in known societies, look at how prices are *actually* formed and then, try to find rules or tendencies on which a theory can be built (or developed). But this requires a lot of work: collecting and processing data, undertaking surveys of not only individual behaviour but also of groups (unions, lobbies, etc.), taking into consideration the legal framework, regulations and cultural factors, and taking an interest in history. It's hard work, rarely thrilling and more often than not will fail to produce 'results' sufficiently general to lead to 'high level' publications or to recommendations of economic policy.

Today's mainstream microeconomists don't do this kind of work. Instead they want to prove 'theorems' (especially, the 'superiority' of the 'market mechanism') and they want to tell us what to do (essentially: suppress 'frictions', wherever possible). It is why they 'solve' the problem of bargaining by supposing that 'prices are given', etc.

My *fifth piece of advice to students studying microeconomics:* Ask the teacher 'Do you agree that behind any price, there is, somewhere, some kind of bargain? Then, please tell me how the neoclassical theory determines the bargaining issue? Oh, and please don't avoid the question by speaking of 'the market mechanism' or of 'competition'.

BARGAINING AND ASYMMETRIC INFORMATION

Beginning in the 1990s, the concept of asymmetric information became fashionable among microeconomists. It became even more so after Ackerlof, Selten and Stiglitz in 2001 won an economics Nobel Prize for their work on it. But this is a typical example of 'discovery' by academic economists of something that is obvious for most people, in this case for anyone who have ever traded or signed a contract with someone with whom they did not have the same information about the objects of the exchange.

Think of the cases of insurance (housing, car, health, etc.), of loans by banks, of used cars (or other durable goods), of labour relations, etc. Insurance companies, banks and employers know that when signing a contract with a customer or an employee they do not know everything they might like to know about her or him. But they have tried to find out as much as they can so as to limit unwanted consequences , resulting from what they call 'moral hazard', 'adverse selection',[7] and so on. Governments act in the same way. For instance when they pass laws to protect consumers. Customs and traditions often act in the same way, even if they are different from one place to another.

What then is the contribution of today's microeconomists, especially that of the prize-winners? Well, they have 'proved' (that is, mathematically) that asymmetry of information is generally a source of 'inefficiencies',[8] and that in some cases it prevents the existence in principle of equilibrium. And so what? One doesn't need mathematics to prove or to understand this. As Stiglitz has correctly insisted, taking asymmetric information into account changes the general theoretical analysis and, of course, the policy recommendations. But this can be done using words: one doesn't need to read Stiglitz's academic papers, full of mathematics, to understand what he says and to approve or disapprove.

WHAT STUDENTS MUST DEMAND

As perfect competition is devoid of interest,[9] students must keep demanding: we don't want to hear anything about it, except in history of economic thought courses (or perhaps eventually in courses about planning).

We want to start at the beginning, as in real life, by studying bilateral relations, by distinguishing between price takers and price makers, by finding at which level the bargaining process takes place, and by trying to determine, if possible, its issue.

We want to study theory, but with real-life examples, and not 'stories' with households and firms described by 'easy to use' mathematical functions and with prices 'emerging' from nowhere.

We know that what we demand is not as reassuring and comforting as exhibiting 'clear' proofs and results – in a mathematical sense. But we want to learn about societies, as they are (or as they have been), and not about clean but uninteresting and non-existent worlds.

9

How Mainstream Economists Model Choice, versus How We Behave, and Why It Matters

PETER E. EARL

UNIVERSITY OF QUEENSLAND, AUSTRALIA

INTRODUCTION

If you compare the theory of consumer behaviour taught in a standard economics course with what is taught as consumer behaviour in a department of marketing, you will find very little overlap. The economists' story is an elegant graphical or mathematical analysis that is presented as an approximation of what goes on when consumers economise in the sense of trying to avoid wasting their scarce budgets on bundles of goods and services that are of less benefit to them than other bundles that they could afford. The whole analysis is remarkably self-contained and, even though it is supposedly focused on how consumers can be thought of as maximizing their well-being, no use is made of anything that psychologists have said about what makes people happy. There *is* a kind of psychology in the theory – the notion of diminishing marginal utility or diminishing marginal rates of substitution – but it is all of the economists' own making. What is also striking about the economists' analysis is that it is of a 'one size fits all' variety, in that there is no suggestion that consumers might make their choices in different ways in different contexts: any choice at all is seen as capable of being approximated in theoretical terms by indifference analysis. Mainstream economists have little to say about habits, for example, even though large-scale empirical work by Houthakker and Taylor (1970) long ago showed just how important habits were in determining demand, as were changes in income, in contrast to the economists' typical focus on responses to changes in relative prices.

The approach to consumer behaviour within marketing, by contrast, is strikingly multi-disciplinary and draws heavily on psychology and sociology, as well as more specialized areas such as semiotics (the study of signs and symbols), communication, and cultural studies. Marketing scholars also keep their eyes open for useful developments from within economics (see for example, Ratchford 1975), comparing marketing approaches to reformulations of mainstream economic analysis in terms of consumers having a demand for product characteristics rather than goods per se – an approach that decades later is still not a central part of the economic mainstream but is standard fare within marketing). The marketing approach is strikingly different in its pluralistic outlook, even in its most prestigious journals such as the *Journal of Consumer Research*: at one extreme, consumer behaviour research can be every bit as formal and quantitative as work by economists whereas, at the other extreme, it can involve much more qualitative approaches, introspection and a hermeneutic approach (the careful analysis of text, such as advertising material). Pluralism extends to the way that choices are seen as being taken in different ways according to context: for example, marketing scholars distinguish between situations that are emotionally charged (high involvement) versus those that do not have great personal significance (low involvement), and between habitual behaviour and discretionary behaviour.

What is particularly strange about the coexistence of such different approaches to consumer behaviour is that there exists a literature within economics that stands somewhere between them but is rarely taught within core economic principles courses. Though economists are prone to dismiss marketing as a 'Mickey Mouse subject', it is clear that in terms of scholarship, the marketing writers are better read and more open-minded. While mainstream economists' work on consumer behaviour remains impervious to work in this area in marketing, marketing writers have drawn extensively on a heterodox approach to economics that draws upon research in psychology and studies of how people actually behave. This approach, known variously as behavioural economics, psychological economics or economic psychology, has major differences with the mainstream approach. The present chapter focuses on four major areas of difference by way of giving students a taste of what they could be missing when they study the microeconomics of choice.

1   Trade-Offs and the Shopping Trolley

Mainstream economics: 'As an approximation to reality, let us assume that consumers consider the pros and cons of having a bit more of one product versus a bit less of any other product and that they do this for all possible combinations of products that are available. Having done this and worked out which bundles of goods they can afford, and which they cannot, they then choose the bundle from their feasible set that gives them the highest utility.'

This perspective assumes that the consumer's information-handling skills do not have any impact on the choices that are made. The trouble is that, in the age of the supermarket, the consumer's choice problem is on an utterly different scale from that faced by much less affluent workers shopping a century or so ago when the essence of today's mainstream approach to choice was first worked out. The century-old perspective might not seem too implausible for poor consumers in a developing country, who face a narrow range of choice in a local market, but it looks much more questionable for supermarket shopping where the consumer faces a choice between over 10,000 distinct product lines. This implies a vast number of potential combinations of ways of spending the weekly shopping budget, plus many more ways of filling shopping trolleys whose cost would exceed the weekly budget. The fact that consumers can actually zip round a supermarket and get their shopping done in an hour or less, rather than spending ages trying to figure out what to do, might be taken by mainstream economists as implying that their approach is a reasonable approximation to what goes on. However, to the behavioural economist, it implies that shopping is being done in a way that does not involve anything like a comprehensive consideration of possible trade-offs.

> *Behavioural economics*: 'People have limited computational powers and can handle only about 10 bits of information per second and they typically can only keep in mind 7 + / − 2 things at a time…'

In the face of such empirically established cognitive limitations, shoppers have to simplify things and make limited comparisons, for example between rival brands of toothpaste, but perhaps not between spending money on toothpaste versus cheese versus olives, etc. Supermarkets are designed to facilitate this, grouping particular categories of products in particular aisles to enable shoppers to make sequential comparisons of like with like and fill their trolleys as they do so – if consumers shopped as pictured in mainstream theory, then products could be placed absolutely anywhere in a store and consumers would walk around the entire store to size up what was available before commencing to make their selections.

Even the comparison of brands may be limited if there are many rivals in the same category, so choice may be affected by advertising and the ability of a brand to grab attention (e.g. by being displayed on a shelf at eye-level or at the end of an aisle, and by having a conspicuous, distinctive type of packaging). Companies that supply grocery products therefore compete to get the best positions for grabbing attention by paying inducements to supermarkets; they also find it worth spending a considerable amount on imprinting their brand symbols on consumers' minds via advertising.

With so many items in stock, and with different shop layouts, supermarkets find it difficult to demonstrate to consumers that they offer a better deal than their rivals. This is why some chains experiment with 'weekly specials' to try to encourage consumers to experiment with shopping in their stores instead of staying at rivals' stores. Other supermarket chains advertise themselves as offering 'everyday low pricing' in order to deter consumers from engaging in the inconvenience of checking the deals offered by their rivals. The different strategies will appeal differently to consumers depending on which *decision rules* they use to simplify their shopping. The implication is that it may be unwise to assume, as mainstream economists do, that all consumers are pretty much the same 'representative agents' and that it may be worth studying the different kinds of shopping strategies that are commonly used.

2   Choice Between Competing Products

> *Mainstream economics*: 'People choose by weighing up a product's good points against its bad points to get an overall view of what it is worth to them, to compare it with other products'.

Although the formal teaching of mainstream consumer theory still normally focuses on choice between rival combinations of goods rather on what these goods have to offer, the mainstream economist's focus on substitution leads to a simple piece of policy advice for firms: 'If you can't sell good goods, sell cheap goods'. This line of thinking has important implications for how a country should deal with a balance of payments problem. To increase exports and reduce imports, the crucial thing is not to change what is being made but to change relative prices. Hence allowing the exchange rate to depreciate is the way to reduce imports and increase exports, since this will change domestic production costs relative to those overseas. In practice, devaluations do not have a brilliant record as means of turning around balance of payments deficits. A mainstream interpretation of this would be that exchange-rate changes tend not to go far enough, whereas from the behavioural perspective the reason might simply be that consumers are choosing on essentially non-price grounds in ways that are at odds with the principle of substitution.

> *Behavioural economics*: 'Consumers may sometimes trade off good points against bad points and form overall evaluations of rival products, but often they may be *intolerant*, choose on the basis of a *priority* ranking, or reject all brands that don't offer *all the features* on their preferred *checklist*.'

There are several plausible reasons why consumers fail to work out overall evaluations of products in the trade-off manner:

- Some kinds of products may get 'ruled out' because consumers see them at odds with how they see their *identities* (as in 'I know it's cheap, functional, or whatever, but it isn't really *me*; I need something that says something about my place in the world, my ability to discern quality, etc. and in the latter terms it simply isn't good enough.').

- They may build their lives around particular *moral* principles (for example, vegetarianism, avoidance of debt, patriotism).

- A product may have *too many* features to keep in mind at once, whereas choice is simplified if one uses a checklist of desired performance standards and does not try to compute an overall value (as with 'I want a DVD player under £100 that is able to play MP3 recordings and JPEG picture CDs, and, ideally, is not made in China'). Experience will enable consumers to judge whether their demands are too restrictive (so nothing is deemed acceptable) or too easy (such that many products get over the set of hurdles and a tie-break rule is needed), and hence what they can reasonably expect to demand. Social inputs may also help in shaping a consumer's mould of tolerance in a particular area.

If price frequently is not a decisive factor, then national policy makers may find balance of payments problems require much more subtle policies than allowing the exchange rate to depreciate, policies such as those aimed at improving the quality of domestic production, making local consumers more patriotic ('Buy British' campaigns in the UK, for example), or setting product standards and bureaucratic hurdles that will make life difficult for importers. In this age of moves towards globalisation via the World Trade Organization (itself driven by mainstream economics), such policies could be problematic; quotas would be a definite 'no-no'.

The behavioural perspective is also relevant for business strategy. Leaving particular features off a product without even making them available as options, or offering inadequate performances in respect of some product features, may mean some consumers will reject it, *regardless of price or performance in other respects*, because they can find something else that is cheap enough which meets their requirements. The consequences even extend to labour market behaviour. For example:

- A car with a very poor rust resistance or reliability record, despite being stylish and sporty (cf. the fate of Lancia in the UK a couple of decades ago, and the difficulties in re-establishing Alfa Romeo as a premium brand)
- An airline with a poor safety record (would you travel with Aeroflot?)
- A restaurant menu with no vegetarian option (a single vegetarian in a group could rule out the restaurant for the entire group)

- A job applicant who cannot meet all the 'required selection criteria' (it is ironic that heterodox economists have a hard time getting jobs in prestigious universities in the UK under the current Research Asssessment Exercise (RAE) system, since they tend not to be able to get articles published in the top ranking journals that the RAE favours when assessing academic departments for research standing and hence funding).

The behavioural perspective may help explain why many highly successful products (and people?) are actually rather bland: the firms that win a big proportion of a market may be those that offer products that offer adequate performances in all respects commonly required even though they are not outstanding in any respect.

3   How Well do People Choose?

Mainstream economics: 'We presume people take decisions consistent with the application of principles from economics and statistics.'

Behavioural economics: 'Research shows that behaviour of actual decision makers is commonly at odds with what economic theory expects but not in an unsystematic manner; in other words, it is subject to a number of commonly observed biases.'

The difference between the perspectives here is rather in terms of normative versus positive economics. For example, a behavioural economist will accept that mainstream advice about what one *should* do in respect of sunk costs is appropriate; however, it is evident that many people *actually* find it difficult to avoid 'pouring good money after bad', falling into the temptation to try to recover money they have already spent on something, rather than focusing on the returns of spending additional money on the same thing versus on something else. (Classic examples include Concorde, the UK's Millennium Dome, playing poker, running an old car, or continuing to go for a workout as a means of 'getting value from gym membership' despite hating the process.) Other kinds of observed behaviour at odds with mainstream theory include cases where:

- People do not treat the value of their time or money consistently and instead 'frame' things mentally in different ways. (For example: taking a quarter of an hour extra to shop for a £10 saving on a car radio, but not haggling for an extra quarter of an hour to save an extra £10 on a car; likewise, advertising £10 off a car will not attract attention in the way that advertising £10 off a much cheaper item will.)

- The value a person places on something is affected by whether or not they already have it (for example, experiments have shown that people who agree to buy something for a particular sum tend to require more to part with the item if it is given to them and the experimenter then offers to buy it back).

- People who mow their own lawns to save paying a lawn-mowing firm £10 to do the job tend not to be prepared to mow their neighbour's lawns to earn £10.

- People tend to be more concerned with *changes* in the value of their wealth than with its absolute value.

- People are prone to addiction and weakness of will, and at the same time to be aware of their personal limitations. If consumers were not aware of their fallibility we would not see them pre-committing themselves to avoid succumbing to temptation, as with Christmas club savings accounts (that are hard to withdraw and tend to offer poor rates of interest), voluntary superannuation schemes (that may perform no better than unit trusts to which the saver has free access), going to health farms, or making their plans public so that a failure to deliver would be humiliating

- People allow their judgment to be affected by vivid pieces of information that they ought to dismiss as statistical outliers or make judgments on the basic of simplistic rules, rather than basing their judgments on large samples of data and easily obtainable expert knowledge. An example of the former is where a consumer allows the tale of a single maverick example of a product to put them off buying it, despite having read consumer magazines that report it is very reliable. As an example of the latter, you might reflect on how you would judge the safety of different types of cars: would you do so in terms of cues such as the size of the car, claims made by manufacturers in advertisements and the manufacturers' reputations, or would you bother to use the internet to check laboratory research findings (for example, those of the European New Car Assessment Programme at http://www.euroncap.com/) or assessments based on actual crash statistics (for example the Swedish Folksam study reported at: http://www.folksam.se/forskning/trafik/sakra_bilar/2003/bilListaEngelsk.htm), and do you find it hard to believe the finding from the latter that the small Toyota Yaris is as safe as a large Volvo and safer than a BMW 5-series?

- People seem to divide their thinking about money into different 'mental accounts', which they treat differently, so they end up scrimping and saving in parts of their lives but spending lavishly any time they come into money by chance.

These kinds of behaviour certainly can cause problems for some firms trying to market their products, but note that firms seeking to shape consumer choice have great potential to exploit their knowledge of how consumers are susceptible to particular kinds of 'non-rational' behaviour. Hence the behavioural perspective implies a need for more active consumer education and protection policies (see the excellent articles by Hanson and Kysar, 1999a, 1999b). However, the area that has attracted the most concerted empirical efforts to date has been the area where most money is at stake, namely in respect of how departures from 'rational' behaviour affect stock market behaviour and give rise to circumstances in which investors can consistently beat the average performance of the stock market, something that standard economics regards as impossible unless the investors have access to 'inside' information.

4   What Determines Overall Happiness?

Mainstream economics: 'An individual's well-being depends on how much they can spend on goods and services; the more you have, the happier you will feel.'

Behavioural Economics: 'Many people do not find more is better, and some, with good reason, don't try to get as many goods and services as they could.'

Our final comparison between mainstream and behavioural economics is perhaps the most significant, particularly because in policy terms the mainstream view promotes a fixation on the pursuit of economic growth with all that this entails in terms of the destruction of the natural environment and depletion of non-renewable resources. As Easterlin notes in the Introduction to his collection of readings on *Happiness in Economics* (2002: ix), the failure of mainstream economists to check the accuracy of their presumption arises, because of 'the heavy hand of a disciplinary paradigm stipulating that what people say is irrelevant to understanding their feelings or behavior' and a belief that 'meaningful interpersonal comparisons of well-being could not be made'. Consequently, most of what is known empirically about the determinants of happiness comes via psychology.

Aside from Easterlin's own work, probably the most famous contribution by an economist challenging the idea that material possessions bring happiness is Tibor Scitovsky's very readable (1976) book *The Joyless Economy*, which draws on physiological psychology with a focus on the impact of new stimuli on arousal. He argues, in essence, that problems arise because consumers do not understand the difference between pleasure and comfort. Affluent Americans often find that their rising wealth does not bring greater happiness because they opt for safe ways of spending their time and money (comfort) rather than enjoying the psychological benefits of taking on challenging activities and getting to grips with them (pleasure). He contrasts their bland entertainment choices, foods, vacations, and so on (nowadays we might think here of McDonald's, Disney and Hollywood as symbols of this) with those of less affluent but culturally more adventurous Europeans. Also evident in this perspective is a recognition that consumers need to experiment and work at developing *skills* in particular areas in order to appreciate the finer things in life: the stereotypical affluent American, by contrast, is prone to outsource such activities to an army of experts (interior design consultants, personal trainers, psychiatrists, and so on).

Two other key themes in the behavioural critique of the 'more is better' viewpoint of mainstream economics are that (a) People tend to judge their well-being not by how much they have in isolation, but by their positions *relative* to other people whom they use as reference points; and that (b) People do not realize that they will soon become *habituated* to better (or worse) standards of living. A long-dreamed-of expensive new car thus may be merely a temporary source of joy unless the manufacturers have managed to build in a lot of design features that will continue to 'surprise and delight' the owner: we soon get used to that standard of motoring and cease marvelling at it, and before long friends and neighbours acquire similar vehicles so it loses its ability to serve as a status symbol.

Given these tendencies, consumers might be far happier if they were less obsessed with trying to get ahead in material terms, with all this entails in terms of work-related stresses, and instead opted for a simpler, free-and-easy lifestyle based on relaxing socially rather than on social competition. In short, striving for economic growth so as to emulate US lifestyles may not result in greater happiness – it might be better to aim for lower stress with less materialistic spending but better education and a vibrant culture.

CONCLUDING COMMENTS

The coverage of differences between mainstream and behavioural approaches to choice presented in this chapter is by no means complete. Even so, the monopolistic domination of the mainstream or neoclassical approach to consumer behaviour may seem rather distressing in the light of the issues that have been raised here, for much time is being taken up teaching and studying this analytical framework at the cost of excluding the empirically far richer behavioural alternative. If you wish to receive training in non-neoclassical research on consumer behaviour but are presently studying with a thoroughly mainstream department of economics, then your best hope is to take enough marketing classes to enable you to take part in a consumer-behaviour course delivered within a department of marketing. It is sad to have to offer such advice right now, but the good news is that the behavioural approach is becoming something that mainstream economists will have trouble ignoring for much longer.

While economists typically paid rather little attention to the award of the 1978 Nobel Prize in Economics to pioneering behavioural economist Herbert A. Simon (who never held an academic post as an economist and at the time of the award was a professor of computing science and psychology), the sharing of the 2002 Nobel Prize by psychologist Daniel Kahneman and experimental economist Vernon Smith received widespread media attention and came hot on the heels of articles in major newspapers (for example, Uchitelle 2001), Lowenstein 2001) about the behavioural approach. Textbook coverage of it can be found in a few cases if you know where to look (Earl 1995, chapters 2 and 4, Frank 2002, chapter 8) and your university library might also subscribe not merely to relevant journals from marketing, such as the *Journal of Consumer Research*, but also to journals that specialize in publishing work in this area, such as the *Journal of Socio-Economics* and the *Journal of Economic Psychology*.

References and Suggestions for Further Reading

Conlisk, J. (1996) 'Why Bounded Rationality?', *Journal of Economic Literature*, 34: 669–700.

Earl, P.E. (1990) 'Economics and psychology: A survey', *Economic Journal*, 100: 718–55.

Earl, P.E. (1995) *Microeconomics for Business and Marketing*, Aldershot, Edward Elgar, chapters 2 and 4.

Earl, P.E. and Kemp, S. (eds.) (1999) *The Elgar Companion to Consumer Research and Economic Psychology*, Cheltenham, Edward Elgar Publishing (paperback 2002).

Easterlin. R.A. (ed.) (2002) *Happiness in Economics*, Cheltenham, Edward Elgar.

Frank, R. (2002) *Microeconomics and Behavior* (5th edn), New York, McGraw-Hill/Irwin.

Hanson, J.D. and Kysar, D.A. (1999a) 'Taking behavioralism seriously: the problem of market manipulation', *New York University Law Review*, 74, no. 3:. 630–749.

Hanson, J.D. and Kysar, D.A. (1999b) 'Taking behavioralism seriously: some evidence of market manipulation', *Harvard Law Review*, 112, no. 7: 1420–572.

Houthakker, H.S. and Taylor, L.D. (1970) *Consumer Demand in the United States: Analysis and Projections* (2nd edn), Cambridge, MA: Harvard University Press.

Lowenstein, R. (2001) 'Exuberance is rational', *New York Times Magazine*, 11 February.

Rabin, M. (1998) 'Psychology and economics', *Journal of Economic Literature*, 36: 11–46.

Rabin, M. (2002) 'A perspective on psychology and economics', *European Economic Review*, 46: 657–85.

Rabin, M. and Thaler, R. (2001) 'Anomalies: risk aversion', *Journal of Economic Perspectives* 15, 1: 219–32.

Ratchford, B.T. (1975) 'The new economic theory of consumer behavior: an interpretive essay', *Journal of Consumer Research*, 2 (September): 65–75.

Scitovsky, T. (1976) *The Joyless Economy*, New York: Oxford University Press.

Uchitelle, L. (2001) 'Some economists call behavior a key', *New York Times*, Business section, 11 February.

10

Managerial Economics: Economics of Management or Economics for Managers?

SASHI SIVRAMKRISHNA

FOUNDATION TO AID INDUSTRIAL RECOVERY, INDIA

This essay is more about 'what's wrong with *managerial* economics' than about 'what's wrong with economics'. I must make it clear that I do not intend to critique neoclassical economics; I am sure that many others will undertake to do so in the present volume. My aim instead is to make clear to students some of the shortcomings of managerial economics, a course that finds a place in almost every management education course. I have articulated my thoughts in relation to the questions raised and concerns expressed by my students, and I hope that the arguments put forth will make the learning experience of other students more meaningful. I also hope that the essay will spark off a debate on what the objectives of a managerial economics course should be. This debate must involve not only teachers but also students and ex-student practicing managers. I sincerely feel that a subject like managerial economics is extremely important and useful to professional managers, but in its present form, valuable time and energy is being wasted.

As students of management, a course in managerial economics could in fact be your first introduction to economics. I found my students coming from diverse backgrounds, from literature to mathematics. Whatever their backgrounds, there is always great enthusiasm to learn economics. Students want to comprehend the radical changes that are transforming our societies. And everyone knows that economics is driving a lot of this. This is even more important in countries like India where there are so many apprehensions about as well as expectations from economic liberalization, privatization and globalization. Managers and entrepreneurs are keen to put all the economic news that bombards them day-after-day into perspective and also develop an informed opinion on various issues. Let me give you a simple example: a few years ago in India one question that grabbed the headlines was whether we should allow the import of used cars. I asked my students for their judgment – most of them were reactionary, but after introducing them to what are the possible gains and losses from free trade, they were able to see that there is never a simple yes-no answer to such questions; economics, like many other subjects, is a struggle of beliefs, the outcome of each step becoming the basis for the next.

Rather than inducing debate and discussion on economic issues, the typical approach of managerial economics is professional, like law or engineering. This is reflected in the objective of a managerial economics course, which is now fairly standardized and exemplified in most textbooks – to provide students with a set of tools that will help them solve decision-making problems that they will face as managers. Consider, for instance, the text by Keat & Young, entitled *Managerial Economics: Economic Tools for Today's Decision-Makers*. The text propagates 'managerial economics as the use of economic analysis to make business decisions involving the best use of an organization's scarce resources'. You are then led to believe that once these tools are acquired, you will be in a position to 'apply' them to, and solve, your business problems.

What follows as the contents of the course, the economics tool kit, is microeconomic optimization theory. Students live under the hope that if they are able to define the market structure within which their businesses function, estimate the demand and cost curves, then *voilà*, they will know in no uncertain terms what quantity of output their firm must produce (Q^*) and at what price (p^*) so as to maximize profit ?*). This approach, where students are made to believe that their managerial economics course will provide them a tool kit, leaves students frustrated because sooner or later they come to realize that these tools cannot be 'used' like engineering formulae. And this realization comes at a significant price; after all, the course demands a lot of effort. Even worse, there is a feeling of emptiness – their economics course never touches upon the economic issues that they would have considered relevant.

As a teacher, this left me dissatisfied and led me to think about why standard microeconomics cannot be 'applied' to business decision-making problems. I soon realized that if managerial economics were to serve as a tool kit, it must begin with an economics *of* management, articulating problems confronting the manager from a manager's perspective, taking into account the constraints they actually face, which must then be related to their decision-making problems. But economics was never developed from the manager's viewpoint or context. As Diamantopoulos & Mathews point out,

> Conventional price theory was never intended to serve as a conceptual framework for the study of pricing of the individual firm...price theory has been primarily developed for use in the analysis of broad economic

changes and the evaluation of social controls... Therefore, it would be
unfruitful (and erroneous) to use conventional price theory as a unified
framework to guide the theoretical and empirical study of price
determination within real-world firms.

(Diamantopoulos and Mathews 1995, p. 11.)

Managerial economics is not based on an economics *of* management–the
latter, I think, is a precondition for it to become useful as a tool kit to managers.
What is done instead is to take a standard microeconomics text, replace all
mathematical subscripts (1, ..., n) with 'real' names, put a few case studies in
boxes as 'applications', and make students feel and reinforce the hope that
these economics tools can be 'used' by them. However, when encountered
with a real problem their tools turn out to be inappropriate because these
*micro*economic models were developed to analyze broad economic and social
systems, not a manager's marketing and sales problems – you cannot hammer
a nail into the wall with a screwdriver.

So why not adapt our usual microeconomic models to a manager's context?
Herein lies the problem. When advocating economics as a bag of tools to
managers, the economist must realize that managerial economics suffers from
a case of asymmetric information – what the economist works with and what
a manager actually has to work with. The result: economics fails to give any
answers to, even articulate, the problems of managers.

What is this information that an economist assumes but that a manager
does not have? Recall Part I of your managerial economics course: the *actual*
demand curve. If you browse through an economics or managerial economics
text, you will notice that the demand curve derived from consumer choice
models is taken as the actual demand curve with a known slope and location –
giving information on what consumers are willing to buy at what price. If the
ceteris paribus assumption is relaxed, the economist also knows by how much
the demand curve will shift. The economist then freely uses this demand curve
when she studies firm behavior; whatever the market structure might be.

The conventional managerial economics text 'cheats' the student by
introducing a chapter on demand curve estimation: a brief, nothing kind of
chapter, on how to estimate demand curves. Even if you are told not to attempt
this exercise yourself, given the dangers of estimating a wrong demand curve,
the student feels that 'it can be done nonetheless'. Students can then go about
the rest of the course feeling assured about the usefulness of the course.
Interestingly, this chapter on demand estimation is missing in many (pure)
economics texts.

As a manager or entrepreneur, are you in the economist's privileged position?
Do you have the actual or estimated demand curve for your product on your
table or computer screen? Obviously not. We need only consider all those

cases that Jack Trout discusses in his book, *Big Brands, Big Trouble*: the failure of New Coke, A.1. Poultry Sauce, Xerox computers, Firestone tires. If these companies, with access to the best resources, could have estimated the demand curves for their products, would they not have done so, and so avoided such failures?

The manager does not know and can never know with certainty where the *actual* demand curve lies. In fact, if she *knows* the actual demand curve for the firm's product, there really isn't much of a management problem. With the actual demand curve, all one has to do is to apply the profit-maximizing rule (MR=MC) or any other rule meeting the firm's objective and the firm's balance sheet could be prepared, not just for the current year, but maybe even for the next year. A manager may still have to motivate employees or obtain raw materials from the cheapest source, but those are not usually the problems with which a manager goes to the economist.

It is useful for the economist to delve into the world of managers and entrepreneurs. Al Ries and Jack Trout can provide some useful tips for the economist trying to understand the Economics *of* Management:

- You can't predict the future. So don't plan on it.
- The fatal flaw in many marketing plans is a strategy based on 'predicting the future'.
- Seldom are the predictions obvious. Usually, they are so buried in assumptions that you need a degree in rhetoric to ferret them out.
- Remember Peter's Law: 'The unexpected always happens'.

(Ries and Tron 1998, pp. 44–5.)

There is something more that an economist needs to learn about management before theorizing about it and that is, management is not about 'predicting' the future, but about 'creating' the future (Ries and Trout 1998). It is not enough that top management 'sees' the demand curve for their product but also create it as they desire it to be. In other words, they must not only know what people want but also make them want it – through advertising, building brands, tactics or whatever. Management decision-making is not only about setting p* and Q* given the demand curve but also shifting the demand curve to meet the company's objectives. In his book on entrepreneurship, 'In the Company of Heroes', Hall comments that 'entrepreneurs do not find high profit opportunities, they create them'. (Hall 1999, p. 38.)

We must, however, be fair to the economist. The idea of the actual demand curve being unknown to a manager is not a novel one in Economics. Diamantopoulos and Mathews quote several economists on this point:

'The most challenging problems occur in attempting to estimate the firm's demand schedule, for typically the pricing executive only knows one point in its demand curve – the number of units being sold for the existing price' (Alpert).

'From the standpoint of decision-making, the relevant demand curve is the one on which management basis its pricing and production decisions. This need not be the actual demand curve. From the decision-making standpoint, it suffices that management behaves *as if* it were the demand curve' (Horowitz).

'The demand curve whose image spurts entrepreneurial action will be referred to indiscriminately as the subjective, or imagined, or anticipated demand curve. It may even be called the *ex ante* demand curve' (Weintraub).

(Diamantoloulos and Mathews 1995, p. 19.)

McKenzie and Lee also point out the problem in knowing the actual demand curve:

Saying that the firm must choose the 'right' price is easier than actually choosing it... Managers can never be completely sure what the demand for their company's product is'. (Chapter 12, p. 290.)

The average-cost pricing model in Economics also recognizes the impossibility of a determinate demand curve:

Tastes in the market change continuously and the reaction of the competitors is impossible to predict. Thus firms cannot estimate their future demand. Past experience does not help much in reducing uncertainty, because extrapolation of past conditions in the future is haphazardous given the dynamic changes in the economic structure. Given this uncertainty average-cost pricing theorists reject the demand schedule as a tool of analysis, thus abandoning half the apparatus of the traditional theory of the firm. (Koutsoyiannis 1994, p. 272.)

But outright rejection of the demand curve really 'reduces' the manager to an accountant. All she must do is to compute average cost and add required mark-up, leaving it to the market to determine sales. As managers, do you then sit back and do nothing? Don't you have to engage with the market? Try to influence demand for your products?

Chamberlin (1969) also talks about an actual demand curve and an expected demand curve, the latter being more elastic (quantity demanded will react more strongly to a given price change) than the former. This expected demand curve assumes a manager to be a naïve individual, always repeating the same mistake of not considering the actions of rivals. Once again this approach may be acceptable if Managerial Economics is about telling managers what economists think of them. But the real world is not this way; or most companies would have economists as their CEOs.

So, if managerial economics cannot be a bag of tools, given that we do not have an Economics *of* Management, then we must take a different approach: the path that I have chosen to take is economics *for* managers. And here we need to be honest and give students plain and simple 'economics', not promising them any bag of tools to be 'applied' to their business problems. If managerial economics means economics *for* managers then this course can be considered supportive in nature, providing awareness, insights and a general understanding of the market system – important ingredients for managerial decision-making – but, let me repeat, *not* a tool kit to solve managerial decision-making problems *per se*. More specifically, the course is not intended to make students believe that MC=MR type rules can be 'applied' to solve business decision-making problems.

With this approach, it is also not necessary to limit the course to neoclassical microeconomics – economic history, political economy, institutional economics and even Marxist theory could all provide invaluable insights of the working of a capitalist economy to managers. I usually begin my managerial economics course with a reading of Heilbroner's 'Worldly Philosophers'. Students must understand that economists, not just the neoclassical ones, try to unravel the mystery of the market system, how it works, when and why it fails, where government intervention may be useful and what are the effects of intervention on societal welfare. Managerial economics must be seen in this light – putting the market system in perspective – the efficiency of the market system in a perfectly competitive structure, the deadweight loss from tariffs and quotas, the inefficiency of monopolies, the need for regulation of natural monopolies, excess capacity in monopolistically competitive markets, price and output of firms in oligopolistic markets, market failure under information asymmetry or externalities like pollution, the importance and role of international institutions like the World Trade Organization. There are also several macroeconomic issues that students are keen to familiarize themselves with: fiscal and monetary policy, financial markets, inflation, and so on. As a manager, don't you have to be aware of what led to the South East Asian crisis? Why budget deficits are a concern of many developing country governments? What the implications of capital account convertibility are?

Though students have come to appreciate this approach to managerial economics, I face a problem of methodology: with just one or two courses of 3 to 4 credits each, it becomes difficult to provide students with both rigorous methods of analyses and an introduction to a wide range of issues. Too much method means that students lose interest, and too little of it means that the discussions become intuitive and shallow. This is a question of balance and is a serious challenge that I have been trying to resolve.

To conclude, teaching managerial economics needs to take a clear stance: is it an *economics tool kit for managers* based on an economics *of* management? Since I think this is not the case, because there really is no economics *of* management, we need a more honest approach, *economics for* managers – and here, we need not restrict course contents to neoclassical theory. We should include a wider understanding of economics and economies (managerial economics will have to be, at least to some degree, country-specific). The problem, however, is to balance the discussion of methods and issues.

This conclusion, however, is not the end, only the beginning of my endeavour to chart out a set of objectives and contents for managerial economics. I would appreciate to receive ideas and suggestions on making this subject more interesting and relevant to students and managers, the world over.

REFERENCES

Edward H. Chamberlin (1969) *The Theory of Monopolistic Competition: A Re-orientation of the Theory of Value*, Harvard, Mass.: Harvard University Press.

Adamantios Diamantopoulos & Brian Mathews (1995) *Making Pricing Decisions: A Study of Managerial Practice*, London: Chapman and Hall.

David Hall (1999) *In the Company of Heroes: An Insider's Guide to Entrepreneurs at Work*, London: Kogan Page Limited.

Robert L. Heilbroner (1980) *The Worldly Philosophers: The Lives, Times, and Ideas of the Great Economic Thinkers*, 5th edn, New York: Simon & Schuster.

Paul G. Keat and Philip K.Y. Young (2000) *Managerial Economics: Economic Tools for Today's Decision Maker*, 3rd edn: Prentice-Hall.

A. Koutsoyiannis (1994) *Modern Microeconomics*, Educational Low-Priced Books Scheme, ELBS, with Macmillar Second Edition Hampshire, 1994.

Richard McKenzie & Dwight Lee, *Microeconomics for MBAs*, http://www.gsm.uci.edu/~mckenzie/onlinebooks.htm

Al Ries and Jack Trout (1998) *Bottom-up Marketing*, McGraw-Hill Company, New Yark.

Jack Trout (2001) *Big Brands Big Trouble: Lessons Learnt the Hard Way*, Madras: East West Books.

PART III

MACRO NONSENSE

11

Why Do We Have Separate
Courses in 'Micro' and 'Macro' Economics?

OZGUR GUN

UNIVERSITÉ DE REIMS CHAMPAGNE ARDENNE

A student in economics would be perfectly warranted in asking his teacher (and himself): 'Why do we have separate courses in microeconomics and macroeconomics? Why not just courses in simple, or elementary, 'economic theory', and then courses in advanced 'economic theory'?'

Textbooks often try to answer these questions – as their authors know that they are inescapable. They generally argue that there exists a kind of ' division of labour ': micro treats of 'relative prices' and 'resource allocation', and macro is interested in 'levels' of production (GNP), of consumption, of investment, general price level, etc. But if this 'division of labour' really holds, why are employment, intertemporal choice (savings and investment) and growth theory studied in macro textbooks? And why are these books nowadays full of maximising households and firms, with given prices, just like micro textbooks are? If everything – including the level of investment – can be reduced to agents' choices, then there is no reason for having a separate course in macroeconomics; there should be no difference between micro and macro.

In fact, the synthesis of micro and macroeconomics is not possible: there is 'no bridge' between them – and there will never be, for (obvious) methodological reasons. Although it is true that certain theoreticians pretend to give 'microfoundations' to macro, they do so by assuming that the economy is reduced to an unique single agent – misleadingly called 'representative agent' – an assumption in contradiction with the very essence of microeconomics: diversity of agents, without which there can be no exchange.

All these points are developed in this chapter.

WHY A SEPARATE COURSE IN MACROECONOMICS?

There is a very simple answer to this question: because microeconomics is of no practical use; as it supposes fictitious agents living in fictitious institutions, it has essentially no relation with the real world around us, present or past (see chapter by Benicourt above). It is purely speculative.

But governments and firms have to take decisions on important economic questions: taxes, public spending, interest rates, production, investment, etc. To do this, they need to be informed about the economic situation in the country – that is why statistics are collected by all sorts of institutions (public and private).They also need theories, and/or models, from which they can deduce, or predict, the consequences of their decisions (policies). These theories, or models, generally start with a few simple relations, valid in the average, obtained from observation of present and past facts. Such is, for example, the case of the 'quantitative theory of money', Keynes's 'consumption function' or the 'investment accelerator' model.

One fundamental point about these relations is that they concern *aggregates*: national income, consumption, investment, saving, employment, money supply, price level, etc., and not specific goods or agents (it is why they can be true only 'on average'). Another point is that they are *observed* (not *deduced*): they are founded on more or less evident 'psychological' facts (as observed behaviours) or 'technical' relations (as capital output ratio); they are generally not deduced from a maximising program (even if behaviours are supposed to be rational, in an elementary way). The parameters (or coefficients) of these macro relations can be estimated by statistical methods (econometrics) applied to (aggregate) data – the theoretician's work consists in selecting which variables are pertinent, and in deciding whether they are endogenous or exogenous.

Traditional macroeconomics was conceived in this global (or 'holistic', as some prefer to say) way. The *IS-LM* model is typical of such an approach: it supposes two (aggregate) behavioural relations (consumption function and the demand for money, money supply being exogenous), and an accounting identity (income is the sum of consumption and saving, or investment). Governments can use the *IS-LM* model to make predictions (of greater or lesser quality) and to determine (with more or less precision) specific policy consequences. The main point here is that macroeconomics was, from the very beginning, conceived to be 'operational' – it tried to explain, using statistical data, what happens in the real world, and was intended to propose policies (or regulations) to transform this real world. Macroeconomics was thus developed *in opposition* to microeconomics and its fictitious worlds.

MICRO AND MACRO: AGGREGATING GOODS

Macroeconomics became increasingly important with the Great Depression that set in after 1929. The consensus according to which all problems would go away if markets were only more 'flexible' (as we say today) and that policies should aim at 'suppressing everything that prevents markets from adjusting – especially labour markets' had broken down. Government intervention was becoming more and more massive in all capitalist countries.

The ideas of theorists like Keynes – who didn't believe in the efficiency of 'market mechanisms' and of *laissez-faire* – became widespread, and even, dominant; their proponents aimed (and still aim) at justifying government intervention. Activist government policies being, in fact, widely accepted, economists got accustomed to macro arguments justifying them and became used to the coexistence (separate existence) of macroeconomics alongside microeconomics. But, at the same time, it was obvious that micro and macro approaches were (and are) fundamentally different, as the former starts from individuals' choices deduced from certain axioms or postulates, whereas the latter takes as its starting point observed relations between aggregates, valid only 'on average'.

Indeed, there seems to exist an easy (or logical) way to bridge the gap between these two approaches: as society is formed of individuals, it should be possible to obtain its (global) production, consumption, investment, growth, cycles, etc. by simply *adding up* individual choices (concerning production, consumption, etc.). If this were to be possible, the distinction between macro and micro would be superfluous: a unified theory would thus be achieved, and methodological individualism (the neoclassical principle according to which all explanation should proceed from individual choices) would be respected. Macroeconomists have not, however, chosen this (apparently obvious) solution because, in any society, there are many goods and many individuals, and they are interested in a *global approach*. That is why they construct aggregates like GNP (gross national product), consumption, investment, capital, and so on.

The main problem with aggregates resides in the fact that they can only be concocted by combining prices *and* quantities. And prices, for instance, depend – if they are not completely arbitrary – on agents' tastes, on technology, resources, customs, laws, bargaining, etc. Aggregates synthesise a lot of information (including social relations). It is then nonsense to treat relations between aggregates as if they were micro relations (i.e. assuming that these aggregates behave 'as if' they were simply quantities of goods). Which is what is regularly done in the case of the (unhappily) famous aggregate production function $F(K, L)$: prices (here, the interest rate and the wage level) are supposed to be deduced from the amount or quantity of capital (through the 'marginal' relation $F'_K(K, L) = r$ and $F'_L(K, L) = w$) ; but the amount or quantity of capital can only be measured by using a system of prices (as capital is, by definition, the *value* of a stock of goods: machines, inputs, etc.). This circular way of reasoning – prices depend on aggregates which themselves depend on prices – has been criticised for a long time (in the famous 'two Cambridge' controversy).

Contemporary textbooks generally ignore the problem involved in aggregating goods. Sometimes, they say that they proceed as if there were *only one good* ('corn' for example); but this doesn't stop them from speaking, later on, of 'markets for goods' (in the *plural*). Sometimes, they make up some stupid imaginary examples, as in Barro and Sala-i-Martin's textbook on *Economic Growth*: 'One way to think about the one-sector technology is to draw an analogy with farm animals, which can be eaten or used as inputs to produce more farm animals. The literature on economic growth has used more inventive examples – with such terms as *shmoos, putty,* or *ectoplasm* – to reflect the easy transmutation [sic!] of capital goods into consumables, and vice versa' (Barro and Sala-i-Martin, 1995, p. 18). No comment…

MICRO AND MACRO: AGGREGATING CHOICES

To deduce macro relations from micro ones, it is thus supposed that there is only one (physical) good – i.e. macro is simply micro in a one-good world. Actual national income, consumption, investment, etc – even if they are evaluated through a system of prices – are considered 'as if' they were amounts of 'corn'. What do households choose, then? They have two decisions to make:

- first, they must decide which part of the product (in 'corn') is consumed – the remaining part is invested (allowing future consumption);
- second, households must choose between work and leisure.

Firms produce corn from corn not consumed ('invested') by households, and from their work. It is then possible to think about 'markets', of 'present' and 'future' corn, and labour. But, as markets presuppose prices, one has to deal with the main (and, in fact, unsolved) problem in microeconomics: price formation.

Just as microeconomists do, macroeconomists also give a prominent place to the so-called 'perfect competition model' – prices in this model are supposed to be 'given', and agents are supposed to act as 'price takers' (see chapter by Benicourt above) Their supplies and demands are then aggregated in a 'macro' perspective to obtain 'global' production, consumption, investment, employment, etc. But for a long time economists have known that it is not possible, generally, to obtain a consistent 'global' choice starting from consistent 'individual' choices – for instance, it is possible that transitive individual preferences are, after aggregation, no longer transitive.

Moreover, it was proved – by Hugo Sonnenschein (1972) – that excess aggregate (competitive) demands can have *any* form whatever, so that when prices and quantities start adjusting 'anything can happen', as it is recognized by Mas-Colell, Whinston and Green (1995) in their advanced textbook *Microeconomic Theory*. One consequence of Sonnenschein's 'theorem' is that it is not possible to 'give microfoundations' to usual macro relations (especially those supposed to describe aggregate behaviour). For instance, aggregated excess demand for a given good need not be a decreasing function of the price of this good. One understands why macro textbooks *never* allude to Sonnenschein's demonstration which destroys intuitive belief about the relation between aggregate supply and demand.

Obviously, it is always possible to *assume* global behavioural relations between aggregates – as is done in Keynes' consumption function – but one doesn't need microeconomics for that (the relations are deduced from direct observation; econometrics can be of some use here). It is quite difficult for neoclassical economists to accept that there is no 'bridge' between micro and macro – and that microeconomics is generally not needed and not useful for studying concrete problems. Indeed, as macroeconomics progressively became a patchwork of some neoclassical ideas combined with some of Keynes' ideas, inconsistencies emerged. As is so usual with neoclassical economists, the 'as if' argument is then invoked to get out of this uncomfortable situation: proceed 'as if' there is only one agent in the economy, call him the 'representative agent', and compare his choices with real economy aggregates, in a 'macro' perspective. And thus, unfortunately, 'New macroeconomics' was born.

NEW MACROECONOMICS: ROBINSON CRUSOE HAS RETURNED

Such a counterintuitive result as Sonnenschein's theorem is possible only if agents are – in some way – heterogeneous (different from each other) so that there are reasons for exchange to take place between them. The easiest way to get rid of Sonnenschein result is, then, to get rid of heterogeneity, by assuming that there is only one agent – or that there are many identical agents. This is the solution retained, at the beginning of the 1970s, by the so-called 'new macroeconomics' – or 'rational expectations revolution'. So, it is said, macroeconomics now has 'microfoundations', and theory is, finally, unified – indeed, macro is absorbed by micro. This so-called 'revolution' is, in fact, a regression, a return, with a lot of 'new' maths, to the old Robinson Crusoe fable.

New-fashion macroeconomists are so amazingly naïve that they don't even try to hide this! For example, Part 1 of Robert Barro's popular textbook

Macroeconomics – about 'microfoundations and the basic market-clearing model' (Barro, 1984, p. 25) – starts with a chapter the title of which is: 'The economy of Robinson Crusoe'. Another famous textbook, Barro and Sala-i-Martins' *Growth Theory*, studies a 'consumer/producer in the Robinson Crusoe style' economy (Barro and Sala-i-Marin, 1995, p. 18). Typically, papers or textbooks of the 'new macroeconomics' kind start with sentences like the following: 'The model economy we consider is populated by a single infinite-life individual (or a constant number of identical individuals) with given initial resources, production possibilities, and tastes. The individual ('Robinson Crusoe') chooses a preferred consumption-production plan...' (Long and Plosser, 1983, p. 43). Or the following: 'There is a large number of identical firms... There is also a large number of identical households... [The firms] are owned by the households' (Romer, 1996, p. 44).

It is easy to find dozens of quotations of the same type. Often, however, they don't use the Crusoe metaphor: they prefer to refer to a 'representative agent' – although it is exactly the same thing, it looks a bit more plausible. But it is misleading. Because, for a normal person, a 'representative' agent must 'represent' a lot of different people – as does a member of Parliament or any elected person. As people are different, their 'representative' is a kind of aggregate, trying to conciliate their interests or projects. However, the 'representative agent' of new macroeconomists is not 'representative' in this way: He is *identical* with the people that he 'represents' – because only *identical* agents are considered. Why are only identical agents considered? Because aggregation of non-identical agents creates problems. But, if people are 'identical', they have no reason for trading (exchange results from *differences*, in tastes, endowments, technologies): the situation is exactly the same if there is one or 'many identical' persons. 'Representative agent' is, thus, another name for Robinson Crusoe: new macroeconomics is 'Crusoe microeconomics' and, therefore, devoid of usefulness–it is even a regression in comparison with the 'old' (IS-LM) macroeconomics. Moreover, it is nonsense. New macroeconomists probably feel this, as they practically *never* try to justify the representative agent assumption. In the alphabetical index, at the end of their books or textbooks, they often 'forget' to mention him (as also happens with the 'auctioneer', in the index of microeconomics textbooks).

Actually, some neoclassical economists – among the most prestigious ones are Robert Solow and Frank Hahn – have distanced themselves from this assumption. Twelve years ago, Alan Kirman – a first-level mathematical economist – published a paper in one of the profession's most popular reviews, *The Journal of Economic Perspectives*, (see Kirman, 1992) in which he explains, from a strictly neoclassical point of view, that a representative agent doesn't 'represent' anything and that macroeconomics is going in a bad direction with this kind of assumption. More than ten years after, we are still waiting for an answer to Kirman from (at least) one among the hundreds of those who publish papers with a 'representative agent'.

'REPRESENTATIVE AGENT' MODELS: NONSENSE

All economics textbooks start by explaining that the first thing to do, in social science, is to distinguish positive from normative propositions. This is an elementary methodological rule. All macro textbooks also explain that representative agent models are derived from Ramsey (1928) and Cass (1965) models, both of which are *normative* (they are interested in a society's *best path* – Cass refers explicitly to the path that an all-seeing central planner would choose). But, at the same time, they present representative agent models as *positive* models, and try to fit the model with existing data (through 'calibration' and other techniques): observed GNP, employment, consumption, investment of a country during, say, 10 years, are thus compared with what a 'representative agent's' intertemporal choice would be – taking into account observed 'shocks'. This is *total nonsense*: How can any reasonable person admit that, for example, the evolution of US aggregates' results from decisions made by a single individual who owns all factories and who decides how much to produce, how much labour to use, how production will be distributed between consumption and investment, and so on? It is quite incredible that the majority of a profession (which pretends to be 'scientific') readily indulges in this kind of absurdity, teaches it, and does a lot of 'research' on it – with maths, statistics, and computers – attempting to specify the representative agent's 'parameters' (that is, coefficients in his utility and production functions) which allow good fits with observed aggregate data.

Indeed, some scholars – especially, (neoclassical) macroeconomists of the old generation – try to protest against this state of things, as Frank Hahn and Robert Solow who complain that in the 'new macroeconomics':

> the actual economy can be read as if it is acting out or approximating the infinite-life discounted utility maximising program of a single, immortal 'representative agent'. The only admissible constraints come from initial resources, a supply of labour, and a well-behaved technology for turning produced means of production and labour into consumer goods and produced means of production. That means that the economy accurately carries out the wishes of the representative agent... It has become good to treat just such a model as a descriptive macro model that needs only be estimated or calibrated and then directly applied to this economy or that... What Ramsey took to be a normative model, useful for working out what an idealised omniscient planner should do, has been transformed into a model for interpreting last year's and next

year's national accounts. (*A critical essay on modern macroeconomics*, Hahn and Solow, 1995, p. 2)[1] .

PERFECT COMPETITION WITH…ONLY ONE AGENT !

Representative agent models are, in their structure, very simple: they study Robinson Crusoe's (intertemporal) choice – that is, they determine the 'consumption-leisure' sequence $(c_t{}^*, l_t{}^*)_{t \in lN}$ which maximises Robinson Crusoe's intertemporal utility function $U(\cdot)$ subject to technological constraints (the product share that is not consumed, at each period, is invested for the next period's production). This is a typical dynamic programming problem – it is formally similar to the program that an engineer has to solve when he wants to determine the 'best path' (minimum use of fuel) for a rocket, given its target. It is a problem for an engineer, *not* for an economist. And, it can be very complicated to solve (as always with non-linear programs). Indeed, generally, it is not possible to find the exact optimal path, but only successive approximations of it (using computers and so on). So, the door is open to a lot of 'work', and 'papers', about maths and econometric techniques that try to get an 'as good as possible' approximation for the optimal path, with different kinds of utility and production functions, and 'shocks'. As unknowns (paths) are sequences or functions (and not numbers, as in common micro problems), Hamiltonians replace Lagrangians, and first order conditions take the form of differential equations; as there is an unlimited horizon, 'transve-rsality' conditions exclude infinite solutions, and so on. These are very complicated problems; but they are Robinson Crusoe's problems – not ours! As economists, we are interested in exchanges, prices, distribution, money, and so on. But, as Robinson Crusoe lives all alone, there are no exchanges, no prices, no money in his world – only quantities of goods, of leisure (or labour).

Now, 'new macroeconomics' papers and books are full of 'prices', 'markets', 'competition', 'money'. How can this nonsense be possible? Well, as Hal Varian naïvely explains in his ('intermediary' or 'advanced') microeconomics textbooks, Robinson Crusoe is in fact 'schizophrenic': he is at the same time a firm and a household – so that he employs himself and sells (and buys) to himself. At what prices ? Well, as everybody is so accustomed with the 'perfect competition' equations : $F'_w(K_t{}^*, L_t{}^*) = w_t$ and $F'_K(K_t{}^*, L_t{}^*) = r_t$, it seems 'natural' to say: Robinson pays himself (and earns) a wage equal to the marginal productivity of labour (the unique good serving as *numéraire*), and pays (to himself) an interest equal to the marginal productivity of capital. Why not, since all this is just an imaginary 'story'?

The problem is that it is a misleading and inconsistent story: in microeconomics courses, students are taught that the main characteristic of perfect competition is that agents are *price takers*, but here Robinson is a *price* *maker*. That is, in 'perfect competition', a relation as $F'_w(K_t, L_t) = w_t$, is read 'from right to left' (i.e. *given* w_t, demand of labour L_t^* is determined); in the 'representative agent' parable it is read 'from left to right': Robinson computes *first* the best intertemporal sequence $(K_t^*, L_t^*)_{t \in IN}$, and *then* deduces wages and interest rates, w_t and r_t, associated with this sequence.

You must be a trained (and motivated) student to understand these subtleties – which are *never* explained in textbooks (and for obvious reasons: because the whole story is absurd). Furthermore, because all your life but especially as an economics student, you have heard that 'competition' is almost synonymous with 'many agents', there are only two alternatives open to you:

1. you can decide that economics is really too difficult a matter to understand ('because of maths') or

2. you can accept the quite evident fact that all these models with a 'representative agent' (called Robinson Crusoe or not) are nonsense.

Obviously, the second possibility is the right one. But it is difficult for a mere, poor student to accept the idea that all these professors and doctors – some of them Nobel Prize laureates – have built their careers on such nonsense.

REPRESENTATIVE AGENT OR CENTRAL PLANNER?

It is common with neoclassical economics that nonsense (or, in other words, the model's 'lack of realism') is hidden or camouflaged by equations. In the 'representative agent' case, confusion comes from the fact that the model is presented in the microeconomic mood:[2] (present and future) prices are given, households and firms 'take prices' and make decisions on supply and demand at these prices. How can this have any sense at all when there is only one household which is also the owner of the unique firm? Well, remember that almost all 'representative agent' models start by supposing that 'there are many identical agents'. A 'trained' economist will then first of all associate the idea 'many' with the idea 'competition', and, secondly, with the idea of 'price taking'. He will then say to himself: 'OK. All this is consistent: since there is perfect competition, it is normal that there are prices'. This is a misleading association of ideas since the important key word here is not 'many', but 'identical'. As people are identical, there are no exchanges, and then, prices are not needed. It is, once again, the 'schizophrenic Robinson Crusoe' – who, now, is split into *three* persons, as he also plays the role of the auctioneer who sets prices, computes (his own) supplies and demands, and determines equilibrium prices.

After many pages dedicated to computing the supplies and demands of the schizophrenic agent, at given prices, and then finding the 'equilibrium' solution, textbook authors arrive at the optimal path $(c_t^*, l_t^*)_{t \in IN}$ (or, equivalently, $(K_t^*,$

$L_t^*)_{t \in \mathbb{N}}$)! That is, a result that could have been obtained directly-without prices, without supplies and demands, and without 'markets' – simply by maximising the 'representative agent' utility function under technological constraints. Obviously, this is not surprising for anybody who knows that the model is of the (one agent) Robinson Crusoe type. Indeed, after having determined the 'competitive equilibrium', textbook authors often admit this, when they write, for example: 'In short, the solution to the social planner's problem is for the initial value of c to be given by the value on the saddle path, and for c and k to then move along the saddle path. That is, the competitive equilibrium maximises the welfare of the representative household' (Romer, 1996, p. 126) or: 'We could also consider that the economy is governed by a benevolent planner who decides choices over time and who intends to maximise the representative agent's utility. If the planner has identical preferences as those assumed before, the solution will then be identical to that of a decentralised economy' (Barro and Sala-i-Martins, 1995, p. 80).

Since this so-called 'decentralised economy' is, in fact, a centralised one (with an auctioneer and price taker agents – see chapter by Benicourt), the situation is the same in both cases – and so also the result. But it takes a very clever student to see that the 'representative agent' model, the 'social (or benevolent) planner' model and the 'competitive' model with 'many identical agents' are, formally and basically, exactly the *same* model. On the other hand a student must be quite foolish to believe that this model 'describes' or 'explains' what happens – or has happened – in the societies in which we live.

ROBINSON MASOCHIST

Representative agent models try to fit real data with those given by the model. To do this, different kinds of 'calibrations' are used – utility and production functional forms, types of 'shocks', etc. But, often, such degrees of freedom are not enough, especially if 'a good fit' concerns many aggregates (production, employment, investment, etc.). Then, to improve the fit and to make the model 'more realistic' (as the expression goes), 'imperfections' are added: in 'real life', there are 'rigidities' such as taxes, government regulations, money controls, and so on. The clever student would ask: 'this is crazy: why would Robinson Crusoe, or identical agents, need all this?' He would be absolutely correct, but this is not enough to change his teacher's mind.

How are these 'imperfections' added to the assumptions? Well, with imagination everything is possible. Robinson can impose a rule on himself, a rule which limits his working day (say, no more than 8 working hours per day). He can decide that he pays taxes to a 'government' (to himself), who uses them in a definite way (that is, independently of Robinson's intertemporal choice). He can invent a 'Central Bank' (himself again), who supplies him with money, and imposes a 'liquidity' constraint on his maximising program. And so on. As Robinson's choices will then depend on a greater number of parameters (length of the working day, money supply, tax level, etc.), there is the possibility of getting better fits with real data – by a parameter's 'calibration'. Obviously, even if the fit is very good, all this is still total nonsense.

CONCLUSION

Students *need* to study macroeconomics – that is, relations between aggregates such as GNP, consumption and investment, price level, unemployment, money supply and so on. Why? Because macroeconomics is concerned with real-life problems and serves as a guide for policy. That means collecting statistics, constructing aggregates, finding relations between them–with the help, at least, of some (simple) theory. But there is *no need* to give 'microfoundations' to macroeconomics. Indeed, it is impossible if there are many goods and agents. And it is ridiculous and nonsensical to proceed 'as if' the whole economy acts as a unique agent–even if he is called 'representative'.

REFERENCES

Barro Robert J. and Sala-i-Martin Xavier (1995), *Economic Growth*, New York, McGraw-Hill.

Cass David (1965), 'Optimum Growth in an Aggregative Model of Capital Accumulation', *Review of Economic Studies*, vol. 32, no. 3, pp. 233–240.

Hahn Frank and Solow Robert (1995), A *Critical Essay on Modern Macroeconomic Theory*, Oxford, Blackwell Publishers.

Keynes John M. (1936), *The General Theory of Employment, Interest, and Money*, Macmillan Cambridge University Press, for Royal Economic Society.

Kirman Alan P. (1992), 'Whom or What Does The Representative Individual Represent?', *Journal of Economic Perspectives*, vol. 6, no. 2, pp. 117–136.

Long John B. and Plosser Charles I. (1983), 'Real Business Cycles', *Journal of Political Economy*, vol. 91, no. 1, pp. 39–69.

Mas-Collel Andrew, Whinston Micheal D. and Green Jerry R. (1995), *Microeconomic Theory*, Oxford, Oxford University Press.

Ramsey F.P. (1928), 'A *Mathematical Theory of Saving*', Economic Journal, vol. 38, no. 152, pp. 543–559.

Sonnenschein Hugo (1972), '*Market Excess Demand Functions*', Econometrica, vol. 40, no. 3, pp. 549–563.

12

The 'Natural' Rate of Unemployment

JAMES G. DEVINE

LOYOLA MARYMOUNT UNIVERSITY, USA

This chapter aims to help us understand the 'natural' rate of unemployment (NRU) and its limitations. This concept is a central part of the neo-liberal or *laissez-faire* view of macroeconomics. This chapter looks at the issue in reference to United States, both theoretically and empirically. The U.S. is probably the best place to understand the issues, since it is the closest to being a closed capitalist economy. There, the NRU theory should apply in the purest form, with a smaller role for exchange-rate fluctuations and the like to confuse inflationary dynamics.

We will start with the history and implications of the NRU. Then, this concept will be described in greater detail, leading up to criticism. Finally, this chapter sketches some conclusions.

FROM FULL EMPLOYMENT TO THE NATURAL RATE

Due to the extreme unemployment encountered during the 1930s, *full employment* (low unemployment) became a major policy goal. But concerns with creeping inflation colored such commitments during the 1950s. This crystallized in the famous Phillips curve, named after economist A.W. Phillips: this was a trade-off between unemployment and inflation. No single 'full employment' unemployment rate exists. Rather, we can 'buy' higher employment only by suffering greater inflation. Or we could obtain lower inflation by enduring higher unemployment.

During the 1970s, the dread disease of 'stagflation' struck Phillips-Curve thinking: for example, unemployment rose from 3.5 to 5 per cent from 1969 to

1970, but inflation stayed high. This combination of high unemployment and inflation rates contradicted the idea of a simple trade-off, making many economists willing to accept the NRU theory, previously developed by *laissez-faire* economists Milton Friedman and Edmund Phelps.

In the NRU view, inflation *accelerates* (gets worse) when the actual unemployment rate persists below the NRU. Something like this happened during the period 1966 to 1969, with unemployment rates below 4 per cent: consumer-price inflation tripled from 1.9 per cent in 1965 to 6.2 per cent in 1969. Going the other way, inflation slows when unemployment stays above the NRU. This *disinflation* was encouraged by unemployment of almost 10 per cent during 1982 and 1983, resulting from the Federal Reserve's high interest rate policy. Inflation rates fell from over 12 per cent in 1980 to about 4 per cent in 1983.

Further, the NRU (somewhere between 5 and 7 per cent of the civilian labor force) is seen as an *economic equilibrium*: if the economy attains it, the inflation rate stays constant, unless there is a shock to the system. This vision returns us to the idea of a unique full-employment unemployment rate. Unlike for earlier thinkers, however, it is not something that's desired. It's something we're stuck with. Thus, economists rarely use the phrase 'full employment' these days.

The NRU corresponds to problems in labor markets that prevent instant adjustment to changes in the economy. These involve classical unemployment (where real wages are too high compared to an assumed equilibrium wage), frictional unemployment (where workers are temporarily between jobs), and structural unemployment (where the economy's dynamic changes leave pockets of workers with skills or in locations that do not correspond to available job openings).

In this view, the economy 'naturally' persists where productive inputs are scarce. So the Central Bank's monetary policy has no permanent effect except on the rate of inflation. Thus, the *only* goal of the Central Bank is to control inflation. As for the other form of demand-management policy (fiscal policy), government deficits simply compete with the private sector for scarce resources and so should be avoided. In theory, such deficits could be used to finance government investment, raising the economy's potential rather than merely crowding out the private sector. But NRU theory is usually part of the broader neo-liberal package, which sees the government as essentially useless beyond its military and police roles. NRU theory also rules out wage and price controls (incomes policies), since they lead to shortages of products, illegal markets, and the like. The bureaucratic costs of such programs correspond to few if any benefits.

Despite its name, the NRU is not fixed. For example, it rises or falls as populations that are more prone to unemployment (such as untrained youth) become more or less represented in the labor force. More crucially, it can (in theory) be reduced by policies that 'reform' labor markets. There is nothing in NRU theory that says that this cannot involve (for example) training of workers for available jobs or even efforts to stop disruptions arising from capital mobility that cause structural unemployment. But these are discouraged by other parts of the neo-liberal package. So the emphasis is on attacking unemployment seen as arising from welfare-state programs, minimum wages, and labor unions. For example, the NRU can be lowered if unemployment insurance benefits are more miserly, undermining the assumed incentive to be unemployed.

UNDERSTANDING THE NRU

The word 'natural' is a rhetorical trick, since there's nothing natural about the NRU. Even its advocates see it as a result of non-natural institutions in labor markets. Other names have been adopted, for example, the inflation-threshold unemployment rate or the long-run equilibrium unemployment rate. For many, it's called the NAIRU, the Non-Accelerating Inflation Rate of Unemployment.

As noted in the references to the late 1960s and early 1980s above, there is some real-world basis for some of the ideas behind the NRU. The key variable is expectations of future inflation, which rise (or fall) based on experience with inflation. They also tend to persist, to have inertia.

Inflation accelerates as the economy persists below the NRU because high inflation becomes a self-fulfilling prophecy. Demand pressure encourages faster inflation than is currently expected. That encourages inflationary expectations to rise as people adapt to perceived reality. Worse, this feeds back to raise the actual inflation rate as people act on their expectations. With persistently high rates of unemployment, on the other hand, inflation moderates. Low demand encourages prices to grow more slowly than expected. So inflationary expectations fall, feeding back to reduce actual inflation. Finally, at some medium rate of unemployment, actual inflation equals the expected inflation rate, so that both stay constant; no acceleration or deceleration of inflation rates occurs.

The subjective nature of inflationary expectations suggests that disinflation is relatively painless. People simply have to change their minds. This perspective opens the way to the *rational expectations* theory, in which high unemployment is seen as an extremely short-lived phenomenon because inflationary expectations have no inertia. People adjust expectations following their understanding of the workings of the economic system (rather than extrapolating past inflation into the future). For example, people might think that money-supply growth is the only source of inflation. So if the Central

Bank slows that growth, this theory says that people will instantly cut their inflationary expectations, reducing actual inflation.

CRITIQUE OF THE NRU THEORY

As the NRU became a fixture in textbooks and policy, critiques arose. Instead of a full survey of this literature, consider only several major points.

Inflationary Persistence: many have emphasized the objective side of inertial inflation. For inflationary expectations to persist, people and institutions must have the *power* to act on their expectations. Thus, inflation is more likely to persist to the extent that corporations are shielded from product-market competition and workers belong to labor unions. Further, the objective inflationary process can take on a life of its own, as in the famous price/wage spiral, which works with, and is reinforced by, inflationary expectations. First, rising prices encourage workers to push for higher money (nominal) wages to avoid or reverse falling real living standards (this may be written into contracts as cost-of-living escalators.) Then employers protect their profit margins by passing on wage increases as higher prices. That, in turn, encourages higher money wages, so the process might continue indefinitely. This process has been described as 'conflict inflation,' since the fight between employers and employees over the creation and distribution of the product can cause inertial inflation. It may be reinforced by 'wage-wage' inflation, in which workers push for nominal wage increases in step with those received by others.

This inertia is not immune to high or low unemployment. But it does tend to persist longer than inflation based solely on subjective expectations. Further, it works asymmetrically. Whereas workers are relatively happy with nominal raises even if they fall behind price inflation, they resent money wage cuts. They thus resist those cuts, discouraging disinflation. This does not rule out disinflation. Rather, it means that efforts to fight severe inflation using only demand restraint can be extremely painful. In the U.S., the 1980s disinflation meant persistent high unemployment, union-busting, and destruction of much of the Northeastern industrial belt. Further, monetary tightness triggered a Latin American debt crisis. In this perspective, incomes policies can reinforce demand-based anti-inflation campaigns, making them more efficient.

Inertial inflation also suggests a larger role for supply shocks (such as the oil-price hikes of the 1970s) than that which is usually allowed in the NRU literature. A rapid increase in oil prices depresses both real wages and profit margins in oil-dependent sectors, intensifying the price/wage spiral. Since the distributional conflict cannot be easily solved with demand-side policies, persistent stagflation results.

The Wide NRU: to Friedman, the NRU corresponds to the level of employment 'which would be ground out by the Walrasian system of general equilibrium...including market imperfections ...the cost of gathering information about job vacancies and labor availabilies, the costs of mobility, and so on' (1968, p. 8). This refers to one of economists' tall tales, that of Léon Walras about an imaginary world where perfect markets are guided by an all-knowing Auctioneer. But then it tries to bring a large number of snakes into this Garden of Eden. Unfortunately, no one has ever combined multiple 'imperfections' with a Walrasian model. Crucially, there is no reason why the NRU should be unique.

Long before Friedman and Phelps, Abba Lerner (1951) developed a version of the NRU theory. Unlike the current orthodoxy, he saw a *range* of full-employment unemployment rates. 'High full employment' (low unemployment) could be attained using incomes policies, but only 'low full employment' (high unemployment) without. If we accept the neo-liberal taboo against incomes policies, we miss much of the economy's potential, while condemning many workers to unneeded misery.

The idea that the NRU is not a unique number has been seen in recent empirical research. Staiger, Stock, and Watson (1997) found that the range of possible values of the NRU (from 4.3 to 7.3 per cent unemployment) was too large to be useful to macroeconomic policy-makers. Robert Eisner (1997) suggested that for 1956–95 there was a zone from about 5 per cent to about 10 per cent unemployment between the low-unemployment realm of accelerating inflation and the high-unemployment realm of disinflation. In between, he found that inflation falls with falling unemployment.

The changing NRU: as noted, there is nothing in NRU theory that says that this threshold is constant. But few if any NRU-oriented economists were ready for the late 1990s, when unemployment persisted at about 5 per cent but inflation rates fell. In response, some pointed to beneficial supply shocks (such as low oil prices or the inflation-suppressing effects of a high dollar exchange rate). Robert J. Gordon (1997) and others tried to save NRU theory by making it vary over time. But this simply repeats one of the major flaws of empirical studies of inflation: because NRU estimates are not based on independent study of labor markets but instead on studies of unemployment/inflation dynamics alone, such estimates tend to follow the actual unemployment rate. If the estimated NRU is based on the path of actual unemployment, that undermines the policy usefulness of the NRU theory.

Further, it makes the hysteresis hypothesis more plausible: contrary to Friedman, for who causation goes only one way, the actual unemployment rate can affect the NRU. As Shaun Hargreaves-Heap (1980) pointed out, persistently high unemployment does not simply undermine inertial inflation. It also encourages a rise in structural unemployment (as, perhaps, in Thatcher-era England), by destroying the value of workers' skills, demoralizing them, and by creating pockets of poverty. The pain created by anti-inflation campaigns can be permanent! Similarly, persistently high demand can erode structural unemployment, lowering the NRU or its range (as perhaps in the U.S. during the 1990s). As he suggests, this re-establishes an inflation/unemployment trade-off.

Recent mainstream research has suggested another reason why the estimated NRU can change. Workers may have 'aspirations' of attaining a specific level of real wages that is above that which is possible currently (given labor productivity). They will thus keep on pushing up nominal wages to attain that desired level, encouraging inertial inflation. Higher unemployment is needed to keep these aspirations from causing accelerating inflation. Ironically, this turn toward the conflict theory of inflation fits well with the Marxian theory, i.e., that some unemployment is needed to undermine the bargaining power of workers and to preserve profitability. This 'reserve army of the unemployed' is an addition to the usual trio of frictional, structural, and classical unemployment. Unlike the last two, this type of unemployment is beneficial to those with the most political and economic power in the system (the capitalists). This theory suggests that, all else constant, estimates of the NRU would be higher when profit rates are low (as in the 1970s), since a larger reserve army would be needed to restore profitability.

CONCLUSION

The history of the 1970s to the 1990s contradicts the NRU theory, suggesting that a new theory will arise. But there is currently no new consensus, so that the NRU theory continues to dominate textbooks. The current theory of the inflation/unemployment connection can be summarized as involving three main elements that can be added up to give the total inflation rate:

1. demand inflation, due to currently low unemployment.

2. supply inflation, due to sudden, large, and persistent increases in the cost of raw materials and/or imported goods.

3. inertial inflation, which can rise due to persistent and extreme low unemployment or due to supply shocks.

All three of these can work in the other direction. Note that the Phillips Curve survives as element #1. Unlike the early version, this curve can shift due to the other two factors.

As for the NRU, the criticisms discussed above suggest that anti-inflation campaigns are far from painless, that this crucial unemployment rate is unknown and could be a range of unemployment rates, changes over time in an uncertain way, and reflects 'sociological factors' such as the balance of class power. This opens the way for the use of incomes policies and the use of government deficits to steer the economy, while making the Central Bank's monetary policy more unfixed and intuitive.

Thus, the avoidance of low unemployment rates by the Central Bank might reflect Michal Kalecki's political theory: low unemployment threatens to undermine worker discipline in the workplace and to offend financiers by causing inflation (Kalecki 1971). If so, that might explain why the NRU theory has been so popular, i.e., that it takes a political issue and tries to end the debate by invoking a 'natural' explanation.

SELECTED REFERENCES

Ball, Laurence and Robert Moffitt (2001) 'Productivity Growth and the Phillips Curve', in Alan B. Krueger and Robert M. Solow, eds, The Roaring Nineties: Can Full Employment Be Sustained?, New York: Century Foundation Press.

Blanchard, Olivier and Lawrence Katz (1997) 'What We Know and Do Not Know about the Natural Rate of Unemployment', Journal of Economic Perspectives, 11 (1) Winter: 51–72.

Burdekin, Richard C. K. and Paul Burkett (1996) Distributional Conflict and Inflation: Theoretical and Historical Perspectives, New York: St. Martin's Press.

Carlin, Wendy and Soskice, David (1990) Macroeconomics and the Wage Bargain: A Modern Approach to Employment, Inflation, and the Exchange Rate, Oxford: Oxford University Press.

Devine, James G. (2000) 'The Rise and Fall of Stagflation: Preliminary Results,' Review of Radical Political Economics, 32 (3): 398–407.

Eisner, Robert (1997) 'A New View of the NAIRU', in Paul Davidson and Jan A. Kregel, eds, Improving the Global Economy, Cheltenham: Edward Elgar.

Friedman, Milton (1968) 'The Role of Monetary Policy', American Economic Review, 58 (1) March: 1–21.

Galbraith, James K. (1997) 'Time to Ditch the NAIRU', Journal of Economic Perspectives, 11 (1) Winter: 93–108.

Gordon, Robert J. (1997) 'The Time-Varying NAIRU and its Implications for Economic Policy' Journal of Economic Perspectives, 11 (1) Winter: 11–32.

Hargreaves-Heap, Shawn P. (1980) 'Choosing the Wrong 'Natural' Rate: Accelerating Inflation or Decelerating Employment and Growth?' Economic Journal, Sept.

Kalecki, Michal (1971) 'Political Aspects of Full Employment' [1943], in Kalecki, Selected Essays on the Dynamics of the Capitalist Economy, Cambridge: University Press.

Lerner, Abba (1951) Economics of Employment, New York: McGraw-Hill.

Pollin, Robert (1998) 'The "Reserve Army of Labor" and the "Natural Rate of Unemployment": Can Marx, Kalecki, Friedman, and Wall Street All Be Wrong?', Review of Radical Political Economics, 30 (3) Summer: 1–13.

Staiger, Douglas, James H. Stock, and Mark W. Watson (1997) 'The NAIRU, Unemployment and Monetary Policy', Journal of Economic Perspectives, 11 (1) Winter: 33–49.

Tobin, James (1980) 'Stabilization Policies after 10 Years', Brookings Papers on Economic Activity: 1.

13

How to Look at Economics Critically: Some Suggestions

RENATO DI RUZZA
UNIVERSITÉ DE AIX-MARSEILLE, FRANCE

JOSEPH HALEVI
UNIVERSITY OF SYDNEY, AUSTRALIA AND UNIVERSITÉ PIERRE MENDÈS FRANCE, FRANCE

INTRODUCTION: JOE STIGLITZ AND...THE SRAFFIANS

Let us start on a light note. Assume not a set of preferences but a Woody Allen type situation in which there is a character resembling very much an economist like Joe Stiglitz. What would such a person say, qua economist, to the psychoanalyst? We surmise that the confession would go along the following lines: 'I am really obsessed by an upward sloping supply curve crossing a downward sloping demand curve, yielding a unique and stable point of equilibrium. That is my dream world which, however, does nor materialize in practice, not even approximately. Yet the world of the sweet dream is necessary for me to transfer the real world into another dream, this time a nightmare, where those two curves, for all sort of reasons, start zigzagging all over the place, generating unpalatable outcomes. This is my economics of an imperfect world, but I cannot have that nightmare unless I first go through the sweet dream'. This is, in a nutshell, the essence of today's mainstream economics. There is nothing remotely factual, observational, or cognitive in it. And if a Joe Stiglitz denounces the major world financial institution as an instrument of impoverishment this should go mostly to his moral credit rather than to his background as an economist.

What economists say in terms of cognition can be said by the lay person as well. Economists do not verify 'laws' or 'relations'. Edmond Malinvaud, a most distinguished Neoclassical believer, thought, by contrast, that they did just that, arguing his case very strongly, also in emotional terms, at a famous international conference on economic methodology held in Paris towards the end of 1992.[1] Yet, perhaps because of the criticisms aired there, Malinvaud later wrote an article where he tried to explain why economists do not make discoveries, precisely by introducing many doubts about the reliability of verification procedures. These shortcomings were seen as deeply rooted rather than contingent upon the immaturity of the state of the art (Malinvaud, 1996). What the economist can do is only to think up an imaginary–not theoretical or abstract-world and then transfer onto it the perceptions he or she receives from the actual environment. In other words, matter never shapes space, as it were. The movement is always one way from the environment to the model leaving the basic theory intact. This is why our Joe Stiglitz's double must tell the psychoanalyst that he believes in the basic supply and demand story as a soothing sweet dream before moving to the nightmare where everything zigzags.

To be fair to the neoclassicists, the case of the actual world either having to adjust to a predetermined imaginary set of postulates or being totally shut out, applies also to some heterodox streams, particularly those which refuse to integrate their research program with historical analysis. Thus, for instance, a well known contributor to the Sraffian research program, Sergio Parrinello, voiced recently the following critical remarks when discussing Sraffa's legacy as continued by the Sraffians themselves:

> It seems as if they were engaged in a sort of division of labour and as if they say: we have done our critical work and we are still doing it; others, perhaps more expert in the fields of historical studies and of non-economic social sciences, should do the rest of the work in order to explain the level and the structure of economic activity and the evolution of these phenomena relative to historically determined factors. But why does such a second field of enquiry not emerge in a complementary way with the Sraffian theory of prices and the assumed methodology of Sraffa? This is a legitimate question 40 years after the publication of Sraffa's book. (Parrinello 2002: 259).

At this juncture two questions spring up in our minds. The first relates to the reasons why most schools in economics are so impervious to becoming relevant for the analysis of the object of their study, namely the economy which, indeed, may not really exist as a set of phenomena, with their imputed variables, in isolation from the rest of the society.

The second question concerns the issue of pluralism behind which lurks the whole ideological and political dimension of economics as a 'theological' discipline. In the next section we shall try to broach some answers to the first question by arguing that the notion of systemic laws and definite tendencies held by classical economics and by Marx, as well as the immanent principles of maximizing behavior held by the neoclassicists, depend on such special (and similar) conditions that the purported cognitive value of the respective theories vanishes in a more complex world. Hence both streams should be looked at as philosophical and political formulations regarding how to 'imagine' rather than to analyze the economy. It will be suggested that perhaps John Maynard Keynes, in his own far from linear way, attempted to express the most that could be said in economic terms by confining himself to the short period and by constructing a point of view not based on hard tendencies. To quote him from memory, in economics it is always the unexpected never the inevitable that happens.

The rest of this chapter will deal with the second question, which we believe is more significant than the first. Economics will continue to exist regardless of its cognitive capacities, since, in today's monetary based world, it performs a central ideological role in shaping power relations. In this way, economics has eliminated the multiple array of moral values in our perceptions of what humanity is and of how to address humankind's existence.

FROM SYSTEMIC TENDENCIES OR IMMANENT BEHAVIOR TO AN
UNKNOWN FUTURE

The nineteenth century witnessed the crystallization of two theoretical orientations aiming at discovering fundamental long-term tendencies in the economy. The first is the classical strand whose importance, we believe, is due to the fact that it culminates in Marx, while the second is what today is called neoclassical mainstream economics. Let us take a brief look at both and we shall immediately see that they collapse when they move from a simple to a complex world.

Marx's coherence lies in that he made every variable of his system interact with capital accumulation. He took the Ricardian theory whereby the value of commodities is determined by the amount of labor time bestowed in producing them. Such a value is independent of distribution which, instead, is determined by variations in the rate of surplus value, that is by changes in the proportions in which total labor time is divided between the amount needed for the workers to buy their means of subsistence and the amount fetched by the capitalist firm as profit. Variations in the rate of surplus value are caused by the relative size of the 'reserve army of labor', i.e. by unemployment, and by technological change, with the latter depending upon the former. Look now at the brilliancy of Marx's dynamics.

Initially the capitalist core is small but its productive forces are dynamically stronger than those of the surrounding system of petty commodity producers. The weight of capitalistic interests, therefore, brings about the end of natural rights over land. Its privatization thus throws throngs of landless peasants onto the labor market whose impact is to lower the general real wage rate. Marx believed very strongly in the Classical, especially Ricardian, tenet according to which a lower wage rate is accompanied by a higher rate of profit and, thus, by a higher rate of capital accumulation. Consequently the transformation of hitherto subsistence peasants into proletarians will enable the stronger forces of production of the capitalist core to forge ahead thereby claiming the space held by urban petty commodity producers. Yet a stage will be reached where the hinterland will no longer have enough people to supply cheap labor.

At this point wages will rise and accumulation will subside bringing a decline in the rate of profits. Operating under competitive conditions, capitalists cannot increase prices in the wake of a general rise in wages. They have only one route left open for salvation: labour-saving technical change which causes technological unemployment. Not all firms will succeed in implementing the change, so that their bankruptcies will throw onto the labor market additional throngs, not of peasants but, this time, of redundant workers and of bankrupt proprietors. The restoration of the 'reserve army' via unemployment will reduce the general wage rate and accumulation will pick up again on an expanded technical basis. The rates of profits and of accumulation recover but, in the long run, from cycle to cycle, the process of labor saving technical change will increase the capitalist intensity of production generating a secular decline in the rate of profit from which, now, there is no cyclical escape. The economy is relentlessly prodded by the iron-clad rule of competition which is the primary motive for capitalists to invest as much as they can:

> [T]he development of capitalist production makes it constantly necessary to keep increasing the amount of the capital laid out in a given industrial undertaking, and competition makes the immanent laws of capitalist production to be felt by each individual capitalist, as external coercive laws. It compels him to keep constantly extending his capital, in order to preserve it, but extend it he cannot, except by means of progressive accumulation (Marx 1967 [1868]: 555).

One cannot but admire the terse logic in which the entire evolution of capitalism, from its inception to its demise, is encapsulated in a limited set of variables interacting with each other.

Yet is it convincing? Unless one believes in the automatic investment of the entire surplus, Marx's story need not hold at all. It is indeed possible to believe in such an automatic mechanism only if the economy is made of corn.

Why should the capitalist farmers pile up (save) corn in their silos without plowing it back into the field? Except for a normal precautionary quantity there is no reason for them to refrain from investing all the corn left over and above consumption. But when the economy is slightly more complicated, firms may simply not be able to invest their surplus. It is enough to introduce a separation between consumption goods and machinery, thereby transforming the economy into a monetary one, in order for savings not to imply investment and accumulation. Thus if the appearance of cheap labor does reduce the average wage rate, the rate of profit may actually fall because of the formation of unused capacity in the consumption goods sector following the reduction in the demand for consumption goods induced by that very decline in the wage rate. Unused capacity in the consumption goods sector will generate excess capacity in the machine sector as well. Indeed orders for capital goods coming from the consumption goods sector will decline, with negative effects on the level of production in the machine sector.

If this phenomenon can occur in a very simple model, imagine how much greater this probability would be in a real economy with millions of mostly heterogeneous products. At this point the economy is simply mired in the short period because it has no long term path to hang on to, unless one is forcibly superimposed upon it. Of course it is always possible to build all sorts of adjustment models depending upon the imagination of the individual author. These are just thought experiments. The moment there are no long term paths, the economist must become a historian versed in the politics, institutions, culture and in the social classes and groups of a particular country and/or of a particular period. A *priori* modeling will not do except for sketching out very tentatively some basic accounting framework.

It is interesting to see that similar, almost identical, conclusions can be arrived at by taking a different road to the study of the path to the future: the route of immanent individualistic maximizing behavior. In opposition to Marx who sought objective laws rooted in historical processes, the neoclassicists attempted to derive outcomes from postulates which they believed were immanent in the behavior of every individual. As noted by John Hicks (1969), who was among the founders of modern General Equilibrium Theory, neoclassical theory does not lend itself to historical contextualization, but this does not mean that neoclassical economists do not believe in the concrete validity of the assumptions, otherwise they could not even begin to zigzag their curves.

Cambridge mathematician Frank Ramsey made the most of the utility maximizing assumption and built on it a formal theory which macroeconomic text-books still use to explain why savings happen at all. For Ramsey the model economy is non-monetary, producing only one commodity, say corn. Under these circumstances the problem for the self-sufficient farmers is how much corn to consume now and how much to save in order to till the land to obtain the next harvest. Given the utility function, the family will decide how much consumption should be forgone in order to have more of it in the future through a larger harvest. The present sacrifice in terms of utility compared to the certain gain in the future should be reflected in the 'real' rate of interest.

As soon as we move out of the corn-based self-sufficient farm, the theory does not hold. In a monetary multi-product economy to save more means, on one hand, to have more money, but, on the other, it entails a reduction in spending and therefore of demand for the other branches of activity. Thus in order to make the whole economy behave as if it were a single self-sufficient farmer, it is necessary to make the absurd assumption that an agent can indeed be conceived as representing the whole society. In modern models, through dynastic transmission, this agent becomes an infinitely long-lived 'thing'; we really dread calling it a human being. In any case there is no relation, let alone identity, between individual and collective behavior, something which has been philosophically ascertained since ancient times but which economists must still labor quite hard to accept (Kirman 1994).

The seemingly conflicting approaches discussed above, equally depend upon the economy being collapsed into one homogeneous sector, thereby enabling the smooth transformation of savings into investment. The smooth transformation defines the path towards the future: via cyclical accumulation in Marx and via intertemporal optimization in Ramsey-type macroeconomics. It is at this point that Keynes's theoretical intuition becomes important because it questions any predetermined tendency. Take for instance the first sentences of chapter 16 of the *General Theory*:

> An act of individual saving means-so to speak-a decision not to have dinner to-day. But it does *not* necessitate a decision to have dinner or to buy a pair of boots a week hence or a year hence or to consume any specified thing at any specified date. Thus it depresses the business of preparing to-day's dinner without stimulating the business of making ready for some future act of consumption. It is not a substitution of future consumption-demand for present consumption-demand, it is a net diminution of such demand. (Keynes 1936: 210).

Yet if:

> saving consisted not merely in abstaining from present consumption but in placing simultaneously a specific order for future consumption, the effect might indeed be different. (*ibid.*)

However there is no reason to believe that to be a normal occurrence, hence:

an individual decision to save does not, in actual fact, involve the placing of any specific forward order for consumption, but merely the cancellation of a present order. (211)

It follows therefore that the cancellation of a present order will contribute to a fall in investment and in employment, exactly the opposite of what an increase in savings was supposed to do. This is Keynes's critique of the neoclassical view of savings. However, the general decline in real wages brought about by the expansion of the 'industrial reserve army' in the Marxian framework is equivalent to a general increase in the capacity to save. Will this phenomenon expand accumulation thanks to the shift in the distribution of income from wages to profits? No, because, if we are to follow Keynes' arguments, such a decline in wages is also a cancellation of orders for a large class of consumption goods.[2] Thus, just as there is no tendency towards a neoclassical intertemporal equilibrium, there is no continuous movement on the postulated cyclical path of Marx's accumulation theory. Both systemic processes are predicated upon investment being predetermined by savings.

The methodological implications concerning the very definition of economic processes are quite drastic. Long-term investment cannot be determined in an acceptably meaningful manner because the system is subjected neither to the iron-clad rules of competition outlined by Marx in the passage quoted hitherto, nor to the optimizing behavior of Ramsey's self-sufficient farmers. In Keynes the impossibility of sketching an acceptable long- term theory of investment related to (unknown) future tendencies in the rate of profits and of accumulation, confines the economist to the short period.[3] To analyze what the next period may look like she would have to get her hands dirty and study how conflicting interests, alliances, or other socio-cultural-political factors that the researcher might find relevant, impact on the day to day evolution of the society under scrutiny.

NO MORALITY, BUT ECONOMICS AS THOUGHT CONTROL

The limitations of the major constructions which aimed at formulating a global, causality-driven theory of economic human behavior, or of growth and accumulation, do not stem from the undeveloped state of macroeconomics as a sub-branch of the discipline. Rather they arise from the failure of micro-relations to come up with a consistent general framework. In other words, the moment a macro-system is broken up into subsectors it no longer holds together, but it cannot be built from the bottom up either.

Here again we find a stark convergence in the inadequacies of the two main opposing bodies of economic thought. In the case of neoclassical General Equilibrium Theory, changes in prices in relation to differences in supply and demand conditions do not necessarily happen according to the principle of substitution since variations in prices change incomes, thereby affecting demand and prices again (Guerrien 1989).[4] Similar problems beset modern day classicists – like the Sraffians – in their search for a long-term position whereby production prices are consistent with uniform rates of profits. The gravitation process may require an immediate response of prices to imbalances in supply and demand – that is, the response must occur at once for the process to unfold towards the long run. Gravitation may also entail wild oscillations between inflation and deflation requiring the adoption of a super-powerful Central Bank, planning credit exactly to avoid those fluctuations (Kubin 1991; Bellino 1999).

All these complications happen in models which do not extend beyond two commodities. How can any of these be taken seriously as devices to understand the economy and its evolutionary transformations? The interesting aspect of the vicissitudes bringing economists working along classical lines onto the same plane as their neoclassical counterparts, is that the former were successful during the construction of the critique but fell into the maze of special cases and of *ad hoc* formulations when they wanted to prove that their approach – gravitation towards production prices-was stronger than the neoclassical one (Cartelier 1993).

Can it be said that there has been no progress in economic theorizing? There has been but in a negative way, as well described in a clear-headed paper by Carlo Benetti and Jean Cartelier (1998) whose observations, we believe, are shared deep-down by many economists of different persuasions. The authors argue that to reach the objective of creating a science, economic theorists sought–since the seventeenth century–to represent society by means of formal theories, based on value and prices without politics and monetary relations in them. Yet, they point out, most analytical developments of the twentieth century did not confirm the conclusions of the founders of the discipline. As a consequence the central questions of economics have yet to receive a satisfactory answer.

In a recent book we maintained that the failure of economics to get a handle on the object of its study is not due to still insufficient research (Di Ruzza and Halevi 2003). It results from the refusal to see what Karl Polanyi emphasized long ago. We wrote that the 'activities and gestures defined as economic ones are 'embedded' (in Karl Polanyi's sense), that is rooted, locked into, inserted, contextualized, in a whole system of references...of an extra-economic nature often dominating and determining those very economic activities. Thus multidisciplinarity must be the very principle underlying their study' (Di Ruzza and Halevi 2003: 126, our translation from French). Our view implies that it is virtually impossible to treat economic variables in isolation and in the abstract. Those constructed variables are not like minerals that can be taken out of the rocks and cut, analyzed, and used industrially. They, instead, are inseparable from the social 'rocks'. But to build a theory of a particular phenomenon, whether real or perceived, it is necessary to isolate a few basic elements precisely in order to ensure the coherence of theory. The problem is that the economy cannot be treated in isolation from politics and other societal elements. The room to construct meaningful economic theories is therefore very limited. No wonder the attempts to construct, rather than find, those laws and behavioral rules have failed.

If we take a hard look at the three major approaches in economics, the Marxian, the Walrasian and that of Keynes, we see that the first appears to be connected to history but its results are fragile, the second is a brilliant metaphysics but its logical outcomes are not robust. The third strand, John Maynard Keynes's own writings, constitutes the most open statement to date that we do not really know, that we must play it by ear, and that we ought not to believe in automatic and symmetric responses. Hence, for Keynes, the whole art of dealing with economic questions is a mixture of politics, journalism, and some 'back of the envelope' quasi-calculations, being always wary of falling into the trap of postulating *a priori* causal relations. But all this also means that Keynes' results, in terms of economics, are very limited and definitely bounded by the conditions of his time.

We can now move one more step away from economics as a structured discipline and advance the proposition that we made, from the floor, in 1992 at the Paris conference on whether economics was becoming a hard science. We stated that anyone can talk about the economy with the same authority as trained economists. When it comes to talking to the public, the discourse of economists is not more informed than that of the lay person who bothers to read quality newspapers, say *Le Monde* or *The Wall Street Journal*. By contrast, not anyone can be a driver of a TGV, or a veterinarian, and not even a lawyer or a chartered accountant. The only element that can give the economist an advantage is the possible role of a priest in the corridors of power, whether private or governmental. The advantage comes from having insider's information. The person's professional profile qua economist is irrelevant. Upon becoming the *conseiller du prince*, or just by positioning himself/herself to be co-opted in that role, our character will start talking in terms of the acceptable jargon involving, in a loose manner, all the causalities belonging to theories which are, to say the least, far from solid. It is unlikely that young, soon to be co-opted, economists will climb the stairs of the Banque de France or of the Bank of New Zealand by waving the major book of the Sorbonne mathematician Bernard Guerrien in which he destroys the concept of flexibility. They will rather enter those buildings thinking of representative agents, of bad rigidities impeding competition, and of bad public sector deficits even when there is a surplus.[5]

More importantly, the role of economics as a thought control process shows up at the crucial junction between what is being said in private-that is: in learned journals, and academic debates-and what is being uttered to the public. The link is represented by university appointments and careers. At the academic level faculty members who are completely aware of the crucial failings of mainstream theorizing, having published papers on the subject, act as gate keepers against heterodoxy, preferring instead the constant reproduction of textbooks' vulgar doctrine. This behavior has had a negative impact on the heterodoxy as well, which, in order to break out of the ghetto, attempted to further professionalize itself by closing its eyes to the imperative of making multidisciplinarity the very principle guiding the study of the economy in society. Among the social sciences and the humanities, the lack of pluralism in economics is unique, and so is the system of reproduction of the established view. The message is simple: zigzag your curves as much as you like but do not question the basic postulates, do not get involved in the social views of Marxism, do not raise any queries about the ideological role of the discipline, look at Keynes as just a set of rigidities, etc., and, especially, do not attempt to look at economic processes as social constructions determined by specific historical and political contexts. Thus, while the conceptual criticism of economics as a failed cognitive discipline encompasses virtually all the theories-because of their inability to connect with the historical context-the political and democratic critique must be exclusively focused on the mainstream component.

REFERENCES

Bellino, Enrico (1999): 'Convergence to Long-Run Equilibrium: On Some Recent Variations of the 'Pure' Cross-Dual Model', *Structural Change and Economic Dynamics*, vol. 10, no. 2, June, 225–37.

Benetti, Carlo and Cartelier, Jean (1998): 'La economia politica como ciencia: la permanencia de una conviccion mal compartida', *Lecturas de Economia*, no. 48, January-June, 7–32.

Cartelier, Jean (1993): 'Prix naturels et prix de marché: A propos du livre d'Ingrid Kubin', *Cahiers d'Economie Politique*, no. 22, 125–32.

d'Autume, Antoine and Cartelier, Jean, eds, (1996): *Is Economics Becoming a Hard Science?* Brookfield, VT: Edward Elgar.

Di Ruzza, Renato and Halevi, Joseph (2003): *De l'économie politique à l'ergologie: lettre aux amis*, Paris: L'Harmattan.

Guerrien, Bernard (1989): *Concurrence, flexibilité et stabilité*, Paris: Economica.

Hicks, J. R. (1939): *Value and Capital*. Oxford: Clarendon.

Hicks, John (1969): *A Theory of Economic History*, Oxford: Clarendon.

Kalecki, Michal (1991): 'Money and Real Wages', in *Collected Works of Michal Kalecki*, Vol. 2, Oxford: Oxford University Press, 21–50.

Keynes, John Maynard (1936): *The General Theory of Employment Interest and Money*, London: Macmillan.

Kirman, Alan (1989): 'The Intrinsic Limits of Modern Economic Theory: The Emperor Has No Clothes', *Economic Journal*, vol. 99, no. 395, Supplement, 126–39.

Kirman, Alan (1994): 'Whom or What Does the Representative Individual Represent?', *The Journal of Economic Perspectives*, vol. 6, no. 2, 117–36.

Kubin, Ingrid (1991): *Market Prices and Natural Prices*, Frankfurt: Peter Lang.

Malinvaud, Edmond (1996): 'Pourquoi les économistes ne font pas de découvertes', *Revue d'Economie Politique*, vol. 106, no. 6, Nov., Dec., 929–42.

Marx Karl (1977) [1868]: *Capital*, vol.1, Moscow: Progress Publishers.

Parrinello, Sergio (2002): 'Sraffa's Legacy in Economics: Some Critical Notes', *Metroeconomica*, vol. 53, no. 3, August, 242–60.

PART IV

ETHICAL VOIDS AND SOCIAL PATHOLOGIES

14

Teaching Economics as if Ethics Mattered

CHARLES K. WILBER

UNIVERSITY OF NOTRE DAME, USA

I have spent the past thirty-five years as a professor of economics. Over the course of my tenure at The American University, in Washington, D. C. (1965–75) and the University of Notre Dame (1975–present), however, I became ever more disenchanted with the capacity of traditional economic theory to enable people to lead a good life. I found myself unable to accept the values embedded in economic theory, particularly the elevation of self-interest, the neglect of income distribution, and the attempts to export these values into studies of the family, the role of the state and so on. As a result I started researching and writing on the nature of economics and the role of ethics in economic theory.

This work has led me to three important conclusions. First is the conviction that economic theory is not value-free as is so often claimed. Rather, it presupposes a set of value judgments upon which economic analysis is erected. Second is the realization that the economy itself requires that the self-interest of economic actors be morally constrained. Third is the recognition that economic institutions and policies impact people's lives requiring that both efficiency and equity be assessed. Teachers of economics need to make use of these insights.

ECONOMISTS, VALUE JUDGMENTS AND ECONOMIC THEORY

Many economists argue that while values might have a place in what is termed normative economics, they should be kept out of the everyday scientific business of the profession-the development and testing of falsifiable propositions – which is often referred to as positive economics. This separation, however, is problematic. Economists, as persons, necessarily work from a viewpoint that structures the questions asked, the methods, the evidence, the answers deemed acceptable. Because there is no direct access to the 'real' world, an economist is forced to see that world through the lenses of theory. Does that mean 'facts' are theory-laden? And if theory-laden, value-laden? What would this mean for economic theory? Ultimately, the question becomes: how does one do economics in a world where facts and values cannot be conveniently disentangled?

In looking for an answer to this question, economics students find to their surprise that they have much to learn from Adam Smith. Smith's economic theory was closely related to his moral thought. For example, while Smith often used the metaphor of the watch in describing how the self-interested actions of individuals worked for the good of the whole, he saw the 'machine' itself as the product of a beneficent God, which moreover depended on the virtues of individual actors to operate smoothly. Smith's *Theory of Moral Sentiments*,[1] written before the *Wealth of Nations*,[2] offers a rich moral vision of society that contrasts with the thin gruel of 'rational economic man.'

Modern economics has selectively adapted Adam Smith's invisible hand metaphor, focusing on the economically wondrous effects of the butcher and baker trading out of their own respective interests and ignoring the prior description of the same deistic hand propelling the creation of a virtuous society. In Smith is a forgotten lesson that the foundation of success in creating a constructive classical liberal society lies in the individuals' adherence to a common social ethics. According to Smith, virtue serves as 'the fine polish to the wheels of society' while vice is 'like the vile rust, which makes them jar and grate upon one another.' Indeed, Smith sought to distance his thesis from that of Mandeville and the implication that individual greed could be the basis for social good. Smith's deistic universe might not sit well with those of post-enlightenment sensibilities, but his understanding that virtue is a prerequisite for a desirable market society remains an important lesson. For Smith ethics is the hero-not self-interest or greed-for it is ethics that defend social intercourse from the Hobbesian chaos.

Since the work of Thomas Kuhn and other historians of science, it has been increasingly recognized that scientists cannot be neutral in matters of value. In an article co-authored with Roland Hoksbergen,[3] I survey what others have had to say about value neutrality in economics, showing that there has been a lively debate on the subject in the years since 1970. One group argues that economists can successfully separate values from facts, which are 'out there' in the world, by adhering to a positivist methodology. According to this group, a failure to maintain this distinction will lead to a disastrous slide into relativism.

Critics of value neutrality, on the other hand, marshal a wide variety of arguments to make their case. It is argued, for example, that there is no access to objective reality except through the lenses of a theory and, therefore, the values shared by the community of economists color their judgment in determining just what the relevant 'facts' are. For example, years of schooling are important facts because they are proxies for human capital, and human capital in turn is important because neoclassical theory says that it is what explains a major portion of income differences. In another theory years of schooling might be replaced by labor-market discrimination and family wealth as more important facts.

I come down on this side of the issue, arguing that neoclassical economists share a 'world view'-a notion of the good, which shapes their analysis of the economy. This world view includes three main elements:

1. People are rational and self-interested.
2. The purpose of life is to pursue happiness as people define it.
3. The ideal world is one in which people are free to compete to achieve their ends and in which market forces lead to optimal equilibrium outcomes.

This is certainly a set of value judgments, in need of justification like any other. If these judgments indeed correctly characterize economics, they should be openly debated, rather than tacitly assumed.

Thus, economists bring certain values to their interpretation of the facts, for example, by imposing a neoclassical template on the world they observe. In an article by Robert Frank and others, they take the argument a step further.[4] They experimentally demonstrate that economists' values can affect the 'real world' itself-and not just economists' interpretations of it. This happens when economists 'export' values into the classroom by teaching the economic theory of rationality. The authors report several experiments, in one of which they put students in a prisoner's dilemma situation, with actual cash at stake. In a regression model of the resulting data, with the decision to defect as the dependent variable, an economics major variable was significantly positive; those who had studied economics the most were more likely to take the most self-interested action. If this kind of effect is common, then even clearly self-interested behavior may not constitute an independent verification of the theory of rational self-interest, but instead may be a *product* of that theory.

An introductory course in economics should provide students with several different approaches to the relationship between facts and values in economics, demonstrating that the role in economics of ideals such as objectivity are unsettled. The debate is a longstanding one, and it continues.

Rationality, Ethics and the Behavior of Economic Agents

After teaching the fundamentals of microeconomics-scarcity, choice, opportunity cost, supply and demand, it is important to discuss the limitations of the microeconomic way of thinking. Basically, economic theory posits that wants are always greater than resources, therefore, scarcity is *the* economic problem. Since by assumption everyone wants to get the most for the least the logic of the model follows. The extensions are particularly troubling-couples choose between a new car and a new baby; elected representatives act so as to maximize the possibility of re-election. Even altruistic behavior is seen as self-interested; people are seen to give money to charity because it makes them feel good or it brings them social approval.

However, all evidence indicates that economic actors (consumers, workers, firms) act out of more than calculated self-interest. Thus the assumption of rationality used in economics may be insufficient in some cases and inappropriate in others. In fact, people's behavior is influenced by many things including ethical norms. Economists have several reasons to be concerned. First, to the extent that economics is based on a faulty theory of human behavior, it will be unable to predict and control. For example, how should government encourage people to behave in socially beneficial ways, say, to donate blood? If people are rational maximizers, government can best achieve its ends by providing a proper set of economic incentives for such behavior. But if economics misconceives the way people are motivated, such incentives might fail to work. In fact, there is evidence that blood donations decline when a system of cash payments is introduced. How can this be?

It is not clear how to account for the decline in contributions, but one possible answer relates to a second, *generative,* role for economic theory. By this is meant its role in generating behavior as opposed to merely predicting or controlling it. Economics can play this role in several possible ways. First, as mentioned earlier, economics can become a sort of philosophy of life for those who study it, leading them to behave in economically rational ways. Second, and more appropriate for the blood-donation case, economically rational ways of behavior can be taught by exposure to social policies and practices that presuppose economic rationality. Thus, even those who initially behave according to social norms about giving blood may come to view blood donation as just another economic transaction, once they see people being paid for their donations. What they once saw as a 'priceless' gift, they now see as a $50 gift. Thus, their non-economic motives are undercut by an economic policy based solely on self-interest.

Another reason to be skeptical regarding the assumption of economic rationality has to do with its normative role. Earlier I noted that the practice of neoclassical economics, despite claims of a positive-normative distinction, commits one to certain moral beliefs. For example, when economics merely identifies and describes certain behaviors as 'rational,' the label of rationality carries a positive connotation that may lead some to see such behavior as desirable or even morally good. Another normative role for the theory of economic rationality is as a benchmark of economic success. Economists measure the success of the economic system by its satisfaction of individual preferences, as opposed to some other measure such as reductions in infant mortality or the elimination of demeaning working conditions. In this 'benchmark' role, the economic theory of rationality is normative because it dictates how policies and behaviors are to be judged.

Thus, there are a number of reasons why one should be concerned about whether the economic theory of rationality is a good one. How would one begin to determine the answer to that question? Certainly it is relevant to ask whether people actually behave according to the theory. One article does just that, using experimental evidence.[5] However, keeping in mind the generative role that theory potentially plays, one must also ask what the *consequences* are of adopting the neoclassical theory of value. In an article I suggest among other things that a society constructed on the basis of pure economic rationality might face overwhelming problems of moral hazard, resulting in a kind of crisis of the moral environment.[6] I examine the problems of organizing society, and, in particular of organizing work, in conditions of imperfect information. In those conditions, as economists have demonstrated, the problem of *moral hazard* can arise. The problem arises when the payoff to one party of a contract depends upon the performance of the other party, and the performance cannot be monitored. For example, there may be a tendency to avoid work when the boss is not looking. Such problems are surely pervasive in our complex society. I argue that ethics can be part of the remedy, diminishing the tendency to 'shirk' in such situations. I argue further that alternative forms of work organization, such as cooperatives, might be effective in eliciting moral behavior under conditions of imperfect information.

Several themes emerge from a study of rationality, ethics, and the behavior of economic agents. As has been seen, one of the crucial issues is the empirical validity of the neoclassical theory. Another issue is the potential consequences of adopting the theory as society's operative theory of human nature. A third issue is the question of exactly *how* people might deviate from the rational model. If people are moral agents in addition to rational maximizers, how *do* they care about the world? For example, do they simply care about the utility of other agents, or do they obey certain moral strictures – like those against lying – regardless of their effect on others' happiness?

What studies make clear is that there is no one form of behavior, whether self-interested or moral, that is dictated by human nature. There is abundant evidence for this. The question then becomes how the various aspects of human nature-economically rational and otherwise-can be elicited so as to create an efficient and just society.

ETHICAL THEORIES

We have examined how the relationship between ethics and economics is important both for the construction of theory and for understanding the behavior of economic agents. We now begin the examination of the third question-how to assess the differential impact of economic institutions and policies. That is, to answer the question of whether outcomes are desirable, ethical evaluations must be applied in addition to economic evaluations. This requires some understanding of available moral theories. A moral theory is needed to provide a framework for responding to the ethical questions that arise in the course of economic activity. For example, if one decides that value-free economics is impossible, which moral values should inform the discipline? If people do not behave simply as rational maximizers, what moral theories might guide their actions? What moral theory should be used to answer applied policy questions? And finally, if individual preference sovereignty is rejected as the overriding goal of the economic system, what moral benchmarks or objectives should take its place? All of these issues cannot be even understood, much less resolved, without some sort of a moral theory as a guide.

There are three main types of moral theory: consequentialist, deontological, and virtue ethics. Consequentialism holds that the right action is the one that results in the best outcomes. One type of consequentialism, utilitarianism, is dominant in economic theory and asserts that the outcomes that matter are utility or preference satisfaction.

Implementing utilitarianism presents certain problems. How does one measure welfare or preference satisfaction, particularly when different individuals must be compared? Do consequences count if they are not expected in advance? Does the welfare of future generations matter? What of animals? How does one compare two different states of affairs in which population levels differ? How does an individual make ethical decisions when quantifying utility is difficult if not impossible? Despite these difficulties, it is argued by many that utility is the only intrinsically good thing. Others argue that utilitarianism is justified on the basis of equal respect among persons. There has been a recent resurgence in the popularity of consequentialism and many economists find it appealing because of its apparent compatibility with neoclassical economic theory.

In deontological ethics by contrast, moral duties or rights sometimes take precedence over outcomes, because those duties or rights are morally valuable in themselves. The deontological position is intuitively appealing as can be seen by means of an example: assume a situation in which you must choose between killing one innocent person yourself and allowing two others to be murdered by another person. The consequences, in terms of the number of lives lost, are not as bad if you commit the murder. But to do so violates the moral obligation not to kill.

Virtue theory traces its roots to Aristotle. Happiness plays a central role in virtue theory, just as in utilitarianism, but virtue theorists mean something different when they refer to happiness. Aristotle used the term to refer to activity in accordance with virtue. Virtues, in turn, are the personal qualities that enable us to do the things that good people do. Of course, the qualities of a good person are complicated and require some kind of agreement on the proper ends of humankind. Unfortunately, an important feature of modern societies is their inability to reach agreement on such matters. But most people will agree that the human virtues include truthfulness, courage, and so on.

Virtue theory might have much to teach modern business people. Businesses might perform better if they concentrated on developing virtues or excellences like quality, rather than focusing exclusively on the bottom line.

Deontological considerations might be used to augment neoclassical economics. The essence of the deontological approach is that while the utilitarian views the person as a unified bundle of preferences, the former sees the self as bifurcated. Each person has a set of desires as well as a separate aspect of the self that judges those preferences in light of moral considerations. The ultimate choices of the individual are the product of both aspects of the self. This notion is consistent with the work of those economists who have introduced 'meta-preferences,' a secondary set of preferences over the domain of all possible preferences. For example, I like grapes but my moral commitment to the United Farm Workers strike kept me from buying them in the 1960s. In addition to the fact that preferences have this dual nature, they respond to experience, and thus are endogenous in an important way. That is, our preferences are not inborn but are learned.

Morality interpenetrates all of economic life; its implications are sweeping and do not apply only to certain areas. For example, in considering work life, the moral value of work, and not just preferences must be taken into account. Moreover, moral behavior undergirds all of the economy, which would quickly disintegrate if large numbers of people attempted to cheat one another or failed to honor their contracts. Thus, moral considerations demand a radical rethinking of all of economics.

Virginia Held[7] addresses another approach to ethics: Is there such a thing as a feminist ethics? Carol Gilligan was one of the first to study this issue. Her work was framed as a criticism of Lawrence Kohlberg, who apparently had found that moral development among girls was less advanced than among boys. Gilligan tried to document that what appears to be a lack of moral development is rather a distinctively 'female' form of moral thought, which is shared by many girls and women, as well as some young boys. Men tend to have what Held calls a 'justice perspective' on morality. This form of morality emphasizes rules and individual conscience. In contrast, women have a 'care perspective,' which centers on meeting others' needs and maintaining relationships, rather than rigid adherence to moral rules.

Following the general lines of Gilligan's approach, Held argues that women tend to share certain ways of thinking, acting and feeling about moral problems. These distinctive forms of female moral experience are in part the product of the activities that women have historically been involved in, especially mothering. To the extent that moral theory is based upon moral experience, Held argues women's distinctive experiences should be included. Held believes that this is especially the case because the experience of mothering is so central and important to human life, compared with the realm of public affairs, which provides the inspiration for many 'male' forms of moral thinking.

Held enumerates several aspects of women's morality. First, it is attentive to the needs of 'particular others,' in contrast to all other people in general. That is, it emphasizes the special obligations we have to those who are close to us, as opposed to all others. Second, a feminist morality de-emphasizes, but does not discard, moral rules and principles. Third, there is more to morality than just knowledge; equally important are the associated feelings and motivations. Fourth, one of the most important female experiences providing inspiration for feminist morality is the process of giving birth; the pain of bearing a child inspires the commitment of the mother, who does not want her suffering to have been in vain. Fifth, a feminist morality emphasizes the survival of children and relations of care and concern. Finally, Held argues that while much of what feminists say about morality has been said before, as some critics have alleged, the important thing is that many problems and experiences specific to women have been largely ignored.

ECONOMIC INSTITUTIONS AND ETHICS

Institutions, such as markets and property rights, impact people's welfare and those impacts need to be evaluated both in economic and ethical terms. Some economists may believe that the market is to be judged only on its efficiency in meeting wants, but Elizabeth Anderson[8] shows that moral concerns should play a part in our evaluations of the market. It is often proposed that markets should be used to allocate goods and services wherever possible because they are more efficient than the alternatives.

How can one evaluate such proposals? Anderson, in 'The Ethical Limitations of the Market,' suggests an answer. She argues that when we allocate a good or service through a certain institution such as the market, we treat it in accordance with the norms of that institution. Those norms may allow us to realize some values, but fail to realize – or even undermine – others. Thus, a good is properly traded on the market if its value is successfully realized by the norms of the market. Also, an institution like the market, together with its associated norms, embodies certain interpretations of ideals, while possibly denying or ignoring other ideals. To determine whether a good is appropriately distributed by the market, one can examine the rival ideals at stake. The way people value things when they are allocated through the market is what Anderson calls *use*. When we *use* something, we treat it in accordance with certain norms of the market:

> First, market relations are impersonal ones. Second, the market is understood to be a sphere in which one is free, within the bounds of the law, to pursue one's personal advantage unrestrained by any consideration of the advantage of others. Third, the goods traded on the market are exclusive and rivals in consumption. Fourth, the market is purely want-regarding: from its standpoint all matters of value are simply matters of personal taste. Finally, dissatisfaction with a commodity or market relation is expressed primarily by 'exit,' not 'voice.' (p. 182)

To determine whether a good should be traded on the market one should consult this list of market norms to see if they are compatible with the full realization of its values.

To illustrate the application of this theory, consider the good of personal relationships. The practice of modern relationships is informed by the ideals of intimacy and commitment, as opposed to the ideal of market freedom embodied in the market. This means that the goods of personal relationships are, to a significant extent, shared ones. So, each partner enjoys those goods and knows that the other also enjoys them. And the goods at stake must be provided in the spirit of a gift, rather than out of narrow self-interest, meaning that they must express a cognizance of and appreciation for the personal characteristics of the recipient.

All of this conflicts with the market norm of *impersonality*, which requires that goods be provided without regard to any characteristics of the buyer other than his or her willingness to pay. Also, the goods of personal relationships cannot be attained if they are given for base motives, like economic gain. Thus, Anderson argues, we can see that sexuality is not appropriately traded on the market. For a prostitute is motivated by monetary gain and, in providing her sexual 'services,' does not respond to the personal qualities of his or her customer. Furthermore, the goods of personal relationships can be seen as 'higher' than those of the market. By implicitly equating the personal goods of the prostitute with the money of the client, a lower good, prostitution, degrades the prostitute. For these and other reasons cited by Anderson, prostitution does not realize the goods of love; thus, sex should not be distributed on the market.

Rational actor theory is more than an empirical theory of behavior. This is perhaps most clearly evident when economists assess the relative efficiency of alternative economic arrangements, and, therefore, the desirability of policies. Since the definition of welfare used is preference satisfaction, the utility function becomes a normative benchmark. In practice economists use the more crude standard – cost-benefit analysis (CBA). In this practice, the merit of projects or policies is determined by adding up their costs and benefits. The benefits are usually measured in terms of the willingness of the affected parties to pay for them; with willingness-to-pay the normatively relevant piece of data because it reflects preferences. Thus, both in theory and in practice, economists rely on the notion that welfare amounts to the satisfaction of observed individual preferences.

Tyler Cowen[9] is critical of the use of preference-satisfaction as a yardstick for policy choice, arguing not that it necessarily always gives the wrong policy recommendations, but that in some cases it fails to issue in any coherent recommendations at all. Cowen's argument is based on the paradox that preferences shift in response to policy. Thus, there is a source of circularity in the use of preferences to guide policy. An example will serve to illustrate the point. Suppose that liberal education instills in students liberal values and a tendency to favor government support for liberal education; while at the same time, those educated in a more authoritarian system tend to support authoritarian educational policies. In this situation, the preference sovereignty standard fails to provide any consistent advice to the policy maker. Which policy satisfies preferences best depends upon which policy is implemented in the first place. Thus, 'preference sovereignty' as a criterion for policy selection is not only incorrect, it is incoherent.

These problems are compounded when considering the problem of how to count the welfare of future generations. The shape (and existence!) of future individuals' preferences are determined in part by the policies adopted today, so again one is faced with the question of which preferences to count.

A related problem arises when dealing with the problem of imperfectly informed preferences. It has been empirically documented that in the real world, preferences are affected by all kinds of irrational influences. How, then can one justify relying on those preferences to guide policy? For example, A person reveals a preference to smoke when buying a pack of cigarettes. At the same time that person wants to quit smoking.

CONCLUSION

In this chapter I have focused on the interaction between ethics and economics, both in economic theory and economic policy. I have examined the three ways in which ethics are important in economics: 1. Economists have ethical values that help shape the way they do economics. 2. Economic actors have ethical values that help shape their behavior. 3. Economic institutions and policies impact people differentially and thus ethical evaluations must supplement economic evaluations. Economics would be greatly enriched if it recognized that there is no alternative to working from a world view. Making explicit the ethical values embodied in that world view would help keep economics more honest and useful.

15
Economics as Ideology and the Need for Pluralism

PETER SÖDERBAUM

MÄLARDALEN UNIVERSITY, SWEDEN

Mainstream neoclassical economics – and no other economics – is taught at university departments of economics and at business schools in all parts of the world. The ideal is to build on one paradigm (theoretical perspective) and to extend this perspective in different directions to cover international economics, environmental economics, health economics and so on. The hope of neoclassical economists is furthermore to offer a useful paradigm that is as close as possible to the philosophy behind physics, chemistry and other natural sciences. Positivism in the sense of objectivity, value neutrality, testing of hypotheses and, whenever possible, mathematical presentation are some of the features of the neoclassical approach. A large number of scholars have vested interests in the monopoly position of the neoclassical paradigm, and since the 1970s, there has even been a Bank of Sweden Prize in Economic Sciences in Memory of Alfred Nobel for extraordinary achievements.

Gunnar Myrdal is one of those who have received the mentioned Nobel Prize. Not unexpectedly, the Nobel committee emphasized his achievements within neoclassical economics, but contrary to other neoclassical economists he – at a certain stage in his career – openly declared his sympathies for institutional economics. He argued that the study of problems related to poverty, health and environment in developing countries and elsewhere has to be based on an interdisciplinary perspective. Myrdal also took an interest in theory of science issues and argued that it is an illusion that economics can be value-free and neutral. 'Values are always with us' in social science research (Myrdal 1978). We have interests in choosing one problem area for our studies rather than another and values are involved when making a choice among possible theories, methods and ways of presenting results. Scientific criteria play a role in making all these choices, but so also do other values that make up the total ideological orientation of the scholar.

The 'fact' that ideology is unavoidably present means that the 'one-paradigm position' at departments of economics becomes untenable. Limiting economics to one paradigm means that one ideological orientation is emphasized at the expense of all others. This position is not compatible with normal ideas of democracy. Departments of economics should avoid the role of being political propaganda centres. With more than one paradigm as part of a pluralistic strategy, the ideological diversity in a democratic society will be better reflected. Furthermore, one specific paradigm, such as the neoclassical one, may perform well in relation to some fields of study while being more of a problem in relation to other fields.

In defence of the neoclassical monopoly position at departments of economics, it could perhaps be argued that there are other social sciences such as economic history, political science, business economics and sociology that are based on paradigms other than the neoclassical one. While this is true, my point here is that the monopoly of the neoclassical paradigm at departments of economics has a considerable impact on the understanding of economics among major actors in society. If their mental maps are largely influenced by neoclassical economics and if some categories of problems cannot be dealt with successfully within the neoclassical perspective, then we have a problem. I will argue that neoclassical economics is not enough – and is even part of the problems faced – in relation to present environmental and development issues.

In this chapter the one-paradigm idea of economics will be questioned. Those acquainted with the history of economic ideas – a subject nowadays often avoided at departments of economics – know that there have been many currents over the years. Among alternatives to neoclassical theory, institutionalism will here be emphasized. Comparing different paradigms, for instance neoclassical theory with institutionalism, is furthermore believed to be an important way of learning. In this way it is possible to illuminate not only differences in some narrow scientific sense but also the ideological tendencies connected with each paradigm.

ON THE MEANINGS OF PARADIGM, IDEOLOGY, PLURALISM AND DEMOCRACY

I have already used concepts that may be unfamiliar to some students. 'Paradigm' here refers to 'theoretical perspective' within a discipline or at an interdisciplinary level. Neoclassical economics with its microeconomics and macroeconomics is a good example of a relatively clear-cut paradigm. Microeconomics refers to individuals as consumers maximizing the utility of alternative bundles of commodities within their monetary budget constraints and to business companies maximizing profits. Individuals and firms interact in markets for commodities and factors of production. Markets are understood in terms of the forces of supply and demand. Macroeconomics refers to the whole national economy where the state may influence all consumers and firms, for instance through monetary and financial policy.

As a paradigm, institutional theory may be less clear-cut. It is more accurate to speak of different versions of institutionalism. According to the one emphasized here, individuals and organizations are understood as 'actors' in the economy. Individuals are guided by their 'ideological orientation' and the same is true of organizations. Neoclassical Economic Man is replaced by a Political Economic Person (PEP), that is, an individual with many roles rather than exclusively the one of being a consumer. To understand the individual in the economy, roles such as the ones of professional, citizen and parent are also judged to be relevant. An organization is similarly understood as a Political Economic Organization (PEO). Firms or business companies are of course important players in the economy but so are governmental agencies, municipalities, environmental organizations, churches and universities. Individuals and organizations alike are understood as actors in a political sense. They all can influence the dialogue about the future of our societies, for instance issues related to taxation, environment and development more generally. They also engage in more limited roles in relation to markets of various kinds.

'Ideology' is here used in a broad sense as 'means-ends philosophy'. Ideology is based on beliefs about 'progress' at the level of society, of organizations and for the individual herself. Normally, each actor has a positive attitude to her 'ideological orientation' and there is no tendency here to use ideology in a derogatory sense. Established political ideologies such as liberalism or socialism are certainly included but also 'issue-related ideologies' such as 'business ideologies', 'health-care ideologies', 'transportation ideologies' or 'environmental ideologies'. According to the ideological orientation of some business actors, only monetary profits and other monetary indicators count while other business actors may point to the importance of a number of non-monetary dimensions, for instance the measurement of social and environmental performance. One health-care ideology may emphasize centralization of health care functions while another may point to the advantages of decentralization. One transportation ideology emphasizes time-savings in transport while another lays stress on the avoidance of negative impacts such as environmental pollution and traffic accidents. A compromise between different objectives is of course as 'ideological' as more 'single objective' ideologies.

Ideologies are seldom reducible to simple mathematical equations. To allow for complexity, the term 'ideological orientation' is preferred as a guiding principle of individuals and organizations. An ideological orientation is typically fragmentary rather than complete; it is uncertain and subject to reconsideration (as part of public and private debate, for instance) rather than certain. The ideological orientation of an actor still serves as a guide with respect to direction of decision-making and behaviour.

'Pluralism' stands for a belief that competition between paradigms and ideologies is good for society. Each actor tends to believe in one paradigm and ideological orientation more than others. This belief can be of a 'fundamentalist' kind or combined with an open attitude in relation to other theoretical perspectives and ideologies. In the latter case of a pluralistic attitude, there is a willingness to listen and learn from advocates of other perspectives.

The opposite of pluralism is monism. In natural science, there is a tendency to believe in one paradigm at a time and then consider the possibility of paradigm-shift in a Kuhnian sense (Kuhn 1970). One paradigm may be abandoned when another is found to be more compatible with the results of empirical experiments etc. Neoclassical economists tend to be 'monists' in this sense. But today even some natural scientists are open to a complementary role for different paradigms in understanding specific phenomena. Paradigms that are incompatible within the current state of knowledge may each contribute to the understanding of a phenomenon, for instance light. In the case of economics, which is our main interest here, 'paradigm co-existence' (Söderbaum 2000: 29–30) appears to be a much more relevant idea than 'paradigm-shift'. The mistake by neoclassical economists is not that they believe in neoclassical economics but rather that they believe in the exclusion of other paradigms. While excluding theoretical perspectives, they at the same time exclude ideological orientations (other than those connected with neoclassical economics) and thereby reduce the possibilities of a constructive dialogue in society.

Most people who follow or participate in the development dialogue globally, regionally or locally understand that mainstream ideas about progress in society are challenged by an increasing number of factors. Simplistic ideas about economic growth as the solution to every problem are no longer convincing (see Hamilton 2003). In relation to poverty, health and the environment, there are a number of unsustainable trends. And it is no longer possible to 'solve' problems in the home region; we all depend on each other at a global level. In this situation of difficult choices we cannot only rely on experts but need a broad dialogue based on ideas of a well functioning democracy.

The meaning of 'democracy' is a big subject and I will here only point to one aspect that appears to be crucial. Each actor in a democratic society may believe in one ideological orientation more than others but should respect the existence of other ideological orientations as long as they do not contradict democracy itself. In attempts to solve present problems, we need to be informed not only by experts in some scientific sense but also by clearly articulated ideological orientations. What is the meaning of Sustainable Development as an alternative to the previous emphasis on economic growth in GNP terms, for instance?

THE IDEOLOGY OF NEOCLASSICAL ECONOMICS

My previous statement that neoclassical economics is not only science but also ideology has to be elaborated a bit. While classical economists such as Adam Smith and David Ricardo always referred to 'political economics' in a broad sense, the neoclassical project starting around 1860 can be seen as an attempt to separate 'economics' from 'politics' and present a 'pure' economics. Following Myrdal, it is here argued that the belief in a value-free economics is an illusion and that the neoclassical project in this respect was a failure. It is now time to return to the 'political economics' vocabulary.

Neoclassical Economic Man assumptions are specific in ideological terms. Some roles and relationships are emphasized while others are excluded. Human beings are regarded as consumers and wage-earners, thereby limited to market relationships. The idea of utility maximization excludes other forms of ethics. Building on Political Economic Person (PEP) assumptions instead means that you do not deny the political and ideological aspect of human behaviour. Each individual is acting in many roles and guided by her 'ideological orientation'. This orientation may be built on utilitarianism, or alternatively on other kinds of social and environmental ethics. Economists have no right to select one ethics as the 'correct' one for purposes of economic analysis. Reference to 'ideological orientation' furthermore suggests that the neoclassical focus on commodities and markets may legitimize a kind of 'market ideology' and 'consumerism' that for many of us appears too limited, if not dangerous, to society. In relation to the current debate about Sustainable Development, something else is needed.

Neoclassical assumptions about profit-maximizing firms are similarly specific in ideological terms. As already argued, the focus on one kind of organization, that is, the firm, appears a bit strange in relation to the present dialogue about development and a well-functioning economy where many kinds of organizations are involved. Excluding Civil Society Organizations, like churches, universities, and public organizations at the national and municipal level, cannot easily be defended if one wishes to understand the functioning of an economy.

For business organizations (and other organizations), monetary performance is of course important but so is non-monetary performance. Environmental Management Systems are a case in point. Stakeholder models of business organizations suggest that rather than just maximization of profits, conflicts of interest and power relationships are also relevant. According to Political Economic Organization (PEO) assumptions, the organization is furthermore 'polycentric' in the sense that each individual connected with the organization is an actor with her specific ideological orientation, which to some extent may depart from that of the leadership of the organization. Such tensions are not only problematic in a negative sense but may as well be a source of learning and reconsideration of the 'core values' or 'business concept' of the organization.

Each individual (or organization) interacts over time with her context. In neoclassical theory, only a market context is taken into account. As part of institutional theory, a multifaceted context is considered which is social, cultural, institutional (markets included), physical, man-made and ecological. Behaviour is guided by ideological orientation and may be habitual or a result of conscious choice, that is, decision-making. In neoclassical microeconomics, decisions are based on some optimization principle (maximum utility or maximum profits) devoid of other ethical considerations. Institutional theory does not deny egoism. Any healthy individual will consider her own best interests. But the individual is at the same time part of a number of 'we-contexts', suggesting that the concern for others is a normal feature in her ideological orientation. Amitai Etzioni has proposed an 'I & We Paradigm' (Etzioni 1988) where egoistic tendencies and concern for others are combined rather than mutually exclusive. Decision-making as part of the institutional perspective is furthermore not exclusively understood as 'optimisation' but rather as a 'matching' process between the ideological orientation of each decision-maker and the expected impact profile of each alternative. In this way not only quantitative but also qualitative and visual aspects of impacts become relevant.

In neoclassical theory, 'markets' are presented in terms of the 'forces' of supply and demand. Contrary to this impersonal view, actors in the market place can be made more visible as part of an institutional perspective. Each market actor is guided by an ideological orientation (according to PEP and PEO assumptions). Fairness and other ethical aspects may be involved in the relationship between two market actors. Each actor may furthermore be part of different networks of cooperation and the relationship between two actors may be cooperative as well as competitive. In business actor-network theory, trust is furthermore an important factor (Ford, ed. 1990). Each market relationship has a history and each market actor is embedded in a social and institutional context (Söderbaum 2002).

In neoclassical theory, 'progress' is assumed to be a matter of GNP growth at the national level, increased profits for organizations and utility-maximization for individuals. The alternative here is an ideologically open attitude to progress at all levels. Some actors are concerned about present environmental, social and institutional problems in society and may, for example, refer to a specific definition of sustainable development as their idea of progress. At the levels of organizations and individuals there may similarly be many ideas of progress rather than one. Monetary and material aspects may be important but how they relate to non-monetary dimensions and ethical considerations has to be the subject of study rather than being veiled over.

CBA AND DEMOCRACY AS A CASE

Neoclassical economists claim to offer clear ideas about 'efficient resource allocation' in the economy. Reference is made to 'welfare theory' and 'applied welfare economics'. The practical instrument or method used is Cost-Benefit Analysis (CBA). Just as the firm considers monetary costs and revenues in attempts to estimate profits from alternative investments, a similar approach is advocated at the national level, that is for society as a whole. What are the costs and benefits in monetary terms of alternative investments in infrastructure such as roads, airports, dams etc.? Not only constructions costs, maintenance cost and benefits directly associated with the project are identified, but also all impacts affecting economic subjects in a nation. The market 'value' of single impacts is estimated with reference to existing markets, prices in comparable real markets or through fictitious markets, using the 'willingness-to-pay' approach. All costs and benefits connected with a project are then aggregated in monetary terms to a 'present value' or 'benefit-cost ratio'.

The claim that neoclassical economics has a clear idea about correct resource allocation as demonstrated in CBA analyses are correct. But this is at the same time a problem. 'Ideology' was previously defined as a means-ends philosophy and 'ideological orientation' was suggested as a guiding principle for different actors. CBA claims to rank mutually exclusive investment proposals. It builds on a specific idea of what is good and best for society in different decision situations and therefore qualifies as an ideology. As ideology, CBA is more precise than most other ideologies. Among all ideologies, CBA is a market ideology of a very specific kind. It is based on the belief that society should be understood in market terms and other frames of reference of a conceptual or ethical kind are thereby automatically excluded. As market ideology, CBA is close to the 'economic growth' ideology (Johansen 1977), an ideology that – as we all know – is not uncontroversial. Should science dictate the correct ideology for politicians, citizens and actors of different kinds? The answer is no. Some other role for science is called for.

What then are the alternatives to CBA? While CBA is a 'highly aggregated' approach one can think of 'highly disaggregated' approaches as alternatives (Table 1). CBA is also 'ideologically closed', whereas there are alternatives that are 'ideologically more open'. This means that there are four possible categories:

Table 1. **Categories of approaches to decision-making**

	Ideologically closed	Ideologically open
Highly aggregated	I	II
Highly disaggregated	III	IV

It is clear that CBA belongs to category I (highly aggregated, ideologically closed). Ezra Mishan, himself the author of a textbook on economics (1971), argues that CBA can only be used if there is a consensus in society about the approach to valuation and progress entailed in CBA (Mishan 1980). If there is no such consensus – and Mishan points especially to disagreements about how to value environmental impacts – the CBA method is no longer useful. If there is a diversity of ideological orientations in society, then CBA is no longer compatible with our ideas about democracy as previously indicated. In a democratic society, each citizen or actor is encouraged to form her own ideological orientation as long as it does not contradict democracy itself. This includes a right to have an opinion about what is good for society and how to relate different policy or project impacts to each other (Söderbaum 2001). The CBA ideology of trading-impacts set against each other in one-dimensional terms at 'correct' prices is just one among possibilities.

In its final report, the World Commission on Dams (2000) expressed scepticism about the use of CBA to legitimise the construction of large dams in various parts of the world. The issue of resettlement of thousands of individuals, in some cases tribal people who have been accustomed to a specific way of living and context, raises issues of ethics that cannot be solved by simplistic cost-benefit calculation. The World Commission on Dams pointed in the direction of Multicriteria approaches (MCA) that are more open-ended (Category II and IV in Table 1) but there are other possibilities as well, for instance Positional Analysis (PA). The latter approach (category IV in Table 1) starts with PEP assumptions, uses 'systems thinking' and 'positional thinking' with the purpose of 'illuminating' a decision situation in relation to different and possibly relevant ideological orientations (Söderbaum 2000).

CONCLUSIONS AND RECOMMENDATIONS FOR EDUCATION IN ECONOMICS

Today, there are many kinds of heterodox economics. Those of us who depart from the neoclassical mainstream do it in many cases for ideological reasons rather than scientific reasons in a narrow sense. We do not like the ideology of neoclassical economics and tend to regard the monopoly position of this specific ideology as an essential part of the problems faced in modern society.

Neoclassical economics is reasonably coherent in logical terms and may be useful for some purposes. While CBA belongs to the weakest elements of mainstream theory, other parts can be considered within the scope of a pluralistic attitude where the parallel existence to competing paradigms is accepted.

In this chapter, the 'political' aspect of economics has been stressed. As already mentioned, 'political economics' was the language used until 1870 when the ideas of a pure economics became dominant. This emphasis on ideology and the political aspects may appear strange to some students. But if ideology is involved and if various actors (such as trans-national corporations, for instance) play a political role in the economy, as I have argued, then this language has to be reintroduced in textbooks and courses in economics. The idea of Homo Politicus or a Political Economic Person has been supported in a number of articles recently (Jakubowski 1999, 2000, Faber *et al.* 2002, Siebenhüner 2000). A textbook on organizational theory discusses 'ideology' in one chapter and 'power' in another (Jackson and Carter 2000). I can understand if some professors and perhaps even students hesitate here, because the expert position of economists in an extreme sense is in danger if you admit that there is ideology in economics. On the other hand, this is a matter of being honest and it is quite possible that a different kind of expertness will restore the legitimacy of economics as a discipline in a democratic society.

Students of economics are normally acquainted with neoclassical theory but they too often know less about the history of economic ideas and about present alternatives to the neoclassical paradigm. Considering the present crisis for neoclassical economics, there are many good reasons to reintroduce courses about early economists and their ideas and to point to the tensions that have always existed between different schools of thought. Students should also have a chance to study institutional microeconomics, ecological economics and other alternative approaches. This means that professors of economics also have to broaden their competence. Present tendencies of conceptual and ideological closure have to be counteracted.

The importance of the 'models' we use in understanding individuals, organizations, decision-making, markets, progress and etc. has been stressed. Textbook writers are in a powerful position to influence future generations of economists and it is a difficult task to open up economics if one generation after another has become accustomed to only one idea of 'correct' economics. This argument about the role of 'models' or 'schemes of interpretation' at the same time furnishes reasons for optimism. While neoclassical economists tend to protect their monopoly in departments of economics, a lot happens in other arenas. Socio-economics, social economics, development economics, ecological economics, institutional economics, political economics, interdisciplinary economics – many labels are used to indicate the existence of alternatives.

'Models' of various phenomena play a role in an ongoing process of change. As part of neoclassical theory, individuals can be regarded as 'consumers' if you are in favour of a consumer society and see globalisation as an extension of market forces to make people happier in all parts of the world. If you instead want to emphasize the role of the individual as citizen (and indeed consider all roles, the one of being a consumer included) with democracy rather than markets as the main ideological priority, then some other form of understanding will follow.

An understanding of the ideological and political character of economics furthermore means that the future of economics is not exclusively a concern for professors and students at departments of economics. While university leaders and university professors are all responsible, politicians, professionals of all kinds and citizens can also contribute constructively. In relation to present environmental problems, and sustainability issues more generally, the European Union and national governments have a role. The present author recently participated in a workshop on 'Sustainability Economics' and 'international institutions for sustainability' at a respected German economics research institute (Deutsches Institut für Wirtschaftsforschung (DIW)). At a meeting with the World Council of Churches, the World Bank and the IMF in Geneva, I was similarly impressed by the position taken, roles played and documents produced by the representatives of churches.

I hope also that environmental organizations and civil society organizations will increasingly come to understand the role of neoclassical economics as a barrier to new thinking in the development dialogue. Behind the present activities of criticized institutions, such as the World Trade Organisation, the World Bank, the IMF and even in some respects the European Union, is a 'mental map' held by the influential actors which is very much connected with neoclassical economics. Only with a pluralistic attitude allowing for more than one paradigm will a better world be possible. A degree of competition rather than monopoly and protectionism seems to be good for society in a number of arenas, universities not excluded.

REFERENCES

Etzioni, Amitai (1988) *The Moral Dimension: Towards a New Economics*, New York: Free Press.

Faber M., T. Petersen and J. Schiller (2002) 'Homo oeconomicus and homo politicus in ecological economics', *Ecological Economics*, vol. 40: 323–33.

Ford, David (ed.) (1990) *Understanding Business Markets: Interaction, Relationships, Networks*, London: Academic Press.

Hamilton, Clive (2003) *Growth Fetish*, Australia: Allen & Unwin, Crows Nest.

Jackson, Norman and Pippa Carter (2000) *Rethinking Organisational Behaviour*, London: Prentice Hall/ Pearson Education.

Jakubowski, Peter (1999) *Demokratische Umweltpolitik: Eine institutionenökonomische Analyse umweltpolitischer Zielfindung*, Frankfurt am Main: Peter Lang.

Jakubowski, Peter (2000) 'Political Economic Person contra Homo Oeconomicus. Mit PEP zu mehr Nachhaltigkeit', *List Forum für Wirtschafts-und Finanzpolitik*, Band 26, Heft 4: 299–310.

Johansen, Leif (1977) *Samfunnsökonomisk lönnsomhet: En dröfting av begrepets bakgrunn og innhold, Industriökonomisk Institutt*, Rapport Nr. 1, Oslo: Tanum-Norli.

Kuhn, Thomas S. (1970) *The Structure of Scientific Revolutions* (2nd edition), Chicago: University of Chicago Press.

Mishan, Ezra J. (1971) *Cost-benefit analysis*, London: Allen & Unwin.

Mishan, Ezra J. (1980) '*How valid are economic evaluations of allocative changes?*' Journal of Economic Issues, Vol.14, No. 1 (March): 143–63.

Myrdal, Gunnar (1978) '*Institutional Economics*', *Journal of Economic Issues*, Vol. 12, No. 4 (December): 771–83.

Siebenhüner, Bernd (2000) '*Homo sustinens–towards a conception of humans for the science of sustainability*', *Ecological Economics*, Vol. 32: 15–25.

Söderbaum, Peter (2000) *Ecological Economics: A Political Economics Approach to Environment and Development*, London: Earthscan.

Söderbaum, Peter (2001) '*Neoclassical Economics, Institutional Theory and Democracy: CBA and its Alternatives*', *Economic and Political Weekly* (Mumbai, India), Vol. 36, No 21, 26 May: 1846–54.

Söderbaum, Peter (2002) '*Business Corporations, Markets and the Globalization of Environmental Problems*', in Havila, Virpi, Mats Forsgren and Håkan Håkansson (eds) Critical Perspectives on Internationalisation, Amsterdam: Pergamon, 179–200.

World Commission on Dams (WCD) (2000) *Dams and Development: A New Framework for Decision-Making* (The Report by the World Commission on Dams), London: Earthscan.

16
The 'Efficiency' Illusion

Richard Wolff

UNIVERSITY OF MASSACHUSETTS, AMHERST, USA

Economists, like other people, get frustrated when different points of view yield clashing conclusions about something important. The frustration can escalate to real anger and conflict when, as often happens, disputing economists are just not persuaded by each others' evidence or reasoning. The disputed issues can be minor: for example, whether to allow a local roadway, factory, or school to expand. Larger social issues likewise divide economists: for example, whether to raise taxes on everyone equally or to graduate tax increases according to tax-payers' ability to pay (that is, according to their incomes and wealth). The great historical issues produce especially intense clashes among contending economists: which economic system better serves a people, capitalism or communism?

As frustration builds, all sides seek to find some way to win the argument, some mechanism that will finally persuade others or at least shut them up. When the larger issues are at stake, intervention from non-economists sometimes resolves the debate with or without any legal justification. For example, a government may kill, imprison, or simply intimidate economists into affirming its preferred position. Likewise, important social institutions do something similar: churches may denounce some points of view while celebrating others or universities may refuse to hire economists favoring one side of the argument and hire only proponents of the other side. Economists who 'win' in this way sometimes pretend that they did so because they had the 'better' case. However, decent economists prefer to win arguments without external intervention. They try to find some 'rational' way to settle frustrating contests between alternative economic arguments, perspectives, and analyses.

The 'rational' procedure most economists use today is an appeal to 'efficiency.' The idea is quite simple. Any disputed issue – a school expansion, a tax, an economic system – is assumed to have both good and bad consequences, usually called benefits and costs. Economists who believe in efficiency propose to identify and measure the benefits and costs of any disputed act, policy, or institution. If the total benefits exceed the total costs of, say, a school expansion or a tax, then it is declared to be efficient. All argument should then stop. The issue is resolved. What has been shown to be 'efficient' is the 'best' for everyone. When economists argue over which is the better of two different acts, policies, or institutions, then a 'comparative efficiency test' resolves the dispute. For example, if capitalism is more efficient (has a greater excess of benefits over costs) than communism, then capitalism is the best economic system for everyone. Efficiency – measured by the difference between benefits and costs – should resolve all debates between economists divided on any issue. No external force needs to intervene in economists' disputes so long as everyone abides by the solution that efficiency dictates.

Economists who differ on issues great and small regularly undertake efficiency measurements to persuade others and win their arguments. In recent decades, efficiency studies have become a major industry. Colleges, universities, and business schools teach courses devoted to 'cost benefit analysis.' Economists sell such analyses to businesses, institutions, and governments. Profits for economic consultants offering efficiency measurements have soared. Everyone with a project opposed by others tries to win the struggle by showing the efficiency (or greater or greatest efficiency) of their project.

Opposing economists challenge each other's efficiency measurements. They accuse their opponents of overlooking significant costs and benefits or improperly measuring them. Most economists never question the very idea of efficiency. Yet, as this chapter will show, efficiency makes little sense and measuring it is impossible anyway. Efficiency turns out to be an illusion; it cannot reasonably decide any dispute. When economists appeal to efficiency, it is their frustration talking. Efficiency arguments only work with those who have never questioned or seen through the efficiency illusion.

THE CONCEPT OF EFFICIENCY

The concept of 'efficiency' holds that economic analysis can and should determine the net balance between the positives (total benefits) and negatives (total costs) that result from any economic act, policy, or institution. When benefits outweigh costs, efficiency is declared; the act, event, or institution is judged to be worthwhile economically for the entire community. When costs outweigh benefits, then the act, event, or institution is declared inefficient and thus contrary to the interests of the community. Disputes should cease because efficiency tests have resolved them.

Such 'efficiency' tests prevail in both micro- and macroeconomic analysis. The building of a factory extension may or may not be *micro*-efficient. An interest rate increase may or may not be *macro*-efficient. At the level of society as a whole, the institution of a 'free market' may or may not be efficient. Likewise in comparative economics, when two or more alternative acts, events or institutions are compared as to their efficiencies. The one with the greatest quantitative net balance of positive over negative aspects is designated the 'more/most efficient.'

This concept of efficiency assumes that an economist can actually identify all the consequences or effects of an economic act, event, or institution. For example, if the disputed issue is whether or not to expand the local hospital, an efficiency analysis must identify all the consequences of that expansion. Such consequences include changes in the number of doctors, nurses, and medical aides living in the local community; their demands for housing, offices, and recreation; the resulting changes in housing prices, rents, and shopping conditions; local traffic patterns near the hospital; the health of area residents; local tax revenues; the average income of local residents; the quality and quantity of toxic medical waste needing safe disposal; and much, much more. The efficiency economist needs to identify the consequences of the hospital expansion for the people whose homes and jobs were destroyed to make room for the expansion. Those consequences include the impact on their childrens' school performances and hence the skill levels they will eventually bring to their jobs; local political change resulting from the hospital expansion may shift which party and which political priorities govern City Hall and may effect the local economy. Since many consequences of a hospital expansion will last for years or only occur in the future, the efficiency economist will need to make guesses about future events.

The changes set in motion by the disputed hospital expansion are infinite in their number, variety, and timing (present and future). No economist or group of economists can identify them all. What efficiency analysis claims to do it cannot do. To declare nonetheless that the hospital expansion 'has been found to be efficient' is a pretense. So too is the opposite claim, that the expansion is 'inefficient.' Efficiency is an illusion.

Moreover, *identifying* all the consequences is only the efficiency economist's first task. The second task is to measure each consequence. That is, the economist must decide whether the consequence is good for the community (a benefit) or bad (a cost) and measure exactly how good or how bad. This is necessary since the efficiency calculation requires comparing the sum of all the good consequences against the sum of all the bad. To compare costs and benefits, the efficiency economist has to put a dollar value on each one. That spells more trouble, since many consequences are very difficult to value in dollars. How, for example, does one put a value on children's difficulties in school or on traffic congestion or, indeed, on most of the countless consequences of a hospital expansion? And the absurdity of even trying to do this is only underlined by the fact that, as noted, many consequences will not occur until the future. So the efficiency economist also must guess the future values of all the future consequences of hospital expansion.

The conclusion is as simple as it is arresting: efficiency analysis is an illusion. Economists cannot identify all the consequences of any act, event, or institution, and they cannot measure them all either. It is not possible. Economists make claims about efficiency – of a hospital expansion or a particular kind of tax or of capitalism versus communism – but logic demands that we reject their claims. No identification and measurement of all the consequences of anything have ever been achieved. Thus no claim of efficiency is or ever has been valid. Efficiency claims cannot reasonably resolve any dispute.

Still other reasons require us to reject the whole idea of efficiency. To see this, let us examine more closely what it means to say that an efficiency economist identifies and measures the consequences of some event. For example, consider a tax cut. An efficiency economist might begin by saying that one consequence of the cut is more spending by consumers and businesses. But here a problem immediately arises. Is it reasonable to assume that rising spending by consumers and businesses resulted from *only* the tax cut? What about all the other influences shaping spending after taxes were cut? After all, the incomes, expectations, politics, and culture shaping consumers and businesses also played their role. In other words, the changed spending by consumers and businesses resulted from countless other forces beside a tax cut. A change in spending cannot and does not measure the efficiency (benefits versus costs) of the tax cut alone. To insist that it does is to deny the effect on consumer and business spending of everything else happening in an economy beside a tax cut. Such insistence, like efficiency analysis itself, is illogical.

EFFICIENCY IN PRACTICE

After our examination dissolves the concept of efficiency into absurdity, we are still left with a question: why has efficiency remained so important in economics? Why do economists hang on to so illogical an idea?

In practice, economists are called upon to help support or defeat all sorts of planned actions, events, and institutions. For example, liberal economists tend to support all sorts of government interventions in the economy, while conservatives usually oppose them. Liberal economists usually show that government intervention is efficient (its benefits outweigh its costs); indeed, showing that is what earns them the name 'liberal.' Conservatives show the opposite. Let us consider how they do this.

The liberal efficiency economist begins by identifying 'consequences' of government intervention and measuring them in dollar terms. This requires proceeding as if each of these consequences resulted from the government intervention alone. Otherwise no efficiency analysis would be possible. Further, the liberal economist limits the list of identified consequences to a manageable number. Consequences that may not show up for years are ignored or else 'guesstimates' are concocted. Since including *all* the possible consequences would make their measurement a task of many lifetimes, in practice the liberal efficiency economist *always selects just a few consequences and measures them.* Among the subset of all consequences selected by the liberal, those that are negative – the costs – are summed and compared to the sum of the positive consequences–the benefits. If total benefits exceed total costs, the liberal happily concludes that government intervention is 'efficient.'

The conservative efficiency economist proceeds in the same basic way but to the opposite conclusion. Once again, the logical problem of attributing a consequence to *only* government intervention is swept under the rug. The conservative economist selects and measures some small subset of all the possible consequences of government intervention in the economy. If the total costs outweigh the total benefits, the conservative declares that government intervention is inefficient.

Liberal and conservative politicians, newspapers, and television companies then use these results to promote their respective agendas. Each side insists that efficiency lies on their side and points to their economists' studies as proof. The entire exercise resembles nothing so much as medieval disputes between opponents who each claimed God to be on their side.

THE RELATIVITY OF EFFICIENCY

Every claim of efficiency depends on which subset (particular few) of all possible consequences were selected for identification and measurement by the economist making the claim. No economist or group of economists could ever have identified and measured them all. The liberal economist usually selects a different set of consequences from that selected by the conservative. Given the huge number of possible consequences, it is hardly surprising that opposed economists would select a different few from so many. The liberal economist usually also measures consequences differently from how a conservative economist evaluates them. Recalling the great difficulty of measurement and the guesstimates about the future unavoidably involved, it is easy to see how measurements would differ. In any case, liberal and conservative economists reach different efficiency conclusions *about the same act, event, or institution* because they select different sets of consequences and/or measure their selected sets differently.

This means that all efficiency claims are relative to the selected consequences and kinds of measurements made. No efficiency claim is absolute. That is, no efficiency claim can be or ever has been based on a complete or comprehensive identification of all consequences. Nor has any system of measurement (including guesstimates of the future) ever won everyone's agreement. Beauty lies in the eye of the beholder, and efficiency lies in the eye of the economist. 'Efficient' – like 'beautiful' – is one way of expressing a positive opinion and nothing more.

A few self-aware efficiency economists admit that they identify and measure only a few consequences of any act, event, or institution to reach their conclusions. They defend their practice on the grounds that the few consequences they select are 'the most important consequences' and that because all the others are far less important, they may safely be neglected in order to reach an efficiency conclusion that everyone should accept. Logic dissolves that argument too. In order to know that the few consequences any economist selects are 'the most important' it would be necessary to identify all consequences and measure all of them. Otherwise, one could not know that those not selected are 'less important' than those that were. In other words, only by identifying and measuring all consequences – which cannot and has not ever been done for any act, event, or institution – can anyone prove that a selected few are the 'most important.'

WHAT LIES BEHIND EFFICIENCY

The illusion of efficiency allows economists to imagine that their disputes are resolvable into a unanimity. Some universally right way for everyone is just around the corner. Proper cost-benefit analyses will reach conclusions valid for everyone (or at least for every 'reasonable' person). Economists cling to the illusion of efficiency by blinding themselves to efficiency's evident logical absurdities.

Our analysis has shown that efficiency claims are moments in struggles between opposing economists (and those who use the economists' claims). Each side seeks to use a claim of efficiency as a way to assert that its particular, partisan goals are really the absolute best for everyone. Each side hopes that the other side(s) will collapse and disappear under the weight of that claim. Those who allow an opponent's claim of efficiency to decide a conflict have been defeated by an illusion. The defeat may be real; the efficiency claim is not. For an economist to accept and practice efficiency economics – to believe in, teach, or perform cost-benefit analysis – is to sustain an illusion that keeps people from recognizing and pursuing their often different and clashing goals and interests.

Economics has always been a terrain on which basically different values, projects, and dreams contest. The contest can be open with alternative perspectives freely able to make their arguments and seek to persuade majorities. Or, one perspective can seek to stifle and repress this contest of differences by disseminating the illusion that some universal 'best' solution exists that everyone must accept. Efficiency economics is one such illusion. The efficiency illusion does not serve the interests of economics as a branch of human thought rich in diversity. It is inconsistent with a democracy based on open discussion of differences in the interest of social progress.

Considering its logical flaws and the dubious contribution it makes to social life, efficiency is a concept long overdue for a well-deserved rejection. It is no compliment to the sophistication of modern economics that it finds this rejection so difficult.

17
'There Are None So Blind...'

SUSAN F. FEINER

DIRECTOR OF WOMEN'S STUDIES & ASSOCIATE PROFESSOR OF ECONOMICS
UNIVERSITY OF SOUTHERN MAINE
PORTLAND, MAINE

INTRODUCTION

Every year, a seemingly endless array of New! Improved! texts parade across our desks, each with its inevitable supporting cast of test banks, overheads, study guides, power points, web sites, and instructors' manuals. But beneath the glamour and the glitter lies a disturbing sameness, a homogeneity that simultaneously produces and reflects both the intellectual commitments of the mainstream paradigm, as well as the lack of diversity in the profession itself.[1] A series of articles published in the 1980s and 1990s revealed the extent to which introductory economics textbooks reproduced stereotypes, failed to consider the range of explanations for differences in economic outcomes by race, gender, and ethnicity, and presented warmed-over Social Darwinism as the 'scientific' pursuit of Truth.[2] It is depressing, but not surprising, to find that standard economics continues to explain the disadvantages correlated with race and gender in terms of the self-congratulatory rationalizations of the Victorian bourgeoisie. Feminist, anti-racist scholars in economics have demonstrated the close connection between contemporary mainstream economics, and the racist and sexist assumptions of Victorian social science. Why then do contemporary economics textbooks continue to reproduce these ideologies?

In earlier discussions of introductory economics textbooks, I analyzed large samples of texts and authors to demonstrate the pervasiveness of racial and sexual biases. I will not repeat that exercise here. Old wine. Old bottles. Instead, I will focus on two texts that bracket the market to show that the practice of mainstream economics necessarily erases the very problems that concern those of us interested in questions of racial, ethnic, and gender equality.

One is hard-pressed to find an economist more committed to mainstream economics than Professor Gregory Mankiw of Harvard University and chair of the Council of Economic Advisors for G. W. Bush. Mankiw, an ardent defender of free markets and free trade, recently reported the unalloyed benefits to the United States of shipping employment overseas. His report triggered a response among Congressional Republicans, some of whom have joined Senate Democrats in the call for his resignation.[3] In contrast, Professor David Colander dedicates his text to Thorstein Veblen,[4] and the well-known radical supplements *Real World Micro*, and *Real World Macro* are cross-referenced to his introductory text.[5] Early on, Colander stresses the economic importance of 'social institutions, such as the family' (14) Elsewhere Colander advocates including issues like race and gender in introductory courses.[6]

Given these indicators of a significant difference in outlook on economics, the near identity of these authors' approach to questions relating to the subordinate economic status of women, people of color, ethnic minorities, gays, and lesbians might seem surprising. Given, however, the theoretical operation of the mainstream paradigm in economics, this is to be expected.

It is important to understand the pedagogical role of textbooks. They are not supposed to push the boundaries of a paradigm nor should they expose students to the unsettled questions or heated debates in the discipline. Instead, textbooks aim to socialize students into the norms and practices of the field.[7] Thomas Kuhn, in his now famous *The Structure of Scientific Revolutions*, gives the *raison d'etre* for the existence of textbooks. 'Textbooks offer a window on "normal science," that is the set of received beliefs that form the foundation for the "educational initiation that prepares and licenses the student for professional practice"'.[8] The nature of the 'rigorous and rigid' preparation helps ensure that the received beliefs are fixed firmly in the student's mind. Scientists take great pains to defend the assumption that scientists know what the world is like. To this end 'normal science' will often suppress novelties that undermine its foundations. Research is therefore not about discovering the unknown, but rather 'a strenuous and devoted attempt to force nature into the conceptual boxes supplied by professional education'.[9]

Instruction in mainstream economics is 'normal science'. The stated purpose of virtually all introductory texts is to teach students to 'think like economists,' which in practice boils down to demonstrating over and over and over again that every aspect of human behavior – marriage, birth, sex, drug use, slavery, and suicide-can be reduced to two timeless, pre-given economic truths. First, every human action is self-interested (else it would not, by definition, occur) and since it is self-interested it must, by definition, make the actor better off. Second, even though we can't actually 'see' this rationality at work, economists attempt to demonstrate that human behavior always and everywhere reflects costs and benefits that can be accurately represented by supply and demand versions of the market.

Taken together these ensure the resulting opinion that markets are largely benevolent. While economists admit that society may, and often does, find market outcomes objectionable, they lament the fact that attempting to improve on market outcomes will almost inevitably make things worse. This 'tough love' approach to social problems, especially such enduring problems as poverty, racial discrimination, and gender inequality renders the policy-maker impotent in face of the power of the market. There is a huge literature (much of it summarized or referenced elsewhere in this volume) demonstrating the flawed logic of this approach. Yet Colander and Mankiw, like virtually all other textbook authors, are content in their ignorance.[10] One result is that the authors of economics textbooks are comfortable presenting explanations of the observed differences in economic outcomes by race, gender, and ethnicity that are not noticeably different from those that circulated in the nineteenth century.

As Susan Feiner and Drucilla Barker argue in *Liberating Economics: Feminist Perspectives on Families, Work, and Globalization*,[11] during the Victorian Era, in the emerging capitalist industrial societies, political, economic, and social pressure produced an ideology that defined women as subservient to men. This subordination rested on the belief that insurmountable differences separated the masculine from the feminine. Consequently, the Victorians imagined that radically different imperatives governed the lives of women and men. Men were *by nature* breadwinners and rule makers, while white women were *naturally* devoted to hearth and home, kith and kin. Laws, editorials, sermons, and scientific research, including that produced by economists, endorsed the view that any woman whose behavior even hinted at autonomous action in the worlds of commerce, politics, religion, or education risked her sanity, her femininity, her fertility, and her very life.[12]

In the same period, Rudyard Kipling coined the racist euphemism 'the white man's burden', which also expressed what seemed to be a self-evident truth about the *nature* of humans of various complexions. This phrase rationalized and apologized for the ruthless exploitation of the peoples of Asia, Africa, and the Americas that took place during the era of formal colonialism. Ideas of racial inferiority, like ideas about women's secondary status, were integral elements of Victorian ideology.[13] Thus, by the end of the nineteenth century, key cultural constructs of Western society included the view that the subordinate social status of women and people of color was *natural*, ordained in the heavens, and useful on earth.

Today many scholars, men as well as women, realize that when views such as these are at the foundation of a discipline's approach to its field of study, the knowledge that results is likely to be one-sided and biased against gender equity, racial/ethnic equality, and social justice. One does not need an advanced degree in textual analysis to show that this critical self-awareness has yet to influence economics. Just a few examples from the Colander and Mankiw texts will illustrate the extent to which these white, privileged (by education if not birth), middle-aged, heterosexual, married male professors at elite schools are unaware of the extent to which their economic narratives reflect their social locations.

TEXTBOOK REPRESENTATIONS OF GENDER, RACE, AND SEXUALITY

Any college sophomore with a B average could, if given the assignment, find the founding articles in feminist economics. Key among these would be Professor Lourdes Beneria's 1995 essay in which she summarizes the major feminist critiques of methodological individualism and market choice, and then shows how these concepts produce misogynist bias in analyses of economic development.[14] Beneria, like many feminists before and since, points out the many problems inherent in assuming harmonious households in which a benevolent (male) income earner makes altruistic decisions for all. The question of who (or what) comprises a household, let alone how households make decisions – an issue of great interest to a wide array of social scientists-is never raised by either Mankiw or Colander. This same student would discover articles by feminist, anti-racist economists like Barbara Bergmann, Robert Cherry, William Darity, Patrick Mason, Julie Nelson, Michelle Pujol, Diana Strassman and Rhonda Williams to name just a few. The questions raised in the *oeuvre* often concern key ontological concepts in economics. Yet both Mankiw and Colander work hard to paint the conceptual building-blocks of mainstream economics as objective, value-free, and scientific.

Feminist economists, like other heterodox economists, disagree. Researching the history of the discipline, feminists have demonstrated that the fundamental categories of economic analysis are not neutral with respect to existing patterns of sexual, racial, and ethnic subordination.[15] The concepts of, for example, rationality and scarcity, maximization and equilibrium, commodities and exploitation, embody historically specific visions of normative masculinity, femininity, whiteness, and heterosexual orientation that are particular to the West. Indeed, the establishment of Anglo-European world dominance depended upon the creation of new patterns of social hierarchy and the intensification of old patterns of domination. Feminist economists have shown how mainstream economics provided (and continues to provide) support for ideologies and policies that justify exploitative social relations fundamental to Western hegemony.

In a nutshell, Victorian visions of appropriate behavior by race, gender, class, and ethnicity continue to be the norm in economic *science*, and this plays out in textbooks in two ways. The usual and less titillating approach is to provide examples designed to prove that inequalities by race, gender, or class are warranted on efficiency grounds. This is Mankiw's *modus operandi*.

Thankfully Mankiw avoids provocative asides about sex, prostitution, slavery, and markets for babies. Instead discussions of income inequality, gender and race (precisely those issues that are most likely to produce critical questioning) are deferred until students have had the mantra 'markets *über alles*' drummed into their heads. In the chapter 'Earnings and Discrimination,' the discussion of the determinants of equilibrium wages includes eight topics, including 'ability, effort and chance' as well as 'the benefits of beauty.' A picture of Brad Pitt shows us that people differ in how 'attractive' and 'handsome' they are. Mankiw then discusses a study published in the *American Economic Review* that estimated 'returns to beauty.' Mankiw never raises the possibility that beauty is a social construct which varies across time, space and culture.[16]

Indeed, the short story 'Coming Apart' and the video *Beyond Killing Us Softly* show, power relations play a huge role in setting beauty standards.[17] Mankiw also neglects to discuss the role of the media in creating beauty standards. Are the preferences that draw large audiences to Brad Pitt's blonde hair and blue eyes truly exogenous, untainted by social norms? Is it a pure esthetic sensibility that produces the result that white supermodels outnumber supermodels who are African American, Hispanic, Native American, or Asian American by over three to one? The point is, as feminist and anti-racist economists have argued, the very factors that are correlated with above-average incomes are themselves the result of a history that has privileged whiteness, maleness, and heterosexuality. In what sense is it scientific to demonstrate that these are precisely the factors valorized by markets?

Mankiw's discussion of discrimination struggles to exonerate markets. He tells us that 'discrimination occurs long before the worker enters the labor market. In this case, the disease is political, even if the symptom is economic' (422). He illustrates this point by referring to research about the segregated streetcars of the Jim Crow south.[18] This research argues that streetcar owners were more interested in profits than in racial apartheid. This logic buttresses the claim that the profit motive inevitably leads to competitive pressure to reduce discrimination. Of course, Mankiw does not balance this presentation with even a passing reference to research by African American economists Professors Darity or Patrick Mason, published in equally prestigious economics journals, that discuss the many audit studies which invariably find that whites (male and female) have advantages over people of color in job application processes, interviews, and housing. This research also traces court awards to plaintiffs in discrimination cases: both the number of awards and the amount of awards has increased. As Darity argues, the conclusion that discrimination will be competed away cannot be inferred from the data, and in contrast the persistence of discrimination can be (and is) observed directly.[19]

The next chapter in Mankiw's book, 'Income Inequality and Poverty', has a similar goal: to demonstrate that the lioness' share of inequality follows directly from individual, self-interested choices. Mankiw begins with a very brief discussion of income inequality in the U.S. (which does not bother to disaggregate the data by race or gender) and then he presents a case study titled 'The Women's Movement and the Income Distribution'.[20] He makes the point that 'when evaluating any change in the distribution of income, policymakers must look at the reasons for that change before deciding whether it presents a problem for society.' Therefore, policymakers ought not try to reverse the recent trend toward more inequality because

> the women's movement has changed the behavior of the wives of high-income men. In the 1950s, a male executive or physician was likely to marry a woman who would stay at home and raise their children. Today, the wife of a male executive or physician is more likely to be an executive or physician herself. The result is that rich households have become even richer, a pattern that increases the inequality in family incomes.

There are at several important points missed in this presentation. First, there is no data showing the large and persistent gap in income between male and female executives, male and female physicians, male and female lawyers. The question of 'the mommy track' is not raised, nor are we asked to think about the consequences of divorce for women and children. Mankiw's sanguine picture also fails to ask, 'what about the kids?' As many feminists point out, a major employment barrier facing women involves the availability, reliability, price and quality of childcare. Typically, private solutions to this public problem involve employing low-income women – many of whom have young children of their own-to take care of the children of the privileged.[21]

For all I find to disagree with in the Mankiw text, at least his tone is serious, and some relevant professional research is cited (although as I've mentioned, his parochial choices are bothersome). This is not the case for Colander. Where Mankiw has half a chapter on discrimination, Colander has three (short) paragraphs. When Mankiw turns to questions of inequality, he discusses segregation, the women's movement, and discrimination in baseball. Colander's discussion of the 'Socioeconomic Dimensions of Income Inequality' is remarkable for its brevity. The section on 'income distribution according to socioeconomic characteristics' contains just five lines. Although the accompanying tables do break down income by occupation, sex, race, and age Colander provides no discussion of the causes of these different economic outcomes. And unlike Mankiw he fails to cite sources.

What impressions are reinforced in students when they read the following assessment of recent US policy changes concerning the demise of AFDC (Aid to Families with Dependent Children) and the establishment of TANF (Temporary Assistance to Needy Families)? 'The general feeling is that the law has significantly increased the incentives to get off and stay off welfare' (402). Even a cursory review of the literature on welfare reform will show that no such general feeling exists among scholars expert in anti-poverty policy.

Other than these brief mentions, much of what Colander chooses to include about gender and/or race come in the form of 'attention grabbers' in what he dubs his 'colloquial style'. He does not seem to have considered the possibility that for some students, these breezy asides may be either tasteless or offensive, and hence an obstacle to learning. For example, early on in the Colander text we encounter an argument that begins with these words: 'if our society allowed individuals to buy and sell babies.'[22] The next sentence completes the syllogism: 'The invisible hand would see to it that the quantity of babies supplied would equal the quantity of babies demanded at some price.' To add emphasis and draw even more attention to the example is the book's second photograph: a set of classified ads about adoption and pregnancy. Is this likely to get a student's attention? Probably. One must wonder what pedagogical purpose is served by including this example so early on.

Colander goes on to write 'Most people, including me, find the idea of selling babies repugnant. But why? It's the strength of social forces reinforced by political forces'. Surely there are other examples that could make the point that 'social and political forces are active in parts of your life…You cannot understand economics without understanding the limitations that political and social forces place on economic actions'. True enough. But as you turn the page the text's first highlighted box grabs the eye. Here, in an OVERSIZED, ALL CAPITALIZED FONT, printed in white (not the usual black) letters, 'Winston Churchill and Lady Astor' are offered as our first lesson in 'applying the tools' of economic analysis. Colander repeats a well-known salacious story. 'Churchill suggested that as a thought experiment Lady Astor ponder the following question: If a man were to promise her a huge amount of money-say a million pounds-for the privilege, would she sleep with him? Lady Astor did ponder the question for a while and finally answered, yes, she would, if the money were guaranteed. Churchill then asked her if she would sleep with him for five pounds. Her response was sharp: 'Of course not. What do you think I am-a prostitute?' This time Churchill won the battle of wits by answering, 'We have already established that fact; we are now simply negotiating about price'.

This vignette illustrates 'one moral' economists 'might' draw; 'economic incentives, if high enough, can have a powerful influence on behavior.' Wow. But so can non-economic incentives: 'most people feel it's wrong to sell sex for money, even if they would be willing to do so if the price were high enough'.

Is this an established fact or Colander's own prejudices trotted out as fact? When I shared this excerpt with a colleague who is an internationally recognized expert on prostitution she wrote: 'The thing I hate the most about the passage as quoted is the editorial note: "Churchill won the battle of wits." Not quite. Rather I'd just say he managed to expose the shame a woman faces when she sees her sexuality as her own and names a substantial price for access to it. If she's willing to commodify it at all then she must be the kind of woman who can be had cheap' (Chapkis to Feiner, February 18, 2004). Clearly perspective matters. As numerous feminist economists have pointed out, members of an interpretive community are most often blind to the fact that their own perspective is as situated as is every other perspective.[23] Colander's text corroborates this point.

After telling readers that, 'many social institutions, such as the family, have economic functions,' the author decides to illustrate the feedback between economic policy and institutional change with the following assertion of causality:

> In the 1960s the United States developed a variety of initiatives designed to eliminate poverty. These initiatives directed income to single parents with children, and assumed that family structure would be unchanged by these policies. But, family structure did not remain unchanged; it changed substantially, and very likely, these policies to eliminate poverty played a role in increasing the number of single-parent families. The result was a failure of the programs to eliminate poverty. [24]

In fact, U.S. anti-poverty initiatives of this form have existed since the 1930s. The above suggests that the rise of single parent households followed from the anti-poverty policies, rather than a rise in the divorce rate, and a growing willingness on the part of women to refuse to marry as the result of a pregnancy.

Toward the end of the book, in a section titled 'Inalienable Rights' is an example of a 'market outcome failure' that stopped me in my tracks. I reproduce it in whole.

> Nice guy wants to save his son who needs an operation that costs $300,000. He doesn't have that kind of money, but he knows that Slave Incorporated, a newly created company, has been offering $300,000 to the first person who agrees to become a slave for life. He enters into the contract, gets his money, and saves his son. Again, the market is working just as it is supposed to. There's no negative externality, and there's no information problem – Nice Guy knows what he is doing and Slave Inc. knows what it's doing. Both participants in the trade believe that it is making them better off.[25]

Discussions like these would be less jarring (and less offensive) if the author bothered to broach substantial discussions of gender and/or racial differences in economic outcomes. Unfortunately, the terms gender, race, discrimination, and segregation do not even appear in the index and a close reading of those sections of the text where such discussions would be likely to occur came up virtually empty.

A HELPFUL ALTERNATIVE

Neva Goodwin, Julie Nelson, Frank Ackerman, and Thomas Weisskopf are to be congratulated for producing a workable text for introductory economics that is far more than a 'kinder, gentler' repackaging of neoclassicism.[26] They have worked for the better part of a decade to put microeconomics 'in context,' by which they mean attending to the human relationships that are always and everywhere a part of economic activity but which are generally either defined out of 'the economic problem' or are forced into the supply and demand framework of rational choice. Goodwin *et al.* go to great lengths to include discussions of 'the core sector of households and communities' including the history of family structures and the role of the cult of domesticity in shaping our norms about who does what-the gender division of labor. They also discuss the 'public purpose sector of governments and non-profits' to avoid reducing all economic activity to the monetary calculus of profit and loss.

Another laudable difference between this text and all others is the attention to questions of sustainability and reproduction. In addition, the text has a remarkably clear discussion of the limitations of the concept of consumer sovereignty, the connection between advertising and consumerism, and the poverty of emphasizing consumables in the definition of wellbeing. Goodwin *et al.* explicitly discuss institutions, power, and history in virtually all chapters. And their final chapter 'Market Systems and Normative Claims' does an excellent job of demonstrating why intelligent, well-trained, thoughtful economists reject the neoclassical orthodoxy.

Do I agree with everything in this text? No. Do I recommend this text? Absolutely. For those of you interested in reading a highly accessible alternative to mainstream texts, this is a fine place to start. Even more importantly, this is the only text that will support you as you develop instructional strategies that are less mechanistic, and more nuanced. And finally this book, far more than any others, does not simply gloss over or ignore the substantive controversies in economics that are associated with race and gender. The model is presented carefully and correctly. But so are important dissenting points of view. Mainstream economists will find no humor in the irony: putting microeconomics in context means students are free to choose.

PART V

MISUSE OF MATHEMATICS AND STATISTICS

18

Can Mathematics Be Used Successfully in Economics?*

Donald Gillies

Professor of Philosophy of Science and Mathematics, King's College London

INTRODUCTION: THE SUCCESS OF MATHEMATICS IN PHYSICS

There is no doubt that mathematics has been extraordinarily successful in physics. Let us take a simple example, namely the calculation of the orbits of planets and comets. Using the mathematical system of mechanics introduced by Newton in 1687, astronomers were able, from some initial data and their theories, to use mathematics to calculate the paths of planets. Moreover their calculations agreed with observation to a very high degree of accuracy. Astronomers were able not just to calculate mathematically the rough orbits of the planets but were able to compute small perturbations. Sometimes Newtonian theory and the mathematical calculations based on it gave results which were slightly (very slightly) wrong. A famous example concerned the motion of the perihelion of the planet Mercury.[1] The motion of the perihelion of Mercury as observed differed from its motion as calculated using Newtonian theory by a small amount. Newcomb in 1898 gave the value of this discrepancy as 41.24' ± 2.09' per century; that is, less than an eightieth part of a degree per century. This is a tiny anomaly, and yet even this anomaly was eliminated by the general theory of relativity which Einstein introduced in 1915. Einstein's calculations using his new mathematics gave a value for the anomalous advance of the perihelion of Mercury as 42.89' per century – a figure well within the bounds set by Newcomb. Of course the successes of mathematics in physics are not limited to astronomy. The mathematics of quantum mechanics has produced equally striking results.

In his famous 1960 paper: 'The unreasonable effectiveness of mathematics in the natural sciences', Wigner poses the question of why mathematics has been so successful in the natural sciences – particularly in physics. There does appear to be something mysterious here which stands in need of explanation.

CAN THE SUCCESS OF MATHEMATICS IN PHYSICS BE REPEATED IN ECONOMICS?

Granted the extraordinary success of mathematics in physics, it is hardly surprising that attempts should have been made to apply mathematics in other areas. Indeed as early as the 1870s, attempts began to develop economics into a mathematical science modelled on physics. One of the pioneers here was the English economist W.S. Jevons,[2] who in his (1871) *The Theory of Political Economy*, wrote (p. 3):

> It is clear that Economics, if it is to be a science at all, must be a mathematical science... Many persons seem to think that the physical sciences form the proper sphere of mathematical method, and that the moral sciences demand some other method – I know not what. My theory of Economics, however, is purely mathematical in character... To me it seems that *our science must be mathematical, simply because it deals with quantities.*'

Jevons' point is that economics deals with money, prices etc., all of which are quantities, and so seem eminently suited to mathematical treatment. We could add that there is a large body of economic data which could be used to test out economic theories, just as astronomical data were used to test out Newtonian mechanics. At first sight then there seems to be a close analogy between physics and economics, and so a good hope of constructing a successful mathematical economics.

Of course not all economists have accepted Jevons' point of view. Perhaps the most famous work of economics in the twentieth century was Keynes' *General Theory* of 1936. Keynes was originally trained in mathematics, but he decided that the mathematical approach to economics was not correct, and generally refrained from using it in his 1936 book. It is true that the *General Theory* does contain a few pages of mathematics. Some of these are at the beginning of chapter 20, but Keynes prefaces them with the following footnote: 'Those who (rightly) dislike algebra will lose little by omitting the first section of this chapter' (Keynes 1973: 280).

While a little later he says:

Too large a proportion of recent 'mathematical' economics are merely concoctions, as imprecise as the initial assumptions they rest on, which allow the author to lose sight of the complexities and interdependencies of the real world in a maze of pretentious and unhelpful symbols. (298)

Despite Keynes' warnings, the last sixty or so years have seen a renewed attempt to develop economics into a mathematical science modelled on physics. Many brilliant mathematicians have worked on this project, and yet unfortunately the results have been hardly very impressive. To exemplify this I will briefly analyse two works of mathematical economics written by leading researchers in the field, namely Samuelson (1947) and Helpman and Krugman (1985).

Samuelson's *Foundations of Economic Analysis* is one of the classics of mathematical economics and has been widely used for teaching purposes in elite universities. Let us ask how it compares with classics of mathematical physics. As we have seen, the great success of mathematical physicists consisted in their being able to use mathematics to calculate from their theories results which could be compared to observational data and which were found to agree with observational data to an often amazingly high degree of accuracy. Now if mathematical economists are even to begin to emulate this success, the first step must be to use mathematics to calculate from their theories results which could be compared to observational data. The extraordinary thing is that Samuelson in his classic book *does not even take this first step*. The book consists, in the edition cited, of 439 pages almost all of them filled with mathematical formulas, but not even one result is derived which could be compared with observational data. Indeed there is no mention of observational data in the entire book. One has to conclude that this book, far from emulating the successes of mathematical physics, seems more like a work of pure mathematics which lacks any empirical content whatever.

Let us now turn to Helpman and Krugman's *Market Structure and Foreign Trade*. The authors are two of the most famous contemporary mathematical economists. Their book is a small improvement on Samuelson's in that out of the 266 pages of the edition cited, one page (173) is actually concerned with results which are obtainable form the general theory and can be compared with observational data. The authors say:

...we suggest the empirical hypothesis that on average the more similar countries are in per capita income, the larger the share of intra-industry trade in their bilateral trade volume. This hypothesis finds support in Loertscher and Wolter (1980) for the year 1978 and in Helpman (1984b) for all the seventies.' (Helpman and Krugman 1996: 173)

Note that this hypothesis is qualitative in character and only weakly supported by data. The authors go on to mention two similar empirical hypotheses on the same page. One cannot help wondering whether it was really necessary to develop 172 pages of complicated mathematics in order to explain a few qualitative results which are poorly supported by empirical evidence. Certainly the situation is very different from that in physics, where, as we have seen, an accuracy of the order of an eightieth part of a degree per century can be achieved in some cases.

This type of economics, characterised by mathematical modelling with little or no empirical content, is fairly common in contemporary research in the field. Indeed, it is the most prestigious part of economics. There are, however, other uses of mathematics in economics. Handling data inevitably involves the employment of numbers and statistics, and the use of mathematics to this extent is largely uncontroversial, except that there might be some argument as to how much statistical processing of economic data is desirable. The problems begin when higher level mathematical models such as those of Samuelson, Helpman and Krugman are developed. In physics such models have been very successful, but they have not proved to be successful in the same sense in economics. Why is there this difference between economics and physics? In the next three sections I will attempt to answer this question.

A SUGGESTED DIFFERENCE BETWEEN PHYSICS AND ECONOMICS

My suggestion is that there is a fundamental difference between physics and economics which could be put like this. The physical world appears on the surface to be qualitative, and yet underneath it obeys precise quantitative laws. That is why mathematics works in physics. Conversely economics appears to be mathematical on the surface, but underneath it is really qualitative. This is why attempts to create a successful mathematical economics have failed. I will deal with the cases of physics and economics in turn.

Let us consider how the behaviour of bodies moving in the air might present itself to a naïve observer. It would surely all seem highly irregular. Leaves flutter slowly to the ground, pebbles fall quickly, clouds float along, and smoke rises. Indeed the first physical theory designed to explain these phenomena (Aristotle's) was qualitative in nature. Galileo, however, was able to show that underlying all these qualitative differences, a single quantitative law was acting, and the differences were due to disturbing factors of various kinds. Thus the apparently qualitative phenomena turned out in reality to be governed by exact mathematical laws.

Let us now consider economics. In contrast to physics, economic phenomena do, as Jevons stressed in the quotation given earlier, appear at first to be numerical and hence mathematical. Thus goods have prices, firms have a market value, and each item in a firm's accounts is given an exact monetary value. Falling pebbles do not come with numbers attached, but stocks and shares and other products do have attached numbers. This would seem at first sight to make economics more suited to mathematics. However my claim is that this appearance is misleading because the numbers attached to economic phenomena are what I propose to call *operational numbers*. Whereas numbers in physics are estimates, which may be more or less accurate, of exact quantities which exist in reality, operational numbers do not correspond to any real quantities. They are a convenient, but sometimes misleading, way of summing up a complicated, qualitative situation. Moreover their values depend to a large extent on conventional decisions and procedures and are therefore arbitrary to a degree. Operational numbers are the numerical surface form of an underlying reality which is qualitative in character. This is essentially my answer to Jevons' claim that economics must be mathematical because it deals with quantities.

AN EXAMPLE OF OPERATIONAL NUMBERS: EXAM RESULTS AND DEGREE CLASSIFICATIONS

I will illustrate the concept of operational number with an example which will be familiar to all students, and then show that many of the salient features of this example apply to the phenomena with which economics deals. The example is that of marking examination papers and classifying degrees. I will take as a specific case a degree with which I have been involved, namely the philosophy and mathematics undergraduate degree at King's College London. The students taking this degree do a mixture of philosophy and mathematics courses, which are all assessed by examination. In the philosophy exams, the students are asked to write 3 essays in 3 hours on 3 topics chosen from a list of about 10 which cover the material of the course. The essays are then marked out of 100, and the total divided by 3 to give a mark out of 100 for the script as a whole. There are four grades: 70+ is a first, 60–69 an upper second, 50–59 a lower second, and 40–49 a third. Below 40 is a fail. Now the thing to note here is that giving a philosophy essay an exact mark out of 100 is a somewhat arbitrary procedure. Of course everyone might agree that some essays are brilliant, some sound but uninspiring, some pretty mediocre, and others positively bad. However to go from this to saying that one essay is worth 47 and another 63 is a rather big step. Nonetheless attempts have been made to introduce criteria so that the marking becomes less arbitrary. Each script is marked independently by two internal examiners, and, if these two examiners cannot agree through discussion, the issue is resolved by an external examiner. Although differences between the two internal examiners do indeed occur, it is perhaps more surprising that there is very often quite close agreement.

The undergraduate degree takes 3 years, and when it is completed the student will have taken a large number of exams for each of which he or she will have been awarded a mark. We now come to the next step which is that of giving the student a classification for the degree as a whole. This again will be first, upper second, lower second, third, or fail. To produce an overall classification, it is obviously necessary to combine all the examination marks using some formula. The simplest idea would be just to take an average of all the student's marks. However, rightly or wrongly, this simple formula is not adopted. There are two arguments against it. First of all, it is thought that the examinations in the third year should count more than those in the second year, and those in the second year more than those in the first year. Thus a weighting is introduced. Secondly it is thought to be unfair to a student that he or she should be brought down by a bad performance in one or two examinations, since these bad performances might have been due to an off day, or to an aversion to a particular subject or teacher. Thus, broadly speaking, the overall assessment is based on the best three quarters of the student's marks. However some account is taken of the remaining quarter of the student's marks.

It will be clear by now that the formula for combining a student's marks to give an overall degree classification must be quite complicated, and this is indeed the case. Moreover King's College London changed the formula for the undergraduate degree in philosophy and mathematics in the period 1999–2001. Previously a formula known as the A-score had been used, but this was phased out and replaced by another formula known as the I-score. The interesting point to note is that a student might get a particular classification, e.g. a first, for his or her degree as a whole on the basis of the A-score, but a different classification, e.g. an upper second, on the basis of the I-score.

All this makes it clear that marks on individual exams, or on degree programmes as a whole, are what I call operational numbers. Their values are produced by conventional procedures which contain much that is arbitrary. Despite this arbitrary character, operational numbers can be a useful shorthand for summing up some salient features of a complicated and qualitative reality. They can, however, mislead if they are taken as estimates of some exact quantity which really exists. I now want to show that some of the quantities with which economics deals are operational numbers in this sense. Indeed there are surprising parallels in some cases to the kinds of procedure which are adopted for assigning marks to exam papers and to degrees.

I propose to consider as my examples of operational numbers in economics, two items which appear on the balance sheets of very many companies these days, and which are always assigned an exact monetary value. These are *goodwill* and *brands*. The two are not wholly distinct, and could be treated together, though, for reasons which will become apparent as we go along, it is often convenient to treat them separately.

Let me start with an example. In 1988 the Swiss Food Corporation Nestlé made a bid for the English confectionery company Rowntree which produced well-known brands such as Polo, Kit-Kat and Quality Street. Eventually Nestlé acquired Rowntree at a price, 83 per cent of which was considered to be for the purchase of goodwill (Smith 1996: 91–3).[3] What does this mean? On purchasing Rowntree, Nestlé obtained a number of factories, buildings, land, stocks of raw materials etc. However items of this sort, which are fairly easily valued, amounted to less than 17 per cent of the price they paid. Rowntree produced various types of sweet such as the mint Polo, the chocolate bar Kit-Kat and the chocolate/toffee selection of Quality Street which were well-known and had loyal groups of consumers. Of course Nestlé could easily have produced a mint similar in shape and taste to Polo, but this would not have been regarded as an acceptable substitute by devoted Polo consumers. To reach this market, Nestlé had to acquire the right to produce 'real' Polos, and this was part of the goodwill for which they were paying such a large sum.

But how could Nestlé estimate the value of this goodwill in order to make their bid? There is no concealing the fact that they had to make a guess, which, though doubtless carefully considered, must at the same time have been highly arbitrary.

Suppose a company like Nestlé purchases a quantity of goodwill. This appears on the accounts as having been paid for, but what happens to that sum of money in later accounts? The answer, in 1996, was that there existed four different conventions for dealing with goodwill operating in different countries. These were (Smith, 1996, p. 159):

US and Canada	Amortise through Profit & Loss A/C – max 40 years
Australia	Amortise through Profit & Loss A/C – max 20 years
Germany	Amortise through Profit & Loss A/C – short period
UK	Immediate write off to reserves.

Let us start with the UK convention. The amount paid for the goodwill is simply deducted from the company's capital reserves. There are two problems with this. First, by reducing the company's capital, it inflates the return on capital, perhaps giving the impression that the company is more efficient than is really the case. Secondly the goodwill, though intangible, really is worth something and so it is not unreasonable that it should be included in some form in the company's assets.

The other three conventions all amortise the goodwill. They differ only in the length of time used for this amortisation. Amortisation was originally introduced for machinery. To take a simple example, let us suppose that a company buys for £100,000, a machine which will last for 10 years. It would seem sensible to deduct £10,000 each year from the value of the machine, so that it is considered as worth £90,000 in the second year, £80,000 in the third etc., and its value has fallen to zero by the time it needs replacing. While this makes perfect sense for a machine, what kind of sense does it make for goodwill? Even if we claim that it is reasonable to amortise goodwill, I can see no rational criterion for preferring one time period rather than another. Inevitably then the value attributed to goodwill in company accounts has to be an operational number established by rather arbitrary decisions and conventions.

Although brands such as Polo, Kit-Kat and Quality Street could reasonably be considered as part of goodwill, they are often valued separately. This is partly because companies such as Cadbury's want to value their own brands, whereas goodwill is often associated with purchasing other companies. Terry Smith gives a description of the method used to value brands, which I will briefly summarise. The first step is to evaluate so-called 'Brand Earnings' which is done as follows:

> Brand Earnings are calculated from the net profit minus profits from own label manufacture. This figure is then manipulated in two ways: firstly figures for the last x years are used and restated at present values, and then a weighted factor is applied to reflect the importance of each year's profits. Often they use the last three years with a weighting of 1/2 to the present year, 1/3 to last year and 1/6 to the year before that. (Smith 1996: 96)

Having obtained 'Brand Earnings', a multiple is then applied and this gives 'Brand Valuation'. To continue Smith's description:

> The multiple applied is derived from a mark given out of 100. The mark is based on the brand's strength in seven areas…each area…weighted in order of importance. These are: *Leadership… Market… Internationality… Trend… Investment…Protection.* Marks are also given for trade marks and patents…' (96–7)

The procedures adopted for brand evaluation are strangely reminiscent of those used for giving an overall evaluation of the worth of a candidate's degree, except that the conventions of degree evaluation seem rather less arbitrary.

Interestingly brand values are not amortised like goodwill. It is argued that this is unnecessary since brand values are maintained by advertising and sales promotion.

Once again it is quite clear that brand values like goodwill values are operational numbers.

It might be thought that I am arguing that the valuation of goodwill or brands is rather absurd and misguided. This is not, however, my opinion. Goodwill and brands do indeed have a value for a company and this value is often much greater than the value of more tangible items such as factories and equipment. It is perfectly reasonable, therefore, that this value should appear on a company's balance sheet. The mistake lies in misunderstanding the nature of the number representing the value of goodwill or of a brand. This number is a rough indication, formed in a somewhat arbitrary and conventional fashion, of a more complicated and qualitative underlying reality. As long as the number is understood in this way it is a useful tool, but the danger lies in taking the number more seriously and regarding it as an approximation to an exact mathematical quantity existing in reality, as would be the case for a similar number in physics.

This example is from the world of firms, but there are many similar ones in macroeconomics. The analysis of the pitfalls in evaluating GDP given by Vaury in his 2003 article is particularly striking. GDP is an excellent example of an operational number.

An important difference between operational numbers and numbers representing measurements in physics is that a thoughtless application of mathematical calculations to operational numbers can easily give results which no longer correspond in any way to reality. A simple example will illustrate what I mean. Consider a set of equations $a_1 = a_2, a_2 = a_3, ..., a_{n-1} = a_n$. Let us suppose that each of these holds within the limits of observational error. Applying a standard mathematical deduction we get $a_1 = a_n$. Yet for large n (say n = 100), $a_1 = a_n$ might be completely false. The invisible errors in each individual case might accumulate to produce a large divergence. This sort of problem can, of course, arise even in physics, but if some account is taken of experimental error, it can be handled in a way which does not cause too many problems. Operational numbers are, however, only rough guides to a more complicated qualitative situation. If we start performing elaborate mathematical calculations with them, the results can all too easily cease to bear any relation to reality. This is one important reason why we should be cautious about applying mathematics in economics, and why the project of creating a mathematical economics similar to physics is a dubious one.

WHAT ARE THE ALTERNATIVES TO MATHEMATICAL ECONOMICS?

But now the question arises: what are the alternatives to mathematical economics? If we eschew the use of mathematics in our economic theorizing, are we not condemning economics to a status of a subordinate subject of little intellectual worth? I do not think we are, because many branches of science have had striking discoveries and great achievements without the use of mathematics. Perhaps economics should model itself more on one of these branches of science than on physics.

A notable example of a huge advance in knowledge without the use of mathematics is afforded by medicine between 1860 and 1945. In 1860 there were no satisfactory theories to explain why the major diseases of the time (tuberculosis, cholera, pneumonia, diphtheria, puerperal fever, etc.) occurred. Surgery was extremely dangerous because a patient's wounds would frequently turn septic, often causing death. Again no one knew why. Yet between 1860 and 1900, Pasteur, Lister, Koch and others had developed the germ theory of disease, and it had been shown that sepsis in wounds and many of the major diseases were caused by bacteria. Indeed the bacterium responsible for each of a whole range of important diseases such as tuberculosis had been identified.

The all important germ theory of disease was a causal but not a mathematical theory. It claimed to identify the causes of a great many diseases and pathological conditions. Until the underlying cause had been found, attempts at prevention and cure had proved fruitless. Once the cause was known, however, prevention became immediately possible through antiseptic precautions. Cure proved harder since it was necessary to find a substance (an antibiotic) which would kill the bacteria in the patient without harming the patient. Most substances which killed bacteria injured the patient as well. Still, in the 1930s the sulphonamide drugs were discovered and in the 1940s penicillin. These achievements would have been unthinkable without it having previously been established that bacteria caused a large number of diseases.

Instead of taking theoretical physics as a model, economics might do better to take as its model medicine between 1860 and 1945. This means in effect adopting a causal rather than mathematical methodology, and trying to explain economic phenomena by looking for their causes rather than by constructing mathematical models.[4] This is hardly a new idea, since the full title of Adam Smith's book was: *An Inquiry into the Nature and Causes of the Wealth of Nations*. Perhaps economists in the last sixty or so years have been seduced by the lure of mathematics into abandoning an older and more fruitful approach.

If economics modelled itself on medicine, it would begin by identifying some problem in the shape of an undesirable economic phenomenon analogous to disease. Attempts would then be made to discover the causes of this phenomenon, and once these were known, they could be used as the basis of policies for putting things right. Keynes's work in economics follows this pattern. His problem was the economic stagnation and mass unemployment of the 1930s. He proposed a qualitative theory which claimed to have identified the principal causes of these undesirable phenomena, and then, on the basis of this theory, suggested policies which could be adopted to put matters right.[5] The specific problem with which Keynes was concerned may not be the main one for the advanced capitalist economies of today. However there are certainly a very large number of other serious problems affecting the world economy at present, and so therefore plenty of scope for applying a causal methodology similar to that of medicine in the attempt to solve them. Moreover medicine should not only combat disease but also promote health. Analogously, economists could study instances of economic success, and analyse their causes with a view to promoting economic success in other countries.

To sum up, then. The application of mathematics to economics has proved largely unsuccessful because it is based on a misleading analogy between economics and physics. Economics would do much better to model itself on another very successful area, namely medicine, and, like much of medicine, to adopt a qualitative causal methodology.

REFERENCES

Gillies, D.A. and Ietto-Gillies, G. (2001) 'Keynes's Notion of *Causa Causans* and its Application to the Globalisation Process', in Philip Arestis, Meghnad.

Desai and Sheila Dow (eds), *Methodology, Microeconomics and Keynes: Essays in Honour of Victoria Chick*, Volume Two, Routledge, 136–48.

Helpman, E. and Krugman, P.R. (1996) *Market Structure and Foreign Trade* [1985], Cambridge, Mass.: MIT Press.

Jevons, W.S. (1965) *The Theory of Political* Economy [1871], New York, Reprints of Economic Classics, Augustus M. Kelley.

Keynes, J. M. (1973) *The General Theory of Employment, Interest and Money* [1936], Volume VII of *The Collected Writings of John Maynard Keynes*, Cambridge: Cambridge University Press.

Pearl, J. (2000) *Causality: Models, Reasoning, and Inference*, Cambridge: Cambridge University Press.

Samuelson, P.A. (1963) *Foundations of Economic* Analysis [1947], Cambridge Mass.:Harvard University Press.

Schabas, M. (1990) *A World Ruled by Number: William Stanley Jevons and the Rise of Mathematical Economics*, Princeton, N.J.: Princeton University Press.

Smith, A. (1937) *An Inquiry into the Nature and Causes of the Wealth of* Nations [1776], New York: The Modern Library.

Smith, T. (1996) *Accounting for Growth: Stripping the Camouflage from Company Accounts*, 2nd Edition, London: Random House Business Books.

Vaury, O. (2003) 'Is GDP a good measure of economic progress?', *Post-Autistic Economics Review*, 20 (3), Article 3, http://www.btinternet.com/~pae_news/review/issue20.htm

Wigner, E.P. (1960) 'The Unreasonable Effectiveness of Mathematics in the Natural Sciences', *Communications on Pure and Applied Mathematics*, XIII: 1–14.

19

Can We Expect Anything From Game Theory?

BERNARD GUERRIEN

UNIVERSITÉ PARIS I, FRANCE

For somebody studying economics, game theory is quite mysterious: almost everywhere, allusions are made to it (for instance, in organisation theory, in labour theory, in international trade economics, in public economics, etc.), but one can obtain a B.A. (and, even, a masters) degree in economics without having followed a special course in this theory – and yet is it assumed to be so important and so full of promise. One can find in recent microeconomic textbooks-Varian and Schotter, for example – one or two chapters on game theory, but they limit themselves to some little stories (almost always the same: prisoners' dilemma, battle of sexes, entry deterrence, store chain paradox, centipede game) and a rough definition of the Nash equilibrium. Indeed, quite surprisingly, these examples seldom lead to clear conclusions or 'results'; on the contrary, they either present dilemmas or paradoxes, or they imply that Nash equilibria are solutions to certain problems.

As they are full of mathematical symbols, game theory books, or textbooks (as Osborne and Rubinstein's, or Fudenberg and Tirole), are very difficult to understand. All game theory presentations, advanced or not, have however a common feature: they *never* give concrete examples, with real data (coming from observed situations and facts). In the place of data, are figured other, more or less complicated stories, that are summarised either by a table (the 'strategic form' of the game), or by a 'tree', with branches and nodes (its 'extensive form'). These stories (almost) always centre on the same question: is there a rational way to make a decision when gains depend on this decision, but also on others' decisions? Indeed, there are a lot of situations where there is no simple answer – or no answer at all – to this question. This is why there are so many 'dilemmas' or 'paradoxes' among game theory stories. Game theory doesn't 'resolve' problems, concrete or not: it highlights the difficulty of characterizing rational behaviour. Ariel Rubinstein, a recognized game theorist, is totally right when he explains that 'game theory is a fascinating and abstract discussion, that is closer to philosophy than to the economic pages of the newspapers' (Rubinstein, 2001). It is for this reason that there are no undergraduate game theory courses: if students in economics are told, from the beginning, that there is often no clear answer to the question: 'what is a rational decision?', even in quite simple – but interdependent – situations, they will then be very sceptical when their professors (specially in microeconomy) tell them that they are going to study 'rational choices' and their consequences. Think of an economic cursus with students criticizing each 'solution' proposed because it doesn't 'really' result from rational behaviour.

GAMES AS STORIES

Game theory has been invented by mathematicians – it is often presented as a branch of mathematics. This is its principal source of prestige: aren't mathematics synonymous with rigour, and their results (theorems) indisputable? But it is also its main weakness: game theory models are always 'stories', like fables or parables, with no relation to real-life situations. When mathematics is used, all aspects of models must be translated into symbols (sets, functions, equations, etc.). But, as no situation in social life can be reduced in such a way, game theorists (as microeconomists) invent stories, called *games* – because they are like parlour games, where people are isolated from the real world, know almost everything about each other and about possible outcomes, and only have to respect imposed rules. If things are so, there can be precise calculations – such as determining the players' payoffs.

Game theory models are thus *all* of the same type; that is, they are *all* formed by three ingredients:

1. *Individuals*, called *players*, who want to maximize their payoffs (they are *rational*).
2. *Sets*, whose elements are called *strategies*. Each player has one set of strategies, and player i is supposed to choose one element s in his set of strategies, S_i ($i = 1, ..., n$, if there are n players).
3. *Rules*, that associate an *outcome* of the game with each *strategy profile* $(s_1, ... , s_i, ... , s_n)$, $s_i \in S_i$, $i = 1, ..., n$, and that assign payoffs to each outcome. Rules are often represented by *payoff functions*. If $g_i(\times)$ is the payoff function for player i, $g_i (s_1, ... , s_i, ... , s_n)$ gives his payoff when the profile of strategies is $(s_1, ... , s_i, ... , s_n)$.

Which strategies will players then choose? Before answering this question, it is necessary to be precise about what each player knows about others, and about the rules of the game (and thus, about payoffs in each outcome).

Game theorists assume, at least for a start, that there is *complete information*: everybody knows everything about everybody, including that they are rational (all this being *common knowledge*).[1]

It is very clear that *there is no real life situation which fulfils these conditions* (1, 2 and 3, plus complete information); it is why game theory models are only stories, without real data-like parlour games.

A FUNDAMENTAL POINT

All game theory models are formed by ingredients 1, 2 and 3 (differences in models come from differences in sets of strategies, in payoff functions and, sometimes, in players' information). When these conditions are fulfilled, players are supposed to choose *separately and simultaneously* one element of their strategy set, and then *the game is over*, the outcome corresponding to these choices (and, thus, players' payoffs) is determined. Assuming that choices are unique and made simultaneously is *fundamental* in game theory; without this assumption, outcomes will not be well defined. But, again, it is quite difficult- or impossible-to find real-life situations where such an assumption can be accepted. And, moreover, usual, or 'popular', presentations of game theory completely ignore this, especially when they explain that, thanks to game theory, it is possible to analyse 'strategic behaviour', 'conflict' or 'cooperation', with 'threats' and 'retaliations', and so on. How can this be possible when players decide – separately and simultaneously – once, and only once?

In fact, confusion proceeds here from two sources: first, game theorists have an interest in 'selling' their models, by insinuating that they can explain many aspects of real life (like 'strategic interactions', 'conflicts', etc.); the other source of confusion comes from the fact that it is possible to construct games fulfilling conditions 1, 2 and 3 with more than one move (sequential games and repeated games), but with simultaneous and unique choices. In this kind of game, strategies are 'lists of instructions', about actions chosen by players at each move (at each node of the game tree). Strategies are, thus, 'conditional', as they are of the kind: 'if I am in this situation, then I will do that; if I am in this other situation, then I will do that'; and so on.

Each player then chooses one list of instructions (a strategy) in his strategy set (whose elements are lists of instructions), all players doing the same, at the same time. When all lists of instructions are chosen, and known by everybody, players – or some kind of referee – determine what happens at each move ('a path in the game tree') and, thus, every player's payoff.

For instance, consider the prisoners' dilemma game, played twice. Each player's strategy set has then four elements, like: 'I won't implicate my colleague at the first move; at the second move, I will implicate him if he has implicated me at the first move but I won't implicate him if he has not implicated me at the first move', or: 'I implicate my colleague at the first move; at the second move, I implicate him again, whatever has he done at the first move'.

Intuition is here misleading: it seems natural to consider that, like in real life, players decide successively, at each move, after observing what has happened in the precedent moves (and then 'learning' from that). But game models don't proceed in this way, and we know why: players are supposed to choose simultaneously one, and only one, strategy (of the conditional type when there is more than one move). *This is not intuitive at all* and, again, there is no real-life situation of this type; for instance, it is impossible to find an example of an oligopoly, an entry with deterrence, or any kind of competition with threats, cooperation, etc. reduced to unique and simultaneous choices – even if textbooks, or books alluding to game theory 'analysis' and 'results', create confusion when they speak of 'dynamics' about game models with many moves. Indeed, these books never present clearly what we have called the fundamental point, i.e. unique and simultaneous choices. If they did so, a normal person would stop reading, as there is no interest (except for fun) to continue with such counterintuitive, and misleading, stories.

ABOUT GAMES 'SOLUTIONS'

Game theory is a collection of stories, that need to satisfy conditions 1, 2 and 3, and thus are irrelevant for real-life situations. But it is always possible to *create* situations such as those described in their stories, and then ask: which strategy will rational players choose in this or that situation ?

If there is a simple answer to this question, then it can be considered as 'the solution' of the game, the outcome predicted by the theory. This can happen if there is an outcome where players' payoffs are bigger than in all other outcomes. But this is a very specific case. Moreover, it is not interesting, as game theory is concerned with conflicts, where players disagree about the game's 'best outcome' (as they each get a bigger payoff with different outcomes).

Prisoners' dilemma is another case, or story, whose solution seems to be obvious... when, in fact, it isn't (it is a 'dilemma')! The story is described in figure 1: the first number in couples (*a,b*) gives player A's payoff, the second number B's payoff.

Figure 1

		B	
		don't implicate	*implicate*
A	*don't implicate*	(1, 1)	(–2, 2)
	implicate	(2, –2)	(–1, –1)

There seems to be an obvious 'solution' for this game, because the strategy 'implicate your colleague' dominates over the strategy 'don't implicate him' – you get greater payoffs if you 'implicate' than if you 'don't implicate', when the other implicates you (–1 > –2) or when he doesn't (2 > 1). If players A and B are rational, they must then both choose to 'implicate' their colleague...but then their payoffs are less than if they had both chosen to stay mute. 'Rational' choice doesn't lead to a 'rational' outcome.

The dilemma is somewhat more dramatic when the prisoners' dilemma is repeated n times (n being 'as big as one wants', but finite). The new game is a game with n moves (each move being described by figure 1) – strategies being then lists of instructions of the conditional type 'implicate (or don't) if ...'. Here too, there is an 'obvious' solution: 'implicate your colleague until the last move, whatever he has done before', as this strategy 'iteratively' dominates the others. Proof is given by *backward induction*: the last move situation is the same as in the 'one move' prisoners' dilemma: whatever has happened in the past, 'implicate' dominates 'don't implicate'. In the $n–1$ move, both players give the instruction 'implicate', as it dominates 'don't', and as they know that what they do then has no influence on the last move decision. The same happens in the $n–2$ move, and so on, until the first move.

Such a solution, apparently so logical, is in fact absurd: prisoners stay all the time in jail (payoff: $–n$) when they could be free (payoff: n)! Is this solution a 'prediction' of the theory – in a positive mood? Or is it the choice proposed by the theorist, in a normative mood? The answer is, of course, 'no' in both cases. Can the theorist predict any other outcome, that could then be considered as a 'solution' of the game? No, as choices depend on expectations: if a player doesn't implicate his colleague in certain moves (certain nodes of the game tree), it is because he expects that he will not be implicated by him. His list of instructions thus depends on his expectations about the list of instructions chosen by his colleague; and as these expectations can be of any form (they depend, among other things, on the opinion that both have of each other), precise predictions are not possible. The same can be said from the normative point of view.

GAMES SOLUTIONS AND RATIONALITY

The prisoners' dilemma played only once has a predictable outcome, because players have a dominant strategy. They both know that, and each expect that, the other will choose his dominant strategy. Consequently, they are even more convinced that they have to choose their own dominant strategy. It is easy to predict what the other's decision will be. But games where every player has a dominant strategy are of a very particular kind. In general, games have no dominant strategies, as in the game described in figure 2.

Figure 2

		a_1	a_2	a_3
			A	
	b_1	(2,2)	(1,6)	(4,1)
B	b_2	(3,3)	(1,2)	(1,0)
	b_3	(2,1)	(7,6)	(3,7)

Is there a solution for this (very simple) game, if by 'solution' we mean a specific outcome (a strategy profile) predicted by theory? No, because all outcomes can be the result of rational players' choices-game theorists say that all players' strategies are *rationalizable*. For instance, A is rational in choosing strategy a_1 if he expects that B will choose b_3; and B is rational in choosing b_3 if he expects that A will choose a_3; this last choice is rational if A expects that B will choose b_2 which is rational if B expects that A will choose a_1, and so on. Indeed, in this game, all strategies are 'rationalizable': there are reasons to choose each of them (actual choices depend on beliefs about others' choices). If 'rationalizability' is the only condition required for the solution of a game, then all outcomes of the game in figure 2 are solutions of this game and no precise prediction is possible (the only prediction is: anything can happen).

From the two very simple examples (or stories) described in figures 1 and 2, we can deduce two important lessons.

1. In general, assuming that players are rational doesn't imply a unique prediction.
2. When there is only one 'rationalizable' outcome, it may not be 'collectively rational', (as in repeated prisoner's dilemma).

Normally, we should stop here, as game theory is interested in determining rational people's 'decisions in interaction', and as, in general, assuming a player's rationality is insufficient to make predictions different than: 'anything, or almost, can happen'.

But game theorists don't do that: they want to publish papers, to get jobs as professors and, probably, they like to invent stories and discuss their 'solutions' or the 'dilemmas' that they can raise. Special attention is then given to particular outcomes, *Nash equilibria*, where expectations are as important as rationality.

NASH EQUILIBRIUM AS A RESULT OF CORRECT EXPECTATIONS

In the figure 2 example, there is a couple of strategies, $\{a_2, b_1\}$, different from other outcomes, in the sense that each player has 'correct' expectations: A chooses a_2 because he thinks that B will choose b_1, and B chooses b_1 because he thinks that A will choose a_2. A couple (or a profile) of strategies where players anticipate correctly what others will do is, by definition, a *Nash equilibrium*. As in a Nash equilibrium each player maximises his payoff, given others' choices, Nash equilibria satisfy in a certain way a rationality condition. But, as with the prisoners' dilemma (simple or repeated), 'individual rationality' doesn't imply 'social rationality': in our example, players' payoffs are bigger with $\{a_3, b_2\}$ than with $\{a_2, b_1\}$. It may then happen that Nash equilibria are not 'best outcomes', thus they cannot be considered as 'solutions' from a normative point of view.

But also, often, they cannot be justified from a positive point of view-that is, Nash equilibria cannot be considered as predictions of what (rational) players will do. This is obvious in repeated prisoners' dilemma (where there is only one Nash equilibrium: each player always implicates his colleague), especially if it is repeated many times (say, more than ten times). In the figure 2 example, it is possible to consider that $\{a_3, b_2\}$ is a prediction at least as good as $\{a_2, b_1\}$ (Nash equilibrium): a_3 is A's choice because he thinks that B is going to choose b_2 where payoffs are, 'in the mean', higher than those that can be obtained with b_1 and b_3 ; there is a risk, for A, that B will choose b_3, but even in this case his payoff is not inferior to that of equilibrium (indeed, $\{a_3, b_3\}$ is also not a bad prediction).

The Cournot duopoly model, one of game theorists' favourite models, gives another example where Nash equilibrium is a very bad prediction. In this model, each duopolist (player) only knows his own *reaction function*, which gives his product supply in response to the other duopolist's supply. As always in game theory, choices (here, supplies) are made *simultaneously* (like in all game models). What can be predicted about duopolists' choices? Nothing: as they don't know anything about the other's choice, the only thing that they can do is to choose randomly their supplies, i.e., anything can happen.

WHY NASH EQUILIBRIUM?

Game theorists, and people who speak about game theory, focus their attention on the Nash equilibrium. They try to see if it exists (in pure or mixed strategies), if it is unique, if it is 'robust' (not too sensitive to parameters' values), etc. But, they seldom answer the question: why give so much importance[1] to the Nash equilibrium? Indeed, the use of the word 'equilibrium' is quite misleading. In general, the idea of equilibrium is associated with that of process-equilibrium being the 'result', the 'outcome' of a process (its 'resting point'). But this is nonsense in game theory, because there are no processes at all, players' choices being, by assumption, unique (and simultaneous).

Cournot's model gives an example of how, often, game theorists and, always, textbooks justify the Nash equilibrium in the wrong way, as the 'solution' of a game. They sketch *both* reaction curves in the *same* figure, and then focus attention on the point where they intersect. Isn't this point the 'obvious' solution of the model? But in fact, the only way to present the model in a correct manner is to draw one figure with one duopolist's reaction curve (this is what this duopolist knows) and *another* figure with the other duopolist's reaction curve. Each duopolist then chooses one point on his reaction curve, and there is no reason that these points are 'precisely' the points where the two curves intersect (indeed, the probability that this happens is zero). It is then clear that the Nash (or Cournot) equilibrium *is not* a prediction of the model, and that there is *no* reason to give it such importance. Often, textbooks present the Cournot equilibrium as the result of a process: one duopolist makes an offer, at random; the other 'reacts' to this offer, and makes his own offer; in his turn, the first duopolist 'reacts' to this offer, and so on, until they reach the equilibrium (the point where reactions curve intersect). But this is nonsense, because rational duopolists will modify their reaction curves as the process goes on (as they notice that their competitor reacts to their offers), and thus the equilibrium (intersection point) changes during the process, as each of them observes how the other reacts (or plays) – equilibrium is 'path dependent', and thus indeterminate.

In summary: in most of their 'stories' (and, especially, in those of the 'imperfect competition' type, such as duopoly models), game theorists are unable to answer the question: why do you pay so much attention to Nash equilibria? They cannot justify, then, all the mathematics that they use in discussing the 'properties' of these specific outcomes (the only justification is that they are interesting, from a mathematical point of view).

GAME THEORY AND 'EXPERIMENTS'

Games, in game theory, are simple stories: they don't describe (even approximately) observed situations. But it is always possible to make 'experiments', asking people to 'play the game', as in parlour games. There have been many 'experiments' of this kind. What are their conclusions? That 'real' people, in flesh and blood, often don't react as the theory predicts (when it predicts anything). Even in the case of the simple prisoners' dilemma, not repeated, there is a minority of people who choose the strategy 'don't implicate', and it seems that they are not rational. When the game is repeated only two or three times, few people choose what seems to be the 'rational' strategy ('always implicate'). But the most famous example is the so-called 'ultimatum game': player A says to player B: 'Somebody will give me a cake only if you accept to share it with me. Now, I propose to give you x per cent of the cake. Do you accept?'

If B is rational, he must accept even if x is tiny (it is better to have something than nothing). If A is rational, and thinks that B is rational too, he will then propose an x near zero: in this case, there is a quite clear prediction. But 'experiments' don't confirm it: in general, people like B don't accept propositions if x is far from 50 per cent, and people like A don't propose a tiny x. Game theorists explain this by sense of equity: if people feel that the share is 'too unfair', they prefer to diminish their gains than to accept. Everybody agrees with them, but we can deduce that if this is true in a such simple situation, it must be true in a lot of real-life situations, where people live together, interact- and where payoffs are not only monetary. Indeed, almost all 'experiments' in game theory fail to confirm the predictions of the theory, even when these predictions are well defined: people don't act as they are supposed to do.

Recent game theory literature is full of another kind of 'experiment' in the so-called, and fashionable, 'evolutionary game theory'. The starting point of this theory is that people *don't choose*: each player is identified with a strategy (often, a conditional one). We are then at the opposite side of the starting point of game theory, which is to try to determine how rational people *choose* (or can choose) one of their (many) strategies.

It's amazing to see that game theorists – so proud of their 'rigour' – use the same words (game theory) to design completely different theories (even if they have some formal similarities). Indeed, in 'evolutionary game theory' each individual is reduced to a strategy, and there are 'tournaments' where strategies are confronted, two by two. Payoffs give a number of 'offspring', who are in their turn confronted in 'tournaments', and so on, until some kind of 'equilibrium', where some (or all) strategies 'survive', is reached.

Countless 'experiments' of this type can be made: only a computer and some imagination are needed! Strategies can be very sophisticated (including some kind of 'learning', decisions in each move depending on what happened before that move) or very simple. The theory doesn't predict anything; theorists only choose the strategies and rules of the 'tournament' that they will play (thanks to computers), and then comment on the 'results' obtained – whatever they are. Mathematicians can try to find which strategies are 'evolutionarily stable' in this or that 'tournament', and so on. But it remains to be proved that these new kinds of 'story' are of any interest-in biology as much as in social science.

MICROECONOMICS AS A BRANCH OF GAME THEORY

Microeconomic textbooks are, like those in game theory, full of little stories with fictitious households and fictitious firms, which interact in fictitious markets – and with no data (when there are some, they are irrelevant, because they are of the aggregate kind). Indeed, microeconomics must be considered as a branch of game theory as its purpose is to study the interactions of rational agents' decisions. Game theorists are, however, more rigorous than current microeconomists, as they give more importance to the rules of the game than to the players' 'tastes' or 'psychology'. When microeconomists speak of 'price mechanisms', 'market forces', 'flexibility', etc., the game theorist asks: 'what do you mean by that? Please, say exactly what the strategic set of each player is, what kind of information they have, how they interact, etc.'

Take microeconomics' preferred model: perfect competition. One of its most important assumptions is that households and firms are 'price takers'; their strategic sets are then bundles of goods. A game theorist asks: 'who sets prices ?', and microeconomists have to recognize that it is (implicitly) supposed that there is 'somebody' setting prices, and that these prices are known, and accepted, by households and firms. The game theorist would pursue by saying: 'OK, but now you have to be precise about the payoffs of this "person"'. The microeconomist (for example, Arrow and Debreu) says: 'Well, it is a benevolent person whose only "satisfaction" is to make as low as possible the value of other agents' total excess demand.' The game is then well defined: households and firms announce bundles of goods, anticipating their prices; the price setter announces a price vector, anticipating (total) goods' excess demand, each one wanting to get a maximum payoff. If, after (simultaneous) announcements, agents notice that they have correctly anticipated other's choices, then there is equilibrium. You can call this (Nash) equilibrium 'competitive' – even if it is not clear at all where there is 'competition' in those simultaneous, and unique, announcements – but it obviously supposes a quite curious institutional arrangement (the game's 'rules') and, incidentally, its probability as an outcome of players' choices is zero (how can anyone predict exactly another's choices, knowing nothing about them?).

CONCLUSION

When somebody speaks of game theory and its 'results', or 'insights', first ask: 'could you please give me a real-life situation with observed facts and data that can be described as a game, in game theory's sense?'. If the answer that you are given is of the kind: theory always simplifies, it tries to explain 'stylized facts', to understand what rational choices can be in different kinds of situations (catching some important aspects of real life), then ask: 'OK, but then, can you tell me what are the predictions of game theory, its proposed "solutions"?' If your interlocutor replies: 'well, the first thing to do is to see if there is (at least) a Nash equilibrium', then insist: 'Do you mean that a Nash equilibrium is the prediction of the model, the result of players' rational choices, or its "solution"?', and wait for the answer... If it doesn't come, or if it is confused, then close your eyes and your ears, and refuse all the figures and maths regarding the 'properties' of Nash equilibria, and so on.

REFERENCES

Guerrien B. (1997), *Dictionnaire d'analyse économique: microéconomique, macroéconomie, théorie des jeux*, Paris: La Découverte.

Guerrien B., This I. (1998), *Les mathématiques de la microéconomie*, Paris: Economica.

Guerrien B. (1999), *La théorie économique néo-classique: tome 1 Microéconomie*, Paris: La Découverte. Paris.

Guerrien B. (2002), *La théorie des jeux*, Paris: Economica.

Fischer F.M. (1989) 'Game economists play: a non cooperative view', *Rand Journal of Economics*, 22, no.1.

Kreps D. (1991) *Game Theory and Economic Modelling*, Oxford: Oxford University Press.

Rubinstein A. (1991) 'Comments on the Interpretation of Game Theory', *Econometrica*, 50.

Rubinstein A. (1999) 'Experience from a Course in Game Theory: Pre- and Post-Class Problem Sets as a Didactic Device', *Games and Economic Behavior*, 28, 155–70.

Rubinstein A. (2001) 'A Theorist's View of Experiments', *European Economic Review*, p. 216.

20

Improbable, Incorrect or Impossible: the Persuasive but Flawed Mathematics of Microeconomics

STEVE KEEN

UNIVERSITY OF WESTERN SYDNEY, AUSTRALIA

The most distinctive feature of economics as a social science is its use of mathematics. Ever since Walras began the program of recasting economics as a mathematical discipline, attitudes to mathematics have defined both its proponents and its detractors. Detractors dispute the feasibility of expressing economic processes in mathematical form, while proponents are dismissive of those whom they believe do not practice mathematics because they do not understand it. As is so often the case, the one who first put this perspective forward also put it best:

> As for those economists who do not know any mathematics, who do not even know what is meant by mathematics and yet have taken the stand that mathematics cannot possibly serve to elucidate economic principles, let them go their way repeating that 'human liberty will never allow itself to be cast into equations' or that 'mathematics ignores frictions which are everything in social science' and other equally forceful and flowery phrases. They can never prevent the theory of the determination of prices under free competition from becoming a mathematical theory. Hence, they will always have to face the alternative either of steering clear of this discipline and consequently elaborating a theory of applied economics without recourse to a theory of pure economics or of tackling the problems of pure economics without the necessary equipment, thus producing not only very bad pure economics but also very bad mathematics. (Walras 1900 [1954]: 47)

The bad economics and bad mathematics has come from Walras and his successors – whom these days we call neoclassical economists – for four main reasons. Firstly, far from using mathematics to analyse the economy, they tried to use mathematics to reach preconceived conclusions. Secondly, they used the wrong types of mathematics. Thirdly, they failed to realise the inherent limitations of mathematics. Fourthly, they made outright mathematical errors which persist in economic analysis and tuition to this day.

Let's take those in reverse order – and if you're an undergraduate economics student who believes that economics is internally consistent, prepare for a shock or two.

MATHEMATICAL ERRORS: DOWNWARD-SLOPING DEMAND CURVES

'While the market demand curve is negatively sloped, the demand curve facing the individual competitive firm is horizontal. Therefore for the competitive firm, marginal revenue is equal to the market price.'

This mantra is a key part of the theory of the firm, and its import is deeper than most economists realise. Without this proposition, a supply curve can't be derived, and supply and demand analysis itself becomes impossible.

Well goodbye supply and demand analysis, because this proposition is mathematically false. Worse, it has been known to be so since at least 1957, when the influential neoclassical economist George Stigler published 'Perfect competition, historically considered' in the leading journal *The Journal of Political Economy*. It took him just one line of calculus to demolish it:

$$\frac{dp}{dq} = \frac{dp}{dQ} \cdot \frac{dQ}{dq} = \frac{dp}{dQ} \tag{1}$$

If that went by you a bit fast, try the English version. This application of the 'Chain Rule', one of the simplest rules in mathematics, translates as 'the slope of the demand curve facing the individual firm equals the slope of the market demand curve, multiplied by how much market output changes given a change in output by a single firm'. Since we're dealing with competitive, non-colluding firms, a change in output by one firm doesn't elicit any reaction by other firms.[1] Therefore the quantity 'how much market output changes given a change in output by a single firm' is one. As a result, the slope of the individual firm's demand curve is exactly the same as the slope of the market demand curve.

The graphical intuition is shown in Figure 1, which shows a market demand curve for an industry with a large number of firms. The overall movement from Q_1 to Q_2 involves a change of $\triangle Q$ in output and $\triangle P$ in price, consisting of changes in the output of each firm of δq that cause a corresponding change of price by δP. The slope of any tiny line segment $\frac{\delta P}{\delta q}$ is equivalent to the slope of the overall section $\frac{\Delta P}{\Delta Q}$. Thus the individual competitive firm's demand curve has exactly the same negative slope as the market demand curve.

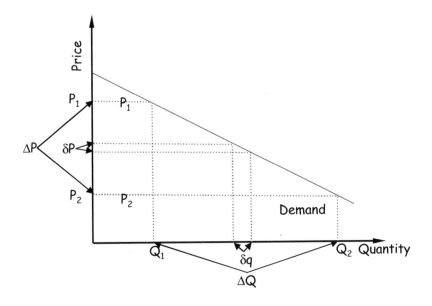

Figure 1: Slope of firm's demand curve is identical to market demand curve

    The 'horizontal firm's demand curve' that adorns so many undergraduate textbooks is thus a travesty of mathematics. Nor can it be 'waved away', as most neoclassical economists try to do, with assertions that the competitive firm is so small compared to the market that it acts 'as if' it faces a horizontal demand curve. If so, then competitive firms are not profit maximisers but profit 'satisficers', and the rest of the theory has to fall apart. Other neoclassicals justify the assumption that the firm's demand curve is horizontal by pointing out that the elasticity of demand for a competitive firm $\left(e = \frac{P}{q} \cdot \frac{dq}{dP} \right)$ is so much larger than the elasticity of demand for the market as a whole $\left(E = \frac{P}{Q} \cdot \frac{dQ}{dP} \right)$ Sure, but this is a red herring. It has nothing to do with the relative slopes of the demand curves (which are identical), but is simply an artefact of the ratio between total industry output (Q) and the output of a single firm (q): $e/E = Q/q$.

    So why do economists persist with a mathematically false model? For the vast majority, the reason is ignorance. Since the texts from which they studied don't mention Stigler's result, they aren't aware that a mathematical error forms a key part of their reasoning. They then continue teaching an error without being aware that they are doing it (have some fun in your next class: find out whether your teacher is aware of Stigler's analysis).

A minority persist because they think that, as well as pointing out an error, Stigler also provided a solution: that though it was strictly false that marginal revenue equals price for the competitive firms, it was approximately true since marginal revenue approaches price as the number of firms increases. Stigler got this result by assuming identical firms and introducing the number of firms (n) and the market elasticity of demand E into the expression for marginal revenue:

$$MR_i(q_i) = P + q_i \cdot \frac{dP}{dQ} = P + \frac{P}{n \cdot E} \tag{2}$$

He argued that 'this last term goes to zero as the number of sellers increases indefinitely' (Stigler 1957: 8), and the minority accept this as a reason to continue teaching a mathematically false proposition to undergraduates. The alternative of telling 'the whole truth' would be just too complicated in first year; let students find out for themselves later (if at all) when they're sufficiently trained in economics to cope with it.[1]

In fact, a solution like this can't eliminate a mathematical error: it simply causes the error to pop up elsewhere. And this relocated mathematical error has a surprising manifestation: the proposition that a firm maximises profits by equating marginal revenue and marginal cost is false.

If that sounds impossible, think about what constitutes a change in revenue for a firm in a multi-firm industry. The conventional formula implicitly assumes that only a change in the firm's output can change the firm's revenue. But with more than one firm in an industry, the ith firm's revenues can change because of the behaviour of the other firms. The ith firm's total revenue is a function not only of its own behavior, but also the behavior of all the other firms in the industry. The true expression for a change in total revenue is therefore not an ordinary differential, as in the conventional formula, but a partial differential. Defining Q_R as the output of the rest of the industry a $\left(Q_R = \sum_{j \neq i}^{n} q_j \right)$ change in revenue for the ith firm is properly defined as:

$$dTR_i (Q_R, q_i) = \left(\frac{\partial}{\partial Q_R} P(Q) \cdot q_i \right) dQ_R + \left(\frac{\partial}{\partial q_i} P(Q) \cdot q_i \right) dq_i \tag{3}$$

The accepted formula ignores the effect of the first term on the firm's profit.[1] When it is taken into account, the true profit-maximising formula turns out to be:

$$MR_i(q_i) - MC_i(q_i) = \frac{n-1}{n}(P(Q) - MC_i(q_i)) \qquad (4)$$

Have you ever noticed that, in conventional economics, everything happens

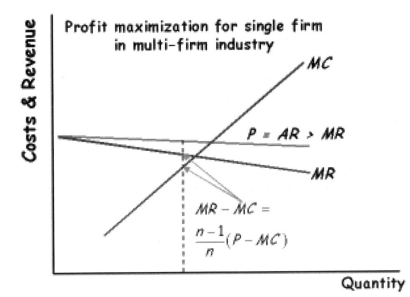

Figure 2: True Profit-Maximisation Level of Output

where two curves cross? This vision is a product of the equilibrium obsession that mars the mathematics economists use, but even on its own terms, it can be wrong – as it is here. As equation (4) shows, only a monopoly (where $n=1$) maximises profits by equating marginal cost and marginal revenue: firms in a multi-firm industry maximise profits by setting their marginal revenue to be *greater than* marginal cost, as illustrated by Figure 2.[1]

So much for the theory of the firm. But surely the theory of consumer behaviour makes sense, right? Don't people utility-maximise?

Not in this universe! The computational power people would need to behave the way economists theorise that they do exceeds not simply the capacity of humans or modern-day computers, but the capacity of the universe itself.

INHERENT LIMITS: UTILITY MAXIMIZATION AND THE REAL WORLD

The proposition that people choose what to consume in order to maximise their utility (given their incomes) sounds intuitively plausible, and economists appear to have codified this in a manner which makes eminent scientific sense.

Starting from the proposition that people know their own preferences, and that these are independent of their incomes (thereby ignoring marketing, peer pressure and a host of other woolly topics more suited for the simpler social sciences), Samuelson codified the economic vision of consumer behaviour into four axioms of rational choice:

- *Completeness*: The consumer knows his/her own subjective ranking of all combinations of goods
- *Transitivity*: If combination A is preferred to combination B, and B to C, then A is preferred to C
- *Non-satiation*: More is always preferred to less.
- *Convexity*: The additional utility that a consumer gets from extra units of each commodity falls.

Given these axioms (plus the assumption that preferences and the budget constraint are completely independent), economists can prove the existence of 'indifference curves' that specify what quantities of commodities a consumer

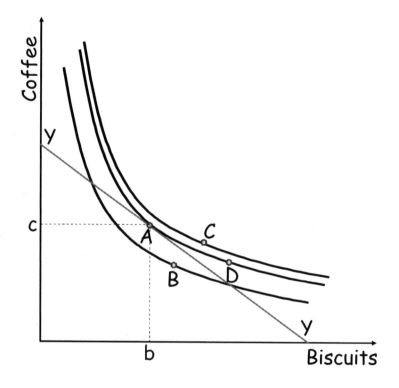

Figure 3: Point of tangency between budget line & indifference map maximises utility

will purchase given different relative prices and incomes. From these they can derive what economists like to call 'well-behaved' demand curves for any commodity: individual demand curves that slope down as price increases.[1] We get the picture of the happy, utility-maximising consumer shown in Figure 3.

This consumer would clearly prefer combination C to combination A – because it lies on a higher indifference curve – but budget YY doesn't allow the consumer to purchase C. She is indifferent between A and D – because they lie on the same indifference curve – but the consumer chooses A because that is within the budget set. Finally the consumer will never purchase B when she can afford A, because it lies on a lower indifference curve than A.

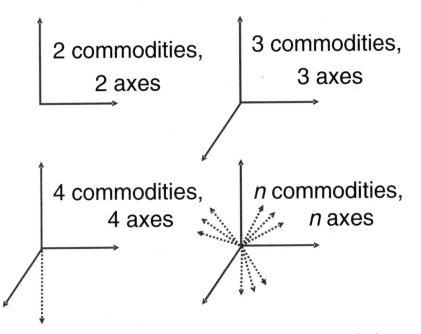

Figure 4: Indifference maps for multiple commodities require multiple axes

Erudite, apparently scientific, and completely wrong: not because of faulty mathematics this time, but because this toy model simply can't scale to the real world. The problem is a well-known dilemma in computational theory called the *curse of dimensionality*.

Take another look at Figure 3: how many commodities does it represent? Just two, of course.

If the 'axioms of revealed preference' scale to the real world, then a rational consumer must have complete preference set rankings for the possible combinations of these thousands of commodities, and must be able to rapidly compute the budgetary implications of purchasing one bundle versus another in order to be able to work out how a given set relates to her budget.

Let's consider a supermarket shopping trip and the simplest possible combination of commodities: the decision whether to buy or not buy each commodity. How many different combinations does the consumer have to have a preference ranking for?

With the standard 2 dimensional (2 commodity) diagram, there are just 4 combinations – (0,0), (1,0), (0,1) and (1,1). With 3 commodities, there are 8 combinations from (0,0,0) through to (1,1,1). With 4 commodities there are 16 combinations, 32 with 5, and so on. The general rule is that the number of feasible consumption sets is equal to:

With a small number of commodities, this isn't a problem. But what happens when the consumer attempts to fulfil the axioms of rational behaviour in the local supermarket? You wouldn't go too far wrong in estimating that the average supermarket contains about 1,000 different commodites. Each 'buy/not buy' bundle thus contains 1,000 entries, so there are 2^{1000} combinations – roughly 10^{300}, or 10 followed by 300 zeros. This is an enormous number, but since most people can't think in exponential numbers, let's compare it to real-world phenomena.

Assume (or pretend, as a student of mine preferred to say) that each human neurone can store preferences for 100 billion combinations, and that each one weighs 10^{-9} grams.[1] How much would the rational consumer's brain weigh? About 10^{280} grams or 10^{274} tonnes. Clearly that's a tad heavier than the average brain. It is, in fact, about 10^{224} times the estimated mass of the universe.[2]

Enough of ridiculous numbers. The point is that, while the axioms of revealed preference *appear* to define rational behaviour, anyone who actually tried to behave that way would be paralysed by the sheer range of choice that is presented by even 30 different commodities – let alone the number in a supermarket. It isn't rational to behave according to the rules of neoclassical micro.

It is therefore no wonder that attempts to empirically verify the neoclassical concept of utility maximisation have been abject failures. The latest and best such study, by Sippel in 1997, led the researcher to tellingly conclude that

> We find a considerable number of violations of the revealed preference axioms, which contradicts the neoclassical theory of the consumer maximizing utility subject to a given budget constraint. We should therefore pay closer attention to the limits of this theory as a description of how people actually behave, i.e. as a positive theory of consumer behavior. Recognizing these limits, we economists should perhaps be a little more modest in our 'imperialist ambitions' of explaining non-market behavior by economic principles.' (Sippel 1997: 1443)

Far from optimising being rational, truly rational behaviour consists in finding ways to reduce the number of bundles you consider to a manageable set. This is common knowledge in computational theory – a branch of knowledge that wasn't available to Walras and his contemporaries, but which should be known to modern economists. Its import is that strict optimisation is impossible in any problem subject to the curse of dimensionality, since no strict optimisation routine could terminate in a meaningful finite time. Sensible computational processes try to find a satisfactory outcome for such problems by finding ways to reduce the complexity to manageable levels without locking in obviously substantially sub-standard outcomes.

We all do this when we shop, using guidelines that economists dismiss as irrational: we *do* use our budgets to limit the commodities we consider. We use habit – we buy largely what we bought last time. These and other heuristic rules enable us to complete a shopping trip in an hour or so, versus the multiple ages of the universe true optimisation would require.

Now's the time to point out an obvious shortcoming to the utility maximisation model: why is consumption not shown as a function of time? Why don't the axes show 'cups of coffee per day', rather than just 'cups of coffee'? It's because neoclassical economics doesn't use the mathematics needed to handle processes that take place in time.

THE WRONG MATHEMATICS: STATICS IN A DYNAMIC WORLD

All first year economics students have suffered through solving simultaneous equations to work out the (irrelevant) intersection of supply and demand. Those doing actual economics degrees (a vastly reduced proportion of the total commerce intake compared to what it used to be) learn some quite sophisticated statistical procedures in the introductory econometrics subject. More senior students learn matrix methods, the method of Lagrange multipliers, etc. Some learn set theory as part of a course on general equilibrium or game theory. But few if any learn the kind of mathematics that should be the starting point of any attempt to apply mathematical analysis to the economy: differential and difference equations (differentiation is not the same thing).

Differential and difference equations are the foundations of the mathematical methods needed to analyse processes that change over time. Clearly the economy is such a process: when was the last time you saw an economy stand still? But the mathematics economists use is by and large restricted to that needed to analyse processes which have ceased: processes that have reached equilibrium and have therefore stopped changing.

The founding fathers of neoclassical economics were aware that economic analysis should use such tools, but they absolved themselves of the responsibility for doing so on the basis that these techniques were so much more difficult than those designed to characterise the nature of equilibrium states. As Alfred Marshall put it,

> ...dynamics includes statics... But the statical solution... is simpler... it may afford useful preparation and training for the more difficult dynamical solution; and it may be the first step towards a provisional and partial solution in problems so complex that a complete dynamical solution is beyond our attainment. (Marshall 1920: xiv).

Marshall, Jevons and Walras contented themselves with the expectation that their successors would develop dynamic methods on the static foundations they laid. The originator of the marginal productivity theory of income distribution, J.B. Clark, was full of hope for the development of dynamic economics in the twentieth century:

> A point on which opinions differ is the capacity of the pure theory of Political Economy for progress. There seems to be growing impression that, as a mere statement of principles, this science will fairly soon be complete... It is with this view that I take issue. The great coming development of economic theory is to take place, I venture to assert, through the statement and solution of dynamic problems. (Clark 1898: 9)

But what happened? Effectively nothing. The vast majority of neoclassical economic methodology is still static, and even those parts (such as game theory) that aspire to some semblance of dynamics are more show than substance (see Guerrien's chapter in this book). This is despite the rapid development of tools for dynamic analysis by other disciplines (mathematics, engineering, physics, biology) since the development of the computer. Economists in general remain blissfully ignorant of the fact that, these days, while still challenging, dynamic analysis is dramatically easier than it was when neoclassical economics first evolved.

Most neoclassicals content themselves in their ignorance with the belief that dynamic processes ultimately converge to an equilibrium, so that in effect 'statics is long run dynamics'. Keynes was aptly dismissive of this in his famous but incompletely quoted 'in the long run' comment, where he observed:

> But this long run is a misleading guide to current affairs. In the long run we are all dead. Economists set themselves too easy, too useless a task if in tempestuous seasons they can only tell us that when the storm is long past the ocean is flat again. (Keynes 1923: 65)

Keynes was of course right. But even on its own terms, the neoclassical faith in equilibrium is misplaced – which brings us to the fourth flaw in the mathematics of microeconomics.

PRECONCEIVED RESULTS AND 'INCONVENIENT' MATHEMATICS: GENERAL
DISEQUILIBRIUM

Walras was correct that opponents of the mathematisation of economics could 'never prevent the theory of the determination of prices under free competition from becoming a mathematical theory'. But he was wrong about the mathematical results that would apply.

Walras commenced with an exchange-only (no production) model in which many agents were both suppliers and demanders of different commodities, and each agent wished to sell a given value of commodities and use the proceeds to buy the same value of other commodities. He realised that, if exchanges occurred out of equilibrium, then some agents would benefit while others lost, thus changing the distribution of income. Each change in the distribution of income would alter the equilibrium, making the equilibrium elusive, non-unique and path-dependent. He therefore invented the fiction of an 'auctioneer', who costlessly jiggled all markets towards equilibrium by a process he called 'tatonnement' ('groping').

The auctioneer would declare an arbitrary set of prices, and using these prices all agents would work out their demands and supplies. Some markets would have more buyers than sellers, others the reverse. The auctioneer would then reduce the prices where supply exceeded demand, and increase prices where demand exceeded supply, until ultimately all markets were in equilibrium: then and only then would the auctioneer let trade occur.

The process sounded plausible, but Walras realised that he could not prove that it would actually converge to equilibrium. He contented himself with the observation that convergence

> will appear probable if we remember that the change from $p'b$ to $p''b$, which reduced the above inequality to an equality, exerted a direct influence that was invariably in the direction of equality at least so far as the demand for (B) was concerned; while the [consequent] changes from $p'c$ to $p''c$, $p'd$ to $p''d$, ...which moved the foregoing inequality farther away from equality, exerted indirect influences, some in the direction of equality and some in the opposite direction, at least so far as the demand for (B) was concerned, so that up to a certain point they cancelled each other out. Hence, the new system of prices ($p''b$, $p''c$, $p''d$, ...) is closer to equilibrium than the old system of prices ($p'b$, $p'c$, $p'd$, ...); and it is only necessary to continue this process along the same lines for the system to move closer and closer to equilibrium. (Walras 1954 [1874]: 172)

Twentieth century mathematics proved Walras wrong: this process need not converge to a unique equilibrium. As one neoclassical author put this dilemma:

From static analysis (going back to Walras and Marshall), it is known that, even under very plausible circumstances, [Walrasian tatonnement] systems...have multiple equilibria... Hence it is not to be expected that, in a reasonably broad class of economic environments (i.e., here, aggregate excess demand functions) every equilibrium point of a Walrasian tatonnement process will be stable.' (Hurwicz 1986: 46–7)

Walras' mechanism is highly unrealistic: there is no such beast as the Walrasian auctioneer (a physicist might compare him to Maxwell's demon), actual trades do occur out of equilibrium, and we necessarily live in a world with production as well as exchange. What about the dynamics of this world – can we expect it to converge to equilibrium?

No. As Jorgenson showed in 1960, such a system is necessarily unstable: either price levels or quantities or both must be in disequilibrium. The simplest possible model with no technical change, no fixed capital, and perfect thrift is:

$$x(t + 1) = A \cdot x(t) \tag{5}$$

For this system to grow stably over time, there has to be a stable rate of growth α% p.a. at which all sectors grow:

$$x(t + 1) = (1 + a) \cdot x(t) \tag{6}$$

These two equations yield three:

$$(1 + \alpha) \cdot x(t) = A \cdot x(t)$$
$$(1 + \alpha) \cdot x(t) - A \cdot x(t) = 0 \tag{7}$$
$$((1 + \alpha) \cdot I - A) \cdot x(t) = 0$$

This is only consistent with non-zero output levels if the determinant of $\left(A^{-1} - (1+\pi) \cdot I\right)$ equals zero.

$$|(1 + a) \cdot I - A| = 0 \tag{8}$$

The market-clearing relative price system for this model economy is given by equation (9)

$$p = (1 + \pi) \cdot p \cdot A \tag{9}$$

Manipulating this to get a compact expression for p yields (10):

$$p = (1 + \pi) \cdot p \cdot A$$
$$p \cdot A^{-1} = (1 + \pi) \cdot p \cdot A \cdot A^{-1}$$
$$p \cdot A^{-1} - (1 + \pi) \cdot p \cdot I = 0 \tag{10}$$
$$p \cdot \left(A^{-1} - (1+\pi) \cdot I\right) = 0$$

This is only consistent with non-zero prices if the determinant of $\left(A^{-1} - (1+\pi) \cdot I\right)$ is zero

$$\left|\left(A^{-1} - (1+\pi) \cdot I\right)\right| = 0 \tag{11}$$

Here's the dilemma that Jorgenson dubbed a 'dual stability theorem', but which is better called a dual instability theorem. The stability of production depends upon the characteristics of the matrix A; the stability of relative prices depends upon the characteristics of its inverse.

By an advanced mathematical theorem known as the Perron-Frobenius theorem, it is known that a matrix like A (with all non-negative entries) has a 'dominant eigenvalue' (largest root) greater than zero. The inverse matrix A^{-1} has the inverse roots. Therefore, the largest root of either A or A^{-1} must exceed one. A dominant eigenvalue greater than one means that the equilibrium is unstable: Hence either quantities or relative prices must be unstable.

This cannot be evaded by considering a nonlinear system, such as a Cobb-Douglas production function,[1] since any such function can be reduced to a polynomial expansion whose first variable term is an input-output matrix. Though the higher polynomial terms may stablilize an unstable system far from equilibrium, the input-output matrix alone determines the stability of the model close to equilibrium.

The 'right thing to do', once this result was proved, was to take to heart the result that Walras was wrong, that equilibrium prices and outputs will not prevail in a real economy, and to develop a theory of disequillibrium, of non-market-clearing prices. Jorgenson himself made such a deduction in a convoluted way: since the equilibrium of a model of spot market prices is necessarily unstable, other non-market-clearing pricing mechanisms are necessary and probably what actually exists in the real world:

> The conclusion is that excess capacity (or positive profit levels or both) is necessary and not merely sufficient for the interpretation of the dynamic input-output system and its dual as a model of an actual economy. (Jorgenson 1960: 893)

But in predictable neoclassical fashion, Jorgenson and others subsequently considered how the system might be made stable by various adjustments, rather than accepting the conclusion that spot market prices must be unstable. Stuff the mathematics: let's assume what we want to assume!

CONCLUSION

Neoclassical economics is a mathematical science? Give me a break! As you should be able to see from above, its so-called mathematical credentials are a myth. Far from using mathematics to elucidate economic issues, neoclassical economics has twisted and distorted mathematics to maintain an ideological vision of the market which proper mathematics shows is unsustainable.

This is a great pity, because – within limits – mathematics can assist economic understanding. But it has to be used as a tool with realism in its foundations, and whose results are accepted rather than evaded when they are inconvenient.

Hopefully some of you young budding economists who read this can contribute to the development of an economics where mathematics is used rather than abused.

REFERENCES

Blatt, J. M. (1983). *Dynamic Economic Systems*. ME Sharpe, Armonk. This contains a good explanation and discussion of Jorgenson's 1960 paper (Jorgenson, D. W., 1960. 'A dual stability theorem', *Econometrica* 28 (892–899).

Hurwicz, L. (1986). 'On the stability of the tatonnement approach to competitive equilibrium', in Sonnenshein, H.F., (ed.), *Lecture Notes in Economics and Mathematical Systems*, Springer-Verlag, Berlin.

Jorgenson, D. W. (1960). 'A dual stability theorem', *Econometrica* 28: 892–899.

Keen, S. (2001). *Debunking Economics: The naked emperor of the social sciences*, Pluto Press & Zed Books, Sydney & London.

Keynes, J. M. (1923 [1977]). 'A Tract on Monetary Reform', in *The Collected Works of John Hayward Keynes*, IV, MacMillan, London.

Manshah, 4. (1920 [1947]). *Principles of Economics*, 8th edition. MacMillan, London.

Shafer, W. & Sonnenschein, H., (1982). 'Market demand and excess demand functions', in Arrow, K.J., & Intriligator, M. D., (eds.), *Handbook of Mathematical Economics* (Vol. II), North-Holland, Amsterdam.

Sippel, R. (1997). 'Experiment on the pure theory of consumer's behaviour', *Economic Journal* 107: 1431–44.

Stigler, G. J. (1957). 'Perfect Competition, Historically Considered', *Journal of Political Economy* 65: 1–17.

Walras, L. (1900 [1954]). *Elements of Pure Economics*, George Allen & Union, London.

21

The Significance of the Economics Research Paper

Stephen T. Ziliak[1]

Roosevelt University, USA

My Father's house of worship has become a den of thieves *stealing in the name of the Lord*. (Reggae lyric)

In 1996 I published with Deirdre McCloskey in the *Journal of Economic Literature* a paper called 'The Standard Error of Regressions' (McCloskey and Ziliak 1996). We gave in that paper the intellectual history of statistical hypothesis testing – significance testing – and showed, with massed observations from the *American Economic Review*, how testing has evolved in the economics research paper. Devolved, to be precise. Significance testing was designed in the eighteenth century to separate random fluctuation from more or less permanent effect; it was not and cannot be used to determine whether a more or less permanent effect is *important* for any other reason. Since 1885, when F.Y. Edgeworth coined the very term 'statistical significance,' a crucial and obvious distinction has been drawn between statistical significance (a concept concerning errors of sampling) and economic or substantive significance (a concept concerning the quantitative magnitude and scientific or ethical importance – the size, the 'what matters' – of the effect (Edgeworth 1885: 187)).[2] A statistically significant difference may not be an economically significant difference and a statistically insignificant difference may be *economically* significant, i.e. important.

It's easy to see why. To fix ideas, suppose you want to test using regression analysis the hypothesis that public assistance – cash welfare - reduces recipient labor supply. I'm not saying it's easy to answer the hypothesis in some clear-cut, final sense: 'guarantee a minimum standard of living,' let's say, because workers are good but exploited, or, 'abolish the dole' because pauperism is a seething social plague. With hypothesis testing it's not like that. Answering a hypothesis in the human sciences, concerning a vision of capitalism, is not like answering a hypothesis concerning a light switch for a person of normal vision. 'Is the switch turned on?' Yes or no. 'Is the light bright?' True or false. In the human sciences, such as economics, you do not ask yes or no or true or false. You have instead to ask *how much*? You have to ask, for example, if welfare payments to the poor increased by 10 per cent, how much was lost in labor supply and GDP? You have to measure the drag of the welfare benefits. (It's some four hundred years since the Elizabethan Poor Law came to the British colonies – the first public welfare in America. Perhaps we're beginning to understand (with Albert Hirschman) that attitudes toward welfare and poverty can rarely be reduced to matters of plain efficiency, labor market or otherwise (Ziliak and Hannon, forthcoming). Just look at today's naked obsession with sex, drugs, and place of birth – that New Victorian gaze of the Other.) In economics research, as here, to throw any light at all you have anyway to measure and interpret the *economic* relationships in your model. Economists and policy makers want to know: how big is the welfare drag?

The answer – ever since Laplace first tested the hypothesis that comets come from outside the solar system – *is found by measuring the size of the regression coefficient against the descriptive statistics*. The answer *cannot be found by looking at t- and other test statistics*. Yet people, highly intelligent people, Nobel Prize winning people, have gotten terribly confused over this crucial distinction, the distinction between statistical and economic significance. They shouldn't.

Imagine a classical linear regression with 300 cross-sectional observations on individual-level labor supply (the dependent variable) and corresponding individual receipts of cash welfare grants (the independent variable). Labor supply is measured continuously by the number of hours an individual works each month and cash welfare is measured by hundreds of dollars or euros or whatever each individual receives per month. To avoid distractions, let's assume that all the usual control variables are included (education, family structure, and so on) and that all the typical holes in econometric practice – such as sample selection bias and oh-my-gosh-I-have-a-lot-of-zeros-on-the-left-hand-side – have been filled with milk and honey. All's well in econometric-land; specification error and other measurable ignorance have been considered and accounted for.

Now, run the regression. Wait! After one more step. To get a definitive answer to a Neyman-Pearson test of a hypothesis you must test a null hypothesis that you believe to be true.[3] Let's say for sake of argument you believe that cash welfare does *not* discourage labor supply. So in your regression you are testing the null $\beta = 0$ against the two-sided alternative that the effect could go either way. (In the nineteenth century the world's leading charities believed that aid to the poor, if properly administered, could actually *increase* labor and build self-reliance: see Ziliak 2004; Humphreys 1995. The idea's alive again: we should watch for it.) Suppose you run the regression and find an estimated coefficient â on the welfare variable = –0.002 with $t = 2.7$.

Should you change your mind about labor supply and the dole? McCloskey and I have found that economists who publish in the most prestigious journal of the profession, the *American Economic Review*, will answer, Yes. The null hypothesis, they observe, is zero effect: that is, the null says that giving cash to poor people does not affect their hours of work. Yet the estimated coefficient is statistically significantly different from zero at the 5 per cent level. Therefore, yes! Change your mind. (If you're not sure why the coefficient is 'statistically significantly different from zero' you might turn in your elementary statistics book to the section on t-testing in large and small samples, and dutifully follow the published tables of t as it leads you through examples. It's not hard.) The typical procedure in the *AER* we've found is to examine the size of the test statistic to discover whether or not a *policy variable* is *economically* significant. As if to say '$t = 2.7$? that's *really* important.'

The problem is that the test statistic cannot say. Economic significance is about the size of economic relationships; it's about how the economy hangs together, quantitatively speaking; it's about the contours of the circular flow, the structure of the American [or French or X] economy. To what *extent* is savings a function of permanent income? That's a question of economic significance (especially in post-1990s Japan). Shockingly, economic significance is about profit and loss in the ordinary business of life. In your research on personal finance you've discovered an enormous rate of return, enough to make a fortune, or you've found tuppence. You have to say which. The government program in Bosnia caused millions in deadweight loss, or was it billions? The Okun's Law trade-off between output and unemployment is between 2.3 and 2.6, you reckon: with what difference for macro policy? What, in economic or human terms, could be lost if the factory is not built? T-tests and the like can't say. Statistical significance, the thing the *AER* is obsessed with, can only say to what degree – under similar observational conditions – the coefficient you've estimated is more or less permanent. That's all. You and your scientific community have to say to what degree your finding is more or less *important*, explaining why with magnitudes.

Look again at the coefficient on welfare: $\beta = -0.002$ ($t = 2.7, N = 300$). In the State of California a cash welfare check can average $800 (US) a month for a single mother. What does the coefficient tell you? It says starting at the point mean (which is what β is), and holding other things equal, a 10 per cent increase in welfare gives an [$80 per month × -0.002] or 0.16 hour reduction in work each month. The reduction in work we find is imputed to be about 10 minutes per month. Ask, is a 10-minute reduction in work per month an economically significant diversion from the hypothesis *no* reduction of work per month? Common sense says no. And so, presumably, does advanced decision theory in the relevant loss functions. In other words, you've so far found no evidence in the data to warrant a change of mind. In 1933 Neyman and Pearson spoke of statistical v. substantive significance in studies of crime and punishment:

> Is it more serious to convict an innocent man or to acquit a guilty? That will depend on the consequences of the error; is the punishment death or fine; what is the danger to the community of released criminals; what are the current ethical views on punishment? From the point of view of mathematical theory all that we can do is show how the risk of errors may be controlled and minimised. The use of these statistical tools in any given case, in determining just how the balance should be struck, *must be left to the investigator.* (Neyman and Pearson 1933: 296; emphasis supplied)

Neyman and Pearson are saying that if your decision-rule leads to a public execution you will before the moment of injection want to reflect humbly on the nature of Type I and Type II error. If on the other hand your decision-rule leads to a slap on the hand you can safely move on to the next problem. To repeat, answering a test concerning cash welfare and labor supply does not complete an answer to the Big Question about the Welfare State (though it's certainly part of an answer. Our example suggests that society can help the children while keeping steady mothers' level of employment.) But one thing is certain: testing means calculating and interpreting the *economic* significance of a diversion from a null. 'From the point of view of mathematical theory all we can do is to show how the risk of errors may be controlled and minimised.

OOMPH

'Quantification,' said Sir Peter Medawar in his *Advice to a Young Scientist*, 'has no merit except insofar as it helps to solve problems' (Medawar 1979: 18). Bingo. As in chemistry and immunology (where Sir Peter earned his Nobel Prize), the meritorious paper in economics will calculate a minimum standard of *oomph* – a reservation price of economic significance that would just make the policy worth pursuing or just make the variable worth discussing. (Medawar got the Nobel for showing how much the body can bear in transplanted parts from another.) The Ziliak-McCloskey standard of oomph can be contrasted graphically with an *AER*-type, empirical proof (Figures 1 and 2):

Authors of the *AER* do not care about oomph but they care a lot for high t values. They will 'accept' a finding as 'significant' if the t-statistic is high,

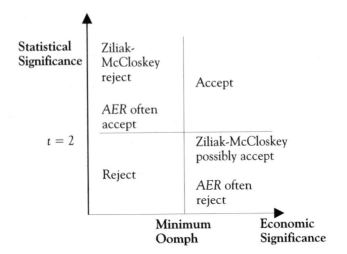

Figure 1: Minimum Oomph is What You're Looking For

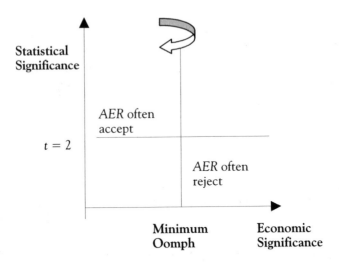

Figure 2: Yet the AER Has Tastes for *t*, with no Oomph

regardless of oomph, regardless of the size of effect (Figure 1 and Figure 2, northwest quadrant). But economic significance is found in the northeast and southeast quadrants; at or above the minimum standard of oomph, regardless of the size of the *t*-statistic. Just how the line of oomph is set is to be determined by the community. For instance, in the history of the United States, 1820 to the present, the average length of time a household takes poor relief lies between 8 and 15 months (Ziliak 2002, 2004). By poor relief I mean public welfare or private charity for the poor; federally funded or locally funded; secular or religious. That seems to be the range. So in a study of poor relief in the United States an investigator would not draw attention to a finding of 10 or 12 months on the welfare rolls. It's not economically significantly different from the norm. A finding of 20 months, however, *may be* economically significant: another half year getting relief and for how many families? With *that* increase the investigator might inquire into the costs and benefits of bringing the rate back down to the normal range. If she's really on the ball she'll talk about the ethics of doing so, too. Like Peter Medawar, in chemistry. Or Stephen Jay Gould, in biology. You'll be able to think up minimum standards of oomph in your own field of macro or trade.

THE AER

What's wrong with significance testing in economics? No oomph. Most economists believe erroneously that statistical significance is a necessary and sufficient condition for economic significance. It's neither. Even the historians and heterodox are not yet angels. The erroneous belief is causing a loss of jobs and justice and even human lives. (In a forthcoming book with McCloskey I'll show how big the problem is in psychology, law, health, biology, management, and medicine. State Supreme Courts have for example a standard of oomph for justice cases: a 5 per cent level of Type I error. You be the judge.)

The problem began years ago, when research workers began to listen to a rhetorical magician named Ronald Aylmer Fisher (1890–1962). Fisher is the prince who invented the 'rule of 2.' Listen as Fisher computes for the masses in 1925 a first test of significance in his *Statistical Methods for Research Workers*:

> The value for which P=.05, or 1 in 20, is 1.96 or nearly 2; it is *convenient* to take this point as a limit in judging whether a deviation is to be considered significant or not. Deviations exceeding twice the standard deviation are *thus formally regarded as significant*. Using this criterion we should be led to follow up a false indication only once in 22 trials, even if the statistics were the only guide available. Small effects will still escape notice if the data are insufficiently numerous to bring them out, but no lowering of the standard of significance would meet this difficulty.

(Fisher 1941 [1925]: 42; emphasis added).

Notice how a standard of 'convenience' rapidly became in Fisher's prose an item to be 'formally regarded.' With Fisher there's no loss function. There's no thinking beyond the statistic. We're 'to take this point as a limit.' Fisher's famous and influential book nowhere confronts the difference between statistical and substantive significance (123–4, 139–40, concerning soporific drugs and algae growth). He provided (and then defended for the rest of his long life against the decision-theoretic ideas of Neyman, Pearson, Wald and every other theorist) the cheapest way to get marketable results. The marginal social benefit of the Fisherian 'rule of 2' is at best equal to its cost of computation.

In the 1996 paper we applied a 19-item questionnaire to all the full-length papers published in the *AER* that used a test of statistical significance, January 1980 to December 1989. The questions were culled from the masters of modern statistics and empirical economics, Edgeworth and Wald to Zellner and Leamer (but not Fisher!) Each question was written so that a Yes answer is 'good,' indicative of serious science in search of economic significance. Table 1 describes the 19 questions and column 3 summarizes the chief findings of the 1980s:

Table 1: The *American Economic Review* Had Numerous Errors In the Use of Statistical Significance, 1980–1999

Survey Question	Percent Yes in 1990s	Percent Yes in 1980s
Does the paper . . .		
1. Use a small number of observations, such that statistically significant differences are not found merely by choosing a very large sample?	67.9	85.7
2. Report descriptive statistics for regression variables?	66.4	32.4
3. Report coefficients in elasticities, or in some other useful form that addresses the question of 'how large is large'?	86.9	66.5
4. Test the null hypotheses that the authors said were the ones of interest?	83.9	97.3
5. Carefully interpret the theoretical meaning of the coefficients? For example, does it pay attention to the details of the units of measurement, and to the limitations of the data?	81.0	44.5
6. Eschew reporting all standard errors t-, p-, and F- statistics, when such information is irrelevant?	12.4	8.3

Survey Question	Percent Yes in 1990s	Percent Yes in 1980s
7. At its first use, consider statistical significance to be one among other criteria of importance?	36.5	47.3
8. Consider the power of the test?	8.0	4.4
9. Examine the power function?[a]	45.5	16.7
10. Eschew 'asterisk econometrics,' the ranking of coefficients according to the absolute value of the test statistic?	32.8	74.7
11. Eschew 'sign econometrics,' which remarks on the sign but not the size of the coefficient?	19.0	46.7
12. Discuss the size of the coefficients?	78.1	80.2
13. Discuss the scientific conversation within which a coefficient would be judged large or small?	54.0	28.0
14. Avoid choosing variables for inclusion solely on the basis of statistical significance?	25.5	68.1
15. Use other criteria of importance besides statistical significance after the crescendo?	28.5	40.7
16. Consider more than statistical significance decisive in an empirical argument?	18.2	29.7
17. Do a simulation to determine whether the coefficients are reasonable?	35.0	13.2
18. In the conclusions, distinguish between statistical and economic significance?	52.6	30.1
19. Avoid using the word 'significance' in ambiguous ways?	37.2	41.2

Source: All the full-length papers using tests of statistical significance and published in the *American Economic Review* in the 1980s (N=182) and 1990s (N=137). Table 1 in McCloskey and Ziliak (1996) reports a small number of papers for which some questions in the survey do not apply.

Notes: a Of the papers that mention the power of a test, this is the fraction that examined the power function or otherwise corrected for power.

The table is rich. But the main point is this: in the 1980s 70 per cent of the papers considered statistical significance to be decisive in an empirical argument (Question 16). In 7 of every 10 papers, that is, scientific matters were decided *only* on the basis of statistical significance. What's worse, of those 70 per cent that relied exclusively on statistical significance, another 70 per cent failed to report descriptive statistics – the means and standard deviations of regression variables. In other words, half the papers in the *AER* supplied *no* evidence, nothing at all, of economic significance.

Since 1996 many colleagues have replied, 'Yes, significance testing turned bad in the 1980s. With our fast PCs, our mullet hairstyles – yessir, we screwed up. But things have gotten better.' Individually and collectively we have many times heard this claim. But like the authors of the *AER* we too are empirical scientists. So we decided to apply the same 19-item questionnaire to all the full-length papers published in the *AER* in the decade just completed, the 1990s.[1] If best practice has improved it would presumably appear in the data. Table 1, column 2, describes the chief findings of the 1990s survey. Unfortunately, best practice has *not* improved. Sadly, in the most crucial variable, it's gotten worse. In the 1990s, we found, *82 per cent* made the crucial error: 8 in 10 papers, that is, mistook statistical significance (or the lack of it) for economic relevance (Question 16). There were improvements, in some areas big, and that's pleasing. But to repeat, the essential problem, the reduction of science to *t*-testing, has gotten worse.

It's not fair to blame the students. We looked at all the textbooks, from advanced econometrics books to elementary statistics for business and economics and found that, with few exceptions, professors propagate the very error we're preaching against (Ziliak and McCloskey 2004; McCloskey and Ziliak 1996). Dear students: show your teachers how to correct the error, politely, and open-handedly, and very patiently (remember: Professor's supposed to *know*). Don't fear. Today you're at worst a victim, tomorrow a saint.

WHAT CAN WE HOPE?

The textbooks are wrong. The teaching is wrong. CNN is wrong. The seminar you just attended is wrong. The most prestigious journal in the profession is wrong. Since you have read this far probably you are searching for ways to avoid being wrong. Perhaps you feel frazzled by what Morris Altman calls the social psychological culture of fear, the deeply entrenched path-dependency, that keeps the abuse in circulation, and want to come out of it. Come.

Significance testing became in the late twentieth century the main tool of empirical economics (and so for most of the life and human sciences). The doctor who does not know statistical significance from substantive significance,

F-stat from heart attack, is like the economist who does not know supply from demand. Actually, it's worse. He's like an economist who's never heard of opportunity cost, or, if he's heard of it, ignores it anyway – the loss function. Accepting or rejecting a test of significance without considering the loss function is like making 'Sophie's Choice' without considering the child. Economists choose now to look the other way, and do not consider the child. They throw out the baby with the bath water.

Some critics, like Ed Leamer, I note, have a look at our findings from the AER and turn nihilistic (though Leamer in a most charming, Harpo Marxian-Friedrich Nietzschean way). I'm optimistic in I'd guess (to make the sentence parallel) a Thomas Carlyle-Dr. Martin Luther King, Jr. kind of way: 'No lie can live forever.' Like McCloskey, like Zellner, like Arrow, like Solow, like Granger, like Friedman (all who've on this matter long seen the light) I believe that a once persuasive though misleading rhetoric was used to inject and defend the incorrect usage of hypothesis testing in economic research. At the peak of modernism in economics, the machine age of economic epistemology, *any* need for human judgment produced in the economist a kind of vertigo, a vertigo he feared and then fled by doping up or tuning out. Like Dr. Strangelove, he let the machine decide. It's the morning after modernism and we've now a different feeling about human judgment. A persuasive and scientific rhetoric – a rhetoric of economic significance – we believe, can be used to dislodge and then replace incorrect usage with correct. Bayesian and frequentist. Classical and subjectivist. Human judgment, human interpretation, we now know, is all that matters. But we've got to get the incentives right.

Hope springs from a frequentist tale. Think of it: Fisher is one of maybe 50 statisticians who've seriously influenced the history of hypothesis testing. That means the long-run relative frequency of Fisher imitations is about 2 per cent. Yet in the twentieth century the relative frequency of Fisher imitations rose far above 2 per cent – to some 95 per cent. I conclude that the percentage of research workers imitating R.A. Fisher will eventually fall to 0 per cent, and for many years over, in order to drive the long-run relative frequency of Fisher imitations down to its equilibrium 2 per cent. This tale assumes, with apologies to Marx, that theory choice is random.

A French naturalist, Count Buffon (1707–1788), flipped a fair coin 4,040 times with the result, heads = 0.5069. While imprisoned by Nazis during World War II an Australian mathematician by the name of John Kerrich flipped a fair coin 10,000 times and with the result, heads = 0.5067 (Moore and McCabe, p. 291). In the 1970s Flip Wilson was a comedian in the United States having nothing at all to do with coins. I cannot conclude with Arnold Zellner that the twentieth century will belong to Bayes. But with so many 'flips' in the twentieth century the next century will likely *not* belong to R.A. Fisher. I hope anyway that in the next century we see reward flowing only to those research papers that find and interpret *economic* significance. It's in truth the only choice, the only choice, that is, if you stand for sanity, humanity, and science.

REFERENCES AND SUGGESTED READING

Berger, J.O. 2003. 'Fisher Lecture: Could Fisher, Jeffreys and Neyman Have Agreed on Testing?' (with discussion), *Statistical Science* 18 (1): 1–32.

Cullenberg, S., J. Amariglio, and D.F. Ruccio, eds (2001) *Postmodernism, Economics and Knowledge*, New York: Routledge.

Edgeworth, F.Y. (1885) 'Methods of Statistics', *Jubilee Volume of the Statistical Society* (Royal Statistical Society of Britain), June 22–24: 181–217.

Fisher, R.A. (1941) *Statistical Methods for Research Workers* [1925], 8th Edition, New York: G.E. Stechart and Co.

Humphreys, R. (1995) *Sin, Organized Charity, and the Poor in Victorian England*, New York: St. Martin's Press.

Jeffreys, H. (1998) *Theory of Probability* [1939], Oxford: Oxford University Press.

Kruskal, W.S. (1968) 'Tests of Statistical Significance' , in David Sills, ed., *International Encyclopedia of the Social Sciences*, 15, New York: Macmillan, 206–24.

Leamer, E. E. (1978) *Specification Searches: Ad Hoc Inferences with Nonexperimental Data*, New York: Wiley.

Leamer, E.E. (1983) 'Let's Take the Con Out of Econometrics', *American Economic Review* 73 (1): 31–43.

McCloskey, D.N. and S.T. Ziliak (1996) 'The Standard Error of Regressions', *Journal of Economic Literature*, XXXIV (March): 97–114.

Medawar, P.S. (1979) *Advice to a Young Scientist*, New York: Basic Books.

Moore, D.S. and G. P. McCabe (1999) *Introduction to the Practice of Statistics*, 3rd Edition, New York: Freeman.

Neyman, J. and E. S. Pearson (1933) 'On the Problem of the Most Efficient Tests of Statistical Hypotheses', *Philosophical Transactions of the Royal Society* A (231): 289–337.

Zellner, A. (1997) *Bayesian Analysis in Econometrics and Statistics*, Cheltenham, UK: Edward Elgar.

Zellner, A. (1984) *Basic Issues in Econometrics*, Chicago: University of Chicago Press.

Ziliak, S.T. (2004) 'Self-Reliance Before the Welfare State: Evidence from the Charity Organization Movement in the United States', *Journal of Economic History*, forthcoming.

Ziliak, S.T. 2002. 'Some Tendencies of Social Welfare and the Problem of Interpretation.' *Cato Journal* 21(3): 499–513.

Ziliak, S.T. (with J.U. Hannon) (2004) 'Public Assistance: Colonial Times to the 1920s', *Historical Statistics of the United States: Colonial Times to the Present*, New York: Cambridge University Press.

Ziliak, S.T. and D.N. McCloskey (2004) 'Size Matters: The Standard Error of Regressions in the *American Economic Review*,' *Journal of Socio-Economics*, forthcoming.

Part VI

Category Mistakes Regarding Wealth and Illth

22

Changing Visions of Humans' Place in the World and the Need for an Ecological Economics

ROBERT COSTANZA

THE UNIVERSITY OF VERMONT, USA

Practical problem-solving in complex, human-dominated ecosystems requires the integration of three elements: (1) active and ongoing envisioning of both how the world works and how we would like the world to be; (2) systematic analysis appropriate to and consistent with the vision; and (3) implementation appropriate to the vision. Scientists generally focus on only the second of these steps, but integrating all three is essential to both good science and effective management. 'Subjective' values enter into the 'vision' element, both in terms of the formation of broad social goals and in the creation of a 'pre-analytic vision' which necessarily precedes any form of scientific analysis.

Research concerning the process of change in various kinds of organizations and communities suggests that a necessary ingredient of moving change in a particular direction is having a clear vision of the desired goal, a vision which is also truly shared by the members of the organization or community (Senge 1990, Wiesbord 1992, Wiesbord and Janoff 1995). Or, as Yogi Berra once said: 'If you don't know where you're going, you end up somewhere else.'

VISIONS OF THE ECONOMY AND ITS RELATIONSHIP TO THE ECOLOGICAL LIFE SUPPORT SYSTEM

Our 'pre-analytic vision' of both how the human economy and society relate to the rest of nature and of the economy itself are changing. The human economy has passed from an 'empty world' era in which human-made capital was the limiting factor in economic development to the current 'full world' era in which remaining natural capital has become the limiting factor (Daly and Cobb 1989, Costanza *et al.* 1997). Basic economic logic tells us that we should maximize the productivity of the scarcest (limiting) factor, as well as try to increase its supply. This means that economic policy should be designed to increase the productivity of natural capital and its total amount, rather than to increase the productivity of human-made capital and its accumulation, as was appropriate in the past when this form of capital was limiting. This implies a very different vision of the economy and its place in the overall ecosystem.

(a) "Conventional" Model of the Economy

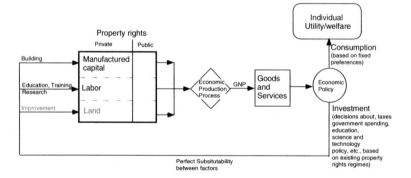

(b) Expanded Model of the Ecological Economic System

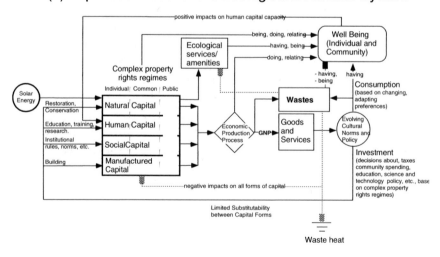

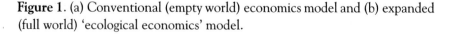

Figure 1. (a) Conventional (empty world) economics model and (b) expanded (full world) 'ecological economics' model.

Figure 1a shows the conventional (empty world) economic pre-analytic vision. The primary factors of production (land, labor, and capital) combine in the economic process to produce goods and services (usually measured as Gross National Product or GNP). GNP is divided into consumption (which is the sole perceived contributor to individual utility and welfare) and investment (which goes into maintaining and increasing the capital stocks). Preferences are fixed. In this model the primary factors are perfect substitutes for each other so 'land' (including ecosystem services) can be almost ignored since one could always substitute more labor or capital for it. Property rights are usually simplified to either private or public and their distribution is usually taken as given. There is nothing in this model that would in any way prevent the economy from growing indefinitely. The main policy question thus becomes: how much should we consume vs. invest in each time period in order to keep the economy growing at the 'optimal' (i.e. fastest possible) rate. If 'welfare' equates to the absolute level of consumption of marketed goods and services then (under this vision) we are maximizing welfare by maximizing the discounted stream of consumption into the future.

Almost all economic policy today is still made based on this vision of the world. If GNP decreases for even a quarter, the 'health' of the economy is thought to be in severe trouble and we have to do everything in our power to get the economy 'growing' again.

What's wrong with this model/vision? The list is long, but here is a brief and partial summary:

- It ignores physical reality, the laws of thermodynamics, and the fact that the economy is a subsystem of the larger global ecosystem. Note that there is no 'waste' in the empty world model. It is a perpetual motion machine that can run forever on its own output.

- It assumes near-perfect substitutability between the main factors of production (land, labor and capital) such that the economy could continue to grow indefinitely, even with no natural resources.

- The view of human psychology embedded in the model is hopelessly simplistic and inaccurate. Psychological research has clearly shown that (beyond a fairly low level) consumption of goods and services is only one of many factors that contribute to human well-being, and that within the consumption factor it is relative rather than absolute consumption that is the more important criteria (Kahneman *et al.* 1999, Kasser 2002).

- It assumes that tastes and preferences are fixed and given, when in fact it is well known that they are evolving and changing in response to a host of influences, including advertising (Norton *et al.* 1998).

- It assumes that humans are rational actors with fixed preferences and perfect information. They value things according to their relative ability to satisfy their individual preferences and there is no interpersonal interaction of one person's preferences with any others'.

- It ignores direct, non-marketed contributions to human welfare by factors such as ecosystem services, a fulfilling job, and family and community social interactions.

- Its view of property rights is simplistic and ignores the many forms of community ownership that have proven effective in many contexts. It also ignores the distribution of these property rights as a problem that is outside the boundaries of economics.

AN ALTERNATIVE MODEL

Figure 1b shows an alternative 'ecological economics' or 'full world' vision of the process (Ekins 1992, Costanza *et al.* 1997) that attempts to address the problems and limitations of the 'empty world' model noted above. Notice that some of the key elements of the conventional model are still present, but much more has been added and many basic assumptions and priorities have changed, including:

1. There is limited substitutability between the basic forms of capital in this model and their number has expanded to four. Their names have also changed to better reflect their roles: (1) natural capital (formerly land) includes ecological systems, mineral deposits and other aspects of the natural world; (2) human capital (formerly labor) includes both the physical labor of humans and the know-how stored in their brains; (3) manufactured or built capital includes all the machines and other infrastructure of the human economy; and (4) social (or cultural) capital includes the web of interpersonal connections, institutional arrangements, rules and norms that allow individual human interactions to occur (Berkes and Folke 1994).

2. Property rights regimes in this model are complex and flexible, spanning the range from individual to common to public property.

3. Natural capital contributes to the production of marketed economic goods and services, which affect human welfare. It also produces ecological services and amenities that directly contribute to human welfare without ever passing through markets.

4. Natural capital captures solar energy and behaves as an autonomous complex system. The model conforms to the basic laws of thermodynamics (conservation of mass and energy, the need for low entropy inputs to keep the system running).

5. There is waste production by the economic process, which contributes negatively to human welfare and has a negative impact on capital and ecological services.

6. Preferences are adapting and changing but basic human needs are constant. Human welfare is a function of much more than the absolute level of consumption of economic goods and services. Welfare involves consumption relative to perceived peers, participation in decisions, a sense of fairness about the distribution of resources, non-marketed benefits from ecosystem services, social interactions at many scales, and other factors.

7. People have limited knowledge and 'rationality' and limited ability to process the information they do have. The value of things has to do with their contribution to the broader conception of human welfare sketched above, rather than the narrow conception embodied in the 'empty world' model.

These visions of the world are significantly different. As Ekins (1992) points out: 'It must be stressed that that the complexities and feedbacks of model 2 are not simply glosses on model 1's simpler portrayal of reality. They fundamentally alter the perceived nature of that reality and in ignoring them conventional analysis produces serious errors...' (151).

One could expand on any of the issues above, and other chapters in this book do just that. In what follows, I'll expand a bit on the valuation issue, as it has been a core concept in economics since its inception.

VALUATION AND SOCIAL GOALS

Valuation ultimately refers to the contribution of an item to meeting a specific goal or objective. A player on a sports team is valuable to the extent that he or she contributes to the goal of the team's winning. In ecology, a gene is valuable to the extent it contributes to the survival of the individuals possessing it, and thus their ability to produce progeny. In conventional economics, a commodity is valuable to the extent it contributes to the goal of individual welfare as assessed by willingness to pay. The point is that one cannot state a value without stating the goal being served. Conventional economic value is based on the goal of individual welfare or utility maximization. But other goals, and thus other values, are possible and may be more important to human welfare, more broadly conceived. For example, if the goal is sustainability, one should assess value based on the contribution to achieving that goal – in addition to value based on the goals of individual utility maximization, social equity, or other goals that may be deemed important. This broadening is particularly important if the goals are potentially in conflict.

There are at least three broad goals which have been identified as important to managing economic systems within the context of the planet's ecological life support system (Daly 1992):

1. assessing and insuring that the scale or magnitude of human activities within the biosphere are ecologically sustainable;

2. distributing resources and property rights fairly, both within the current generation of humans and between this and future generations, and also between humans and other species; and

3. efficiently allocating resources as constrained and defined by 1 and 2 above, and including both marketed and non-marketed resources, especially ecosystem services.

Several authors have discussed valuation of ecosystem services with respect to goal 3 above – allocative efficiency based on individual utility maximization (e.g. Farber and Costanza 1987, Mitchell and Carson 1989, Costanza et al. 1989, Dixon and Hufschmidt 1990, Pearce 1993, Goulder and Kennedy 1997). We need to explore more fully the implications of extending these concepts to include valuation with respect to the other two goals of (1) ecological sustainability, and (2) distributional fairness (Costanza and Folke 1997). Basing valuation on current individual preferences and utility maximization alone, as is done in conventional analysis, does not necessarily lead to ecological sustainability or social fairness (Bishop 1993).

A Kantian or intrinsic rights approach to valuation (see Goulder and Kennedy 1997) is one approach to goal 2, but it is important to recognize that the three goals are not 'either-or' alternatives. While they are in some senses independent multiple criteria (Arrow and Raynaud 1986) they must all be satisfied in an integrated fashion to allow human life to continue in a desirable way. Similarly, the valuations that flow from these goals are not 'either-or' alternatives. Rather than an 'utilitarian or intrinsic rights' dichotomy, we must integrate the three goals listed above and their consequent valuations.

A two-tiered approach that combines public discussion and consensus building on sustainability and equity goals at the community level with methods for modifying both prices and preferences at the individual level to better reflect these community goals may be necessary (Rawls 1971, Norton 1995, Norton et al. 1998). Estimation of ecosystem values based on sustainability and fairness goals requires treating preferences as endogenous and co-evolving with other ecological, economic, and social variables.

VALUATION WITH SUSTAINABILITY, FAIRNESS, AND EFFICIENCY AS GOALS

Thus, we can distinguish at least three types of value which are relevant to the broader goal of maintaining human welfare. These are laid out in Table 1, according to their corresponding goal or value basis. Efficiency-based value (E-value) is based on a model of human behavior sometimes referred to as 'Homo economius' – that humans act independently, rationally and in their own self-interest. Value in this context (E-value) is based on current individual preferences, which are assumed to be fixed or given (Norton *et al.* 1998). No additional discussion or scientific input is required to form these preferences (since they are assumed to already exist) and value is simply people's revealed willingness to pay for the good or service in question. The best estimate of what people are willing to pay is thought to be what they would actually pay in a well-functioning market. For resources or services for which there is no market (like many ecosystem services) a pseudo-market can sometimes be simulated with questionnaires that elicit individual's 'contingent' valuation.

Fairness based value (F-value) would require that individuals vote their preferences as a member of the community, not as individuals. This different 'species' (*Homo communicus*) would engage in much discussion with other members of the community and come to consensus on the values that would be fair to all members of the current and future community (including non-human species), incorporating scientific information about possible future consequences as necessary. One method to implement this might be Rawls' (1971) idea of the 'veil of ignorance', where everyone votes as if they were operating with no knowledge of their own individual status in current or future society.

Table 1. Valuation of ecosystem services based on the three primary goals of efficiency, fairness, and sustainability (Costanza and Folke 1997)

Goal or Value Basis	Who votes	Preference Basis	Level of Discussion Required	Level of Scientific Input Required	Specific Methods
Efficiency	*Homo economius*	Current individual preferences	low	low	willingness to pay
Fairness	*Homo communicus*	Community preferences	high	medium ignorance	veil of
Sustainability	*Homo naturalis*	Whole system preferences	medium	high	modeling with precaution

Sustainability-based value (S-value) would require an assessment of the contribution to ecological sustainability of the item in question. For example, the S-value of ecosystem services is connected to their physical, chemical, and biological role in the long-term functioning of the global system. Scientific information about the functioning of the global system is thus critical in assessing S-value, and some discussion and consensus-building is also necessary. If it is accepted that all species, no matter how seemingly uninteresting or lacking in immediate utility, have a role to play in natural ecosystems (Naeem *et al.* 1994, Tilman and Downing 1994, Holling *et al.* 1995), estimates of ecosystem services may be derived from scientific studies of the role of ecosystems and their biota in the overall system, without direct reference to current human preferences. Humans operate as *Homo naturalis* in this context, expressing preferences as if they were representatives of the whole system. Instead of being merely an expression of current individual preferences, S-value becomes a system characteristic related to the item's evolutionary contribution to the survival of the linked ecological economic system. Using this perspective we may be able to better estimate the values contributed by, say, maintenance of water and atmospheric quality to long-term human well-being, including protecting the opportunities of choice for future generations (Golley 1994, Perrings 1994). One way to get at these values, would be to employ systems-simulation models that incorporated the major linkages in the system at the appropriate time and space scales (Costanza *et al.* 1993, 2002, Boumans *et al.* 2002). To account for the large uncertainties involved, these models would have to be used in a precautionary way, looking for the range of possible values and erring on the side of caution (Costanza and Perrings 1990).

In order to fully integrate the three goals of ecological sustainability, social fairness, and economic efficiency we also need a further step, which Sen (1995) has described as 'value formation through public discussion'. This can be seen as the essence of real democracy. As Buchanan (1954: 120) put it: 'The definition of democracy as 'government by discussion' implies that individual values can and do change in the process of decision-making.' Limiting our valuations and social decision-making to the goal of economic efficiency based on fixed preferences prevents the needed democratic discussion of values and options and leaves us with only the 'illusion of choice' (Schmookler 1993). So, rather than trying to avoid the difficult questions of valuation, we need to acknowledge the broad range of goals being served as well as the technical difficulties involved. We must get on with the process of value formation and analysis in as participatory and democratic a way as possible, but one which also takes advantage of the full range and depth of scientific information we have accumulated on system functioning. This is not simply the application of the conventional pre-analytic vision and analyses to a new problem, but will require the new, more comprehensive, more integrated, pre-analytic vision discussed above, and new, yet to be developed, analyses and valuation techniques that flow from it. This will be an enormously important challenge for the next generation of ecologists and economists working together in the transdisciplinary field of ecological economics.

REFERENCES

Arrow, K. J. and H. Raynaud (1986) *Social Choice and Multicriterion Decision-Making*, Cambridge: MIT Press.

Boumans, R., R. Costanza, J. Farley, M. A. Wilson, R. Portela, J. Rotmans, F. Villa, and M. Grasso (2002) 'Modeling the Dynamics of the Integrated Earth System and the Value of Global Ecosystem Services Using the GUMBO Model', *Ecological Economics* 41: 529–60.

Berkes, F., and C. Folke (1994) 'Investing in Cultural Capital for a Sustainable Use of Natural Capital', in *Investing in Natural Capital: the Ecological Economics Approach to Sustainability*, edited by A.M. Jansson, M. Hammer, C. Folke, and R. Costanza, 128–49. Washington DC: Island Press.

Bishop, R.C. (1993) 'Economic efficiency, sustainability, and biodiversity', *Ambio* 22: 69–73.

Buchanan, J. M. (1954) 'Social choice, democracy, and free markets' *Journal of Political Economy* 62: 114–23.

Costanza, R. and C. Folke (1997) 'Valuing ecosystem services with efficiency, fairness and sustainability as goals' in G. Daily (ed.), *Nature's Services: Societal Dependence on Natural Ecosystems* Washington, DC: Island Press, 49–70.

Costanza, R. and C. Perrings (1990) 'A flexible assurance bonding system for improved environmental management' *Ecological Economics*, 2: 57–76.

——, S. C. Farber, and J. Maxwell (1989) 'The valuation and management of wetland ecosystems', *Ecological Economics* 1: 335–62.

——, J. C. Cumberland, H. E. Daly, R. Goodland, and R. Norgaard (1997) *An Introduction to Ecological Economics*, Boca Raton: St. Lucie Press.

——, L. Wainger, C. Folke, and K.-G. Mäler (1993) 'Modeling complex ecological economic systems: toward an evolutionary, dynamic understanding of people and nature' *BioScience*, 43: 545–55.

——, A. Voinov, R. Boumans, T. Maxwell, F. Villa, L. Wainger, and H. Voinov (2002) 'Integrated ecological economic modeling of the Patuxent River watershed, Maryland' *Ecological Monographs*, 72: 203–31.

Daly, H. E. (1992) 'Allocation, distribution, and scale: towards an economics that is efficient, just, and sustainable' *Ecologial Economics*, 6: 185–93.

—— and Cobb, J. (1989) *For the Common Good: Redirecting the Economy Towards Community, the Environment, and a Sustainable Future*, Boston, Beacon Press.

Dixon, J. A. and M. M. Hufschmidt (1990) *Economic Valuation Techniques for the Environment: a Case Study Workbook*, Baltimore: The Johns Hopkins University Press.

Ekins, P. (1992) 'A four-capital model of wealth creation' in P. Ekins and M. Max-Neef, *Real-Life Economics: Understanding Wealth Creation*, London: Routledge, 147–55.

Farber, S. and R. Costanza (1987) 'The economic value of wetlands systems', *Journal of Environmental Management*, 24: 41–51.

Golley, F.B. (1994) 'Rebuilding a humane and ethical decision system for investing in natural capital', in *Investing in Natural Capital: the Ecological Economics Approach to Sustainability*, ed. A.M. Jansson, M. Hammer, C. Folke, and R. Costanza, Washington DC: Island Press, 169–78.

Goulder, L.H., and D. Kennedy (1997) 'Valuing ecosystem services' in *Ecosystem Services: their Nature and Value*, ed. G. Daily, Washington D. C.: Island Press, (in press) 23–48.

Holling, C.S., D.W. Schindler, B.W. Walker, and J. Roughgarden (1995) 'Biodiversity in the functioning of ecosystems: an ecological synthesis' in *Biodiversity Loss: Economic and Ecological Issues*, eds C. Perrings, K.-G. Mäler, C. Folke, C.S. Holling, and B.-O. Jansson, New York: Cambridge University Press, 44–83.

Kahneman, D, E. Diener, and N. Schwarz (eds) (1999) 'Well-being: the foundations of hedonic psychology' New York: Russell Sage Foundation.

Kasser, T. (2002) *The High Price of Materialism*, Cambridge, MA: MIT Press.

Mitchell, R. C. and R. T. Carson (1989) *Using Surveys to Value Public Goods: the Contingent Valuation Method*, Washington D.C: Resources for the Future.

Naeem, S., L. J. Thompson, S. P. Lawler, J. H. Lawton, and R. M. Woodfin (1994) 'Declining biodiversity can alter the performance of ecosystems', *Nature*, 368: 734–7.

Norton, B., R. Costanza, and R. Bishop (1998) 'The evolution of preferences: why "sovereign" preferences may not lead to sustainable policies and what to do about it', *Ecological Economics* 24: 193–211.

Norton, Bryan G. (1995) 'Ecological integrity and social values: at what scale?' *Ecosystem Health* 1: 228–41.

Pearce, D. (1993) *Economic Values and the Natural World*, London: Earthscan.

Perrings, C. A. (1994) 'Biotic diversity, sustainable development, and natural capital' in *Investing in Natural Capital: the Ecological Economics Approach to Sustainability*, ed. A. M. Jansson, M. Hammer, C. Folke, and R. Costanza, Washington D. C.: Island Press, 92–112.

Rawls, J. (1971) *A Theory of Justice*, Oxford: Oxford University Press.

Schmookler, A. B. (1993) *The Illusion of Choice: How the Market Economy Shapes Our Destiny*. Albany: State University of New York Press.

Sen, A. (1995) 'Rationality and social choice', *American Economic Review*, 85: 1–24.

Senge, P. M. (1990) *The Fifth Discipline: the Art and Practice of the Learning Organization*, New York: Currency-Doubleday.

Tilman, D., and J. A. Downing (1994) 'Biodiversity and stability in grasslands' *Nature* 367: 363–5.

Weisbord, M. (ed.) (1992) *Discovering Common Ground*, San Francisco: Berrett-Koehler.

Weisbord, M. and S. Janoff (1995) *Future search: an Action Guide to Finding Common Ground in Organizations and Communities*, San Francisco, Berrett-Koehler.

23
Ecological Economics:
The Concept of Scale and Its Relation to Allocation, Distribution, and Uneconomic Growth

HERMAN E. DALY

UNIVERSITY OF MARYLAND, USA

INTRODUCTION

My discussion is in three parts. First, I look at the main features and issues in ecological economics, noting differences and questions under debate with mainstream neoclassical economics. Second, a look at the meanings of economic growth, and the specific issue of economic growth versus uneconomic growth in the scale of the physical economy. Third, some policy implications from ecological economics about avoiding uneconomic growth by seeking a steady-state economy at or near the optimum scale.

ECOLOGICAL ECONOMICS IN GENERAL AND COMPARED TO NEOCLASSICAL ECONOMICS

Ecological economics is mainly about three issues: allocation of resources, distribution of income, and scale of the economy relative to the ecosystem – especially the third. A good allocation of resources is *efficient* (Pareto optimal); a good distribution of income or wealth is *just* (a limited range of acceptable inequality); a good scale does not generate 'bads' faster than goods, and is also ecologically *sustainable* (it could last a long time, although nothing is forever). Allocation and distribution are familiar concepts from standard economics for any given distribution of income there is a different optimal efficient allocation of resources with its corresponding optimal set of prices. A Pareto optimal allocation is one in which it is impossible to reallocate resources in a way that makes someone better off without making someone else worse off – a very minimalist definition of efficiency. Standard economics focuses primarily on the allocation issue, but pays secondary attention to distribution, first because a given distribution is logically necessary for defining efficient allocation, and second because distributive fairness is important in its own right. It is fair to say, however, that ecological economists consider the issue of distributive fairness more pressing than do most neoclassical economists.

The third issue of 'scale', by which is meant the *physical* size of the economy relative to the containing ecosystem, is not recognized in standard economics, and has therefore become the differentiating focus of ecological economics.

Ecological economists' pre-analytic vision of the economy as an open subsystem of a larger ecosystem that is finite, non growing, and materially closed (though open with respect to solar energy), immediately suggests several analytical questions regarding scale: How large *is* the economic subsystem relative to the earth ecosystem? How large *could* it be, i.e., what is its maximum scale? And most importantly, How large *should* the subsystem be relative to the ecosystem? Is there an optimal scale (less than the biophysical maximum) beyond which physical growth of the economic subsystem (even if possible) begins to cost more at the margin than it is worth, in terms of human welfare? You will not find these questions in standard economics textbooks.

If the economy grew into the Void it would encroach on nothing, and its growth would have no opportunity cost. But, since the economy in fact grows into and encroaches upon the finite and non growing ecosystem, there *is* an opportunity cost to growth in scale, as well as a benefit. The costs arise from the fact that the physical economy, like an animal, is a 'dissipative structure' sustained by a metabolic flow from and back to the environment. This flow, called 'throughput', begins with the depletion of low-entropy, useful resources from the environment and ends with the return of high-entropy polluting wastes. Depletion and pollution are costs – 'bads' rather than goods. Not only does the growing economy encroach spatially and quantitatively on the ecosystem, it also qualitatively degrades the environmental sources and sinks of the metabolic throughput by which it is maintained.[1]

The scale of the economy has two measures: (1) the throughput flow of physical resources that constitute the material component of the annual flow of goods and bads, and (2) the accumulated stock of goods in the form of wealth, and of bads in the form of 'illth' (to employ a useful a word coined by John Ruskin to designate the opposite of wealth). The throughput flow measure is emphasized because it is what affects ecosystem sources (depletion) and sinks (pollution) at the margin.

We would of course prefer not to produce bads or allow them to accumulate in illth, but since we live in a finite world governed by the laws of thermodynamics, and since we and the artifacts we produce are dissipative structures, we cannot avoid producing bads along with goods. If we stop depleting, we and our economy die of starvation; if we stop polluting, we die of constipation. If, however, we keep the throughput within the natural capacity of the ecosystem to absorb wastes and regenerate depleted resources, then the scale of the economy is ecologically 'sustainable'. There are many sustainable scales. The particular sustainable scale that maximizes the difference between wealth and illth (i.e., equates marginal goods produced with marginal bads), is the optimal scale. If we grow beyond this point then growth becomes uneconomic, and GNP becomes, in Ruskin's terms, 'a gilded index of far-reaching ruin.'

As growth pushes us from an empty world to a full world the limiting factor in production will increasingly become natural capital, not manmade capital – e.g., the fish catch today is no longer limited by manmade capital of fishing boats, but by the complementary natural capital of fish populations in the sea; irrigated agriculture is limited not by the manmade capital of pumps and pipes, but by the natural capital of aquifers and rivers, etc. As we move from the empty world into a full world, economic logic remains the same, namely to economize on and invest in the limiting factor. But the identity of the limiting factor changes from manmade capital to remaining natural capital, and our economizing efforts and policies must change accordingly. Therefore it becomes more important to study the nature of natural capital, of environmental goods and services – are they rival or non rival, excludable or non excludable – in order to know the extent to which they can be allocated by markets.

Ecological economics has no quarrel with the standard analysis of allocative efficiency, given prior social determination of the distribution and scale questions. Although the main difference has been the focus on scale, that difference has entailed more attention to distribution, especially to two often neglected dimensions of distribution: namely intergenerational distribution of the resource base, and distribution of 'places in the sun' between humans and all other species (biodiversity). Also as more vital natural resources and services cease being free goods, and are allocated by the market whenever possible, the fairness of the assumed distribution underlying efficient market allocation becomes more critical.

One question sure to be asked is: what is the relation between ecological economics and the fields of resource economics and environmental economics? The difference is that the latter two are both sub-fields of neoclassical economics, do not consider scale an issue, have no concept of throughput, and are focused on efficiency of allocation. Resource economics deals with the efficiency of allocation of labor and capital devoted to extractive industries.

It develops many useful concepts, such as scarcity rent, user cost, and Hotelling's rule. Likewise, environmental economics also focuses on efficiency of allocation and how it is disrupted by pollution externalities. Concepts of internalizing externalities by Pigouvian taxes or Coasian property rights are certainly useful and policy-relevant, but their aim is allocative efficiency via right prices, not sustainable scale. Ecological economics connects resource and environmental economics by connecting depletion with pollution by the concept of throughput.[2] It also pays much more attention to impacts on, and feedbacks from, the rest of the ecosystem induced by economic activities that cause depletion, pollution and entropic degradation, chief among which is the growing scale of the human economy.

Within this overall context of a difference in basic vision, there are in addition some important specific issues of debate between ecological and neoclassical economists. Below I list seven important ones.

1 *Whether natural and manmade capital are primarily substitutes or complements.* Ecological economics sees them as basically complements, substitutable only over a very limited margin. Neoclassical economics regards them as overwhelmingly substitutes. If complements, the one in short supply is limiting; if substitutes, there is no limiting factor. The phenomenon of limiting factor greatly increases the force of scarcity. For example, the scarcity of fish in the sea reduces the value of the complementary capital of fishing boats.

2 *The degree of coupling between physical throughput and GNP.* Ecological economics sees this coupling as by no means fixed, but not nearly as flexible as neoclassicals believe it to be – in other words, the 'dematerialization' of GNP and the 'information economy' will not save growth economics by forever reducing material intensity of GNP. We can certainly eat lower on the food chain, but we cannot eat recipes! While throughput per dollar of GDP has recently declined somewhat in some OECD countries, the absolute level of throughput continues to increase as GDP increases.

3 *The degree of coupling between GNP and welfare.* Here ecological economists consider the coupling very loose, at least beyond some minimum amount. Since many non-economic sources of welfare are damaged by growth in GNP, yet are not subtracted from GNP, the gap between Welfare and GNP widens as we move from the empty world to the full world. Neoclassical economists invariably advocate policies based on the assumption that welfare increase is rigidly coupled to GNP growth, even though in theory they allow themselves a few doubts. *In sum, ecological economists see GNP as tightly coupled*

to throughput and loosely coupled to welfare, while neoclassicals believe that GNP is only loosely coupled to throughput but tightly coupled to welfare. There is clearly room for empirical work here!

4   A deeper philosophical issue is the *relative importance in production of 'value added' versus 'that to which value is added'*. Value is added *to* the throughput flow of natural resources, and it is added *by* the transforming services of labor and capital. In Aristotle's terms labor and capital are the *efficient cause* of production (transforming agent), while natural resources are the *material* cause (that which is transformed). Neoclassical economists evidently do not believe in material causation because their production functions usually say that output is a function only of labor and capital inputs – a recipe that includes the cook and her kitchen, but no list of ingredients. When they occasionally do include resources as an input in the production function, they almost always do it in a way that contradicts the first law of thermodynamics.[3]

This error is repeated with admirable logical consistency in national income accounting where GNP is defined as the sum of all value added by labor and capital. *No valuable contribution from nature is recognized.* Natural resources in the ground are of zero value. When extracted they are valued by the marginal cost of capital and labor needed to extract them. Yes, there are royalties paid to resource owners, and that seems like a price for resources in the ground, but royalties are determined by savings on labor and capital costs of extraction whenever the owner's mine or well is richer or more accessible than the marginal mine or well. Resources are considered a free gift of nature, but some free gifts are easier to unwrap than others, and earn a rent determined by their relative ease of 'unwrapping' or extraction, as measured by labor and capital costs saved. Labor and capital remain the source of all value, nothing is attributed to nature.

Ecological economics recognizes that it is a lot easier to add value to low-entropy natural resources than to high-entropy waste, and that this extra receptivity to the addition of value by labor and capital should count as 'nature's value, value-added'. Low-entropy matter/energy is our ultimate means without which we cannot satisfy any of our ends, including that of staying alive. We cannot produce low entropy in net terms, but only use it up as it is supplied by nature. It is scarce and becoming more so. To omit this necessary contribution from nature both from our theory of production and from our accounting of value is a monumental error.

5   Growth has been treated as a macroeconomic issue, and frequently justified in terms of *GNP accounting*. If macro policies are designed to promote growth in GNP, then *ex post* accounting issues become relevant to *ex ante* policy in the next time period. Ecological economists have argued that whole categories being measured in GNP are mistakenly conceived, even if the prices by which the value of the category is measured are correct. I consider three such category mistakes in GNP accounting in the next section.

6   Although ecological economics focuses on the physical or real economy, *monetary issues* are also relevant. Under our current fractional reserve banking system, favored by the neoclassical mainstream, the money supply is a by-product of private commercial activities of lending and borrowing, rather than a public utility for effecting exchange. Over 95 per cent of our money supply is created by the private banking system (demand deposits) and bears interest as a condition of its existence. Unless loans are repaid at interest and renewed, the money supply will shrink and transactions will be more difficult. Fractional reserve money is therefore not neutral with respect to the scale of the physical economy – it requires growth of GDP to keep the money supply from declining. And GDP growth correlates positively with throughput growth. Furthermore the seigniorage (profit to the issuer of fiat money) now goes largely to the private sector (banks and their customers), rather than to the public sector, the government, the legitimate supplier of the public utility of money. A public good has been subjected to 'enclosure' – converted to a private good – just like the common pastures of England. Ecological economists also welcome the local reclaiming of money as a public utility by the various supplementary local currency movements. Local currencies allow people, especially in depressed areas, to make local exchanges (to employ each other) without first having to compete or be employed in the national economy just to get the money that allows them to avoid the enormous inconvenience of even local barter. Also seigniorage from local money can be used to finance local public goods.

7   Ecological economists' preference for the local is also expressed by their advocacy of internationalization and opposition to the globalization so favored by neoclassicals. *Internationalization* refers to the increasing importance of relations between nations: international trade, international treaties, alliances, protocols, etc. The basic unit of community and policy remains the nation, even as relations among nations, and among individuals in different nations, become increasingly necessary and important. *Globalization* refers

to global economic integration of many formerly national economies into one global economy, by free trade, especially by free capital mobility, and also, as a distant but increasingly important third, by easy or uncontrolled migration. *Globalization is the effective erasure of national boundaries for economic purposes.* As nations encounter limits to the scale of their national economies they seek to grow into the global commons, and into the ecological space of other nations. Global integration is an attempt by all economies to expand their national scale simultaneously. Global boundaries are of course not erased, and the result is that all countries now integrated will hit the limits to growth more simultaneously and less sequentially than before, with less opportunity to learn from the experience of others.

There are other issues, of course, but these seven illustrate the range and importance of the differences, and provide a research agenda for at least several years.

ECONOMIC GROWTH AND UNECONOMIC GROWTH

Economic growth is the major goal of most countries today. But what exactly do we mean by economic growth? Usually growth in GNP. But is economic growth so measured a holy icon of the *summum bonum*, or a statistically graven image of Mammon? It can be either because there are two very different meanings of economic growth in common usage, often confused, and certainly conflated in the measure of GNP:

1 'Economic growth' in sense (1) is simply the expansion of what we call 'the economy', i.e., production and consumption of goods and services. The economy is basically the human niche within the ecosystem, what we have called its scale. It is measured either by the stock of people and their artifacts, or by the flow of resources necessary to maintain and add to this stock. That, in physical terms, is the economy. When it gets bigger in scale we have growth of the economy, and refer to it in quite normal English usage as 'economic growth'.

2 'Economic growth' in sense (2) is any change in the economy for which extra benefits are greater than extra costs. Benefits and costs are not physical concepts, but refer to psychic experiences of increased or decreased welfare or enjoyment of life. The changes in the economy that cause changes in costs and benefits may themselves be either physical or nonphysical. Whatever profits us, whatever yields net benefits, is 'economic growth'. In public discourse we shift easily from one meaning of 'economic growth' to the other, and

thereby introduce a lot of confusion. Quantitative increase in size and qualitative improvement in wellbeing are very different things, and should not be lumped together, as done in calculating GNP.

As discussed earlier, there are *three* economic problems (allocation, distribution, and scale), not just one (allocation). Let us consider each in its relation to the two meanings of economic growth.

Economic growth as physical expansion of the economy (sense 1) clearly refers to the third problem (scale). Economic growth occurs when the economy gets physically larger, as measured either in its stock or flow dimensions. Since the economy grows into the rest of the finite ecosystem, not into the infinite Void, the economy becomes larger not only absolutely, but relative to its enveloping ecosystem. That is what is meant by scale increase, the first of the two common senses of 'economic growth.' The second sense of 'economic growth' – an increase in net benefit – may or may not result from growth in the first sense. More on that later.

Net benefit can result from an improvement in allocative efficiency – redirecting the same scale of resource use from low-value uses to high-value uses – this is economic growth in sense (2), but not in sense (1). Ecological economists have no problem with this kind of growth. But GNP does *not* distinguish growth based on greater allocative efficiency from growth based on larger scale.[4]

Let us turn now from scale and allocation to distribution – what is the relation of distribution to economic growth? Redistribution does not involve growth in sense (1) – scale stays the same. But does it involve economic growth in sense (2) – an improvement in net benefit? It does not involve a Pareto improvement because someone is made worse off in any redistribution, so neoclassical economists would disallow redistribution as a source of net social benefit.

But Vilfredo Pareto was not God, and many people, including some economists, think it perfectly reasonable to say that a dollar redistributed from the low marginal utility uses of the rich to the high marginal utility uses of the poor increases total social utility – i.e., signals an increase in net social benefit (economic growth in sense (2)).

The conclusion is inescapable if we assume the law of diminishing marginal utility, and the democratic principle that everyone's utility counts equally. Carried to its extreme this argument implies complete equality in the distribution of income, which is why many economists backed off from it. But principles need not be carried to extremes. For that matter, the Pareto principle has its own extreme – one person could have all of the surplus and everyone else live at subsistence (or die for that matter!), and there would still be no case for arguing that redistribution would increase net social benefit. Within limits, therefore, it is reasonable to say that redistribution can give us economic growth in sense (2), but not in sense (1) – another reason why ecological economists pay more attention to distribution than do neoclassicals.

Does economic growth in sense 1(scale) imply economic growth in sense 2 (net benefit)? No, absolutely not! Growth in the economy, sense (1) (expansion), *can be* economic growth in sense (2) (net benefit), but does not have to be. It can be, and in some countries probably already is, '*uneconomic growth*' – physical expansion that increases costs by more than benefits, thus reducing net benefit. Or, to recall John Ruskin's more colorful language, the economy becomes a net producer of 'illth', not wealth, and GNP would become, in Ruskin's terms, 'a gilded index of far-reaching ruin'. I think this is more than a logical possibility – it is a reasonable characterization of the actual state of affairs in some countries.

One will surely ask: What makes you think that growth has become uneconomic, say in the US? Some empirical evidence is referenced below,[5] but an equally fair question is to ask what makes economists think that benefits of growth are greater than costs at the current margin? GNP measures only benefits and not costs. Moreover GNP accounting commits several category mistakes – mistakes that count as benefits what are in fact costs. Three examples are discussed below.

Regrettably necessary defensive expenditures are what national income accountants call those expenditures we make to defend ourselves from the unwanted side effects of production and consumption by others. To escape the congestion and pollution of the city one buys another car and more gasoline to commute from the suburbs. This is a voluntary expenditure, but regrettable. Alternatively, one can remain in the city and regrettably spend more on soundproof windows, security services, and air filters. Regrettably necessary defensive expenditures are more coerced than voluntary, even though they are, strictly speaking, voluntary in the sense that no one had a gun at your head. Some reject such a distinction, arguing that all expenditure is defensive – food defends us against hunger, clothes defend us against cold, etc. True, but hunger and cold are not the consequences of other peoples' production and consumption – they are natural background default conditions. Defensive expenditures are '*anti-bads*' rather than goods. They counteract or neutralize the negative effects of other production. They *should be* counted as a cost of production of the activity that made them necessary, thereby increasing the price and reducing the amount purchased of that activity, and reducing scale. Instead we count them as purely voluntary purchases and *add* them to GDP. This may be economic growth in sense 1(expansion), but not in sense 2 (net benefit).

Monetization of previously non monetized production. A young colleague told me that he and his wife must make more money so that they can pay the woman who looks after their children enough to enable her to pay someone to look after her children while she is caring for theirs, etc. Childcare, housekeeping, cooking, and other household production used to be non-monetized. Now they have largely been shifted to the monetary sector and thus counted in GDP. Simply counting what was previously uncounted, even though it existed, is likely not to be economic growth in either sense (1) or (2).

Counting consumption of capital as income. Running down stocks of natural capital reduces future capacity to produce, even while increasing current consumption. Depleting nonrenewables is like running down an inventory without replacing it; consuming renewable stocks beyond sustainable yield is like failing to maintain and replace depreciating machinery. The same applies to failure to maintain social overhead capital such as roads, bridges, etc. Some would consider the costs of dishonesty, whether on the level of Enron or of local robbery, as the cost of having allowed the depletion of traditional social standards of honesty, or 'moral capital'. Mis-counting capital consumption as income increases economic growth in sense (1), but not in sense (2), at least in the long term.

The above cases are examples of uneconomic growth in GNP even with correct prices – they involve accounting category mistakes rather than measurement errors – counting intermediate as final production, counting traditional but newly monetized production as if it were new production, and treating capital drawdown as if it were income. Each of these categories may be priced correctly, but the categories are misused. A job not worth doing is not worth doing well.

More convincing to me than empirical measures, which I along with others have attempted, is the simple theoretical argument that as the scale of the human subsystem (the economy) expands relative to the fixed dimensions of the containing and sustaining ecosystem, we necessarily encroach upon that system and must pay the opportunity cost of lost ecosystem services as we enjoy the extra benefit of increased human scale.

As rational beings we presumably satisfy our most pressing wants first, so that each increase in scale yields a diminishing marginal benefit. Likewise, we presumably would sequence our takeovers of the ecosystem so as to sacrifice first the *least* important natural services. Obviously we have not yet begun to do this because we are just now recognizing that natural services are scarce. But let me credit us with capacity to learn. Even so, that means that increasing marginal costs and decreasing marginal benefits will accompany growth in human scale. At some point increasing marginal cost will equal declining marginal benefit. That is the optimum scale. Beyond that point growth becomes uneconomic in sense (2) – the economy becomes a net producer of a current flow of bads and an accumulating stock of illth.

If we add to the limits of finitude and non-growth of the total system the additional limits of entropy and ecosystem complexity, then it is clear that the optimal scale will be encountered sooner rather than later. Additionally, if we expand our anthropocentric view of the optimum scale to a more biocentric view, by which I mean one that attributes not only instrumental but also some degree of intrinsic value to other species, then it is clear that the optimal scale of the human presence will be further limited by the duty to reserve a place in the sun for other species, even beyond what they 'pay for' in terms of their instrumental value to us. 'Biodiversity' is an empty slogan unless we are willing to limit human scale. And of course the whole idea of 'sustainability' is that the optimal scale should exist for a very long time, not just a few generations. Clearly a sustainable scale will be smaller than an unsustainable scale. For all these reasons I think that, for policy purposes, we do not really need exact empirical measures of the optimal scale.

Consider a thought experiment. Imagine an economy in which all prices were right – at the initial scale of the economy air and water are free goods so their right price is zero. Now suppose scale increases – population and per capita resource use both triple, so scale goes up nine-fold (roughly what has happened in my lifetime). Now air and water are scarce, so their right prices are no longer zero, but positive numbers, which are, let us assume, accurately set. In both cases right prices give us a Pareto optimal allocation and the neoclassical economist is happy. But are people indifferent between the two cases? Should they be? Some will agree with John Stuart Mill that:

> It is not good for a man to be kept perforce at all times in the presence of his species... Nor is their much satisfaction in contemplating a world with nothing left to the spontaneous activity of nature; with every rood of land brought into cultivation... every flowery waste or natural pasture plowed up, all quadrupeds or birds which are not domesticated for man's use exterminated as his rivals for food, and every hedgerow or superfluous tree rooted out, and scarcely a place left where a wild shrub or flower could grow without being eradicated as a weed in the name of improved agriculture.[5]

To bring Mill up to date we need only extend the predicament of the wildflower to the traditional agricultural crops that replaced it. These crops are now in danger of being eradicated by their genetically engineered cousins, designed to grow faster and be more resistant to both pests and pesticides.

The difference between Mill's view and that of his opposites, such as Julian Simon and Peter Huber, runs deep. Some will consider Mill old fashioned and agree with Huber, who says:

Cut down the last redwood for chopsticks, harpoon the last blue whale for sushi, and the additional mouths fed will nourish additional human brains, which will soon invent ways to replace blubber with olestra and pine with plastic. Humanity can survive just fine in a planet-covering crypt of concrete and computers... There is not the slightest scientific reason to suppose that such a world must collapse under its own weight or that it will be any less stable than the one we now inhabit.[6]

Huber does admit that such a world might not be as pretty, but it is clear that on balance he likes it better than Mill's world.

Neither side will be comforted by the neoclasssical economist pointing out that in both cases right prices will give us a Pareto-optimal allocation. Some will want a larger scale, some a smaller – but it seems that only the neoclassical economist is indifferent.

Some say that it is idle to talk about maintaining a steady state at some limited scale unless we first know the optimal scale at which to be stable. On the contrary, unless we first know how to be stable, it is idle to know the optimal scale. Such knowledge would only enable us to recognize and wave goodbye to the optimal scale as we grew through it! If one jumps from an airplane one needs a parachute more than an altimeter.

TOWARDS POLICY

So let us begin to search for some parachutes to arrest the free-fall of growth in scale.

We measure growth of the macroeconomy by GNP. Does that measure reflect economic growth in sense (1) (scale) or in sense (2) (net benefit)? As we have seen it conflates the two. But by historical design and intention it mainly reflects sense (1), growth in the physical scale of aggregate production. However, economists soon began to treat GNP also as a measure of growth in sense (2), any change yielding net benefits. They reasoned that for something to count in GNP, someone had to buy it, and consequently that person must have judged that the item benefited her more than it cost her, so its production must represent economic growth in sense (2) as well as in sense (1). Consequently, for most economists the concept of 'uneconomic growth in GNP' makes no sense. There is no separate problem of scale. The free market is thought to optimize scale and allocation simultaneously.[7] Presumably you could temporarily have uneconomic growth in the scale of the economy (sense 1), but if it were truly uneconomic growth (sense 2), it would cost people more than it was worth and they would learn not to buy it, and therefore it would not be counted in GNP, and whoever was making it would go out of business, and scale would decline.

This individualistic, consumer-sovereign judgment of costs and benefits has its obvious strengths, but also some less obvious weaknesses. It assumes that *individual* costs and benefits coincide with *social* costs and benefits – in other words that the prices faced by the consumer are a good measure of opportunity cost, not just to the individual consumer, but to society as a whole. However, our economy has a bias toward privatizing or internalizing benefits and socializing or externalizing costs, in the interest of maximizing private profits, thus driving a wedge between private and social.

Collecting and selling poisonous mushrooms no doubt has greater social costs than benefits. But if the costs fall on the public who cannot distinguish poisonous from non poisonous varieties, while the benefits all accrue to me, then I will find the activity privately profitable. Frequently the prices individuals pay are an underestimate of full social opportunity cost, so it is true that much stuff is purchased only because the prices are wrong – too low. Therefore some growth in GNP is uneconomic due to wrong prices. The economists' answer is admirably straightforward – get the prices right! I certainly agree. But note that getting prices right does not mean that GDP can grow forever – it means that growth as measured by GDP based on right prices would presumably have stopped sooner, when it became uneconomic – when it began to cost more than it was worth as measured by corrected prices – when the price of my poisonous mushrooms was high enough to pay wrongful death claims to my customers' survivors. By then I would be out of business. Right prices are all to the good. However, whether right prices are by themselves *sufficient* to avoid uneconomic growth requires further consideration.

Indifference to scale is only one neoclassical reaction. Somewhat contradictorily, neoclassical economists frequently argue that scale will automatically be optimized along with allocation. The first view, indifference to scale, is logically consistent with neoclassical theory, but inconsistent with the facts (people are not indifferent to scale). The second view, that scale is automatically solved along with allocation, is either logically inconsistent or requires absurd premises to be consistent. Regarding this view, it is inconsistent for neoclassicals to claim that the same set of prices that optimizes allocation would also optimize scale. That would sin against the mathematical condition that we cannot maximize simultaneously for two independent variables, as well as against Jan Tinbergen's policy rule that for every independent policy goal we need a separate policy instrument. If we use relative prices to solve the allocation problem, we cannot simultaneously use prices to solve the scale problem (or the distribution problem).

The only way out of this logical difficulty, and a way taken by some economists, is to claim that the allocation and scale problems are not independent, but merely the same problem. The way to reduce scale to allocation is to assume that scale is total. Everything is economy, nothing is environment. Everything in creation, every whale and every amoeba, is conceptually yoked to pull the human wagon, and their services are allocated according to pecuniary calculation of present value maximization. The scale of the economy would not be a separate issue because there is nothing that is external to the economy. This is the result of carrying the principle of internalization of costs and benefits to its extreme. When everything is internalized, then nothing is external, the scale of the economy is 100 per cent by definition.

One of the saving graces of neoclassical economists has been their humility when faced with the information requirements of a centrally planned economy. The information requirements of 'centrally planning' the entire biosphere, even with liberal use of markets, is so utopian that honest neoclassicals will blush at the very thought.

Given prior social decisions on scale and distribution, the market can, as always, determine allocatively efficient prices. Indirectly these prices would then reflect socially imposed scale and distributive limits and therefore may be thought of as, in a sense, 'internalizing' the values of sustainability and justice that have previously been decided politically, independently of prices.

Another way to make the point is to distinguish *price-determining* from *price-determined* policy actions. Allocation is price-determined. Distribution and scale are, or should be, price-determining. What then determines distribution and scale? Social values of justice and of sustainability. Once these social values are reflected in constraints on the market, then the allocative prices calculated by the market will reflect, and in a sense 'internalize' these external constraints. We cannot use these corrected allocative prices to calculate the cost and benefit of a change in scale or distribution, because we first had to set the distribution and scale to get the corrected allocative prices.

The way to get prices to reflect the values of just distribution and sustainable scale is to impose quantitative restrictions on the market that limit the degree of inequality in distribution of income and wealth to a just range; and that limit the scale of physical throughput from and back to nature to a sustainable volume. These imposed macro-scale limits reflect the social values of justice and sustainability, which are not personal tastes and cannot be reflected in the market by individualistic actions. The market can, however, recalculate allocative prices that are consistent with the *imposed* scale and distribution constraints, thereby in a sense 'internalizing' these social values into prices. Scale and distribution limits are our 'parachutes'. Allocative prices are more like an altimeter.

Finally it is worth emphasizing a general policy consequence of these considerations: namely, 'frugality first, efficiency second'. By frugality I mean limiting scale by limiting quantity of throughput. Limited throughput will drive up resource prices (the rents can be captured as public revenue and used to finance the reduction of other taxes). Higher resource prices will induce greater efficiency. If on the other hand we continue to follow the usual policy of 'efficiency first' we do not induce frugality as a secondary consequence. Instead, efficiency improvements make frugality less necessary. A more efficient car is equivalent to discovering more oil. It will have the same consequence, namely reducing the price of oil. That will induce more use of oil than before. True, the oil will be burned more efficiently, but more will be used. We will have become more efficient and less frugal. We must become *more* frugal. If we seek frugality first by limiting scale, we will get efficiency as a bonus.

Standard economics strains out the gnat of allocative inefficiency while swallowing the twin camels of unjust distribution and unsustainable scale. As distribution becomes more unjust big money buys political power and uses it to avoid any redistribution. A favorite political ploy for avoiding redistribution is to emphasize economic growth. Growth in sense (1) leads to an unsustainable scale and uneconomic growth in sense (2). But if growth is uneconomic then it makes us poorer, not richer. Growth is then no longer the cure for poverty and cannot substitute for redistribution. Consequently, the concepts of uneconomic growth, accumulating illth, and unsustainable scale have to be incorporated in economic theory if it is to be capable of expressing what is happening in the world. This is what ecological economists are trying to do.

24

What's Wrong with GDP and Growth? The Need for Alternative Indicators

JEAN GADREY[1]

UNIVERSITÉ LILLE, FRANCE

It is customary to say that developing countries are looking for growth. On the other hand, it might reasonably be suggested that developed Western countries are now looking for what might be termed post-growth development and the intellectual tools to denote, conceptualise and evaluate such development.

At first sight, however, the key indicator that developed societies use in formulating their overall judgements on progress or their anxieties about the future is still, perhaps more than ever, the standard indicator of economic growth, that is the one that measures variations in GDP (gross domestic product) or some variant of that notion, which remains the cornerstone of national accounting. Thus what is being monitored and measured is the total 'volume' of goods and services produced each year and the variations therein.

There are of course other major indicators that regularly attract attention in public debate and in the media, notably the unemployment and inflation rates and, more recently, the leading stock exchange indices. However, the level of GDP and growth remain the major symbols of success and progress. This was clearly demonstrated at the beginning of 2002 by the 'storm' aroused by the publication of dubious EUROSTAT statistics comparing the level of per capita GDP in EU member states and the changes in the rankings of member states since 1990.

The domination of these criteria has been a target of criticism since the 1970s. Such criticism has, on occasions, emanated from economists but usually from other 'anti-establishment' actors, some of whose protests have had a social slant (growth is not necessarily to be equated with social progress) while others have been more concerned with environmental issues (growth can destroy non-renewable natural resources). However, these criticisms have had little impact until now, at least as far as the institutionalisation of alternative indicators is concerned.

There are several reasons for the ineffectualness of this criticism. The main one is that, even though it is true that growth is not the answer to all problems, many people believe, quite rightly, that it can open up room for manoeuvre and improve certain aspects of daily life, employment, etc. In the short and medium term, therefore, it is regarded positively by large sections of the population. This widespread acceptance of the benefits of growth is, incidentally, further reinforced by the fact that it is encapsulated in one final figure (the rate of growth achieved or hoped for) that ignores the qualitative aspect of growth (what has improved?). Great care is taken to avoid specifying, for example, who has received what (the 'distribution of value added').[2] And even less mention is made of certain problems of measurement which are, nevertheless, quite formidable and would undoubtedly undermine the religion of the growth rate if they were ever to become the focus of public attention.[3]

However, there are other explanations for the relatively small impact these criticisms have had. One of them consists of the theoretical and methodological weaknesses of the alternative indicators that have been suggested in the past, and their inability to produce meaning.

Nevertheless, it would seem that recent years have seen genuine advances in the search for indicators that are both theoretically 'defensible' and capable of producing an alternative meaning (an extended vision of wealth). This is one of the most dynamic and innovative areas of contemporary socio-economics. Following an investigation of the limits of the concepts of GDP and growth in part 1, part 2 of this chapter will be given over to an initial assessment of these innovations.

1. WHAT'S WRONG WITH GDP AND GROWTH?

The calculation of growth is based on the definition of what is termed the gross domestic product. GDP is made up of two parts. The first is the market value of all the goods and services sold in a country in the course of a year (to be precise, I should say the market value *added*, but that does not change anything I say subsequently) of all the goods and services sold in a country in the course of year. This market value is then supplemented by a second part, namely the cost of producing the non-market services provided by government bodies: state education, central and local government services, and so on. Thus – and this is a crucial point – economic wealth measured in this way, that is GDP, is purely market and monetary wealth. And growth is defined as the increase in GDP, that is the increase in the volume of goods and services that are sold or costed in monetary terms. Once again, I'm simplifying somewhat, since in order to evaluate GDP in volume (or in 'real') terms, account must be taken of inflation, etc. However, this too has no effect on what follows.

This is all that it is necessary to know in order to understand what the main issues at stake are. Indeed, this way of measuring national wealth has three major consequences:

- everything that can be sold and has monetary value added will bump up GDP and growth, irrespective of whether or not it adds to individual and collective well-being;

- many activities and resources that contribute to well-being are not counted, simply because they are not market activities or resources or because they do not have a direct production cost expressed in money terms;

- GDP measures only outputs. It takes no account of 'outcomes', which are more important in assessing progress. It indicates how much 'having' there is in a society, not its well-being. Nor does it take account of the distribution of the wealth it measures, or of inequalities, poverty, economic security, etc., despite the fact that they are virtually unanimously regarded as aspects of a society's well-being.

1.1   The Defence Put Up By Orthodox Economists

Before examining several examples of the limits of GDP, a slight digression might be useful. If you question economists and experts in national accounting on this matter, they all adopt a simple line of defence: we know perfectly well that GDP and growth do not measure well-being! That's not what they're intended to do! Your accusation is unfounded! Nobody's stopping you suggesting indicators of well-being in addition to GDP and using them! Just leave us to get on with our work and you do whatever you want to do!

These economists are absolutely right-and absolutely wrong. They're absolutely right, because the current measure of GDP is indeed not designed to assess well-being. It is not an indicator of well-being, of human development or of sustainable development. Such indicators have, therefore, to be constructed in different ways and in parallel with GDP. However, they are also absolutely wrong, for three reasons.

Firstly, if the current measure of GDP is not designed for this purpose, what is stopping us from developing it, from redefining it so that it encompasses the forms of wealth it currently ignores? After all, national accounting has evolved since its early days and some activities or services that were ignored at the beginning have subsequently been included. Why can other enlargements not be considered?

Secondly, why do economists and experts in national accounting (encouraged by policymakers, who commission these statistics) devote 100 per cent of their efforts to measuring and using GDP and economic growth instead of directing only 50 per cent of their efforts in that direction and reserving the other 50 per cent for developing and diffusing alternative indicators that better reflect notions such as well-being, human development, social development, sustainable development and so on? Are they not imprisoned in a very narrow vision of what really counts and what should be counted?

Thirdly, economists state that they do not confuse economic growth with growth in well-being and that if others confuse the two, it's nothing to do with them. That may be so, but if it is why is it that, in the media and in public debates, we hear incessantly of economic growth as the indispensable lynchpin of progress, while there is little if any mention of indicators of social health, of well-being or environmental protection? Do economists have no responsibility for this unbalanced situation, in which a country's health is judged virtually exclusively in terms of its economic health?

I come now to a few examples that will help us better understand how far removed the notions of GDP and economic growth are from those of well-being and development.

1.2   Growth of What?

The damage caused by the current growth model is not counted and is not deducted from the evaluation of wealth produced.

By way of a first example, let us take a society in which there are many road accidents, which require medical care, vehicle repairs, emergency services etc. Such a society will tend to have a higher GDP than a society in which people drive carefully (all other things being equal, of course). More precisely, it will tend to direct a large share of its economic resources and activities towards the repair of damage, *without any overall increase in well-being*, rather than towards the production of additional well-being.

Imagine: if a county paid 10 per cent of its population to destroy goods, make holes in roads, damage vehicles, etc., and another 10 per cent to make good the damage, it would have the same GDP as a country in which the same 20 per cent of employment (whose effects on well-being cancel each other out) was given over to improving health life expectancy, educational levels and participation in cultural and leisure activities.

The same idea can be applied to expenditure incurred in making good environmental damage linked to human activity. This is what ecologists call defensive expenditure. From this perspective, expenditure (and the corresponding output) incurred in repairing the damage caused by human actions should not be counted as a positive contribution to 'real' wealth. If such damage (pollution, crime, road accidents, etc.) reduces well-being and makes it necessary to produce goods and services (whose value is X) in order to repair or defend against this reduction, there can be no question of X being counted as a positive item in any measurement of 'real' wealth. And since the conventional measure of GDP counts the defensive output X as a positive item, which is acceptable from a purely economic perspective, X must be deducted from GDP in order better to identify 'real' wealth (that which contributes to well-being). If households are purchasing more and more anti-burglary equipment or anti-pollution devices in response to increasing risks, the corresponding expenditures should be deducted from GDP (or their standard of living) if it is desired to depict the variations in their well-being more accurately. There is no need for such equipment in countries in which the incidence of burglary or of pollution is very low. As Fred Hirsch wrote in a superb book[4], if the outside temperature drops and the heating is turned up in order to maintain the inside temperature at a constant level, there is no increase in well-being. This holds true if 'outside temperature' is replaced by 'pollution, crime, accidents, uncontrolled urbanisation, etc.' and "turning the heating up' by 'increasing reparative or defensive output'.

Let us take a second example. The organised destruction of the Amazon rainforest is an activity that increases global GDP. Nowhere is any account taken of the resultant loss of natural resources, or of the various effects on climate, biodiversity, the long term and the needs of future generations. GDP takes no account of losses of natural resources. On the contrary, it counts the organised destruction of such resources as a positive item on the balance sheet. Similarly, a company that pollutes a river in order to ensure its own economic growth and thereby contribute to GDP causes damage that reduces some people's well-being. Such damage is not included in any measure of economic wealth.

In all the previous examples, what emerges is the fact that nowhere are the damage and destruction (and losses of well-being) linked to economic growth accounted for. Thus we have indicators that incessantly add and add economic wealth as soon as production and monetary sale take place, without any concern for what is lost on the way, which may not have any market value but may be of enormous value for our current well-being and that of future generations.

A. Positive contributions essential to well-being are not counted

In addition to these examples in which no account is taken of losses of well-being, there are other in which gains, that is contributions essential to well-being, are not counted. A few examples are listed below.

First, if, in order to achieve high growth rates, people are forced or encouraged to work more and more and to enjoy less and less leisure and free time, this phenomenon will be reflected only in an increase in GDP, since an increase in free time is not regarded as an asset worthy of being included in the measure of national wealth. I have not selected this example at random. In the United States, average annual working time per person has increased by the equivalent of five weeks of work (204 hours) since 1980. This contrasts with what has happened in virtually all European countries, where there has been a significant reduction. This is an excellent example of an essential contribution to well-being, namely free time, that does not appear in measures of wealth.

A second example of a contribution that is disregarded is voluntary work, which is not included among the activities that contribute to national wealth as defined by GDP precisely because it is free and non-monetary. Does this form of work not produce wealth and well-being in the same way as paid work?

The third and final example of a forgotten contribution is even more significant. It is domestic work, the work carried out in the private sphere, mostly by women, which is not the least of the reasons why it is ignored. This is invisible work *par excellence*. And yet enormous volumes of such work are performed, and there is no doubt that it contributes to well-being in the same way as paid work. It is estimated that the total time devoted to unpaid domestic work in developed countries is of the same order of magnitude as that spent on paid work. If it was decided, for example, to attribute to it the same monetary value per hour of work, GDP would be doubled overnight! And even if it were given a lower value, for example one equivalent to the hourly cost of a cleaning lady or a home help, there would still be considerable amounts of wealth being disregarded.

B. GDP is concerned only with outputs and not with the outcomes of economic activity in terms of well-being

It is no secret that having a great deal is not the same as well-being. This latter notion can be approached in two ways. The first is to evaluate subjective well-being by means of opinion polls or satisfaction surveys. These are, it is true, tricky to interpret but they do at least reveal very considerable discrepancies between the evolution of living standards and perceptions of the evolution of well-being. Numerous surveys conducted in several countries have shown that this is so. For example, 'when Canadians were asked in 1998 how the overall financial situation of their generation compared to that of their parents at the same stage of life, less than half (44 per cent) thought that there had been an improvement, despite an increase of approximately 60 per cent in real GDP per capita over the previous 25 years.'[5]

The other approach to well-being is to assess objective well-being on the basis of a range of criteria such as good health and life expectancy, access to education and knowledge, economic security, the incidence of poverty and inequalities, housing and working conditions, etc. Now GDP measures only volumes of outputs (the volume of goods and the quantity of services consumed) and is not concerned with these outcomes. For example, the contribution of health services to growth is measured only in terms of the volume of consultations, hospital admissions, treatment etc. and never in terms of the contribution such services make to improvements in health and living conditions. With the present type of measurement method, an effective policy on the prevention of health risks would tend to reduce the contribution of health services to growth whereas it would probably increase well-being.

1.3 Growth for Whom?

Besides the question of 'growth for what?', there is also the question of 'growth for whom?', that is the question of inequalities. Now the same growth rate of 2 or 3 per cent per annum over a number of years may go hand in hand, in certain cases, with a widening or a reduction in social inequalities. And yet these phenomena have no part in the prevailing concept of wealth. Is this normal? Does the fact of living in a society in which vast numbers of poor people coexist with a handful of very rich individuals have no impact at all on our well-being? Does not a Euro or dollar's worth of growth in a poor man's pocket produce more well-being than the same sum added to Bill Gates' wallet? And yet this is the hypothesis advanced by those who regard GDP, wealth and progress as one and the same thing.

2. Alternative, Synthetic Indicators

Since the beginning of the 1990s, there has been a proliferation of attempts on a global scale to produce alternative visions of wealth and indicators thereof, a sure sign of increasing protest. It will take time to establish new norms, but it would seem that an increasingly powerful wave is on the move and beginning to affect the major international institutions. I have selected four of these innovations on the grounds that they are well known internationally and could possibly be used by economists seeking alternatives to current practice.

They all involve the use of synthetic indicators with the aim of encapsulating in a single final figure, like GDP but with considerably more uncertainties, various aspects of progress that others prefer to present separately in the form of reports or 'dashboards'. However, as Amartya Sen has shown with regard to the UNDP Human Development Index, which was the first major international alternative indicator, these two approaches should not be pitted against each other. Provided there is sufficient transparency, they can both improve the quality of public debate, mutually reinforce each other and contribute to the formation of individual and collective assessments of progress.

2.1   The UNDP Indicators

Since 1990, the United Nations Development Programme (UNDP) has published a Human Development Report,[6] which includes the celebrated, albeit rudimentary Human Development Index, whose diffusion throughout the world has been a spectacular success beyond the developing counties for which it was initially intended. This indicator is quite simply the average of three indicators that classify countries on a scale of 0 to 1: GDP per capita (expressed in purchasing power parities[7]), life expectancy at birth and a knowledge index (measured by a weighted combination of the adult literacy rate and the gross enrolment ratio). The UNDP has subsequently published other synthetic indicators each year. Of these, only the GEM (Gender Empowerment Measure, an indicator of women's participation in economic and political life) and the HPI (Human Poverty Index) will be examined here. For developed countries, this latter indicator is based on four criteria that are all given the same weighting: probability at birth of not surviving to age 60, percentage of adults lacking functional literary skills, percentage of people living below the poverty line and long-term unemployment rate.

Table 1 shows the ranking of the 20 leading countries (only 17 in the case of the HPI, for lack of data for some countries) by, respectively, the HDI, HPE and the GEM that appeared in the 2003 report. In addition, column 2 ranks the countries in the first column by the single criterion of GDP per capita.

The UNDP indicators, particularly the HDI, have attracted some strong criticism. Critics have pointed, among other things, to imperfections, sometimes enormous, in some of the data, which for some countries produce results that are simply counterintuitive, to the allegedly 'arbitrary' weightings used to produce the synthetic indicators (in general, the various component indices are given equal weighting) and to a 'third world' bias, which renders the HDI unsuited to producing significant differences between rich countries (in 1999, the 20 leading countries all exceeded 0.9 on the scale, the maximum value being 1). All this is true, but it is also defensible and to some extent surmountable, as the adjustments made over the years have shown. Nevertheless, it remains the case that any comparative approach using statistics that attempt to cover every single country will inevitably come up against limitations with respect to relevance and reliability. Thus we need to turn to other approaches (the ones that will be outlined below) that do not seek to be global in their scope and may consequently provide a basis for making more detailed and accurate evaluations of each country or of a limited number of countries.

Whatever their limitations may be, these indicators already show many things, even in the case of developed countries. It is not without significance, for example, to note that the Nordic countries achieve an excellent ranking for inequality reduction (poverty, gender inequalities) while retaining a decent ranking when economic wealth comes into play (as one component of the HDI). Nor is it entirely without interest to observe those countries whose social performance (in terms of ranking) is significantly better than their raw economic performance (the Nordic countries once again). It is also worthy of note that the four countries ranked lowest in terms of the incidence of poverty (albeit in a list made up of only 17 countries) are, in descending order, Australia, the UK, Ireland and the USA.

Table 1 Developed countries ranked by four indicators (UNDP report 2003)

HDI (2001) ranking	Ranking by GDP/capita	Poverty HPI-2 (2001)	Gender empowerment GEM (2001)
1. Norway	5	1. Sweden	1. Iceland
2. Iceland	4	2. Norway	2. Norway
3. Sweden	18	3. Finland	3. Sweden
4. Australia	12	4. Netherlands	4. Denmark
5. Netherlands	8	5. Denmark	5. Finland
6. Belgium	11	6. Germany	6. Netherlands
7. USA	2	7. Luxembourg	7. Austria
8. Canada	9	8. France	8. Germany
9. Japan	14	9. Spain	9. Canada
10. Switzerland	7	10. Japan	10. USA
11. Denmark	6	11. Italy	11. Australia
12. Ireland	3	12. Canada	12. New Zealand
13. UK	19	13. Belgium	13. Switzerland
14. Finland	17	14. Australia	14. Spain
15. Luxembourg	1	15. UK	15. Belgium
16. Austria	10	16. Ireland	16. Ireland
17. France	20	17. USA	17. UK
18. Germany	13		18. The Bahamas
19. Spain	24		19. Costa Rica
20. New Zealand	28		20. Barbados
21. Italy	16		21. Portugal

Reading the table: for each of these four indicators, the country ranked highest is the one that performs 'the best'. Thus in terms of poverty, Sweden is ranked first in the sense that it is the country where, according to this indicator, there is least poverty.

2.2 The Index of Social Health

In 1996 two American researchers (Marc and Marque-Luisa Miringoff) produced and launched a debate on a global indicator of 'social health' for their country.[8] Their indicator was the average of 16 existing indicators, each of which has values ranging from 0 to 100. For each of these 16 variables, a mark of 0 is given for the 'worst value' achieved during the reference period for the index (generally two or three decades) and a mark of 100 is given for the 'best value'.

The criteria used in constructing the index relate to health, education, unemployment, poverty and inequalities, accidents and various risks (see Table 2). It amounts to a sort of summary of what these researchers see as the major contemporary social problems, taking into account the relative significance of these issues in the ongoing public debate in the USA. This indicator has achieved a certain degree of fame in North America and elsewhere as a result of the publication in the magazine *Challenge* in 1996 of a fairly striking graph depicting both the curve of economic growth (the evolution of GDP, base 50 in 1959) and that of the index of social health since 1959, with the two diverging spectacularly from 1973–74 onwards (Graph 1 below).

Graph 1 Index of Social Health and Economic Growth, USA, 1959–1996

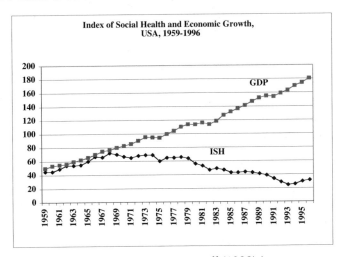

(Source: M. Miringoff and M. G. Miringoff (1999).)

Table 2 The components of the index of social health

Children	Youth	Adults	Elderly	All ages
Infant mortality	Youth suicides	Unemployment	Persons 65 and over in poverty	Violent crime
	Drug use	Average weekly earnings	Life expectancy aged 65+	Alcohol-related traffic fatalities
Child abuse	High-school dropouts	Health Insurance coverage		Affordable Housing
Child poverty	Teenage births			Inequality in family income

2.3 The Index of Economic Well-Being

The index of economic well-being constructed by the Canadians Osberg and Sharpe is undoubtedly one of the most promising initiatives, particularly because it links national accounts and certain sets of social statistics. It takes the average of four component indicators, which are themselves synthetic, relating respectively to consumption flows broadly defined (including household production, leisure and other unmarketed goods and services), stocks of productive resources (economic, human and environmental capital), economic inequalities and poverty and economic insecurity (economic risks linked to unemployment, illness and old age and those incurred by single-parent households). The economic and social dimensions play a very important role, a significantly greater one than environmental issues. However, since this method of construction is very transparent, there is no reason why, after discussion, other weightings could not be selected.[1] These researchers have applied their method to various OECD countries. Graphs 2 and 3 show two very contrasting cases, that of the UK and that of Norway, for the period 1980–1999 (base 1 in 1980 for each country). In the former, the index of economic well-being (bottom curve) stagnates then dips before beginning to climb again (from 1991 onwards) but without regaining its 1980 level, even though economic growth (as reflected in the evolution of GDP per capita depicted in the top curve) was, on average, good. It is the economic equality and security indices (not shown here) that caused the overall index to take a downward turn. It may be no coincidence that Thatcher's long period as prime minister, which lasted 11 years, came to an end in late 1990. In the case of Norway, economic growth (which was slightly higher than the UK's over the same period) and 'economic well-being' evolved in unison.

Graph 2 United Kingdom: Index of Economic Well-Being (IEWB) and GDP per capita, 1980–1999

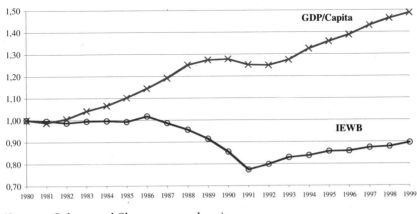

(Source: Osberg and Sharp, www.csls.ca)

Graph 3 Norway: Index of Economic Well-Being (IEWB) and GDP per capita, 1980-1999

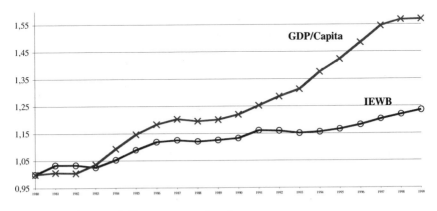

(Source: Osberg and Sharp, www.csls.ca)

2.3 Sustainable Development and the Genuine Progress Indicator

In 1987, the World Commission of Environment and Development, known as the Brundtland Commission after its chair, put forward a definition of sustainable development that is now widely cited but lacks precision: 'development that meets the needs of the present without compromising the ability of future generations to meet their own needs'.

This notion is clearly in need of clarification, and the trend that is now emerging at international level, which was vigorously reaffirmed at the 2002 Earth Summit in Johannesburg, is to seek to do so by taking into account the economic, environmental and social aspects of sustainability. This is what is reflected in the various synthetic indicators of sustainable development that have been produced in the last ten years under various names (Green National Product, Index of Sustainable Economic Welfare, Dashboard of Sustainable Development) and by a multiplicity of actors (NGOs such as Friends of the Earth, various foundations, national environmental institutes, etc.). In all cases, the method of aggregation adopted is the monetarisation of the component variables.

A good example of an indicator of this type, constructed after much careful thought as to the method, is the Genuine Progress Indicator (GPI), which Redefining Progress, a Californian institute that campaigns and researches on environmental and sustainability issues, has been developing since 1995. The method (which draws on earlier, and controversial, work by Nordhaus and Tobin in 1972) takes as its starting point the traditional measure of household consumption. To this are added various contributions to 'real' wealth and well-being, including voluntary activity and domestic work. The estimated value of 'lost wealth' is then subtracted; the main element here is natural resource depletion (destruction of the ozone layer, other environmental damage, destruction of non-renewable resources) but a social dimension is also included (social cost of unemployment, crime, road accidents, increasing inequality). This 'extended national accounting system' seeks to calculate (as far as possible) a monetary value for all these added or subtracted effects, e.g. the value added of voluntary work, the (lost) value of environmental damage, etc.

The result of these calculations is no less spectacular than those of the previous indicators, as is shown by the example of the USA between 1950 and 1998. While gross economic wealth (GDP) per capita virtually tripled in 50 years, net economic, social and environmental wealth (GPI) per person barely increased at all, and actually declined from 1980 onwards.

CONCLUSION

It has to be conceded that all these alternative indicators (particularly those that attempt to put a monetary value on sustainable development) depend on questionable conventions, but this is not sufficient reason to ignore them. Firstly, indicators other than those outlined above that also seek to combine the economic, social and environmental dimensions, in very different

Graph 4   GDP and GPI per capita, USA, 1950–1998

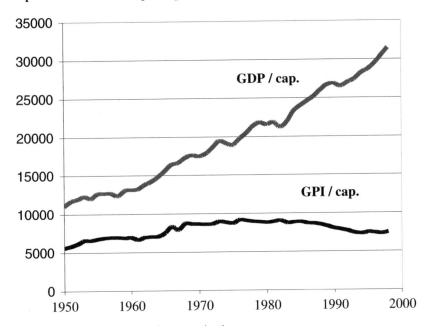

(Source: www.rprogress.org/projects/gpi)

proportions and using very different methods, actually provide fairly similar diagnoses, particularly over long observation periods. Secondly, it is difficult to see how 'questionable conventions' can be dispensed with in attempting to construct indicators encompassing the environment, quality of life and social progress and hence value systems. Even the 'serious' economic indicators are riddled with questionable conventions, as the debates on the very considerable uncertainties about the comparisons of GDP per capita in Europe demonstrated. Finally, the emerging international debate on these questions can be expected to improve matters.

One day, perhaps, the European and international criteria used to evaluate 'convergence' and 'good governance' will take as much account of such alternative indicators as of countries' economic and financial performance. Well, we can dream, can't we?

A FEW WEBSITES ABOUT THE NEW INDICATORS

- On the UNDP indicators: www.undp.org
- On the Index of Social Health: no website, but an excellent book: M. and M.L. Miringoff, *The Social Health of the Nation*, Oxford: Oxford University Press, 1999.
- On Osberg and Sharpe's index of economic well-being: www.csls.ca

- On the indicators of sustainable development, include the GPI, see Friends of the Earth's British website : www.foe.co.uk
- The GPI : www.rprogress.org/projects/gpi
- The dashboard of sustainable development: http://esl.jrc.it/dc

PART VII

GLOBALIST DISTORTIONS

25

What is Wrong with the 'Official History of Capitalism'?

With Special Reference to the Debates on Globalisation and Economic Development[1]

HA-JOON CHANG

CAMBRIDGE UNIVERSITY, UK

HOW RELEVANT IS ECONOMIC HISTORY FOR CONTEMPORARY ECONOMIC PROBLEMS?

Economic history courses have been disappearing from classrooms across the world. Once a compulsory part of economics education, they have been relegated to the remote corners of 'options' and even closed down. With increasing emphasis on mathematical and statistical techniques, historical knowledge is becoming an insignificant extra for young economists today, something they can ill afford to spend their valuable time acquiring.

Perhaps deplorable from an intellectual point of view, one may say, but not a big deal. Does it matter, it may be asked, all that much if economists do not know much about what happened in the nineteenth century? My answer is: it actually does matter a lot, especially in relation to the debates on globalisation and on economic development. Why do I say that? The mainstream (neo-classical) economists have a very clear recipe for the economic development of the poorer countries in today's globalising world–such as liberalisation of trade and investment and strong patent law. Their belief in their own recommendation is so absolute that in their view it has to be imposed on the developing countries through strong bilateral and multilateral external pressures, even when these countries don't want them. In taking this position, the proponents of this recipe argue that they have not only economic theory but also history on their side. After all, they argue, these are the policies and the institutions that the developed countries had used in the past in order to become rich. In this way, what mainstream economists (think they) know about the history of today's rich countries hugely affects their view on economic development.

However, the understanding of the economic history of today's rich countries held by the mainstream economists – or what I call the 'official history of capitalism' – is seriously flawed. Contrary to the conventional wisdom, the historical fact is that the rich countries did not develop on the basis of the policies and the institutions that they now recommend to, and often force upon, the developing countries. Unfortunately, this fact is little known these days because the 'official historians' of capitalism have been very successful in re-writing its history.

THE OFFICIAL HISTORY OF CAPITALISM AND GLOBALISATION

The 'official history of capitalism' starts from the eighteenth century. At the time, Britain started to 'get ahead of the pack' because it broke with the period's 'mercantilist' convention of the time and started using proved free-market and free-trade policies.

Through such policies that unleashed the entrepreneurial energy of the nation, it beat interventionist France, its main competitor at the time, and established itself as the supreme world economic power. Especially once it had abandoned its deplorable agricultural protection (the Corn Law) and other remnants of old mercantilist protectionist measures in 1846, it was able to play the role of the architect and hegemon of a new 'Liberal' world economic order.

In its quest for a Liberal global order, Britain's ultimate weapon was its economic success based on a free-market–free-trade system, which made other countries realize the limitations of their mercantilist policies and adopt free (or at least freer) trade from around 1860. However, Britain was also greatly helped in its project by the works of its classical economists such as Adam Smith and David Ricardo, who proved theoretically the superiority of *laissez-faire* policy, especially free trade.

This Liberal world order, perfected around 1870, was based on: *laissez-faire* industrial policies at home; low barriers to the international flows of goods, capital, and labour; and the macroeconomic stability, both nationally and internationally, guaranteed by the Gold Standard and the principle of balanced budgets. A period of unprecedented prosperity followed.

Unfortunately, according to this story, things started to go wrong with the onset of the First World War. In response to the ensuing instability of the world economic and political system, countries started to erect trade barriers again. In 1930, the USA abandoned free trade and enacted the infamous Smoot-Hawley tariff, which the famous free-trade economist Jagdish Bahgwati describes as 'the most visible and dramatic act of anti-trade folly'.[2] Countries like Germany and Japan erected high trade barriers and also started creating powerful cartels, which were closely linked with fascism and their external aggression in the following decades. The world free-trade system finally ended in 1932, when Britain, hitherto the champion of free trade, succumbed to the temptation and re-introduced tariffs. The resulting contraction and instability in the world economy and then finally the Second World War destroyed the last remnants of the first Liberal world order.

After the Second World War, so the story goes, some significant progress was made in trade liberalization through the early GATT (General Agreement on Trade and Tariffs) talks. However, unfortunately, *dirigiste* approaches to economic management dominated the policy-making scene until the 1970s in the developed world, and until the early 1980s in the developing world (and the Communist world until its collapse in 1989).

Fortunately, it is said, interventionist policies have been largely abandoned across the world since the 1980s with the rise of neo-liberalism, which emphasised the virtues of small government, *laissez-faire* policies, and international openness. Especially in the developing world, by the late 1970s economic growth had begun to falter in most countries outside East and Southeast Asia, which were already pursuing 'good' policies. The ultimate crowning glory of this trend towards liberalization and opening up was the fall of Communism in 1989, which finally ended what may mainstream economists regard as a 'historical anomaly'[3] of a closed world trading system that had prevailed in the early postwar years.

When combined with the establishment of new global governance institutions represented by the WTO, these policy changes at the national level have created a new global economic system, comparable in its (at least potential) prosperity only to the earlier 'golden age' of Liberalism (1870–1914). Renato Ruggiero, the first Director-General of the WTO, argues that thanks to this new world order we now have 'the potential for eradicating global poverty in the early part of the next [twenty-first] century – a utopian notion even a few decades ago, but a real possibility today'.[4]

A CRITICAL LOOK AT THE OFFICIAL HISTORY OF CAPITALISM

The story told by the Official History paints a fundamentally misleading picture, but no less a powerful one (for further details, see Chang, 2002). And it should be accepted that there are also some senses in which the late nineteenth century can indeed be described as an era of *laissez-faire*.

To begin with, as we can see in Table 1, there was a period in the late-nineteenth century, albeit a brief one, when liberal trade régimes prevailed in large parts of the world economy. Starting from 1846 with the repeal of the Corn Law, Britain made a decided shift to a unilateral free-trade regime (which was accomplished by the 1860s), although this move was based on its then unchallenged economic superiority and intricately linked with its imperial policy. Between 1860 and 1880, many European countries reduced tariff protection substantially. At the same time, most of the rest of the world was forced to practice free trade through colonialism, and, in the cases of a few nominally 'independent' countries (such as the Latin American countries, China, Thailand [then Siam], Iran [then Persia], and Turkey [then the Ottoman Empire]), unequal treaties. Of course, the obvious exception to this was the USA, which maintained a very high tariff barrier even during this period. However, given that the USA was still a relatively small part of the world economy, it may not be totally unreasonable to say that this is as close to free trade as the world has ever got (or probably ever will).

More importantly, the scope of state intervention before the Second World War (or at least before the First World War) was quite limited by modern standards. For example, before the 1930s, both the hegemony of the doctrine of balanced budget and the limited scope for taxation (given, among other things, the absence of personal and corporate income taxes in most countries) severely limited the scope for active budgetary policy. The narrow tax base restricted government budgets, so large fiscal outlays for developmental purposes were difficult, even if the government had the intention to make them—railways being an obvious exception in a number of countries. In most countries, fully–fledged central banking did not exist until the early twentieth century, so the scope for monetary policy was also very limited. On the whole, banks were privately–owned and little regulated by the state, so the scope for using 'directed credit programmes', which were so widely and successfully used in countries like Japan, Korea, Taiwan, and France during the postwar period, was extremely limited. Measures like the nationalization of industry and investment planning, practices that served many European countries (especially France, Austria, and Norway) well in the early postwar years, were regarded as unthinkable outside wartime before the Second World War. One somewhat paradoxical consequence of all these limitations was that tariff protection was far more important as a policy tool in the nineteenth century than it is in our time.

Table 1. Average Tariff Rates on Manufactured Products for Selected Developed Countries in Their Early Stages of Development
(weighted average; in percentages of value)[1]

	1820[2]	1875[2]	1913	1925	1931	1950
Austria[3]	R	15–20	18	16	24	18
Belgium[4]	6–8	9–10	9	15	14	11
Denmark	25–35	15–20	14	10	n.a.	3
France	R	12–15	20	21	30	18
Germany[5]	8–12	4–6	13	20	21	26
Italy	n.a.	8–10	18	22	46	25
Japan[6]	R	5	30	n.a.	n.a.	n.a.
Netherlands[4]	6–8	3–5	4	6	n.a.	11
Russia	R	15–20	84	R	R	R
Spain	R	15–20	41	41	63	n.a.
Sweden	R	3–5	20	16	21	9
Switzerland	8–12	4–6	9	14	19	n.a.
United Kingdom	45–55	0	0	5	n.a.	23
United States	35–45	40–50	44	37	48	14

Source: Bairoch 1993: 40, Table 3.3.

Notes:

R=Numerous and important restrictions on manufactured imports existed and therefore average tariff rates are not meaningful.

[1] World Bank (1991: 97, Box table 5.2) provides a similar table, partly drawing on Bairoch's own studies that form the basis of the above table. However, the World Bank figures, although in most cases very similar to Bairoch's figures, are *unweighted* averages, which are obviously less preferable to *weighted* average figures that Bairoch provides.

[2] These are very approximate rates, and give range of average rates, not extremes.

[3] Austria-Hungary before 1925.

[4] In 1820, Belgium was united with the Netherlands.

[5] The 1820 figure is for Prussia only.

[6] Before 1911, Japan was obliged to keep low tariff rates (up to 5 per cent) through a series of 'unequal treaties' with the European countries and the USA. The World Bank table cited in note 1 above gives Japan's *unweighted* average tariff rate for *all goods* (and not just manufactured goods) for the years 1925, 1930, 1950 as 13 per cent, 19 per cent, 4 per cent.

Despite these limitations, virtually all of today's developed countries actively used interventionist industrial, trade, and technology policies aimed at promoting their new ('infant') industries against the competition from the established industries based in more advanced countries. And, interestingly,

Britain and the USA, the two countries that are supposed to have reached the summit of the world economy through their free-market, free-trade policy, are actually the ones that had most aggressively used protection and subsidies.

Contrary to the popular myth, Britain had been an aggressive user, and in certain areas a pioneer, of activist policies intended to promote its industries. Such policies, although limited in scope, date back to the fourteenth (Edward III) and the fifteenth centuries (Henry VII) in relation to woollen manufacturing, the leading industry of the time. At the time, England was an exporter of raw wool to the Low Countries, and Henry VII for example tried to change this by taxing raw wool exports and poaching skilled workers from the Low Countries.

Particularly between the trade policy reform of its first Prime Minister Robert Walpole in 1721 and its adoption of free trade around 1860, Britain used very *dirigiste* trade and industrial policies, involving measures very similar to what countries like Japan and Korea later used in order to develop their industries. During this period, it protected its industries a lot more heavily than did France, the supposed *dirigiste* counterpoint to this 'free-trade, free-market' system. Given this history, argued Friedrich List, the leading German economist of the mid-nineteenth century, Britain preaching free trade to less advanced countries like Germany and the USA was like someone trying to 'kick away the ladder' with which he had climbed to the top.

List was not alone in seeing the matter in this light. Many American thinkers shared this view. Indeed, it was American thinkers like Alexander Hamilton, the first Treasury Secretary of the USA, and the (now-forgotten) economist Daniel Raymond, who first systematically developed the so-called infant industry argument–namely, the argument that governments of less developed countries need to provide tariff protection and subsidies in order to help their new ('infant') industries establish themselves in the face of competition from their competitors based in more developed countries. Indeed, List, who is commonly known as the father of the infant industry argument, in fact started out as a free-trader–he was an ardent supporter of the free-trade agreement among the German states, that is, the German customs union (*Zollverein*). He learnt about the infant industry argument only during his exile in the USA during the 1820s.

Little known today, the intellectual interaction between the USA and Germany during the nineteenth century did not end there. The German Historical School – represented by people like Wilhelm Roscher, Bruno Hildebrand, Karl Knies, Gustav Schmoller, and Werner Sombart – attracted a lot of American economists in the late nineteenth century. The patron saint of American neoclassical economics, John Bates Clark, in whose name the most prestigious award for young (under 40) American economists is given today, went to Germany in 1873 and studied the German Historical School under Roscher and Knies, although he gradually drifted away from it. Richard Ely, one of the leading American economists of the time, also studied under Knies and influenced the American Institutionalist School through his disciple, John Commons. Ely was one of the founding fathers of the American Economic Association; to this day, the biggest public lecture at the Association's annual meeting is given in Ely's name, although few of the present AEA members would know who he was.

Between the Civil War and the Second World War, the USA was literally the most heavily protected economy in the world (see table 1). In this context, it is important to note that the American Civil War was fought on the issue of tariff as much as, if not more, on the issue of slavery. Of the two major issues that divided the North and the South, the South had actually more to fear on the tariff front than on the slavery front. Abraham Lincoln was a well-known protectionist who cut his political teeth under the charismatic politician Henry Clay in the Whig Party, which advocated the 'American System' based on infrastructural development and protectionism (thus named in the recognition that free trade acts for British interests). One of Lincoln's top economic advisors was the famous protectionist economist, Henry Carey, who once was described as 'the only American economist of importance' by Karl Marx and Friedrich Engels in the early 1850s but has now been almost completely air-brushed out of the history of American economic thought. On the other hand, Lincoln thought the blacks were racially inferior and slave emancipation was an idealistic proposal with no prospect of immediate implementation–he is said to have emancipated the slaves in 1862 as a strategic move to win the War rather than out of some moral conviction.

In protecting their industries, the Americans were going against the advice of such prominent economists as Adam Smith and Jean Baptiste Say, who saw the country's future in agriculture. However, the Americans knew exactly what the game was. They knew that Britain reached the top through protection and subsidies and therefore that they needed to do the same if they were going to get anywhere. Criticising the British preaching of free trade to his country, Ulysses Grant, the Civil War hero and the US President from 1868 to 1876, retorted that 'within 200 years, when America has gotten out of protection all that it can offer, it too will adopt free trade'. When his country later reached the top after the Second World War, it too started 'kicking away the ladder' by preaching free trade and forcing it on the less developed countries.

The UK and the USA may be the more dramatic examples, but almost all the rest of the developed world today used tariffs, subsidies and other means to promote their industries in the earlier stages of their development. Cases like Germany, Japan, and Korea are well known in this respect. But even

Sweden, which later came to represent the 'small open economy' to many economists had also strategically used tariffs, subsidies, cartels, and state support for R&D to develop key industries, especially textile, steel, and engineering.

There were some exceptions like the Netherlands and Switzerland that have maintained free trade since the late eighteenth century. However, these countries were already on the frontier of technological development by the eighteenth century and therefore did not need much protection. Also, it should be noted that the Netherlands deployed an impressive range of interventionist measures up till the seventeenth century in order to build up its maritime and commercial supremacy. Moreover, Switzerland did not have a patent law until 1907, flying directly against the emphasis that today's orthodoxy puts on the protection of intellectual property rights (see below). More interestingly, the Netherlands abolished its 1817 patent law in 1869 on the ground that patents are politically created monopolies inconsistent with its free-market principles – a position that seems to elude most of today's free-market economists – and did not introduce another patent law until 1912.

The story is similar in relation to institutional development. In the earlier stages of their development, today's developed countries did not even have such institutions as a professional civil service, central bank, and patent law, which the mainstream economists regard as 'basic'. It was only after the Pendleton Act in 1883 that the US federal government started recruiting its employees through a competitive process. The central bank, an institution dear to the heart of today's free-market economists, did not exist in most of today's rich countries until the early twentieth century – not least because the free-market economists of the day condemned it as a mechanism for unjustly bailing out imprudent borrowers. The US central bank (the Federal Reserve Board) was set up only in 1913 and the Italian central bank did not even have a note-issue monopoly until 1926. Many countries allowed patenting of foreign inventions until the late nineteenth century. As I mentioned above, Switzerland and the Netherlands refused to introduce a patent law despite international pressure until 1907 and 1912 respectively, and thus freely 'stole' technologies from abroad. The examples can go on.

One important conclusion that emerges from the history of institutional development is that it took the developed countries a long time to develop institutions in their earlier days of development. Institutions typically took decades, and sometimes generations, to develop. Just to give one example, the need for central banking was perceived at least in some circles from at least the seventeenth century, but the first 'real' central bank, the Bank of England, was instituted only in 1844, some two centuries later.

Another important point that emerges is that the levels of institutional development in today's developed countries in their earlier period were much lower than those in today's developing countries. For example, measured by the (admittedly highly imperfect) income level, in 1820 the UK was at a somewhat higher level of development than that of India today, but it did not even have many of the most 'basic' institutions that India has today. It did not have universal suffrage (it did not even have universal *male* suffrage), a central bank, income tax, generalised limited liability, a generalised bankruptcy law, a professional bureaucracy, meaningful securities regulations, or even minimal labour regulations (except for a couple of minimal and hardly-enforced regulations on child labour).

REVISING THE OFFICIAL HISTORY AND ITS IMPLICATIONS FOR ECONOMIC DEVELOPMENT

If the policies and institutions that the rich countries are recommending to the poor countries are not the ones that they themselves used when they were developing, what is going on?

We can only conclude that the rich countries are trying to 'kick away the ladder' that allowed them to climb where they are. It is no coincidence that economic development has become more difficult during the last two decades when the developed countries started turning on the pressure on the developing countries to adopt the so-called 'global standard' policies and institutions.

During this period, the average annual per capita income growth rate for the developing countries has been halved from 3 per cent in the previous two decades (1960-80) to 1.5 per cent. In particular, Latin America virtually stopped growing, while Sub-Saharan Africa and most ex-Communist countries have experienced a fall in absolute income. Economic instability has increased markedly, as manifested in the dozens of financial crises we have witnessed over the last decade alone. Income inequality has been growing in many developing countries and poverty has increased, rather than decreased, in a significant number of them. What can be done to change this?

First, the historical facts about the historical experiences of the developed countries should be more widely publicised, both through improved economic history education and through the mass media. This is not just a matter of 'getting history right', but also of allowing the developing countries to make more informed choices.

Second, the conditions attached to bilateral and multilateral financial assistance to developing countries should be radically changed. It should be accepted that the orthodox recipe is not working, and also that there can be no 'best practice' policies that everyone should use.

Third, the WTO rules should be re-written so that the developing countries can more actively use tariffs and subsidies for industrial development. They should also be allowed to have less stringent patent laws and other intellectual property rights laws.

Fourth, improvements in institutions should be encouraged, but this should not be equated with imposing a fixed set of (in practice, today's – not even yesterday's – Anglo-American) institutions on all countries. Special care has to be taken in order not to demand excessively rapid upgrading of institutions by the developing countries, especially given that they already have quite developed institutions when compared to today's developed countries at comparable stages of development, and given that establishing and running new institutions is costly.

By being allowed to adopt policies and institutions that are more suitable to their conditions, the developing countries will be able to develop faster. This will also benefit the developed countries in the long run, as it will increase their trade and investment opportunities. That the developed countries cannot see this is the tragedy of our time.

SUGGESTED FURTHER READING

Bairoch, P. (1993) *Economics and World History–Myths and Paradoxes*, Brighton: Wheatsheaf.

Chang, H. J. (2002) *Kicking Away the Ladder: Development Strategy in Historical Perspective*, London: Anthem Press.

Hirst, P. & Thompson, G. (1999) *Globalisation in Question*, 2nd edition, Cambridge: Polity Press.

List, F. (1885) *The National System of Political Economy* [1841], trans. by Sampson Lloyd, London: Longman, Green, and Company.

Sachs, J. & Warner, A. (1995) 'Economic Reform and the Process of Global Integration', *Brookings Papers on Economic Activity*, 1995, no. 1.

26

Should the Study of Transnational Companies Be Part of the Economics Syllabus?

GRAZIA IETTO-GILLIES[1]

LONDON SOUTH BANK UNIVERSITY, UK

INTRODUCTION

The transnational companies (TNCs)[2] are here, there and everywhere. They are also the talk of the town: everybody talks about them, blames or hails them or protests against them. Most ordinary people consider them to be a (the?) main player in the contemporary economic system.

Yet most economics curricula[3] will have very little or nothing about transnational companies as such: the talk of the town they may be, but they ain't the talk of economics lectures. Units in industrial economics deal with some of the characteristics of large companies – size, impact on market structure, mergers, organizational issues – but not much time is devoted to the trans-national character and activities of many companies.

A brief and superficial internet search on the range of units offered by some of the most prestigious universities in the English-speaking world gives the following results. In Britain, at the University of Cambridge I could detect nothing on this topic in the official syllabus, nor in the teaching content provided by the individual lecturers. This in spite of the fact that there are some academics who are currently doing – or have done in the past-research in the field. One of the most prestigious courses in the land, the University of Oxford degree in Philosophy, Politics and Economics (PPE) does not appear to contain anything on the TNCs. Neither could I find any evidence in the various units offered by the London School of Economics (LSE). I had more luck when I searched the offerings of the University of Warwick Department of Economics. A unit on 'The Industrial Economy' for Term I lists 'Multinationals and international investment' in the syllabus and indeed suggests a well-known text on multinational companies (MNCs) in the reading list. Moreover, the University offers a full unit at the Master level taught by a well-known researcher in the field.

On the other side of the Atlantic, the Massachusetts Institute of Technology (MIT), as part of its PhD programme in economics, offers a unit on 'International Economics I' dealing with 'Theory of international trade and foreign investment…'. I could not find anything on TNCs at the undergraduate level. Harvard University offers a unit on 'International Trade and Investment' to both undergraduate and graduate students. There is also a unit on 'International Trade' for graduates only, dealing with '…international trade, direct foreign investment and trade policy'.

These observations must be considered with great caution because: (a) the sample is not representative, though it is indicative of practice in top institutions and such practices may cascade down to lesser universities; (b) the information gathered is not fully satisfactory because some universities and departments give only general titles for their units rather than syllabuses.[4]

Nonetheless the overall feeling I am left with is that the activities of transnational corporations do not form an integral part of the curriculum for economics degrees. Most undergraduate students are lucky to get a few lectures as part of an industrial economics syllabus; sometimes as part of the international trade curriculum. Is this unreasonable? And if so why?

This chapter proceeds as follows. The next section puts the case for why it is not reasonable to expect more material on TNCs in the economics curricula. Section three argues the opposite case and the last section summarises and considers some implications.

IS A SPECIAL STUDY OF TNC'S NECESSARY IN ECONOMICS?[5]

There is a large body of research and literature on the TNCs and their activities going back to the 1950s and 60s with the works of Steven Hymer – a Canadian economist working for a doctorate at the MIT – and, on this side of the Atlantic, with those of John Dunning of the University of Reading.

The literature deals with why companies internationalise; why and in what circumstances they may choose to do so via exports or licensing or direct production abroad; what effects are produced on the industries they operate in or the countries from which they originate (home countries) or in which they invest (host countries); what effects the activities of TNCs have on the performance of firms, industries or the macroeconomy. Specifically, what effects are produced on growth and development, on employment, trade, the balance of payments or on the development and diffusion of innovation and technology.

Much of this literature has remained at the margin of mainstream economics for decades. There are signs that this may be changing and mainstream prestigious journals are now more likely to host articles on this topic. Part of the reason for this is the fact that the subject has, in the last fifteen years, been taken up by exponents of 'New Trade Theories' and developed within the framework of general equilibrium analysis (Krugman 1985; Markusen 1984; 1995; Helpman 1985; Helpman and Krugman 1985). New trade theories (Krugman 1985; 1991; 1998) give prominence to issues of economic geography and locational agglomeration and it was, therefore, inevitable that economists interested in these theories should begin to ask questions about the TNC, that is about the agent most responsible for the international location of production.

This may account for the more recent interest of mainstream economics researchers in TNCs and their activities. However, the interest is still relatively low and relegated to issues of location and trade; it has not yet touched on issues involving industrial structures or the macroeconomy. Moreover, the economics curricula do not seem to have been affected and, as mentioned in the previous section, it is possible for someone to gain a degree in economics from a top university in the US or UK without ever having learn anything about TNCs, their activities or effects. Is this unreasonable? Do we need a special study of TNCs to understand what is going on in our current economic systems?

These questions may appear extraordinary to men and women in the street. Yet they are not such absurd questions.

Most economics texts ignore the TNCs and therefore ignore the domestic versus foreign character of the investor or producer, or more specifically, ignore the actual nationality of the investor. Instead, concentration tends to focus on such issues as the following: the firm in general or in relation to its size or organization; the market structure of an industry; the production, investment or trade of the macro economy independently of the nationality of the firm producing, investing or trading. This is exactly what we do when we study, for example, trade theory: we analyse the comparative conditions and advantages of the trading countries and/or the impact of trade on them independently of the national character/identity of the exporter firm. Why should we bother with such characteristics when the exporter is someone *investing* abroad? In fact, we do not attach much relevance to the identity of the investors when they originate from other regions within the same nation-state; for example when a Texan firm invests in California or a firm from Lombardy invests in Sicily. Why should we consider the origin of the firm as relevant when it is from a foreign country?

What I mean is that the case for a special study of the TNC is not obvious. Traditionally, economists have looked into the specific characteristics of the investor, when studying investment by public firms. However, the reason for this is clear: the public investor is assumed to have different *objectives* compared with the private one and thus the identity private/public does matter. But this is not the case when the investor is a TNC. Whether the firm is foreign or domestic, whether it is a transnational or a uninational firm, the objectives are not different; they are profit objectives.

In fact the reason why in our case the uni- or multi-national character of the investor matters has nothing to do with objectives but with *strategies*. It is on the basis of strategic issues that the case for more prominence to the study of TNCs rests. The case will be made in the next section.

WHY TRANS-NATIONAL ACTIVITIES MATTER

There are three main dimensions to operations across national frontiers:

1. *Spatial/geographical dimension.* The distance between locations in different nation-states is often greater than the distance between locations within the same nation-state. But this is not always the case. For example, the distance between Milan and Reggio Calabria is greater than the one between Milan and Geneva. Similarly, the distance between Boston and San Francisco is far greater than the distance between Boston and Montreal. The spatial distance – whether within or across nations – affects the costs of transportation.

2. *Cultural and linguistic dimension.* The cultural distance is usually greater between nation-states than between regions of the same nation-state. But again, this is not always the case. The cultural distance between Milan and Geneva is probably lower than the one between Milan and Reggio Calabria. Cultural and linguistic distance affects costs of business operations as managers have to learn and adapt to different cultural business environments.

3. *Regulatory régimes dimension.* By regulatory régime I mean the sets of all laws, regulations and customs governing the economic, social and political life of a country. It therefore includes the sets of rules governing production, markets and the movement of resources across countries. Each country has specific regulatory régimes and thus specific sets of rules and regulations which often have historical origins and connotations. Countries differ – often substantially – in terms of their specific regulatory régimes. However, the regulatory régimes tend to be fairly – though not completely – homogeneous and consistent within each nation-state. In particular, different nation-states have different:

   ● Currency régimes
   ● Tax régimes
   ● Rules and regulations regarding the social security system and in particular different régimes regarding labour and its organisation.

Dimensions one, two and three are all important elements in decisions and strategies related to international business activities. However, it is particularly the third dimension that characterizes each nation-state though the other two can also contribute to the differences between states. Moreover, it is the third dimension that generates opportunities – as well as some costs – for taking advantages of economic activities across frontiers.

The existence of different frontiers may generate additional costs for business activities. They are associated mainly with the first two dimensions, though the third dimension may also generate costs. For the TNCs, organizing and managing under different laws, regulations, cultures, may also be costly; uncertainty over exchange rates may be a disadvantage of operations across countries. There may also be costs of forgone economies of scale, if production is spread in too many locations.

However, the third dimension may also give rise to specific advantages of transnationality *per se*. Here these advantages will be considered from two perspectives: (1) the possibility that such advantages can be actively created by the firm's strategic behaviour and in a variety of fields; (2) the possibility that strategic behaviour to create advantages can be used not only towards rival firms–as envisaged in many theories[6] but also towards other players in the economic system such as labour or governments.

The following are specific advantages of transnationality linked to the existence of different regulatory régimes:

- Advantages regarding different currency and tax régimes
- Advantages towards labour
- Advantages in negotiations with governments
- Advantages of risk spreading

Companies that can truly plan, organise, control activities and assets across frontiers can also develop strategies to take advantage of differences in regulatory régimes across frontiers. Thus the existence of different *currencies and taxation laws* may, for example, give them the opportunity to develop location and intra-firm transfer strategies that give them the benefit of transfer prices manipulation and therefore of higher profits than they would otherwise have achieved.

Transfer prices are the prices charged by one part of the company to another for material products–usually components of final products – or services transferred internally to the company though across national frontiers. Such prices can be set at 'arm's length', that is at the same level as they would be set on the open market to an external firm. However, transfer prices might be 'manipulated' (i.e. set at levels other than arm's length) in order to give the company as a whole larger profits than it would have if the transfer prices were set at arm's length. The most common reason for the manipulation of transfer prices has to do with minimizing the company's overall tax liability. If different countries have different rates of corporation tax, it is in the interest of the company as a whole to declare most of its profit in the country with the lowest tax rate and have zero or low declared profits in countries with high tax rates. From the accounting point of view, this can be achieved by a strategic setting of transfer prices.

The procedures are illegal and therefore no company would own to them; however, it is well known that they do occur and that they have considerable effects at the micro and macro levels. The company which successfully indulges in this type of manipulation will see its profits increase. However, there are also macro effects and policy implications. Surplus is arbitrarily moved from country to country: the low tax-rate country will see more profits and tax revenue imputed to it than warranted by its production and exchange activities. The opposite is the case for high tax-rate countries. Moreover, there is an overall transfer of surplus from the public to the private sphere as lower tax revenue is received by the world's public finances and more is allocated to private profits.

There are also other reasons for the possible manipulation of transfer prices, such as market penetration or the circumvention of laws on the repatriation of profits.

The literature on large firms – whether TNCs or not[7] – gives some emphasis to strategies towards rival firms, in particular in the context of oligopolistic market structures. The advantage of transnationality can be used – and has at times been used-to analyse advantages in relation to rivals. However, strategic behaviour towards other players in the economic system such as labour or governments has been given less weight. Yet it is with respect to these other players that the advantages of transnationality can be used most effectively.

It is particularly with regard to *labour* that the opportunity to develop advantageous strategies arises. Unlike the TNC, labour has, so far, been unable to organise itself across frontiers and, indeed, labour solidarity across frontiers tends to be much lower than within frontiers. This means that whenever a TNC has production spread into many nation-states it faces a labour force working for it that is more fragmented/segmented and less able to organise and resist the demands of corporate capital. This situation should be assessed in comparison with one in which the same labour force were all to be employed by the same company to produce the same amount of output in one single country. The latter situation would make labour organisation and resistance much stronger. Thus a strategy of international location may also be a *strategy of labour fragmentation*.[8]

A strategy of fragmentation/segmentation weakens the power of labour to resist in any conflict with capital. This effect is compounded by another type of fragmentation strategy which has been pursued in the last two decades by large uni- and multi-national organisations in both the private and public sector. I refer to organisational fragmentations in which businesses (private and/or public institutions) outsource part of their activities thus forcing the labour force, previously all working for the same organisation, to work for a variety of enterprises. This organizational fragmentation makes it more difficult for labour to organise and resist the pressures of capital for poor and divisive pay and conditions.

Transnational companies can – and do – play *governments* of different countries or regions against each other with the objective of raising the offer of financial incentives for the location of inward FDI (Oman 2000; Phelps and Raines 2002). The fact that the company operates with a large multinational internal network makes any threat of relocation of production very credible as it could be achieved with relatively low costs. Thus the TNC with a production network spreading into many countries[9] has a strong element of bargaining power towards both governments and labour force.

Moreover, location of production in several countries will *spread the risks*, particularly those associated with political or labour unrest. It may also enhance the company's innovative power as it learns from different environments (Cantwell 1989 and 1995; Frenz and Ietto-Gillies 2003; Castellani and Zanfei 2003).

The conclusion is that the transnational company: by virtue of operating effectively across different nation-states and thus across different regulatory régimes-has wider opportunities for developing strategies designed to improve its position vis-à-vis other actors in the economic system who have been less able – so far – to operate across frontiers as effectively as the TNC.[10] In this approach the spread of production into many countries becomes one of the strategies for achieving long-term profits.

So the reason why we must study the TNC and why the nationality of the company matters is not due to its having different objectives from other firms (as in the case of private versus public companies) but to its having different and wider *opportunities for strategies* to pursue its profits aims.

When we are dealing with large and powerful organisations, a strategic approach is necessary for the understanding of their activities, their motivations and implications. However, we must move away from a strategic approach focused only on strategies towards rivals, in the direction of an approach that considers also TNCs' strategies towards other players in the economic system such as strategies towards labour or governments or supplier firms. Success in the latter types of strategy is also likely to give the firm a competitive advantage towards its rivals.

SUMMARY AND IMPLICATIONS

The chapter starts with some facts – albeit limited to some of the most prestigious universities in the English-speaking world – on the extent to which syllabuses for economics curricula deal with the TNCs and their activities. The case for why such a topic might not need a special treatment in economics is dealt with in section two; this is followed (section three) by arguments in favour of the opposite point of view.

The arguments for a special study of TNCs are built around the following: (a) analysis of specific dimensions of operations across frontiers; (b) emphasis on advantages – as well as possible costs – of such operations; (c) a strategic approach to the analysis of TNCs, their motivations and behaviour; and (d) emphasis on strategic behaviour towards labour and governments as well as towards rival firms.

Several implications derive from this approach, particularly with regard to research, teaching and policy. I shall not deal with the research implications here. The interested reader will find this issue dealt with in the conclusions to Ietto-Gillies (2003).

The implications for *teaching and syllabuses* are obvious. There is now a large body of literature and knowledge about the TNCs and their activities. Even if most of the relevant theories are not fully integrated into the working of the economics system as a whole and more research is needed on this issue, the existing knowledge should be part of the economics curriculum and students should be given the opportunity to learn about it. This will give them the chance to deal with more realistic issues relating to economic systems.

A further reason why this topic should be part of the curriculum is that the TNCs and their activities have relevant *policy implications* of which economics graduates should be aware. Policy implications arise with respect to the effects of transfer prices manipulation or the offer of incentives for inward investment, or competition issues, or the regulation of social and labour issues.

FURTHER READING

Dicken, P. (2003) *Global Shifts: Reshaping the Global Economic Map in the Twentieth Century*, London: Sage Publications.

Ietto-Gillies, G. (2001) *Transnational Corporations: Fragmentation amidst Integration*, London: Routledge: Chapters 2, 6 and 9.

Ietto-Gillies, G. (2005) *Transnational Firms and International Production. Concepts, Theories and Effects*, Aldershot: Edward Elgar (forthcoming): Part 1, selected chapters of part III (according to interests) and part IV.

Pitelis, C. N. and Sugden, R. (2000), *The Nature of the Transnational Firm*, London: Routledge: particularly chapter 2, though 4, 5 and 8 may also be of interest.

REFERENCES

Cantwell, J. (1989) *Technological Innovation and Multinational Corporations*, Oxford: Blackwell.

Cantwell, J. (1995) 'The globalisation of technology: What remains of the product cycle model?', *Cambridge Journal of Economics*, 19, 1: 155–74.

Cantwell, J. (2000), 'A survey of theories of international production' in C. N. Pitelis and R. Sugden (eds), *The Nature of the Transnational Firm*, London: Routledge', 10–56.

Castellani, D. and Zanfei, A. (2003), 'Innovation, foreign ownership and multinationality. An empirical analysis of Italian manufacturing firms' Paper presented at the International Workshop on Empirical Stusied on Innovation in Europe, University of Urbino, 1–2 December 2003.

Chesnais F. and Saillou A. (2000), 'Foreign direct investment and European Trade', in Chesnais, F., Ietto-Gillies, G. and Simonetti, R. (eds), *European Integration and Global Corporate Strategies,* London: Routledge, ch. 2.

Cowling, K. and Sugden, R. (1987), *Transnational Monopoly Capitalism,* Brighton: Wheatsheaf.

Frenz, M. and Ietto-Gillies, G. (2003), 'The Impact of Multinationality on the Propensity to Innovate. An Analysis of the UK Community Innovation Survey 3' Paper presented at the International Workshop on Empirical Studies in Innovation in Europe, University of Urbino, 1–2 December 2003.

Graham, E. M. (1978), 'Transatlantic investment by multinational firms: a rivalristic phenomenon? *Journal of Post-Keynesian Economics*, 1, 1 (Fall).

Graham, E. M. (1990), 'Exchange of threats between multinational firms as an infinitely repeated non-cooperative game', *International Trade Journal*, 4, 3: 259–77.

Helpman, E. (1985) 'Multinational Corporations and Trade Structure', *Review of Economic Studies*, July: 443–58.

Helpman, E. and Krugman, P. (1985), *Market Structures and Foreign Trade: Increasing Returns, Imperfect Competition and the International Economy*, Cambridge, MA: MIT Press.

Hymer, S. H. (1976) *The International Operations of National Firms: a Study of Direct Foreign Investment* [1960], Cambridge, MA: MIT Press.

Ietto-Gillies, G. (1988) Internationalization of production: an analysis based on labour. *British Review of Economibc Issues*, 10 (23): 19–48.

Ietto-Gillies, G. (2001) *Transnational Corporations. Fragmentation amidst Integration,* London: Routledge.

Ietto-Gillies, G. (2003) 'The nation-state and the theory of the transnational corporation' presented at the Conference on 'Economics for the Future' organised by the Cambridge Journal of Economics, Cambridge, 17–19 September.

Knickerbocker, F. T. (1973) *Oligopolistic Reaction and Multinational Enterprise*, Cambridge, M. A.: Division of Research, Graduate School of Business Administration, Harvard University.

Krugman, P. (1985), 'Increasing Returns and the Theory of International Trade', *National Bureau of Economic Research Working Papers*, No. 1752, November.

Krugman, P. (1991a), *Geography and Trade*, Cambridge, MA: The MIT Press.

Krugman, P. (1998), 'What's new about the new economic geography?', *Oxford Review of Economic Policy*, 14, 2: 7–17.

Markusen, J.R. (1984), 'Multinationals, Multi-Plant Economies and the Gains from Trade', *Journal of International Economics*, 16, 3/4: 205–24.

Markusen, J. R. (1995), 'The Boundaries of Multinational Enterprises, and the Theory of International Trade', *Journal of Economic Perspectives*, 9, 2: 169–89.

Oman, C. P. (2000), *Policy Competition for Foreign Direct Investment: A study of Competition among Governments to Attract FDI*, Paris: OECD Development Center.

Peoples, J. and Sugden, R. (2000), 'Divide and rule by transnational corporations', in Pitelis, C. N. and Sugden, R. (eds.), *The Nature of the Transnational Firm*, 2nd edition, London: Routledge, 174–92.

Phelps, N. and Raines, P. (eds), (2002), *The New Competition for Inward Investment*, Aldershot: Edward Elgar.

Sengenberger, W. and Wilkinson, F. (1995), 'Globalization and Labour Standards', in Michie, J. and Grieve Smith, J. (eds), *Managing the Global Economy*, Oxford: Oxford University Press, 111–34.

United Nations Conference on Trade and Development (1996), *World Investment Report 1996: Investment, Trade and International Policy Arrangements*, Geneva: United Nations.

Vernon, R. (1966) 'International investment and international trade in the product cycle', *Quarterly Journal of Economics*, 80, 190–207.

27

Would a Latin American Economics Make Sense?

ANA MARIA BIANCHI

UNIVERSITY OF SAO PAULO, BRAZIL

In his latest book, Geoffrey Hodgson (2001) argues in favor of the importance of history in the social sciences. He questions the possibility of a universal theory applicable to human economic behavior in all societies and all times. At the ontological level, he claims, universal laws are often of limited use when it comes to the detail of specific contexts and situations. There is a problem of historical specificity posed by the fact that a fundamentally different reality requires a different theory.

As much as I agree with this general point of view, how far can this argument be extended? Should the social sciences abandon the pretense of constructing theories that are universally applicable? Would something like a Latin American (African, Asiatic, Third World or whatever) economics make sense?

My answer to the two last questions is negative, and I will try to argue why. To make the whole argument more concrete, I will turn to two different approaches to economic development that were inspired by the Latin American experience, where economists faced the challenge of building an economic theory specially attuned to the continent´s conditions. My case studies are: i) the Latin American School of Economics, which corresponds to the approach developed by the United Nations Economic Committee for Latin America and the Caribbean (ECLAC) in the mid-twentieth century, under the leadership of the Argentinean economist Raúl Prebisch; ii) the linkage approach to development, proposed by Albert Hirschman in the 1950s, according to which the maintenance of disequilibria is an essential ingredient in development processes. These two different approaches basically developed outside the mainstream of the profession and were never fully integrated into its academic textbooks. Nevertheless, they constitute a significant contribution to development economics, throwing light on new perspectives on the mechanisms that foster development and, in more general terms, on the functioning of economic systems throughout the world.

In the concluding remarks, I claim that the ECLAC writers ('*cepalinos*', as they are known) and Hirschman did not abandon the pretense of building an universalizing theory. Rather, they tried to combine it with an explicit consideration of the institutional circumstances in which theories were born and to which they were to be applied. They agreed on the necessity of making the necessary qualifications to the general theories from which they departed, questioning their usefulness for specific social contexts.

THE LATIN AMERICAN SCHOOL OF ECONOMICS

In the mid-twentieth-century, concern with economic development became an important issue in the agenda of Latin American economists. In this section, I proceed to sum up the main ideas defended by Raúl Prebisch and other ECLAC economists, with a specific focus on two documents that were published in the 1940s and 1950s, which are representative of their conception.

In 1947, the United Nations Economic and Social Council established its first regional economic commissions for Europe and for Asia and the Far East. Their mission was to provide information concerning the economic trends and special problems of each region. This was followed by a movement to create a similar organization for Latin America, a proposal that led to the establishment of the Economic Commission for Latin America in 1948, with its headquarters in Santiago, Chile. Raúl Prebisch, who had held important positions in the Central Bank of Argentina and who was then teaching economics at the University of Buenos Aires, was invited to join the newly-born institution. He entered the entity's secretariat in 1949 and two years later was designated its chief executive. Under the leadership of Prebisch, the ECLAC became a think tank for the generation of heterodox ideas that fostered the industrial development of Latin America.[1]

By the time Prebisch became executive secretary of the ECLAC, he had formed his own conception of the growth processes in Latin America, which was to become the basis of the Latin American School of Economics. This conception is developed in one of his early essays, entitled '*Desarollo Económico de América Latina y sus Principales Problemas*' (hereafter, '*Manifesto*') and in the introduction to the ECLAC annual report, called '*Estúdio económico de América Latina 1949*' (hereafter, '*Estúdio*'), published a few months later.

The main thesis in both essays is that the 'peripheral countries', as exporters of raw materials and primary products in general to 'central' industrialized countries, suffered from a long-term decline in their terms of trade. This general thesis finds support in four specific propositions based on statistical evidence about the performance of Latin American economies, namely; i) since the 1930s, the absolute demand for primary goods exported by Latin American countries had been declining; ii) Latin America was selling its exports at prices that were not keeping pace with the corresponding variations in the prices of the manufactured goods it purchased in the international market; iii) due to market imperfections, which included labor-union pressures and rigidities of wages, the gains in productivity caused by technological improvements did not result in decreasing prices for industrial goods bought by Latin America in the international trade market; iv) the resulting balance of payment deficits were detrimental to the economic growth of Latin America, as receipts deriving from exports did not create the import capacity needed to provide the region with goods that were essential to develop its industrial sector. The overall scenario that resulted from this asymmetrical relationship between peripheral and central countries maintained the former in a vicious circle of low productivity and a low rate of savings.

According to Prebisch, the process of 'universal dissemination of the capitalistic technique of production' comprised two different stages: the first, in the nineteenth century, corresponding to the development of the central countries; the second, in the twentieth century, corresponding to the development of the Latin American countries (Prebisch 1950: 65). The complexity of the whole process had substantially increased in this second phase, resulting in a widening gap of income and productivity levels between central and peripheral countries. Given the conditions prevalent in the twentieth century, the technology adopted in the industrialization process imposed large coefficients of capital per unit of labor, demanding a level of savings that was incompatible with the income levels that prevailed in the less developed regions of the world. Peripheral economies also suffered from the fact that their economies were both specialized and heterogeneous: specialized due to the excessive degree of specialization of their foreign trade; and heterogeneous because they faced serious unemployment problems and had a large percentage of their workforce employed in low productivity sectors.

In order to overcome this situation, Latin American countries needed to protect their foreign trade and concentrate on the production of an array of manufactured goods that were formerly imported. For the *cepalinos*, import substitution was a necessary condition for peripheral growth, in association with structural reforms in the national economies. Although exportations were considered crucial to guarantee the foreign exchange that the countries needed to import capital goods, the hallmark of this model was the focus on the domestic market. Within Latin America, economic integration between countries would allow them to take advantage of economies of scale, in the sense of providing larger markets and favoring the dissemination of modern technologies.

The industrialization of 'latecomers' thus required a significant degree of State supervision in order to succeed. Prebisch and ECLAC saw development not as a result of a natural evolution, but as a result of policy. A deliberate set of measures that could stimulate an import-substituting industrialization was the only way out of poverty and underdevelopment. In the fulfillment of this goal, national states were expected to play a major role. Adapting protectionist measures, they would create the proper environment needed to estimulate the take-off and consolidation of the industrial sector. In this sense, later ECLAC official documents presented planning and planification as a crucial requisite to ensure that resources were adequately allocated for development priorities.

The *cepalinos* found the empirical support for their theses on a careful collection of statistical data about the various Latin American countries and their patterns of foreign trade. It its important to note that this was not a widespread procedure in the first half of the twentieth century. Up to the 1950s, few essays written by Latin American economists showed a systematic concern with the use of statistical evidence to support economic analysis, a pattern that was broken by Prebisch and others from the Latin American School. In fact, concern with empirical evidence was present in the very spirit that led to the creation of ECLAC. The entity's staff was put in charge of assembling statistical data about Latin America, in order to compensate for the chronic deficiency in this area.

Another important characteristic of Prebisch's early writings is the critical attitude that he took towards the mainstream theory of international trade, both in its Ricardian and neoclassical versions. He expressed reservations about the basic tenets of this theory, not only from the viewpoint of its theoretical significance but in what concerned its policy implications as well. He acknowledged the usefulness of its basic analytical tools – which included concepts such as income elasticity of demand, capital-product ratio and multiplier, among many others – but claimed that some important qualifications were necessary in order to adapt this general theory to Latin America's specific historical and geographical contexts.

In the *Manifesto* and in the *Estúdio* Prebisch argued that the main mistake of conventional neoclassical economics was to attribute a general character to something that was geographically circumscribed. Statistical evidence on Latin America refuted the assumptions of perfect mobility of the production factors and of the universal advantages of free trade. The data showed, instead, an uneven distribution of the benefits of trade between the two groups of countries mentioned above, the central and the peripheral ones. From the viewpoint of the periphery, conventional economics suffered from 'a false sense of universality', and tended to fall into the trap of 'dogmatic generalizations' (Prebisch 1949: 7) The real economic world was very different from this abstract world, and the free action of market forces was unable to eliminate the wide differences in income between central and peripheral countries. (Prebisch 1950: 84)

It was therefore necessary to modify the mainstream economic theory, introducing qualifications derived from the experience of peripheral countries. The severe crises faced by the world economies after World War I, coupled with the specificities of the Latin American countries, required 'a serious effort of theoretical revision'. (Prebisch 1950: 60) This investigative effort was an essential step towards achieving a correct diagnosis of Latin American problems, from which the adequate policy recommendations could be derived. Not that the *cepalinos* thought that the new generations of Latin American economists should start all over again, working on a entirely different economic theory. On the contrary, they recommended the building of educational institutions where Latin American economists would learn traditional economic theory. Acquaintance with the basic tenets of this theory would allow them to make the necessary adaptations, tailoring it to meet the specific conditions of peripheral economies. (Prebisch 1949: 54, 94)

In his concluding remarks to the *Estúdio*, Prebisch argued once more that the worth of the mainstream theory of trade depended on the attention that it would be able to pay to the particularities of the peripheral economies. Working on this task would not be a wasted effort: rather, it would enable the economists to build a theory that would eventually acquire an universal significance (84).

Perhaps one of the most important features of the Latin American School is the fact that its authors were thoroughly concerned with the practical relevance of their writings. They recognized the prescriptive nature of economics and the direct link between building a theory and making policy recommendations. Besides this impulse to bridge the gap between what was taught in the textbooks and 'the world out there', their writings show an explicit commitment to values such as economic development, social welfare and equity.

A LINKAGE APPROACH TO DEVELOPMENT

The focus here is Albert Hirschman's writings that resulted from his professional experience in Colombia, Brazil, Chile and other Latin American countries, during the 1950s and 1960s. These writings include *The Strategy of Economic Development* (1958), among many other books and articles published by the author in the same period.[2]

When Hirschman first arrived in Latin America, in 1952, Colombia was a very poor country, with a population of 12.6 million people. Life expectancy at birth was 50.6 years and the annual rate of population increase exceeded 3 per cent, one of the highest rates in the world. The Colombian economy was primarily agricultural, with the agricultural sector being responsible for 40 per cent of the GDP and 60 per cent of the population living in rural areas. While the country´s exports were based on highly inelastic primary products, with limited opportunities for expansion, the production of industrial and agricultural consumer goods was contingent on imports of intermediate and capital goods, for which there was little foreign exchange.

So Hirschman went to Colombia in 1952 and stayed for almost five years. After working directly with the Colombian Government during the first two years, he spent the rest of his stay serving as a private economic and financial adviser. In 1956 he returned to the United States, where he settled at Yale University. But he made several other trips to Central and South America, to visit World Bank finance projects. The same interest in development economics took him to developing countries in Asia and Africa.

This is the overall scenario which inspired Hirschman to write the *Strategy*. The book builds on some basic processes making for economic progress in developing countries. It favors the establishment of industries with strong backward linkages, as a strategy to promote development. This approach caused much controversy, although in a formalized version it is now common knowledge among economists who concentrate their research efforts in the field of development economics.

From the viewpoint of its central thesis, the main chapter in *The Strategy* is chapter 4, where Hirschman put forward the idea of an unbalanced development strategy. The chapter´s title ('Unbalanced growth: an espousal') expesses commitment to the idea that maintaining disequilibria was essential for the development process:

> …our aim must be to *keep alive* rather than eliminate the disequilibria of which profits and losses are symptoms in a competitive economy. If the economy is to be kept moving ahead, the task of development policy is to maintain tensions, disproportions, and disequilibria. That nightmare of equilibrium economics, the endlessly spinning cobweb, is the *kind* of mechanism we must assiduously look for as an invaluable help in the development process. (Hirschman 1958: 66)

This bold proposition emphasizes the disorderly nature of economic development. It challenges the generalizations and theoretical viewpoints that prevailed among economists dealing with development problems up to that point in time. In the previous chapter ('Balanced growth: A critique') Hirschman had attacked the balanced growth thesis that was advocated by his forerunners in the field. He argued that problems of industrialization did not require a simultaneous solution, as claimed by economists such as

Rosenstein-Rodan, Nurkse, Lewis and Scitovsky. Quite the opposite: new industrialization processes would allow for a number of sequential solutions which where essentially different from those followed by the older industrial countries. Instead of emphasizing the various obstacles to economic progress – land tenure systems, family structure, administrative instability, lack of savings and so on – Hirschman chose to stress the need for inducement mechanisms. In his view, the fundamental problem of development consisted in generating and channeling human energies into a desired direction (Hirschman 1958: 25).

Hirschman used the term 'linkage' to denote interrelations in a general equilibrium system, where everything depends on everything else; he applied it to a variety of multiplier effects, including spillover and other external effects. In *The Strategy*, the concept acquired a more specific and concrete meaning, standing for inducement mechanisms at work within the sector of directly productive activities. Backward linkages corresponded to the stimuli going to sectors that supplied the inputs required by a particular activity, whereas forward linkages were the inducement to set up new activities utilizing the output of the proposed activity. The main source of development would be activities with high potential linkage effects, mainly backward ones.

The idea that industrial development should (and in fact would) proceed largely through backward linkages was quite revolutionary at the time: instead of doing things in the conventional way, industrial development would work its way from the 'last touches' to intermediate and basic industry. Industrialization of certain leading sectors would pull along the rest of the economy. In this sense, it was not be feasible nor desirable to suppress the tensions and disequilibria created by the development process, since there was a 'creative virtue' on them.

It is worthwhile mentioning that Hirschman's conception of development did not result from purely theoretical considerations. On the contrary, its inspiration came out of the experience of underdeveloped countries who were already undergoing an industrialization process. Their history showed that the industrial sector was working its way backward from 'the final touches' state to the domestic production of intermediate products, and finally to that of basic industrial inputs. In turn, industry served as a powerful stimulus to the development of the agricultural sector.

If disequilibrium was an intentional mechanism, how could balance be restored? Hirschman pictured it as the outcome of pressures, incentives and compulsions. He suggested that the efficient path toward economic development was often found in circumstances where the country had to find solutions for bottlenecks and shortages of skills, facilities, services, and products.

In Chapter 8 ('Efficiency and growth of the individual firm') Hirschman looked at the empirical evidence concerning the industrialization process that was just beginning in Colombia. Learning from this evidence, he suggested that less developed countries might have a comparative advantage in tasks such as the running of airlines, as compared to activities such as building and maintaining highways. Why would that be so? Because in the latter the compulsion to maintain is not strong – lack of maintenance leads to a slow deterioration in the quality and quantity of output or to temporary damages to a few machines, without immediate drastic consequences. In contrast, lack of maintenance in the airlines sector implies severe penalties, including the massive loss of life and property. The conclusion logically follows: contrarily to common sense, underdeveloped countries might achieve considerable success in ventures with a complicated technology. The maintenance habit could be acquired and from there spread to the rest of the economy (Hirschman 1958: 142).

Hirschman then proceeded to a generalization: under certain circumstances, it could be rational for governments in underdeveloped countries to concentrate on 'show-pieces', since large ventures were likely to be planned much more carefully than small ones. Because of their strong backward linkages, certain highly capital-intensive industries were particularly well suited for underdeveloped countries. Those 'cart-before-the-horse' sequences could be efficient, and were indeed characteristic of the process of economic and social development of latecomers.

In the conclusion of *The Strategy*, Hirschman made some cautionary remarks about the bold theses that he had proposed in the previous chapters. He admitted a certain uneasiness about the importance and creative virtue attributed to pressures, tensions, and disequilibrium, and conceded that the response to such situations might at times be destructive. But he added that this did not imply that such tensions were undesirable and should not occur (209). How could one make the most of this positive relation between development and the tensions it creates? By means of extending technical assistance and policy advice to underdeveloped countries, answered the author.

This points to another very interesting idea that Hirschman began to conceive in *The Strategy*, one that he would further develop in other writings and would later call 'the visiting-economist syndrome'. Specialist missions sent to underdeveloped countries with the aim of giving them technical assistance often succumbed to this syndrome. In a nutshell, it consisted on issuing policy recommendations without a close examination of the empirical conditions prevailing in the region. Hirschman questioned the automatic application of orthodox remedies to the problems of underdevelopment. Instead of relying on general principles and abstract prescriptions, the foreign adviser should carry 'an empirical lantern' and make 'a visit to the patient' before being able to diagnose what was wrong with him (Hirschman 1998: 88). This general attitude involved regular conversations with Latin American policymakers and entrepreneurs, so that foreign specialists could acquire a perception about the way investment decisions were taken.

Overcoming the visiting-economist syndrome implied an attitude of suspicion against any system of ideas that pretended to have all the answers to the complex problems faced by Latin American societies. Rather than assuming from the outset that the road to development depended on a previously defined kit of techniques, the foreign consultant needed to 'understand the understanding' that Latin Americans had of their own reality. He should begin his work by engaging on a thorough empirical research of his 'cases', in order to understand their peculiarities and unusual aspects.

CONCLUDING REMARKS

Besides the substantive content of their approach, there are many differences between Prebisch and the *cepalinos*, on the one hand, and Albert Hirschman on the other. Prebisch studied economics in his home country, Argentina; Hirschman was born in Germany and went to the École des Hautes Études Commerciales, in France, and to the London School of Economics. Prebisch was basically concerned with the economic dimension of development processes, whereas Hirschman was also much attracted to its political, anthropological and psychological aspects. A third important difference comes from the fact that the Latin American School was never assimilated into mainstream economic theory. There are few mentions of its work outside Latin America, and those that there are tend to be critical. As for Hirschman, notwithstanding his heterodoxy, a formalized version of the concept of linkages was assimilated by mainstream economic thought, which adopted development indices to identify key sectors in the economy.

In spite of their many differences, however, Hirschman, Prebisch and the *cepalinos* shared a few characteristics. First of all, they were all very concerned with the empirical grounding of their theoretical effort. Whereas the *cepalinos* basically relied on statistical material, Hirschman concentrated attention on the historical and institutional aspects of his case studies. In both cases, however, the authors fully recognized the need to substantiate their theoretical claims with a wide array of empirical evidence.

The second similitude comes from the fact that Hirschman and the *cepalinos* had a clear commitment to finding practical solutions for the problems which they pinpointed in their writings. Theirs was not a purely intellectual endeavor. On the contrary, theory-building and policymaking were directly connected, and mobilizing some broad-based economic expertise was essential to promote economic and social changes. Hirschman, Prebisch and the *cepalinos* concluded that available theories were highly simplified in comparison with the messy complexity of reality, and that there was no single magic formula that could lead to a definitive solution to the problems associated with the development of the Third World.

The third and final characteristic shared by Hirschman and the *cepalinos* has a clear epistemological implication. Basically, they did not abdicate from the idea of building an universal theory, but argued that a social theory cannot acquire an universal scope without paying due respect to the historical, geographical and institutional diversity of its subject matter. Like all social phenomena, economic activities are necessarily embedded in culture, which includes all kinds of social, political and moral institutions that shape human behavior.

In this connection, it is worth pointing to a very interesting remark made by Hirschman at a later point in his career. He realized that he had set up out to build an economic theory specially suited to the underdeveloped countries and ended up by finding a valid approach for understanding change and growth in other developing and advanced countries as well. Looking for the specific, he went full circle and met the universal. I close this chapter by quoting from him:

> It appears, therefore, that the very characteristics on which I had sought to build an economics specially attuned to the underdeveloped countries have a far wider, perhaps even a universal, range and that they define, not a special strategy for the development for a well-defined group of countries, but a much more generally valid approach to the understanding of change and growth. In other words, *I set out to learn about others, and in the end learned about ourselves.* (Hirschman 1984: 95 – emphasis added)

REFERENCES

Bianchi, Ana Maria (2002) 'For different audiences, different arguments: economic rhetoric at the beginning of the Latin American School', *Journal of the History of Economic Thought*, vol. 24, no. 3: 291–305.

Hirschman, Albert O. (1958) *The Strategy of Economic Development*, New Haven, Conn.: Yale University Press.

Hirschman, Albert O. (1984) 'A Dissenter´s Confession: *The Strategy of Economic Development* Revisited' in G.M. Meier and D. Seers, *Pioneers in Development*, Oxford: Oxford University Press.

Hirschman, Albert O. (1998) *Crossing Boundaries: Selected Writings*, New York: Zone Books.

Hodgson, Geoffrey, (2001) *How Economics Forgot History*, London and New York: Routledge.

Prebisch, Raúl, (1949) 'The Economic Development of Latin America and its Principal Problems.' UN E CN.12/89/Rev.1, 1950.

Prebisch, Raúl, (1950) 'Introducción' in: Naciones Unidas, Commissión Económica para la América Latina, *Estúdio Económico de América Latina 1949*. Santiago: Secretaria Geral (published in English as *Economic Survey of Latin America 1949*, UN, 1951).

Notes

Introduction:

1 Stiglitz, Joseph E. (2002) 'There Is No Invisible Hand', *The Guardian*, December 20, 2002.

2 All the student petitions discussed are available at www.paecon.net

3 For further information about the PAE, see *The Crisis in Economics: The Post-Autistic Economics Movement: The first 600 days*, Edward Fullbrook (editor), London: Routledge, 2003.

Chapter 2: Modern Economics: the Problem and a Solution

1 For helpful comments on an earlier draft I am grateful to Steven Pratten and Roy Rotheim.

2 Sometimes a function defined in X with values in Y is called a transformation or mapping of X into Y.

Chapter 3: The Pitfalls of Mainstream Economic Reasoning (and Teaching)

1 Milton Friedman *Essays in Positive Economics*, Chicago: University of Chicago Press, 1953.

2 See David P. Levine, *Economic Studies: Contributions to the Critique of Economic Theory* (Preface), London: Routledge and Kegan Paul 1977.

Chapter 4: Neoclassical Economic Theory: a Special and Not a General Case

1 See, for example Kirman, A. 'The economy as an interactive system' in *The Economy as an Evolving Complex System*, eds. W. B. Arthur, S. N. Durlauf, D. A. Lane, Proceedings of Santa Fe Institute, vol. XXVII, Reading, Mass., Addison-Wesley, 1997; W. B. Arthur, 'Competing technologies, increasing returns and lock-in by historical events', *Economic Journal*, 1989; E. L. Glaeser, B. Sacerdote, and J. A. Scheinkman, 'Crime and social interactions', *Quarterly Journal of Economics*, vol.CXI, no.2, 1996: 507–48; and P. Ormerod, C. Mountfield and L. Smith 'Non-linear modelling of burglary and violent crime in the UK', in *Modelling Crime and Offending*, Home Office Occasional Paper no. 80, London: Home Office, 2003.

2 Kershaw, C., N. Chivite-Matthews, C. Thomas and R. Aust, *British Crime Survey 2001: First Results*, London: Home Office Statistical Bulletin, October 2001.

3 See, for example, K. Hansen and S. Machin 'Modelling crime at police force level' in *Modelling Crime and Offending*, Home Office Occasional Paper no. 80, London: Home Office, 2003.

4 Sutton, J. *Marshall's Tendencies: What Can Economists Know?*, Cambridge, MA: MIT Press, 2000.

5 For example, G. Akerlof, 'The Market for "Lemons": Quality Uncertainty and the Market Mechanism', *Quarterly Journal of Economics*, August 1970; and S. Salop and J. Stiglitz, 'Bargains and Rip-Offs: A Model of Monopolistic Competitive Price Dispersion', *Review of Economic Studies*, vol. 44, 1977: 493–510.

6   Ormerod, P. *Butterfly Economics*, Faber and Faber, 1998

7   see, for example, D. Khaneman and A. Tversky, 'Prospect theory: an analysis of decision under risk', *Econometrica*, 47, 1979: 263–91, and V. L. Smith 'Constructivist and ecological rationality in economics', *American Economic Review*, 93, 2003: 465–508.

8   Radner, R. 'Competitive Equilibrium Under Uncertainty', *Econometrica*, 36, 1968.

9   Kirman, A. 'The Behaviour of the Foreign Exchange Market', *Bank of England Quarterly Bulletin*, August 1995.

10 Arrow, K. *Guardian* newspaper, 3 January 1994, London.

11 ibid.

Chapter 5: Where Do Economies Come From? The Missing Story

1   Mankiw, N. Gregory *Essentials of Economics*, third edn, Mason, Ohio: Thomson-Southwestern, 2004 (3rd edition), p. 4.

2   *Ibid.*, p.4.

3   Wrightson, Keith *Earthly Necessities: Economic Lives in Early Modern Britain*, New Haven and London: Yale University Press, 2000, Chapter 2.

4   Polanyi, Karl *The Great Transformation*, Boston: Beacon Press, 1957.

5   See Chapter 2 of Wrightson for an excellent account of how the rational strategies listed by Mankiw were employed in the very different setting of sixteenth-century England.

6   The web address for the US agency for International Development is http://www.usaid.gov.

7   'In a Hostile Land, Trying Whatever Works; U.S. Officials in Iraq Learn to Adapt to Local Rules,' *Washington Post*, December 23, 2003.

8   'Iraqis Face Tough Transition to Market-Based Agriculture', *Washington Post*, January 22, 2004.

Chapter 6: Can Economics Start from the Individual Alone?

1   Solow, Robert M. 'Economic History and Economics', *American Economic Review (Papers and Proceedings)*, 75(2), May 1985, pp. 328–31.

2   Haavelmo, Trygve 'Econometrics and the Welfare State' (1989 Nobel Lecture), *American Economic Review*, 87 (supplement), December 1997, pp. 13–17.

Chapter 8: Five Pieces of Advice for Students Studying Microeconomics

1   These properties lead to propositions like: 'if the preference relation has such properties, then the demand curve can be decreasing–on condition that the income effect isn't too big in comparison to the substitution effect'.

2   For other ludicrous examples concerning the justification of the 'substitutability of factors', see 'What is the use of microeconomics', www.autisme-economie.org

3   Both Varian's and Kreps' books have very detailed indexes, but the term 'auctioneer' figures in neither of them.

4   A 'Pareto-optimal' state of the economy is considered as 'efficient' in the sense that it exhausts all possibilities of mutually beneficial exchanges (i.e. no-one's situation can be improved without adversely affecting someone else's).

5   Indeed, if there are many persons polluted, then there is the 'free rider' problem (each one expects that others will pay).

6   In this case, the model often supposes that the wage is 'pushed down' by 'competition' to the workers' reservation level. This can be accepted by a marxist, but not by a neoclassical theorist, for whom society consists of 'agents' with the same status. Firms can also be 'pushed by competition' to their reservation wage- the highest they can pay (all the surplus going then to the worker). And, if everybody is 'pushed by competition', here again, there is indeterminacy.

7   Moral hazard for an insurance company consists in the possibility that people are less cautious once they are insured. Adverse selection reflects the tendency that the people more exposed to a risk are likely to insure themselves against it than people less exposed to it.

8   In general, asymmetric information models suppose a bilateral relation (between an ' informed' person, and an 'uninformed' one) that comes down to a bargaining process, and then to an indeterminate outcome. For the neoclassical economist, the asymmetric case differs from those where bargainers have the same (complete) information only in that there can be 'inefficient' outcomes. Microeconomists then pay attention solely to the 'efficient' cases – always taking the normative point of view – but the indeterminacy remains.

9   This is true even for partial equilibrium analysis: 'competitive' supply and demand curves suppose (implicitly) that there is an auctioneer.

Chapter 11: Why Do We Have Separate Courses in 'Micro' and 'Macro' Economics ?

1   As for Solow's growth model, it is of the 'representative agent' kind; the only difference from the models of the 'new macroeconomics' is that it assumes a non-sophisticated choice by the 'community' (as Solow says): at each period, production is divided into consumption and investment according to a fixed rule (a part s is saved, the rest, 1–s is consumed).

2   The only difference is that there is only one 'physical' good (present and future), and labour-leisure–these being the 'reason' for distinguishing macro from micro.

Chapter 13: How to Look at Economics Critically: Some Suggestions

1   The Conference proceedings are in d'Autume and Cartelier (1996). Yet they do not convey the heated discussions and challenges from the floor where the present writers and Fréderic Catz, a mathematician and a colleague from the University of Grenoble, were the very bad boys of an otherwise most respectful audience.

2   The best argument why a general fall in wages will probably lead to a fall in profits, output and employment was made in 1939 by Michal Kalecki (1991).

3   See chapter 12 of the *General Theory*, aptly titled 'The State of Long-Run Expectations'. In it Keynes writes: 'The outstanding fact is the extreme precariousness of the basis of knowledge on which our estimates of prospective yield have to be made. Our knowledge of the factors which will govern the yield of an investment some years hence is usually very slight and often negligible' (Keynes 1936: 149).

4   Mainstream economists teach that when demand exceeds supply, price will increase thereby eliminating the excess demand. In their search for stability, mathematical economists produced a set of theorems, known as the Sonnenschein-Mantel-Debreu theorem, showing that such an equilibrium result is not a likely one. This is due to the fact that interdependencies among agents and sectors are prone to give more weight to the income effect than to the substitution effect. John Hicks, who in 1939 mapped out the research program in neoclassical economics, was fully aware

of the problem. He formulated the condition that for price adjustments to be consistent with equilibrium, gross substitutability must always prevail (Hicks 1939). But those considerations and results were never studied, until the Sorbonne's Bernard Guerrien wrote his 1989 book, in terms of their catastrophic implications for mainstream microeconomic theory. The reader can find some hints in a paper by Alan Kirman (1989), a Briton who teaches economics in France, but not with the same depth and breadth as in Guerrien's original and pioneering work.

5   On this last issue the experience of the United States is completely schizophrenic since politicians and their cohort of economists, including those of the Virginia School, who lambasted government expenditures, generated, under President Reagan's tenure, the first major deficits since WW2.

Chapter 14: Teaching Economics As If Ethics Mattered

1   Adam Smith *The Theory of Moral Sentiments* [1759], D. D. Raphael and A. L. Macfie, eds., in *The Glasgow Edition of the Works and Correspondence of Adam Smith*, Vol. 1, General eds D. D. Raphael and Andrew Skinner, Oxford: Clarendon Press, 1976.

2   Adam Smith *An Inquiry into the Nature and Causes of the Wealth of Nations* [1776], ed. W. B. Todd, in *The Glasgow Edition of the Works and Correspondence of Adam Smith*, Vol. 2.

3   Charles K. Wilber and Roland Hoksbergen 'Ethical Values and Economic Theory: A Survey,' *Religious Studies Review*, 12:3/4 (July/October, 1986), pp. 205–14.

4   Robert H. Frank, Thomas Gilovich, and Denis T. Regan 'Does Studying Economics Inhibit Cooperation?', *Journal of Economic Perspectives*, Vol. 7, No. 2 (Spring 1993),159–71.

5   Robin M. Dawes and Richard H. Thaler 'Cooperation,' *Journal of Economic Perspectives*, Vol. 2, No. 3 (Summer 1988), pp. 187–97.

6   Charles K. Wilber 'Trust, Moral Hazards and Social Economics: Incentives and the Organization of Work,' in *On the Condition of Labor and the Social Question One Hundred Years Later: Commemorating the 100th Anniversary of Rerum Novarum and the Fiftieth Anniversary of the Association for Social Economics*, eds Thomas O. Nitsch, Joseph M. Phillips, Jr. and Edward L. Fitzsimmons, Toronto Studies in Theology, Vol. 69, The Edwin Mellen Press, 1994, 173–84.

7   Virgina Held, 'Feminist Transformations of Moral Theory,' *Philosophy and Phenomenological Research*, Vol. 50, supplement (1990): 321–44.

8   Elizabeth Anderson 'The Ethical Limitations of the Market,' *Economics and Philosophy*, Vol. 6, No. 2 (October 1990): 179–205.

9   Tyler Cowen 'The Scope and Limit of Preference Sovereignty,' *Economics and Philosophy*, Vol. 9, No. 2 (October 1993): 253–69.

Chapter 17: 'There Are None So Blind . . .

1   Becker, W. and M. Watts state that 'The typical U.S. economics instructor is a male (81 per cent in 2000 and 83 per cent in 1995), Caucasian (89 per cent in 2000 and 89 per cent in 1995), with a Ph.D. (84 per cent in 2000, 86 per cent in 1995)' ('Teaching methods in undergraduate U.S. economics courses', *Journal of Economic Education*, Vol. 32, No. 3 (2001): 275.

2   S. Feiner and B. Morgan, 'Women and Minorities in Introductory Economics Textbooks: 1974 to 1984.' *Journal of Economic Education*, Vol. 18, No. 4 (Fall 1987): 376–392.

—— and B. Roberts, 'Hidden by the invisible hand: neoclassical economic theory and the textbook treatment of minorities and women', *Gender & Society*, Vol. 4, No. 2 (June 1990): 159–181.

—— and R. Bartlett, 'Balancing the economics curriculum: method, content and pedagogy', *The American Economic Review*, Vol. 82, No. 2 (May 1992): 559–64.

—— 'Women and minorities in introductory economics textbooks: an overview of the last 15 years', *The Journal of Economic Education* (Spring 1993): 145–62.

—— and R. Cherry, 'Discrimination in Economics Journals and Economics Textbooks: 1972 to 1987', *The Review of Black Political Economy*, Vol. 21, No. 2 (Fall 1992): 99–118.

—— and B. Roberts, 'Using an Alternative Paradigm to Teach Race, Gender and Critical Thinking', *The American Economic Review*, Vol. 85 (May 1995): 367–371.

3   See N. Gregory Mankiw 2004, *Principles of Microeconomics*, Thamson/Southwestern 3rd edition, Reported in *The New York Times*, February 12th 2004, 'Hastert Faults Report on Exporting Jobs', Article available at: http://www.nytimes.com/2004/02/12/politics/12BBOX.html

4   David C. Colander, 2004, *Principles of Microeconomics*, McGraw-Hill/Irwin 5th edition, Veblen, himself a radical critic of mainstream economics, was also an early feminist.

5   This is from the advertising for *Real World Micro*: 'And while *Real World Micro* is an excellent supplement to any mainstream text, its articles have been keyed to David Colander's popular textbook, *Economics*, 5th edition, and its microeconomics 'split." (http://www.dollarsandsense.org/bookstore/infomicro.html)

6   David C. Colander. *J. Economic Education*. "Integrating Sex, and Drugs into the Principles Course: Market Failures Versus Failures of Market Outcomes." Vol. 34, No. 1. Winter 2003. p. 82–91. 'The central argument of this article is that the current micro principles course is structured around an approach to policy that avoids many of the controversial, but central, issues of policy.'

7   Interesting aspects of this are discussed in the article, Kenneth N. Ehrensal 'Training Capitalism's Foot Soldiers,' in Eric Margolis, ed., *The Hidden Curriculum of Higher Education*, London: Routledge, 2001 pp. 97–114. For those of you not familiar with the concept of the 'hidden curriculum' you can find an abbreviated version of Jean Anyon's classic 1981 article at http://www.pipeline.com/~rgibson/hiddencurriculum.htm.

8   Thomas Kuhn and the structure of scientific revolutions. Accessed 7 June 2004. http://csmres.jim.edu/geollab/fichter/geol 364/kuhn.pdf

9   This fine summary of Kuhn's argument can be found on line at http://www.emory.edu/EDUCATION/mfp/kuhnsyn.html

10 The literature critical of the demand side analysis is as large and compelling as is the literature critical of the supply side analysis. If you are reading this book you should know both lines of argumentation. For a fine overview see James Galbraith, 'How the Economists Got it Wrong'. Accessed on 7/04 http://www.prospect.org/print/VII/7/galbraith-j.htm.

11 Forthcoming, Ann Arbor: University of Michigan Press, Fall 2004.

12 The work of feminist historian Carroll Rosenberg-Smith, *Disorderly Conduct: Visions of Gender in Victorian America* (Oxford: Oxford University Press, 1986) remains a classic work on these topics. The path-breaking work of the late Michelle Pujol demonstrates the formative role economists and economic theory played in the

creation of the cult of domesticity. See Michelle Pujol, *Feminism and Anti-Feminism in Early Economic Thought* , Edward Elgar, 1988.

13 Rhonda Williams forcefully argues this point in her essay, 'Race, Deconstruction, and the Emergent Economic Theory' in *Beyond Economic Man*, Marianne A. Ferber and Julie A. Nelson, eds, Chicago: Chicago University Press, 1993, 144–52.

14 Beneria, Lourdes 'Toward a greater integration of gender in economics', *World Development*, Vol. 23, Issue 11 (Nov. 1995): 18–39.

15 see Pujol, Nelson, and others.

16 Mankiw, 2004, Chapter 19, pp. 411–428, especially p. 416.

17 Alice Walker, 'Coming Apart', in *You Can't Keep a Good Woman Down*, Harvest Books, 1982, 41–53. *Beyond Killing Us Softly: The Strength to Resist*, Fort Washington, PA: Cambridge Documentary Films, 2001.

18 Professor Darity, asked to comment on Mankiw's presentation said, this: 'but it required an extensive (and somewhat dangerous) consumer strike by blacks to produce a serious conflict between profits and Southern racial norms for streetcar owners (or owners of downtown businesses in Southern cities). Plus the private market can be used to preserve Jim Crow, e.g. the rise of private white academies throughout the south as an exit route for white parents who did not want their kids in school with blacks. The market doesn't inherently promote desegregation out of profitability.'

19 Relevant articles by Professor William Darity can be found in *Southern Economic Journal* (1998) and *American Journal of Economics and Sociology* (2001), and with Patrick Mason in *Journal of Economic Perspectives* (1998).

20 Mankiw, 2004, pp. 431–432.

21 The Global Nanny Chain' by Arlie Hochshild does a fine job of exposing this problem. A very good video, *Chains of Love*, First Run/Icarus Films, also explores these questions.

22 Colander, 2004, pp. 10–11, 13. All quotations from the subsequent vignette are drawn from these pages.

23 This argument is made especially well by feminist economist Diana Strassman. See Diana Strassman, 'The stories of Economics and the power of the strory teller', History of Political Economy, Vol. 25, No. 1 (1993): 147–166.

24 Colendar, 2004, p. 16.

25 The text goes on as follows: 'Many people's view of the trade will likely be different; they would regard such a market outcome-an outcome that allows slavery-as a market outcome failure. That is why governments have developed laws that make such trades illegal.'

26 Houghton Mifflin, 2003.

Chapter 18: Can Mathematics Be Used Successfully in Economics?

*   An earlier version of some of the material in this chapter was read in March 2002 at the conference on 'Karl Popper and the role of the Social Scientist' at LUISS, Rome. I am very grateful for the comments received on that occasion as well as for comments on an earlier draft from Grazia Ietto Gillies and Margaret Schabas. These comments have led to several improvements.

1   The perihelion of a planet is the point at which it is closest to the Sun.

2   An excellent account of Jevons' work and his role in promoting mathematical economics is contained in Margaret Schabas (1990) A World Ruled by Number. William Stanley Jevons and the Rise of Mathematical Economics.

3   My main source of information about the accountancy treatment of goodwill and brands is Terry Smith's amusing and informative book: Accounting for Growth: Stripping the Camouflage from Company Accounts, 2nd Edition, 1996.

4   It might be argued that this is a false dichotomy since there have been some recent attempts e.g. Pearl (2000) to mathematise causality. However, what I am arguing for here is the use of economics of the traditional qualitative concept of causality rather than the use of some of the recent mathematical versions of causality whose value has yet to be established.

5   Keynes himself makes implicit use of this analogy between his work in economics and standard procedures in medicine. For details and a discussion, see Gillies and Ietto-Gillies (2001).

Chapter 19: Can We Expect Anything From Game Theory?

1   They also consider 'incomplete information' games, which are not fundamentally different, but much more complicated (it is supposed that there are player (or payoff) 'types', with some probabilities-both being common knowledge), especially because some kind of beliefs are included in models' parameters, or 'fundamentals'.

2   The same can be said about equilibrium in the Stackelberg model (where one of the players is 'cournotian' and then chooses his supply randomly). In the other duopole model, Bertrand's, rational players will never choose Nash equilibrium strategies, where payoffs are equal to zero: if they propose a price bigger than the equilibrium price, they can have a strictly positive payoff (it depends on the price proposed by the other duopolist).

Chapter 20: Improbable, Incorrect or Impossible: the Persuasive But Flawed Mathematics of Microeconomics

1   They might well change their output later given the impact of the change in market output, but since they aren't colluding or managed collectively, no firm will instantaneously change its output as a result of changes in output by any other firm.

2   They might well change their output later given the impact of the change in market output, but since they aren't colluding or managed collectively, no firm will instantaneously change its output as a result of changes in output by any other firm.

3   It also ignores the fact that in a multi-firm industry with independent firms, the firm cannot know either term on the right hand side of equation (4) – all it can know is the sum of the two. So it has no way of knowing 'its' marginal revenue in the first place.

5   The results here elaborate on the arguments in Chapter 4 of Debunking Economics. To read the full argument, go to www.debunking-economics.com/Papers/ TheoryOfTheFirm.pdf

6   Of course, even if all consumers have individual demand curves like this, the market demand curve that is derived from adding up these individual demand curves can have any shape at all, including sections where demand rises as price rises, kinks, etc. (unless we assume that all consumers have identical tastes). What do you

mean, you didn't know that? Didn't your lecturer tell you? And what do you mean, your textbook doesn't say that? Read Chapter 2 of *Debunking Economics*, or consult the (almost) original authors: Shafer & Sonnenschein (1982).

7   The average human brain consists of 100 billion neurones (10^{11}), and the average brain weights about 1.35kg. If the entire mass of the brain were neurones (which it's not), each neurone would weigh about 10^{-8} grams.

8   The sun weighs under 10^{27} tonnes, it's an average size star and there are 100 billion (10^{11}) stars in the Milky Way; the Milky Way is on the large size as galaxies go, and there are about 125 billion (10^{11}) galaxies. Visible matter constitutes about 10 per cent of the universe's mass (the rest is called 'Dark Matter').

9   The Cobb-Douglas production function much beloved of neoclassical economists is another pseudo-scientific concept. As Anwar Shaikh and others have shown, the Cobb-Douglas 'production function' is simply a transformation of the national income identity *Income = Wages + Profits* under conditions of relatively constant income shares. Its 'impressive correlation' with economic growth data occurs because it is a correlation of X with approximately X.

Chapter 21: The Significance of the Economics Research Paper

1   Associate Professor of Economics, School of Policy Studies, Roosevelt University, Chicago, IL 60605. Email: sziliak@roosevelt.edu. The author thanks Erik Thorbecke for suggesting here the figures on oomph. And for comments on a talk at the meetings of the American Economic Association (2004) he thanks Morris Altman, Kenneth Arrow, Clive Granger, Joel Horowitz, Ed Leamer, Deirdre McCloskey, Tony O'Brien, Erik Thorbecke, Arnold Zellner, and the members of an encouragingly large audience.

2   It's a shame that the history of economic thought has been dropped from so many curricula. It means you're likely never to hear or read about for example Francis Ysidro Edgeworth (1845–1926), who earned distinction in economics, philosophy, and statistics. Edgeworth invented among other things ?indifference curve analysis,'a device detested and nearly buried by Alfred Marshall. It's now used lavishly by today's price theorists, many who'd like to bury Marshallian analysis. But what could an old controversy have to do with the *practice* of science?

3   Truth and falsehood are as trendy today as a wool bra. You probably know something about it (the genealogy, that is, of truth and falsehood since Nietzsche, and especially since the rise of postmodernism). A splendid introduction is S. Cullenberg, J. Amariglio, and D.F. Ruccio, eds., *Postmodernism, Economics and Knowledge* (2001).

4   Ziliak and McCloskey, 'Size Matters: The Standard Error of Regressions in the *American Economic Review*,' *Journal of Socio-Economics* (forthcoming, 2004). 'Size Matters' is being published in a volume devoted exclusively to the resurrection of economic significance. The volume includes comments on our papers by Clive Granger, Arnold Zellner, Takeshi Amemiya, Edward Leamer, Joel Horowitz, Jeffrey Wooldridge, and other leading theorists and users of econometrics. And record this happy and serious fact: on the basic point, *every one* of them agrees with us.

Chapter 23: Ecological Economics: the Concept of Scale and its Relation to Allocation, Distribution, and Uneconomic Growth

1   See Nicholas Georgescu-Roegen, *The Entropy Law and the Economic Process*, Cambridge, MA: Harvard University Press, 1972.

2   Curiously the World Bank in WDR 2003, *Sustainable Development in a Dynamic World*, has adopted ecological economist's vocabulary of 'sources' and 'sinks', but does not tie them together by the concept of throughput – the entropic flow from source to sink. Much less do they consider the scale of the throughput or its entropic directionality. In dismissing the idea of overconsumption they say, 'But the overall level of consumption is not the source of the problem. It is the combination of the specific consumption mix and the production processes that generates the externality. And for these there are well-established policy prescriptions from public finance' (196). So much for scale – it is not important – allocative efficiency via right prices is everything!

3   That is, as a multiplicative form that analytically describes the process of production as the multiplication of capital times labor times resources (each factor is raised to an exponent, but that is not important to the point I am making). In this representation we can hold output constant and reduce resources as much as we wish (though not to zero), as long as we increase labor or capital by the required amount. We can supposedly make a hundred-pound cake with only five ounces of flour, sugar, eggs, etc., if only we stir hard enough, and bake in a big enough oven! In mathematics a 'product' is yielded by multiplying 'factors'. In production there is no multiplication, only transformation of resources (material cause) by labor and capital (efficient cause) into a final good. Have we been misled by the mathematical terms of 'factors' and 'products' to see a process of multiplication where there is none?

4   Indeed, GNP does not reflect efficiency very well. Greater efficiency by itself leads to lower cost and lower price. This would by itself reduce GNP, unless the quantity sold of the good increases sufficiently to offset the price decline – i.e. unless the demand for the good were elastic. Similarly, a fall in efficiency and an increase in price for a good with inelastic demand will perversely register an increase in GNP.

5   John Stuart Mill, Principles of Political Economy, Vol. 2 (London: John W. Parker, 1857, p. 326).

6   For critical discussion and the latest revision of the ISEW, see, Clifford W. Cobb and John B. Cobb, Jr., *et al.*, *The Green National Product*, New York: University Press of America, 1994. For a presentation of the ISEW see Appendix of H. Daly and J. Cobb, *For the Common Good*, Boston: Beacon Press, 1989; second edition 1994. See also Clifford W. Cobb, *et al.*, 'If the GDP is Up, Why is America Down?, *Atlantic Monthly*, October, 1995; Manfred Max-Neef, Economic Growth and Quality of Life: A Threshold Hypothesis, *Ecological Economics*, 15, (1995): 115–18; Phillip A. Lawn, *Toward Sustainable Development* (An Ecological Economics Approach), Boca Raton, FL: Lewis Publishers, 2001; Clive Hamilton, *Growth Fetish*, NSW, Australia: Allen and Unwin, 2003.

7   *Hard Green: Saving the Environment from the Environmentalists* (A Conservative Manifesto by Peter Huber), New York: Basic Books (A Manhattan Institute Book), 2000, p. 81.

8   In spite of the fact that mathematicians tell us that we cannot maximize a function for more than one variable!

Chapter 24: What's Wrong with GDP and Growth? The Need for Alternative Indicators

1   This chapter has been written to be accessible to beginners in economics, or even to those who have never studied the subject at all. Nevertheless, it contains references that may assist the interested reader to enquire further.

2   And yet Simon Kuznets, the father of national accounting in the USA, said as early as 1934, in a statement to Congress, that, 'The well-being of a nation can scarcely be inferred from any measurement of national income', that a distinction had to be made between 'the quantity and quality of growth' and that the key decisions that had to be taken in this regard related to 'growth of what, and for whom'.

3   See Jean Gadrey, 'Croissance et productivité: des indicateurs en crise larvée', *Travail et Emploi*, no. 91, July 2002: 9–17.

4   *Social Limits to Growth*, London: Routledge, 1995 (first edition 1976).

5   L. Osberg and A. Sharpe, Estimates of an Index of Economic Well-Being for OECD Countries, web site www.cls.ca, 2000.

6   See the website: www.undp.org

7   Example: if the same basket of goods representative of French and American consumption costs 0.9 Euros in France and 1 dollar in the USA, the purchasing power parity between the two countries is said to be 1 dollar for 0.9 Euros and French GDP can be expressed in dollars (and vice versa).

8   See *The Social Health of the Nation*, Oxford University Press, 1999.

9   All the data can be downloaded in Excel format from the researchers' website: www.csls.ca

Chapter 25: What is Wrong with the 'Official History of Capitalism'? With Special Reference to the Debates on Globalisation and Economic Development

1   This chapter is based on Ha-Joon Chang, *Kicking Away the Ladder: Development Strategy in Historical Perspective*, London: Anthem Press, 2002. Further details and references can be found in the book.

2   Jagdish Bhagwati, *Protectionism*, Cambridge, Mass.: MIT Press, 1985, 22, n. 10.

3   Jeffrey Sachs & Andrew Warner, 'Economic Reform and the Process of Global Integration', *Brookings Papers on Economic Activity*, 1995, no. 1: 3

4   Renato Ruggiero, 'Whither the Trade System Next?' in J. Bhagwati & M. Hirsch (eds), *The Uruguay Round and Beyond–Essays in Honour of Aurthur* Dunkel, Ann Arbor, The Michigan University Press, 1998, 131.

Chapter 26: Should the Study of Transnational Companies Be Part of the Economics Syllabus?

1   Emerita Professor of Applied Economics, London South Bank University; Visiting Research Professor, The Open University. Email: iettogg@lsbu.ac.uk

2   It is more common to name companies with direct activities in more than one country as multinational companies (MNCs). The term transnational companies is preferred here because it expresses better the idea that activities, their planning, control and organization takes place *across* national frontiers. Moreover, the emphasis on trans-nationality avoids being stuck into the issue of how many foreign countries are necessary to have direct activities in, for a company to be classified as MNC. TNC is also the expression used by the United Nations Conference on Trade and Development (UNCTAD).

3   Curricula for business studies degrees – at both under and post graduate levels – are much more likely to have units dealing wholly or partly with the activities of TNCs.

4   For some universities I was able to gather more information by looking at the teaching of individual lecturers.

5   The current and next sections draw on material in Ietto-Gillies (2003).

6   A strategic approach towards rival firms can be detected in Hymer (1960); Vernon (1966); Knickerbocker (1973); Cowling and Sugden (1987); Cantwell (1989). An exposition of these and other theories of TNCs and international production is in Ietto-Gillies (2005) while Cantwell (2000) gives a concise summary.

7   But, of course, most large firms are transnationals because operations abroad is part of growth strategies and often a condition for growth.

8   This issue was considered in Ietto-Gillies (1988) and further developed in Ietto-Gillies (2001: ch. 6). Cowling and Sugden (1987) and Peoples and Sugden (2000) talk of 'divide and rule' strategies of TNCs' towards labour.

9   On the theoretical and empirical analyses of international networks of the world's largest TNCs cf. Ietto-Gillies (2001: chs 3, 4 and 5).

10 On this issue Sengenberger and Wilkinson (1995: 111) write of a '...mismatch between the economic and social space...'.

Chapter 27: Would a Latin American economics Make Sense?

1   In Bianchi 2002 the reader can find a more complete account of the ECLAC doctrine, with bibliographical references that would be useful for further readings.

2   For an overall picture of Hirschman´s writings, see Meldolesi (1995), where the reader will find many useful references.

NAME INDEX